FOLKLORE OF THE SANTAL PARGANAS

FOLKLORE OF THE SANTAL PARGANAS

TRANSLATED BY

CECIL HENRY BOMPAS
OF THE INDIAN CIVIL SERVICE

GYAN PUBLISHING HOUSE
New Delhi - 110002

FOLKLORE OF THE SANTAL PARGANAS

ISBN : 9788121207546

Reprinted in 2016 in India by

Gyan Publishing House
5, Ansari Road
New Delhi—110002
Phones : 9811692060
E-Mail : books@gyanbooks.com
Website: www.gyanbooks.com

Leser type setting at : Apex Computers Delhi 110053
Printed at : Mehra Offset Printers

CONTENTS

PART I

PART II

PART III

PART IV

PART V

PART VI

PREFACE

The Santals are a Munda tribe, a branch of that aboriginal element which probably entered India from the North East. At the present day they inhabit the Eastern outskirts of the Chutia Nagpore plateau.

Originally hunters and dwellers in the jungle, they are still but indifferent agriculturists. Like the Mundas and Hos and other representatives of the race, they are jovial in character, fond of their rice beer, and ready to take a joke.

Their social organization is very complete; each village has its headman or manjhi, with his assistant the paranik; the jogmanghi is charged with the supervision of the morals of the young men and women; the naeke is the village priest, the godet is the village constable. Over a group of villages is the pargana or tribal chief. The Santals are divided into exogamous septs—originally twelve in number, and their social observances are complex, *e.g.* while some relations treat each other with the greatest reserve, between others the utmost freedom of intercourse is allowed.

Their religion is animistic, spirits (*bongas*) are everywhere around them: the spirits of their ancestors, the spirit of the house, the spirit dwelling in the patch of primeval forest preserved in each village. Every hill tree and rock may have its spirit. These spirits are propitiated by elaborate ceremonies and sacrifices which generally terminate in dances, and the drinking of rice beer.

The Santal Parganas is a district 4800 sq. miles in area, lying about 150 miles north of Calcutta, and was formed into a separate administration after the Santals had risen in rebellion in 1856. The Santals at present form about one-third of the population.

The stories and legends which are here translated have been collected by the Rev. O. Bodding, D. D. of the Scandinavian Mission to the Santals. To be perfectly sure that neither language nor ideas should in any way be influenced by contact with European mind he arranged for most of them to be written out in Santali, principally by a Christian convert named Sagram Murmu, at present living at Mohulpahari in the Santal Parganas.

Santali is an aggulatinative language of great regularity and complexity but when the Santals come in contact with races speaking an Aryan language it is apt to become corrupted with foreign idioms. The language in which these stories have been written is beautifully pure, and the purity of language may be accepted as an index that the ideas have not been affected, as is often the case, by contact with Europeans.

My translation though somewhat condensed is very literal, and the stories have perhaps thereby an added interest as showing the way in whcih a very primitive people look at things. The Santals are great story tellers; the old folk of the village gather the young people round them in the evening and tell them stories, and the men when watching the crops on the threshing floor will often sit up all night telling stories.

There is however, no doubt that at the present time the knowledge of these stories tends to die out. Under the peace which Birtish rule brings there is more intercourse between the different communities and castes, a considerable degree of assimilation takes place, and old customs and traditions tend to be obliterated.

Several collections of Indian stories have been made, *e.g.*, Stokes, Indian Fairy Tales; Frere, Old Deccan Days; Day, Folk Tales of Bengal; and Knowles' Folk Tales of Kashmir, and it will be seen that all the stories in the present collection are by no means of pure Santal origin. Incidents which form part of the common stock of Indian folklore abound, and many of the stories professedly relate to characters of various Hindu castes, others again deal with such essentially Santal beliefs as the dealings of men and *bongas*.

The Rev. Dr. Campbell of Gobindpore published in 1891 a collection of Santal Folk Tales. He gathered his material in the District of Manbhum, and many of the stories are identical with those included in the present volume. I have added as an appendix some stories which I collected among the Hos of Singhbhum, a tribe closely related to the Santals, and which the Asiatic Society of Bengal has kindly permitted me to reprint here.

My task has been merely one of translation; it is due solely to Mr. Bodding's influence with, and intimate knowledge of, the people that the stories have been committed to writing, and I have to thank him for assistance and advice throughout my work of translation.

I have roughly classified the stories: in part I are stories of a general character; in part 2, stories relating to animals; in part 3, stories which are scarcely folklore but are anecdotes relating to Santal life; in Part 4, stories relating to the dealings of *bongas* and men. In part 5, are some legends and traditions, and a few notes relating to tribal customs. Part 8 contains illustrations of the belief in witchcraft. I have had to omit a certain number of stories as unsuited for publication.

C. H. Bompas.

PART I

In these stories are many incidents which appear in stories collected in other parts of India, though it is rather surprising that so few of them appear elsewhere in their entirety. We have however, instances of the husk myth, the youngest son who surpasses his brother, the life of the ogre placed in some external object, the jealous stepmother, the selection of a king by an elephant, the queen whose husband is invariably killed on his wedding night, etc. etc.

Few of the old Indian stories found in the Katha Sarit Sagara or the Buddhist Birth stories appear in recognizable form in the present collection.

I. BAJUN AND JHORE

Once upon a time there were two brothers named Bajun and Jhore. Bajun was married and one day his wife fell ill of fever. So, as he was going ploughing, Bajun told Jhore to stay at home and cook the dinner and he bade him put into the pot there measures of rice. Jhore stayed at home filled the pot with water and put it on to boil; then he went to look for rice measures ; there was only one in the house and Jhore thought " My brother told me to put in three measures and if I only put in one I shall get into trouble." So he went to a neighbour's house and borrowed two more measures, and put them into the pot and left them to boil. At noon Bajun came back from ploughing and found Jhore stirring the pot and asked him whether the rice was ready. Jhore made no answer, so Bajun took the spoon from him, saying "Let me feel how it is getting on", but when he stirred with the spoon he heard a rattling noise and when he looked into the pot he found no rice but only three wooden measures floating about; then he turned and abused Jhore for his folly, but Jhore said "You yourself told me to put in three measures and I have done so." So Bajun had to set to work and cook the rice himself and got his dinner very late.

Next day Bajun said to Jhore, "You don't know how to cook the dinner; I will stay at home to-day, you go to plough, and take a hatchet with you and if the plough catches in a root or anything, give a cut with the hatchet." So Jhore went ploughing and when the plough caught in anything and stopped, he gave a cut with his hatchet at the legs of the bullocks; they backed and plunged with the pain and then he only chopped at them the more until he lamed them both. At noon Bajun saw the bullocks come limping back and asked what was the matter with them. "O," said Jhore, "that is because I cut at them as you told me' "You idiot," said Bajun, "I meant you to give a cut at the roots in which the plough got caught, not at the legs of the bullocks; how will you live if you do such silly things? You cannot plough, you must stay at home and cook the rice. I will show you this evening how it is done." So after that Jhore stayed at home and cooked. Bajun's wife grew no better, so one day Bajun, before he went to the fields, told Jhore to warm some water in order that his wife might wash with it. But Jhore made the water boiling hot and then took it and began to pour it over his sister-in-law as she lay on her bed; she was scalded and shrieked out " Don't pour it over me," but Jhore only laughed and went on pouring until he had scalded her to death. Then he wrapped her up in a cloth and. brought her dinner to her and offered it her to eat, but she was dead and made no answer to him, so he left it by her and went and ate his own rice. When Bajun came back and found his wife scalded to death he was very angry and went to get an axe to kill Jhore with; thereupon Jhore ran away into the jungle and Bajun pursued him with the axe.

In the jungle Jhore found a dead sheep and he took out its stomach and called out, "Where are you, brother, I have found some meat." But Bajun answered, " I will not leave you till I have killed you." So Jhore ran on and climbed up inside a hollow tree, where Bajun could not follow. Bajun got a long stick and poked at him with it and as he poked, Jhore let fall the sheep's stomach, and when Bajun saw it. he concluded that he had killed his brother. So he went home and burned the body of his wife and a few days later he performed the funeral ceremonies to the memory of his wife and brother; he smeared the floor of the house with cowdung and sacrificed goats and fowls. Now Jhore had come back that day and climbed up on to the rafters of the house, and he sat there watching all that his brother did. Bajun cooked a great basket of rice and stewed the flesh of the animals he had scarified and offered I it to the spirits of the dead and he recited the dedication "My wife I offer this rice, this food, for your purification," and so saying he scattered some rice on the ground; and he also offered to Jhore, saying, Jhore, my brother, I offer this rice, this food, for your purification," and then Jhore called out from the roof " Well, as you offer it to me I will take it." Bajun had not bargained to get any answer, so he was astounded and went to ask the villagers whether their spirits made answer when sacrificed to: and the villagers told him that they had never heard of such a thing. While Bajun was away on this errand, Jhore took up the unguarded basket of rice and ran away with it; after going some way he sat down by the road and ate as much as he wanted, then he sat, and called out " Is there anyone on the road or in the jungle who wants a feast? " A gang of thieves who were on a thieving expedition heard him and went to see, what he meant ; he offered to let them eat the rice if they would admit him to their company; they agreed and he went on with them to steal; they broke into a rich man's house and the thieves began to collect the pots and pans but Jhore felt about in the dark and got hold of a drum and began to beat on it. This woke up the people of the house and they drove away the thieves. Then the thieves abused Jhore and said that 'they could not let him stay with them: "Very well", said he, "then give me. back the rice you ate." Of course they could not do this. So they had to let him stay with them. Then they went to the house of a rich Hindu who had a stable full of horses and they planned to steal the horses and rice, away with them; so each thief picked out a horse, but Jhore got hold of a tiger which had come to the back of the stable to kill one of the horses; and when the thieves mounted their horses, Jhore mounted on the tiger, and the tiger ran off with him towards the jungle. Jhore kept on' calling out, Keep to the road, you Hindu horse, keep to the road, you Hindu horse.' But it dragged him through the briars and bushes till he was dead and that was the end of Jhore.

II. ANUWA AND HIS MOTHER

Once there was a young fellow named Anuwa who lived with his old mother, and when he was out ploughing his mother used to take him his breakfast. One day a jackal met her on her way to the field with her son's breakfast and told her to put down the food which she was carrying or he would knock her down and bite her; so she put it down in a fright and the jackal ate most of it and then went away and the old woman took what was left to her son and told him nothing about what had happened. This happened several days in succession; at last one day Anuwa asked her why she brought so little rice and that so untidily arranged; so she told him how she was attacked every day by the jackal. Then they made a plan that the next day the mother should take the plough afield, while Anuwa should dress up as an old woman and carry the breakfast. This they did and the jackal met Anuwa as usual and made him put down the breakfast basket, but while the jackal was eating, knocked him head over heels with his stick and the jackal got up and fled, threatening and cursing Anuwa. Among other things the jackal as he ran away, had threatened to eat Anuwa's *malhan* plants, so Anuwa put a fence of thorns round them and when the jackal came at night and tried to eat the pods he only got his nose pricked.

Foiled in this the jackal called out, "Well, I will eat your fowls to-morrow;" but Anuwa the next night sat by the fowl house with a sickle and when the jackal came and poked in his head, Anuwa gave him a rap on the snout with the sickle, so the jackal made off crying "Well, Anuwa, your fowls have pecked me on the head, you shall die". So the next day Anuwa pretended to be dead and his mother went about crying; she took her way to the jungle and there she met the jackal and she told him that Anuwa had died in consequence of his curse and she invited him to the funeral feast, saying that he used to eat the rice which she had cooked and he had become like a son for her. The, Jackal gladly promised to attend, and had collected a timber of his friends and at evening they went to Anuwa's house and sat down in the courtyard. then the old woman came out and began to bewail her son: but the jackal said, "Stop crying, grannie, you cannot get back the dead: let us get on to the feast." So she said that the would fry some cakes first, as it would take some time before the rice was ready. The jackals approved of this but they asked her to tie them up with a rope 'first lest, they should get to fighting over the food, so the old woman brought a thick rope and tied them all up 'and tightest of all she tied up the jackal which had cursed Anuwa; then she went inside and put an iron pan on the fire and from time to time she sprinkled water on it and when the jackals heard the water hissing they thought that it was the cakes frying and jumped about with joy. Suddenly

Anuwa came out with a thick stick and set to beating the jackals till they bit through the ropes and ran away howling; but the first jackal was tied so tightly that he could not escape, and Anuwa beat him till he was senseless and lay without moving all night. The next morning Anuwa took the jackal and tied him to a stake near the place where the village women drew water and he put a thick stick beside it and every woman who went for water would give the jackal one blow with the stick. After a few days beating the body of the, jackal became all swollen and one night some other jackals came there and asked him what he ate that he had got so fat and he said that every one who came to draw water gave him a handful of rice and that was why he was so fat; and if they did not believe him they could take his place and try for themselves.

So one jackal agreed to try and untied the first jackal and let himself be tied in his place, but in the morning five women came down and each gave him a blow with the stick till he jumped about for pain, and seeing him jumping other women came and beat him till he died.

III. LEDHA AND THE LEOPARD

Once upon a time a boy named Ledha was tending cattle with other boys at the foot of a hill, and these boys in fun used to call out "Ho, leopard: Ho, leopard," and the echo used to answer from the hill " Ho, leopard. Now there really was a leopard who lived in the hill and one day he was playing hide and seek with a lizard which also lived there. The lizard hid and the leopard looked every where for it in vain. At last the leopard sat down to rest and it chanced that he sat right on top of the lizard which was hiding in a hole. The lizard thought that the leopard meant to hurt it and in revenge bit him and fastened on to his rump so that he could not get it off, so that day when the boys came calling out "Ho, leopard," he ran towards them to get their help: but when they saw the leopard they all fled for their lives. Ledha however could not run fast because he was lame, and the leopard headed him off and begged him to remove the lizard. This he did after the leopard had sworn not to eat him, and before they parted the leopard made him promise to tell no one that the lizard had bitten him, and said that if he told then he would be carried off and eaten. So Ledha rejoined his companions and told them nothing of what had passed between him and the leopard. But that night when they had all gone to bed, Ledha's sister-in-law began to worry him to tell her what the leopard had said to him, when it had caught him. He told her that the leopard would eat him if he told, but she coaxed him and said that no one could hear them inside the house; so at last he told her that he had taken off a lizard which was hanging on to its rump. Then they went to sleep; but the leopard was hiding at the back of the house and heard all that they said; and when they were all asleep, he crept in and carried of Ledha's bed with Ledha in it on his head. When Ledha woke up towards morning, he found himself being carried through dense jungle and he quietly pulled himself up into one of the trees I which overhung the Path. Thus when the leopard put down the bed and was going, to eat Ledha, he found it empty. So he went back on his track and by and bye came to the tree in which Ledha was hiding. The leopard begged Ledha to come down 'as he had something to say to him, and promised not to eat him; but directly Ledha reached the ground and the leopard said "Now I am going to eat you." Ledha was powerless, so he only asked to be allowed to have one chew of tobacco before he died; the leopard assented and Ledha felt in his cloth for his tobacco, but the tobacco did not come out easily and as Ledha felt about for it the dry tobacco leaves crackled; the leopard asked what the crackling sound was, and Ledha said "That is the lizard which bit you yesterday;" then the leopard got into a terrible fright and ran away as hard as he could, calling out "Don't let it loose: Don't let it loose."

So Ledha was saved from the leopard, but he did not know his way out of the jungle. He wandered about, till he came to the place where the wild buffaloes used to sleep at night, and he swept up the place and made it clean and then took refuge in a hollow tree; he stayed there some days, sweeping up the place daily and supporting himself on the fruit of a fig tree. At last one day the buffaloes left one cow behind to watch and see who it was who swept up their sleeping place. The cow pretended to be too ill to rise, and Ledha after watching for some time came out and swept the ground as usual, and then tried to pull the sick cow up by the tail; but she would not move so he went back to his hollow tree. When the buffaloes returned they heard that it was a kindhearted man who cleaned their sleeping place; so they called Ledha out and said that they would keep him as their servant to clean their sleeping place and to scrub them when they bathed in the river; they made him taste the milk of all the cows and appointed the cow whose milk he liked best to supply him. Thenceforward he used to wander about with the buffaloes and he made a flute and used to play on it.

One day after scrubbing the buffaloes he washed his head in the river and some of his hairs came out; so he wrapped them up in a leaf and set the packet to float down the stream. Lower down the stream two princesses were bathing with their attendants, and when they saw the packet they tried who could fish it out and :it was the younger princess who caught it. Then they measured the hairs and found them twelve cubits long. The princess who had taken the packet from the water went home and took to her bed and said that she would not eat until the man was found to whom the hairs belonged. Her father, the Raja, sent messengers in all directions to search for the man but they could not find him. Then he sent a parrot and the parrot flew up high and looking down saw Ledha with the buffaloes in the forest; but it did not dare to go near, so the parrot returned and told the Raja that the man was in the forest but that no messenger could approach for fear of the wild buffaloes. However a crow said, "I can bring him if any one can," so they sent the crow and it went and perched on the backs of the buffaloes and began to peck them; then Ledha threw stones at it, but it would not go away; then he threw a stick at it and last of all he threw his flute. The crow caught up the flute and flew up to a tree with it. Ledha ran after it, but the crow kept flying on a short distance and Ledha still pursued until he came to the Raja's city. The crow flew on till it entered the room where the princess lay, and dropped the flute into the hands of the princess. Ledha followed right into the room and they shut him in and the princess, gave him his flute after he had promised to marry her.

So he stayed there a long time, but meanwhile the Buffaloes all got weak and ill for want of some one to look after them. One day Ledha set off to the jungle with his wife to see them and when he saw how ill the buffaloes were, he decided to build a house in the jungle and live there. And the Raja sent them money and horses and cattle and elephants and servants and they built a palace and Ledha subdued all the jungle and became a great Raja; and he made a highway to his father-in-law's home and used to go to and fro on it.

IV. THE CRUEL STEPMOTHER

There was once a Raja whose wife died leaving him with one young child. He reared It with great care and when it could toddle about it took a great fancy to a cat; the child was always playing with it and carrying it about.

All his friends begged the Raja to marry again, but he said that he was sure that a stepmother would be cruel to his child; at last they persuaded him to promise to marry again, if a bride could be found who would promise to care for the child as her own, so his friends looked out for a bride; but though they found plenty of girls who were anxious to marry the Raja, not one would promise to care for his child as her own. There was a young window in a certain village who heard of what was going on, and one day she asked whether a bride had been found for the Raja and she was told that no one was willing to take charge of the child. "Why don't they agree," said she,, I would agree fast enough. If I were Rani I should have nothing to do but look after the child and I would care for it more than its own mother could." This came to the ears of the Raja and he sent for the widow and was pleased with her looks, and when she promised to love his child as her own, he married her.

At first no one could be kinder to the child than she was, but in the course of time she had a child of her own and then she began to be jealous of the elder child and she thought daily how she could get rid of him. He was still devoted to his cat and one day when he came back to the house, he asked his stepmother where the cat was. She answered angrily, "The cat has bewitched the boy ! It is "cat, cat," all day long."

At this the child began to cry; so she found the cat and threw it to him, saying, "Here is your cat: you are mad about your cat." But the boy hugged it in his arms and kept on crying at his stepmother's cross words. As he would not keep quiet his stepmother got more angry still; and catching hold of the cat she scratched her own arms and legs with the cat's claws until the blood flowed; then she began to cry and scold and when the neighbours came to see what was the matter, she told them that the boy had let his cat scratch her; and the neighbours saw that she was not loving the boy as she promised.

Presently the Raja came in and asked what was the matter; she turned and scolded him saying: "You have reared the accursed cat and it has scratched me finely; look, it has taken all the skin off; this is the way the boy repays me for all my trouble. I will not stay with you; if I stay the boy will injure me like this again." The Raja said, "Don't cry like a baby; how can a simple child like that know better? when he grows up I will scold him." But the woman persisted and declared that she would go away with her own child unless the Raja promised to kill his elder son. The Raja refused to do this, so the Rani took up her baby and went out of the house with it in a rage. Now the Raja was deeply in love with her and he followed and stopped her, and said that he could not let her take away his younger child; she answered, "Why trouble about the child? it is mine; I have left you your boy, if you don't kill him, when he grows up, he will tell you some lie about me and make you have me beaten to death." At last the Raja said, "Well, come back and if the boy does you any harm I will kill him." But the Rani said. "Either kill him now or let me go." So at last the Raja promised and brought her back to the palace. Then the Raja called the boy and gave him his dinner and told him that they were going on a visit to his uncle's: and the child was delighted and fetched his shoes and umbrella, and off they set, and a dog came running after them. When they came to a jungle the Raja told his son to' sit under a tree and wait for him, and he went away and killed the dog that had followed them and smeared the blood on his axe and went home, leaving the child.

When his father did not return, the child began to cry, and Thakur heard him and came down, and to frighten the boy and make him leave the jungle he came in the guise of a leopard; but the child would not move from where. he was; then Thakur appeared as a bear and as a snake and an elephant and in many other forms but the child would not move; so at last Thakur took the form of an old woman, who lifted him in her arms and soothed him and carried him to the edge of the jungle and left him on the outskirts of a village.

In the morning a rich Brahman found him and took him home, and as no one claimed the child he brought him up and made him his goat-herd, and they gave him the name of Lela. The Brahman's sons and daughters used to go school, and before he took his goats out to graze Lela used to carry their books to the school. And going to the school every day Lela got to know one or two letters and used to draw them in the sand while minding his goats; later he got the children to give him an old book saying that he wanted to pretend to the other boys that he could read and out of this book he taught himself to read: and as he grew up he became quite a scholar. One day he picked up a letter and found that it was from one of the village girls arranging to elope that very evening with a young man. At the appointed time Lela went to the rendezvous and hid himself in a tree; soon he saw the Brahman's daughter come to the place, but as her letter had not been delivered her lover did nor appear. The girl got tired of waiting and then she began to call to her lover, thinking that perhaps he was hiding for a joke. When she called, Lela answered from the tree and she thought that it was her lover and said "Come down and let us be off." Lela came down and they started off together; when day dawned she saw that it was Lela who was with her and she sat down and upbraided him for deceiving her. Lela said that they had met by chance; he had not enticed her away, no harm had been done and she could go home if she liked or come away with him if she liked. The girl considered but she saw that if she went home now she would be disgraced and her family would be outcasted, so in the end she agreed to run away with Lela.

They went on and after travelling some days they came to a great city, where they took up their quarters in a tumble-down house and the next morning Lela went into the city to look for work. He went to the cut cherry and enrolled himself as a *muktear* (attorney) and soon the litigants and the magistrates found out how clever he was and he acquired a big practice. One day the Raja said, "This fellow is very handsome, I wonder what his wife is like?" And he sent an old woman to see; so the old woman went and got into conversation with Lela's wife and returned to the Raja and told him that none of his wives was so beautiful as Lela's wife; so the Raja determined to go and see her himself, and as the old woman said that she would hide herself in the house if she saw the Raja coming, he disguised himself as a poor man and went and saw her; he found that the old woman had not exaggerated and he determined to possess himself of Lela's wife. He had first to get Lela out of the way, so he sent for him and said, "You are a fine fellow and have given me satisfaction. I have one more commission for you, if you perform it I will give you half my kingdom and my sister in marriage." Lela said that he must hear what it was before he made any promise. The Raja said "It is this: in a certain mountain grows the Chandmoni Kusum flower; bring it to me and I will give you what I have promised:"—but the Raja felt sure that if Lela went to the mountain he would be eaten by the Rakhas (ogress) who dwelt there. Lela said that he would go if the Raja gave him a written bond in the presence of witnesses; and this the Raja willingly did. Then Lela went and told his wife and she said, "This is excellent: I have a younger sister in the mountain, her name is Chandmoni and it was she who planted the Chandmoni Kusum flower; when you get there call her by her name and she will certainly give you the flower."

So Lela started off and when he was gone his wife fell ill, and her body became a mass of sores. Directly Lela was out of the way, the Raja sent the old woman to see what his wife was doing and she brought back word that she was afflicted with illness; so the Raja sent medicines and told the old woman to nurse her. Lela went off and came to the cave in the mountain where Chandmoni lived with the Rakhas; and the Rakha. was away hunting men, so Lela called out Chandmoni' and told her who he was and begged her to hide him; then they planned how they should kill the Rakhas, and she hid him in the cave; presently the Rakhas returned and said to Chandmoni "I smell a man: where is he? "But Chandmoni said that there was no one there but herself; and that the smell was probably due to the Rakhas having been eating human flesh and recommended her to anoint herself with hot ghee. The Rakhas agreed: so Chandmoni put a great iron pan of ghee on to boil, and when it was boiling she called the Rakhas, and as the Rakhas was leaning over the pan, Lela ran out and pushed her into the boiling ghee and she died. Then Chandmoni asked Lela why he had come, and he told her, "to fetch the flower." She promised to give it to him but asked what was to become of her now that the ogress with whom she lived was dead. Lela promised to take her with him, so they cut off the tongue and ears and claws of the Rakhas and returned to the city. And directly Lela returned, his first wife recovered from her illness.

Then the Raja saw that it was useless to contend with Lela, and he gave him half his kingdom and married him to his sister according to his bond. So Lela lived with his three Ranis and they bore him children and after some years he told them that he was the son of a Raja and he wished to visit his own country and see whether his father was alie. So they set out in great style with horses and elephants and came to the town where Lela's father lived. Now five or six days after abandoning Lela, his father had become blind and he made over the management of his kingdom to a Dewan, and the Dewan and the Rani managed everything. When the Dewan heard that Lela had come with a great force he thought that he would loot the country and he ran away in fear. Then Lela sent word to his father to come to him, as he was the son who had been abandoned in the jungle, so the Raja set forth joyfully and after he had gone a few paces he began to see dimly, and by the time that he came to Lela's camp he had quite recovered his eyesight. When they met, father and son embraced and wept over each other; and Lela ordered a feast to be prepared and while this was being done a maidservant came running to say that the wicked Rani had hanged herself, so they went and burned the body and then returned and enjoyed the feast. Then the Raja resigned his kingdom to Lela and the ryots begged him to stay and rule over them; so he remained there and lived happily ever after.

V. KARMU AND DHARMU

There were once two brothers Karmu and Dharmu. Karmu was a farmer and Dharmu was a trader; once when Dharmu was away from home Karmu gave a religious feast and did not invite Dharmu's household; when Dharmu returned and learnt this, he told his wife that he also would perform the ceremonies in his house, so they set to work and were employed in cooking rice and vegetables far into the night; and Karam Gosain came down to see what preparations Dharmu was making in his honour, and he watched from the back of the house.

Just then Dharmu strained off the water from the cooked rice and threw it out of the window, and it fell on Karam Gosain and scalded him, and as the fhes and insects worried the wound, Karam Gosain went off to the Ganges and buried himself in the middle of the stream. As he had thus offended Karam Gosain, all Dharmu's undertakings failed and he fell into deep poverty, and had not even enough to eat, so he had to take service with his brother Karmu. When the time for transplanting the rice came, Dharmu used to plough and dig the ditches and mend the gaps along with the day labourers. Karmu told him not to work himself but act as overseer of the other labourers, and the labourers also told him that it was not suitable for him to work' as a labourer himself, but Dharmu said that he must earn his wages and insisted on working; and in the same way Dharmu's wife might have acted as overseer of the women, but she was ashamed not to work too.

One day they were transplanting the rice and Karmu brought out breakfast for the labourers; he told Dharmu and his wife to wash their hands and come and eat; but they answered that they belonged to the household and that the hired labourers should be fed first. So labourers ate and they ate up all the rice and there was nothing left for Dharmu and his wife. When midday meal was brought same thing happened, Dharmu and his wife got nothing; but ,they hoped that it would be made up to them when the wages were paid, and worked on fasting. At evening when they came to pay the wages in kind, Dharmu name was called out first, but he told his brother to pay the labourers first, and in doing this the paddy was all used up and there was nothing left for Dharmu and his wife; So they went home sorrowfully and their children cried for food and they had nothing to give them. In the night Dharmu's wife said "They promised to pay us for merely looking after the work and instead, we worked hard and have still got nothing. We will not work for them anymore; come, let us undo the work we did today, you cut down the embankments you repaired, and I will uproot the seedlings which I planted." So they went out into the night to do this. But whenever Dharmu raised his spade a voice called out "Hold, hold" And whenever his wife put out her hand to pull up the rice a voice called out "Hold, hold'!" Then they said "Who are you who stop us?" And the voice answered "You have done evil and offered Karam Gosain by scalding him; this is why you -have become poor and to-day have worked without food and without wages; he has gone to the Ganges and you must go and propitiate him." And they asked how they should propitiate him, and the voice said "Grind turmeric and put it on a plate, and buy new cloth and dye it with turmeric and make ready oil and take these things to the Ganges and call on Karam Gosain." And they believed the voice and the next day did as it commanded, and set off, leaving their children in charge of Karmu on the way they came to a fig-tree full of figs and they went to eat the fruit; but when they got near they found that all the figs were full of grubs, and they sang:—

"Exhausted by hunger we came to a fig-tree,
And found it full of grubs,
O Karam Gosain, how far off are you? "

Then they came to a mango tree and the same thing happened. And they went on and saw a cow with a calf; and they thought that they would milk the cow and drink the milk, but when they went to catch it, it ran away from them and would not let itself be caught;, and they sang:—

"We go to catch the cow and it runs away,
We go to catch the calf and it, runs away,
O Karam Gosain how far off are you?"

But the cow said to them—"Go to the banks of the Ganges." Then they came to a buffalo and went to milk it, but it lowered its head and charged them; and Dharmu cried but his wife said "Don't cry" and sang:—

"If you go to catch the buffalo, Dharmu, It will kill you.
How shall- we drink milk? How shall we drink milk?"
How far off are you, O our Karam Gosain?"

And the buffalo said, "Go on to the bank of the Ganges." Then they came to a horse and they thought that they would catch it and mount it, but it kicked and snorted; and they sang:—

"Dharmu tries to catch the horse:
But it kicks and runs away.
How shall we reach the Ganges ?

O Karam Gosain, how far off are you ? "

And the horse said, "Go to the banks of the Ganges. " Then they saw an elephant but it would not let them approach, so they decided to push on straight for the river; and they saw under a banyan tree a large pot full of rupees, but they were so disheartened that they made no attempt to touch it; then they met a woman who asked where they were going and when she heard, she said "For twelve years I have had a *pai* measure stuck on my throat; ask Karam Gosain for me how I am to get rid of it," and they promised; and going on they met a woman with a bundle of thatching grass stuck to her head; and she made them promise to ask Karam Gosain how she could be freed; then they met a woman with both her feet burning in a fire and another with a stool stuck fast to her back and they promised to enquire how these might be delivered.

So at last they came to the Ganges and they stood on the bank and called to Karam Gosain; and when he came they caught hold of him and he said "Fie, 'what low caste person is touching me? " But they said. "It is no low caste person, but Dharmu." Then they bathed him and anointed him with oil and turmeric and wrapped him in the new cloth which they had brought, and thus they persuaded him to return; so they rose up to go back, and Dharmu asked about the women whom they had met, and Karam Gosain said: The woman has a stool stuck to her back because when visitors came she never offered them a seat; let her do so in future, and she will be freed; and the woman has her feet burning in the fire because she pushed the fuel into the fire with her foot; let her not do so in future, and she will be freed; and the woman has the thatching grass stuck to her head because when she saw a friend with straw sticking in her hair she did not tell her about it; let her do so in future and she will be freed; and the woman has the *pai* measure stuck to her throat because, when her neighbour wanted to borrow her measure, she would not lend it; let her do so in future and she will be freed." And Karam Gosain asked whether they had seen an elephant and a horse and a buffalo and a cow and money and mangoes and figs and Dharmu said " Yes," but that he had not been able to catch the animals and the fruit was bad. Karam Gosain promised them that on their way back they should take possession of all; and they did so and mounted on the elephant and returned to their home with great wealth. On their way they met the four women and told them how they could be saved from their troubles. The villagers welcomed Dharmu and he arranged a great feast and gave paddy to all the villagers to husk; but where they had boiled it the weather became cloudy so that. they could not dry it, so they prayed to the sun and he at once shone out and dried the paddy.

Then a day was fixed and they prepared rice beer, and worshipped Karam

Gosain and they danced all night and got very drunk and enjoyed themselves.

VI. THE JEALOUS STEPMOTHER

There was once a man whose wife died leaving him with one son and after a year he married again. The second wife was very jealous of the son and she told her husband that she would not stay with him unless he killed the boy; at first he refused but she insisted and then he said that he was frightened to do the deed, but she might kill the boy herself if she liked. She said " No: he is your son and you must kill him; if he were mine I would do it. You need not be frightened; when you take him out ploughing make him drive the front plough, and you sharpen your plough pole to a point and drive it into him from behind and till him and then it will seem to be an accident." So the man promised and made a sharp point to his plough pole but wherever they ploughed the son drove his plough so fast that the father could not catch him up and so the boy was not killed; then the woman abused her husband and said that he was deceiving her. So he promised to finish the business the next day and told her to give the boy a good hot Breakfast before they started, so that he might receive one last kindness, and he said that they must find some other way of killing him because all the ploughing was finished; but his wife told him he could plough down their crop of *goondli* the bullocks would stop to eat the *goondli* as they went along and so he would easily catch up his son. Accordingly the next morning, father and son took out the ploughs and the boy asked where they should plough, and the father said that they would plough down the field of *goondli*. But the boy said. " Why should we do that? It is a good crop and will be ripe in a day or two; it is too late to sow again, we shall lose this crop and who knows whether we shall get anything in its place ?"

And the father thought 'What the boy says is true; the first crop is like the first child, if I kill him who will support me in my old age ? Who knows whether my second wife will have children. I will not kill him however angry she be;' so they unyoked their ploughs and went home. He told his wife that he would not kill the boy and scolded her and ended by giving her a beating. Then she ran away in a passion but he did not trouble to go and look for her and in a few days her father and brothers brought her back, and her husband told them what had happened and they also scolded her and told her to mend her ways.

VII. THE PIOUS WOMAN

There was once a very pious woman and her special virtue was that she would not eat or drink on any day until she had first given alms to a beggar. One day no beggar came to her house, so by noon she got tired of waiting, and, tying in her cloth some parched rice, she went to the place where the women drew water. When she got there she saw a Jugi coming towards her, she greeted him and said that she had brought dried rice for him. He said that omens had bidden him come to her and that he came to grant her a boon: she might ask one favour and it would be given her. The woman said:, "Grant me this noon to know where our souls go after death, and to see it the time of death how they escape, whether through the nose or the mouth, and where they go to; and tell my when I shall die and where my soul will go to; this I ask and no more. Then the jugi answered, "Your prayer is granted, but you must tell no one; if you do, the power will depart from you." So saying he took from his bag something like a feather and brushed her eyes with it and washed them with water. Then the woman's eyes were opened and she saw spirits—*bongas, bhuts, dains, churins*, and the souls of dead men; and the jugi told her not to be afraid, but not to speak to them lest men should think her mad; then he took his leave, and she returned home.

Now in the village lived a poor man and his wife and they were much liked because they were industrious and obedient; shortly afterwards this poor man died and the pious woman saw men come with a palankin and take away the poor man's soul with great ceremony. She was pleased at the sight and thought that the souls of all men were taken away like this. But shortly afterwards her father-in-law died. He had been a rich man, but harsh, and while the family were mourning the pious woman saw four sipahis armed with iron-shod staves and of fierce countenance come to the house and two entered and took the father-in-law by the neck and thrust him forth; their bound him and beat him, they knocked him down and as he could not walk they dragged him away by his legs. The woman followed him to the end of the garden and when she saw him being dragged away, she screamed. When her husband's relatives saw her screaming and crying they were angry and said that she must have killed her father-in-law by witchcraft, for she did not sit by the corpse and cry but went to the end of the garden. and after the body had been burnt they held a council and questioned her and told her that they would hold her to be a witch, if she could not explain. So she told them of the power which the Jugi had conferred on her and of what she had seen, and they believed her and acquitted her of the charge of witchcraft; but from that time she lost her power and saw no more spirits.

VIII. THE WISE DAUGHTER-IN-LAW

There was once a rich man who had seven sons, but one day his wife died and after this the family fell into poverty. All their property was sold and they lived by selling firewood in the bazar. At last the wife of the eldest son said to her father-in-law " I have a proposal to make: Do you choose one of us to be head of the family whom all shall obey; we cannot all be our own masters as at present." The old man said, "Well, I choose you," and he assembled the whole family and made them promise to obey the wife of his eldest son.

Thereupon she told them that they must all go out into the fields and bring her whatever they found. So the next day they went out in different directions and the old man found some human excrement and he thought "Well, my daughter-in-law told me to bring whatever I found" so he wrapped it up in leaves and took it home; and his daughter-in-law told him that he had done well and bade him hang up the packet at the back of the house. A few days later he found the slough of snake and he took that home and his daughter-in-law told him to tie a clod of earth to it to prevent its being blown away, and to throw it on to the roof of the house.

Some years after the Raja of the country was ill with cancer of the face and none of the *ojhas* could cure him. At last one *ojha* said that there was only one medicine which could effect a cure, but he saw no chance of obtaining it and that was human excrement 12 years old. Then the Raja sent messengers throughout the kingdom offering a reward of 200 Rupees to any one who could supply excrement twelve years old; and when a messenger came to the village where this family lived the daughter-in-law produced the packet which the old man had brought home and received the reward of 200 Rupees; and they were all delighted at making so much money by what the old man had brought home in jest.

And again it happened that the son of a Raja was bathing and he left his gold belt on the bank and a kite thought it was a snake and flew off with it. The prince was much distressed at the loss but the Raja told him not to grieve as the kite must have dropped it somewhere and he would offer a reward of a thousand rupees for it. Now the kite had soon found that the belt was not good to eat and seeing, the snake's skin which the old man had thrown on to the roof of the house, it dropped the belt and flew off with the skin; and the daughter-in-law picked up the belt and when criers came round offering a reward she produced it and received the money. And they praised her wisdom and by this means the family became rich again.

IX. THE OILMAN AND HIS SONS

There was once an oilman with five sons and they were all married and lived jointly with their father. But the daughters-in-law were discontented with this arrangement and urged their husbands to ask their father to divide the family property. At first the old man refused, but when his sons persisted, he told them to bring him a log two cubits long and so thick that two hands could just span it, and he said that if they could break the log in two, he would divide the property; so they brought the log and then asked for axes, but he told them that they must break it themseves by snapping it or twisting it or standing on it; As they tried and failed. Then the old man said, "You are five and I make six; split the log into six." So they split it and he gave each a piece and told them to break them, and each easily snapped his stick; then the old man said " We are like the whole log: we have plenty of property and are strong and can overcome attack; but if we separate we shall be like the split sticks and easily broken." They admitted that this was true and proposed that the property should not be divided but that they should all become separate in mess. But the father would not agree to this for he thought that people would call him a miser if he let his sons live separately without his giving them their share in the property as their own. So as they persisted in their folly he partitioned the property.

But in a few years they all fell into poverty and had not enough to eat nor clothes to wear, and father and mother were no better off; then the old man called all his sons and their wives and said "You see what trouble you have fallen into; I have a riddle for you, explain it to me. "There are four wells, three empty and one full of water; if you draw water from the full one and pour it into the three empty ones they will become full; but when they are full and the first one is empty, if you pour water from the three full ones into the empty one it will not be filled; what does this meant" And they could not answer and he said, "The four well mean that a man had three sons, and while they were little he filled their stomachs as the wells were filled with water; but when they separated they would not fill the old man's stomach."

And it was true, that the sons had done nothing to help their father and they were filled with shame and they agreed that as long as their father lived they would be joint with him and would not separate again until he died.

X. THE GIRL WHO FOUND HELPERS.

Once upon a time there were seven brothers and they were all married, and they had one sister who was not married. The brothers went away to a far country for a whole year, leaving their wives at home. Now the wives hated their sister-in-law and did their best to torment her. So one day they gave her a pot full of holes and told her to bring it back full of water; and threatened that if she failed she should have no food. So she took the pot to the spring and there sat down and cried and sang:—

"I am fetching water in a pot full of holes,
I am fetching water in a pot full of holes,
How far away have my brothers gone to trade."

After she had cried a long time, a number of frogs came up out of the water and asked her what was the matter, and she told them that she must fill the pot with water, and was not allowed to stop the holes with clay or lac. Then they told her not to cry, and said, that they would sit on the holes and then the water would not run out; they did this and the girl dried her eyes and filled the pot with water and took it home. Her sisters-in-law were much disappointed at her success, but the next day they told her to go to the jungle and bring back a bundle of leaves, but she was to use no rope for tying them up. So she went to the jungle and collected the leaves and then sat down and cried and sang:—

"I am to fetch leaves without a rope,
I am to fetch leaves without a rope,
How far have my brothers gone to trade?"

and as she cried a *buka sobo* snake came out and asked why she was crying, and when she told it, it said that it would coil itself round the leaves in place of a rope. So it stretched itself out straight and she piled the leaves on the top of it and the snake coiled itself tightly round them and so she was able to carry the bundle home on her head. Her sisters-in-law ran to set how she managed it, but she put the bundle down gently and the snake slipped away unperceived. Still they resolved to try again; so the next day they sent her to fetch a bundle of fire wood, but told her that she was to use no rope to tie it with. So she went to the jungle and collected the sticks and then sat down and cried:—

"I am to bring wood without tying it,
I am to bring wood without tying it,
How far have my brothers gone to trader?"

and as she cried a python came out and asked what was the matter, and when it heard, it told her not to cry and said that it would act as a rope to bind up the sticks; so it stretched itself out and she laid the sticks on it and then it coiled itself round them and she carried the bundle home.

As the sisters-in-law had been baffled thus, they resolved on another plan and proposed that they should all go and gather sticks in the jungle; and on the way they came to a *machunda* tree in full flower and they wanted to pick some of the flowers. The wicked sisters-in-law at first began to climb the tree, but they pretended that they could not and kept slipping down; then they hoisted their sister-in-law into the branches and told her to throw down the flowers to them. But while she was in the tree, they tied thorns round the trunk so that she could not descend and then left her to starve. After she had been in the tree a long time, her brothers passed that way on their return journey, and sat down under the tree to rest; the girl was too weak to speak but she cried and her tears fell on the back of her elder brother, and he looked up and saw her; then they rescued her and revived her and listened to her story; and they were very angry and vowed to have revenge. So they gave their sister some needles and put her in a sack and put the sack on one of the pack-bullocks,. And when they got home, they took the sack off gently and told their wives to carry it carefully inside the house, and on no account to put it down. But when the wives took it up, the girl inside pricked them with the needles so that they screamed and let the sack fail. Their husbands scolded them and made them take it up again, and they had to carry it in, though they were pricked till the blood ran down. Then the brothers enquired about all that had happened in their absence, and at last asked after their sister, and their wives said that she had gone to the jungle with some friends to get firewood. But the brothers turned on them and cold how they had found her in the *machunda* tree and had brought her home in the sack, and their wives were dumb-founded. Then the brothers said that they had made a vow to dig a well and consecrate it; so they set to work to dig a well two fathoms across and three fathoms deep; and when they reached water, they fixed a day for the consecration; and they told their wives to put on their best clothes and do the *cumaura* (betrothal) ceremony at the well. So the wives went to the well, escorted by drummers, and as they stood in a row round the well, each man pushed his own wife into it and then they covered the well with a wooden grating and kept them in it for a whole year and at the end of the year they pulled them out again.

Another version of this story gives three other tasks preliminary to those given above and begins as follows:-

Once upon a time there was a girl named Hira who had seven brothers. The brothers went away to a far country to trade leaving her alone in the house with their wives; these seven sisters-in-law hated Hira and did what they could to torment her; one day they sowed a basketful of mustard seed in a field and then told her to go and pick it all up; she went to the field and began to lament, singing:—

"They have sown a basket of mustard seed !
Oh, how far away have my brothers gone to trade."

As she cried a flock of pigeons came rustling down and asked her what was the matter, and when they heard, they told her to be comforted; they at once set to work picking up the mustard grain by grain and putting it into her basket; soon the basket was quite full and she joyfully took it home and showed it to her sisters-in-law. Then they set her another task and told her to bring them some bear's hair that they might weave it into a hair armlet for her wedding. So she went off to the jungle and sat down to cry; as she wept two bear cubs came up and asked what was the matter; when she told her story they bade her be of good cheer and took her into cave and hid her. Presently the mother bear came back and suckled her cubs, and when they had finished they asked their mother to leave them some of hair that they might amuse themselves by plaiting it while she was away.

She did so and directly she had gone off to look for food, the cubs gave the girl the hair and sent her home rejoicing. The sisters-in-law were only made more angry by her success and plotted how to kill her, so they ordered her to bring them some tiger's milk that they might make it into curds for her wedding. Then she went off to the jungle and began to weep, singing:—

"I brought the hair of a bear:
How far away have my brothers gone to trade."

At the sound two tiger cubs came running up and asked what was the matter; they told her to be comforted and they would manage to give her what she wanted; and they took her and hid her near where they were lying. Presently the tigress came back and suckled her cubs and as she did so she declared that she smelt a human being, but the cubs laughed at her and said that it must be they whom she smelt; so she was satisfied, and as she was leaving them they asked her to leave some of her milk in an earthern pot so that they might have something to drink if she were long in coming back. The tigress did so and directly she was gone the cubs gave the milk to the girl who took it home.— The story then continues as before.

XI. HOW TO GROW RICH

Once upon a time there was a woman whose husband died while she was pregnant, and she was very unhappy and used to pray daily to Singh Chando to give her a man child in place of her husband; she was left well off and among her property were three gold coins, and as she was afraid of these being stolen she decided to place them in the care of the village headman. So she took them to him and asked him to keep them till her child was born; and no one was present at the time but the headman's wife. In due time her child was born and by the mercy of Singh Chando it was a son; and when the boy had grown a bit and could run alone his mother decided to take back the gold coins, so she went to the headman and asked him for them; but he and his wife said: " We do not understand what you are talking about? We know of no gold coins: where are your witnesses? You must have had witnesses in such a business." And they drove her out. She went away crying and called the villagers together and asked them to decide the matter. So they qestioned her and the headman but as it was word against word they could come to no decision; so they settled to put the parties on oath, but the headman and the woman both swore that they had spoken the truth, saying, "May we die if we have spoken falsely." Then the villagers made them swear by their children and the woman and the headman laid their hands on the heads of their sons and swore; and when the woman swore her son fell down dead and she took up the dead body in her arms and ran away with it.

The villagers were very sorry for what had happened but the headman and his wife abused them for not having believed their word. The woman had not gone very far before she met a stranger who asked why she was crying and when she told him, he said: "Do not cry; you told one falsehood and so your son has died. 'Take your child back to the villagers and tell them that it was five gold coins and not three that you gave to the headman and if you do this the child will come to life again."

So the woman hastened back and found the villagers still assembled and she told them as the stranger had directed; and she agreed to be sworn again an the body of the child, and the headman promised to pay five gold pieces if the child were restored to life. So the woman laid her hands on the dead child and swore, and it was restored to life. Then the headman was dumbfounded and reluctantly brought out five gold pieces and gave them to the woman. She gave five rupees to the villagers and they made the headman give them ten rupees for having deceived them, and they bought pigs and had a feast.

In the course of time the boy grew up and his mother urged him to marry. He asked her if she knew how to choose a wife and also what sort of cattle to buy, and she said that she did not know; her husband had not told her this. So the youth said that he would go to Singh Chando and ask.

His mother washed his clothes for him and gave him food for the journey and he set out. On the way he met a man who asked him where he was going and he answered that he was going to make a petition to Singh Chando. "Then," said the man, "make a petition for me also. I have so much wealth that I cannot look after it all; ask him to take away half from me." The youth promised and went on and he met another man who said that he had so many cattle that he could not build enough cow-houses for them and asked to petition Singh Chando to diminish their number; and he promised, and went on and came to Singh Chando, and there he asked how to choose a wife and how to buy cattle. And Singh Chando said, "When you buy a bullock first put your hand on its quarter and if it shrinks and tries to get free, buy it; and when you want a wife enquire first as to the character of her father and mother; good parents make good children." Then the youth asked about the two men he had met; Singh Chando said, Tell the first man when he is ploughing to plough two or three furrows beyond the boundary of his field and his wealth will diminish and tell the second man to drive away three or four of his cattle every day and their number will decrease." So the youth returned and met the man who had too many cattle and told him what Chando had said, and the man thought "If I drive away three or four head of cattle every day I shall soon become poor" so from that time he looked out for any straying cattle and would drive them home with his own; if the owner claimed them, he gave them up, but if no claimant appeared, he kept them and so he became richer than ever. And the youth went on and met the man who was too rich, and when he heard what Chando had said he thought, If I plough over the boundary on to my neighbour's land it will be a great sin and I shall soon become poor;" and he went to his ploughmen and told them never to plough right up to the edge of the field but to leave two of three furrows space, and they obeyed and from that time he grew richer than ever. And the youth returned to his mother and told her all that had happened and they understood the meaning of the advice which Chando had given to the two men and acted accordingly. And it is true that we see that avaricious men who trespass across boundaries become poor.

XII. THE CHANGED CALF

There was once a cowherd named Sona who saved few rupees and he decided to buy a calf ; so as to have something to show for his labours ; and he went to a distant village and bought a bull calf and on the way home he was benighted. So he turned into a Hindu village and went to an oilman's house and asked to be allowed to sleep there. When the oilman saw such a fine calf he coveted it and he told Sona to put it in the stable along with his own bullock and he gave him some supper and let him sleep in the verandah. But in the middle of' the night the oilman got up and moistened some oil cake and plastered it over the calf; he then untied his own bullock and made it lick the oil cake off the calf, and as the bullock was accustomed to that oil cake it licked at greedily; then the oilman raised a cry, "The bullock that turns the oil mill has given birth to a calf." And all the villagers collected, and saw the bullock licking the calf and they believed the oilman. Sona did not wake up and knew nothing of all this, the next morning he got up and went to untie his calf and drive it away, but the oilman would not let him and claimed the calf as his own. Then Sona called the villagers to come and decide the matter: but they said that they had seen him bring no calf to the village and he had not called any of them to witness it, but they had seen the bullock licking the calf; why should the bullock lick any but its own calf. No one ever saw a bullock lick a strange bullock or cow and so they awarded the calf to the oilman. Then Sona said that he would call someone to argue the matter and he went away meaning to get some men from the next village: but he lost his way in the jungle and as he went along a night-jar flew up from under his feet; he called out to it to stay as he was in great distress, and the bird alighted and asked what was the matter, and Sona told it his trouble.Then the night-jar said that it would argue the matter for him but it must have colleague and it told Sona to go on and ask the first living being he met to help; so he went on and met a jackal and the jackal agreed to help the night-jar, and they told him to call the villagers to the edge of the jungle and not to let them bring any dogs with them. So Sona brought all the villagers to the jungle and the night-jar and jackal sat side by side on a stone.

Then Sona asked the villagers whether they would let him take away the calf or no, and they persisted in their previous opinion. At last one man said, "What are your advocates doing? It seems to me that they are asleep." And at this the two woke up with a start and looked about them, and the night-jar said "I have been asleep and dreamed a dream: will you men please hear it and explain its meaning?"

And the jackal said, "I too have had a dream, please explain it for me. If you can explain the meaning you shall keep the calf and, if not, the boy shall have it." The villagers told them to speak and the night-jar said, I saw two night-jar's eggs and one egg, was sitting on them, tell me what this means." And the jackal said, "I saw that the sea was on fire and the fishes were all being burnt up, and I was busy eating them and that was why I did not wake up, what is the meaning of this dream?" And the villagers said. "The two dreams are both alike: neither has any meaning; an egg cannot sit on an egg, and the sea cannot catch fire." The jackal said, "Why cannot it be? If you won't believe that water can catch fire why do you say that a bullock gave birth for a calf? Have you ever seen such a thing? Speak." And they admitted that they had never seen a bullock have a calf, but only cows. " Then," said the jackal," explain why you have given the oilman a decree." And they admitted that they were wrong and awarded the calf to Sona and fined the oilman five rupees for having deceived them.

XIII. THE KOERI AND THE BARBER

There was a well-to-do man of the Koeri (cultivating) caste and opposite his house lived a barber who was very poor; and the barber thought that if he carried on his cultivation just as the Koeri did he might get better results; so every day he made some pretext to visit the Koeri's house and hear what work he was going to do the next day, and with the same object he would listen outside his house at night; and he exactly imitated the Koeri: he yoked his cattle and unyoked them, he ploughed and sowed and transplanted just when the Koeri did and the result was good, for that year he got a very fine crop. But he was not content with this and resolved to continue to copy the Koeri; the Koeri suspected what the barber was doing and did not like it. So he resolved to put the matter to the test and at the same time teach the barber to mind his own business. In January they both planted sugar cane, and one day when the crop was half grown the barber was sitting at the Koeri's house and the Koeri gave orders to his servants to put the leveller over the crop the next day and break it down; this was only a pretence of the Koeri's, but the barber went away and the next day crushed his sugar cane crop with the leveller, the whole village laughed to see what he had done; but it turned out that each root of the barber's sugar cane sent up a number of shoots and in the end he had a much heavier crop than the Koeri.

Another day the Koeri announced that he was going to sow *but* (pulse) and therefore ordered his servants to bring out the seed and roast it well, that it might germinate quickly; and the barber hearing this went off and had his seed *but* roasted and the next day he sowed it, only a very few seeds germinated, while the crop of the Koeri which had not really been roasted sprouted finely. The barber asked the Koeri why his crop had not come up well, and the Koeri told him that it must be because he had not roasted the seed enough; the few seeds that had come up must have been those which had been roasted most. But in the end the laugh was against the Koeri, for the few seeds of the barber's which germinated, produced such fine plants that when he came to thresh them out he had more grain than the Koeri, and so in 3 or 4 years the barber became the, richer man of the two.

XIV. THE PRINCE WHO ACQUIRED WISDOM

There was once a Raja who had an only son and the Raja was always urging his son to learn to read and write in order that when he came to his kingdom he might manage well and be able to decide disputes that were brought to him for judgment; but the boy paid no heed to his father's advice and continued to neglect his lessons. At last when he was grown up the prince saw that his father was right and he resolved to go away to foreign countries to acquire wisdom; so he set off without telling anyone but his wife, and he took with him a purse of money and three pieces of gold. After travelling a long time, he one day saw a man ploughing in a field and he went and got some tobacco from him and asked him whether there were any wise men living in that neighbourhood. What do you want with wise men?", asked the ploughman.The Prince said that he was travelling to get wisdom. The ploughman said that he would give him instruction if he were paid. Then the Prince promised to give him one gold piece for each piece of wisdom. The ploughman agreed and said. "Listen attentively ! My first maxim is this: You are the son of a Raja; whenever you go to visit a friend or one of your subjects and they offer you a bedstead, or stool, or mat to sit on, do not sit down at once but move the stool or mat a little to one side; this is one maxim: give me my gold coin." So the Prince paid him. Then the ploughman said. "The second maxim is this: You are the son of a Raja; whenever you go to bathe, do not bathe at the common bathing place, but at a place by yourself; give me my coin," and the Prince did so. Then he continued, "My third maxim is this: You are the son of a Raja; when men come to you for advice of to have a dispute decided, listen to what the majority of those present say and do not follow your own fancy, now pay me;" and the Prince gave him his last gold coin, and said that he had no more. "Well," said the ploughman, "your lesson is finished but still I will give you one more piece of advice free and it is this: "You are the son of a Raja; Restrain your anger, if anything you see or hear makes you angry, still do not at once take action; hear the explanation and weigh it well, then if you find cause you can give rein to your anger and if not, let the offender off."

After this the prince set his face homewards as he had spent all his money; and he began to repent of having spent his gold pieces on advice that seemed worthless. However on his way he turned into a bazar to buy some food and the shopkeepers on all side called out " Buy, buy," so he went to a shop and the shopkeeper invited him to sit on a rug; he was just about to do so when he remembered the maxim of his instructor and pulled the rug to one side; and when he did so he saw that it had been spread over the mouth of a well and that if he had sat on it he would have been killed *; so he began to believe in the wisdom of his teacher. Then he went on his way and on the road he turned aside to a tank to bathe, and remembering the maxim of his teacher he did not bathe at the common place but went to a place apart; then having eaten his lunch he continued his journey, but he had not gone far when he found that he had left his purse behind, so he turned back and found it lying at the place where he had put down his things when he bathed; thereupon he applauded the wisdom of his teacher, for if he had bathed at the common bathing place someone would have seen the purse and have taken it away. When evening came on he turned into a village and asked the headman to let him sleep in his verandah, and there was already one other traveller sleeping there and in the morning it was found that the traveller had died in his sleep. Then the headman consulted the villagers and they decided that there was nothing to be done but to throw away the body, and that as the Prince was also a traveller he should do it. At first he refused to touch the corpse as he was the son of a Raja, but the villagers insisted and then he bethought himself of the maxim that he should not act contrary to the general opinion; so he yielded and dragged away the body, and threw it into a ravine.

Before leaving it he remembered that it was proper to remove the clothes, and when he began to do so he found round the waist of the body a roll of coin; so he took this and was glad that he had followed the advice of his teacher.

That evening he reached the boundary of his own territory and decided to

* This is why Santals when going to eat, move the stool that is offered to them before they sit down ors it

press on home although it was dark; at midnight he reached the palace and without arousing anyone went to the door of his wife's room. Outside the door he saw a pair of shoes and a sword; at the sight he became wild with rage and drawing the sword he called out: "Who is in my room ?"

As a matter of fact the Prince's wife had got the Prince's little sister to sleep with her, and when the girl heard the Prince's voice she got up to leave; but when she opened the door and saw the Prince standing with the drawn sword she drew back in fear; she told him who she was and explained that they had put the shoes and sword at the door to prevent anyone else from entering; but in his wrath the Prince would not listen and called to her to come out and be killed.

Then she took off her cloth and showed it to him through the crack of the door and at the sight of this he was convinced: then he reflected on the advice of his teacher and repented, because he had nearly killed his sister through not restraining his wrath.

XV. THE MONKEY BOY

There was once a man who had six sons and two daughters and he died leaving his wife pregnant of a ninth child.

And when the child was born it proved to be a monkey.

The villagers and relations advised the mother to make away with it, but she refused saying "Chando knows why he has given me such a child, but as he has done so I will rear it."

All her relations said that if she chose to rear a monkey they would turn her out of the family. However she persisted that she would do so at all costs. So they sent her to live with her child in a hut outside the village, and the monkey boy grew up and learned to talk like a human being.

One day his elder brothers began to clear the jungle for cultivation and the monkey boy took a hatchet and went with them; he asked where he could clear land for himself and in fun they showed him the place where the jungle was thickest. So he went where and drove his hatchet into the trunk of a tree and then returned and watched his brothers working hard clearing the scrub, and when they had finished their work he went and fetched his hatchet and returned home with them. Every day he did the same--and one day his brothers asked why he spent all his time with them, but he said that he only came to them when he was tired of cutting down trees; they laughed at this and said that they would like to see his clearing, so he took them to the place and to their astonishment they saw a large clearing, bigger than they had been able to make for themselves. Then the brothers burnt the jungle they had cut down and began to plough the land.

But the monkey boy's mother had no plough or cattle nor any seed rice; the only thing in the house was a pumpkin, so he took the seed out of the pumpkin and sowed it in this clearing. His brothers asked what he had sown and he told them—Rice.

The brothers ploughed and sowed and used to go daily to watch the growing crop, and one say they went to have a look at the monkey boy's crop and they saw that it was pumpkins and not rice and they laughed at him. When their crop was ripe the brothers prepared to offer the first fruits and the monkey boy watched them that he might observe the same ceremonies as they. One day they brought home the first fruits and offered them to the *bongas*, and they invited the monkey boy and his mother to come to the feast which followed the offering.

They both went and enjoyed themselves; and two or three days later the monkey boy said that he would also have a feast of first fruits, so he told his mother to clear the courtyard and invited his brothers and he purified himself and went to his clearing and brought home the biggest pumpkin that had grown there; this he offered to the spirits; he sliced off the top of it as if it were the head of a fowl, and as he did so he saw that the inside was full of rice; he called his mother and they filled a winnowing fan with the rice and there was enough besides to nearly fill a basket; they were delighted at this windfall but kept the matter secret lest they should be robbed. The monkey boy told his mother to be sure and cook enough rice so that his brothers and their wives might have as much as ever they could eat, and not merely a small helping such as they had given him, and if necessary he would go and fetch another pumpkin; so his mother boiled the rice. When the time fixed for the feast came, nothing was to be seen of the brothers because they did not expect that there would really be anything for them to eat; so the monkey boy went and fetched them, and when they came to the feast they were astonished to have as much rice as they could eat. When the crop was quite ripe the monkey boy gathered all the pumpkins and got sufficient rice from them to last for the whole year.

After this the brothers went out to buy horses, and the monkey boy went with them and as he had no money he took nothing but a coil of rope ; his brothers were ashamed to have him with them and drove him away, so he went on ahead and got first to the place where the horse dealer lived. The brothers arrived late in their evening and decided to make their purchases the following morning and ride their horses home, so they, camped for the night. The monkey boy spent the night hiding on the rafters of the stable; and in the night the horses began to talk to each other and discussed which could gallop farthest, and one mare said " I can gallop twelve *kos* on the ground and then twelve kos in the air." When the monkey boy heard this he got down and lamed the mare by running a splinter into her hoof. The next morning the brothers bought the horses which pleased them and rode off. Then the monkey boy went to the horse dealer and asked why the mare was lame and advised him to apply remedies. But the dealer said that that was useless: when horses got ill they always died; then the monkey boy asked if he would sell the mare and offered to give the coil of rope in exchange; the dealer, thinking that the animal was useless, agreed, so the monkey boy led it away, but when he was out of sight he took out the splinter and the lameness at once ceased. Then he mounted mare and rode after his brothers, and when he had nearly overtaken them he rose into the air and flew past his brothers and arrived first at home. There he tied up the mare outside his house and went and bathed and had his dinner and waited for his brothers.

They did not arrive for a full hour afterwards and when they saw the monkey boy and his mount they wanted to know how he had got home first. He boasted of how swift his mare was and so they arranged to have a race and match their horses against his. The race took place two or three days later and the monkey boy's mare easily beat all the other horses, she gallopped twelve *kos* on the ground and twelve *kos* in the air. Then they wanted to change their horses for his, but he said they had had first choice and he was not going to change.

In two or three years the monkey boy became rich and then he announced that he wanted to marry; this puzzled his mother for she thought that no human girl would marry him while a monkey would not be able to talk; so she told him that he must find a bride for himself. One day he set off to look for a wife and came to a tank in which some girls were bathing, and he took up the cloth belonging to one of them and ran up a tree with it, and when the girl missed it and saw it hanging down from the tree she borrowed a cloth from her friends and went and asked the monkey boy for her own; he told her that she could only have it back if she consented to marry him; she was surprised to find that he could talk and he conversed she was bewitched by him and let him pull her up into the tree by her hair, and she called out to her friends to go home and leave her where she was. Then he took her on his back and ran off home with her.

The girl's father and relations turned out with bows and arrows to look for the monkey who had carried her off but he had gone so far away that they never found him. When the monkey boy appeared with his bride all the villagers were astonished that he had found anyone to marry him, but everything was made ready for the marriage as quickly as possible and all the relations were invited and the wedding took place and the monkey boy and his wife lived happily ever after.

XVI. THE MISER'S SERVANT

Once there was a rich man who was a miser. Although he kept farm servants they would never stay out the year with him; but ran away in the middle. When the villagers asked why they ran always and so lost their year's wages, the servants answered, "you would do the same in our place: at the busy time of the year he speaks us fair and feeds us well, but directly the crops are gathered he begins to starve us; this year we have had nothing to eat since September."

And the villagers said "Well, that is a good reason, a man can stand scolding but not starvation; we all work to fill our bellies, hunger is the worst disease of all." The news that the miser made his servants work for nothing spread throughout the neighborhood so he could get no servants near by and when he brought them from a distance they soon heard of this character and ran away. Men would only work for him on daily wages and because of his miserliness they demanded higher wages than usual from him and would not work without. Now there was a young fellow named Kora who heard all this and he said,"If I were that man's servant I would not run away. I would get the better of him; ask him if he wants a servant and if he says, yes, take me to him." The man to whom Kora told this went to the miser and informed him that Kora was willing to engage himself to him; so Kora was fetched and they had a drink of rice beer and then the miser asked Kora whether he would work for the full year and not run away in the middle. Kora said that he would stay if he were satisfied with the wages. The master said " I will fix your wages when I see your work; if you are handy at every thing I will give You 12 *Kats* of rice and if you are only a moderate worker then 9 or 10 *Kats* besides your clothes. How much do you ask for?"

And Kora said " Well, listen to me: I hear that your servants run away in the middle of the year because you give them so little to eat, all I ask for my wages is that you give me once a year one grain of rice and I will sow it and you must give me low land to plant all the seed that I get from it,, and give me one seed of maize and I will sow it for seed, and you must give me upland to sow all the seed I get from it; and give me the customary quantity of clothes, and for food give me one leaf full of rice three times a day. I only want what will go on a single leaf, you need not sew several leaves together into a plate. I will ask for no second helping but if you do not fill the leaf full I shall have the right to abuse you, and if I do not do all the work you give me properly, then you can abuse me and beat me. If I run away from fear of hard work you may cut off the little finger of my right hand, and if you do not give me the wages we have agreed upon then I shall have the right to cut off the little finger of your hand. What do you say to this proposal: consult your friends and give me your answer." Then the miser answered "I engage you on these terms and if I turn you off without reason you may cut off my little finger." Then Kora turned to the man who had fetched him and said, "Listen to all this: if there is any dispute hereafter you will be my witness."

So Kora began to work and the first day they gave him rice on a. single sal leaf and he ate it up in one mouthful: but the next day he brought a plantain leaf (*which is some three feet long*) and said" Give me my rice on this and mind you fill it full.,' And they refused: but he said,"Why not? it is only a single leaf " and they had to give in because he was within his rights; so he ate as much as he wanted, and every day he brought a plantain leaf till his master's wife got tired and said to her husband " Why have you got a servant like this-he takes a whole pot of rice to himself every day," but he answered " Never mind: his wages are nothing, he is working for his keep alone; so the whole year Kora got his plantain leaf filled and he was never lazy over his work so they could find no fault with him on that score, and when the year was up they gave him one grain of rice and one seed of maize for his wages for the year. Kora kept them carefully, and his, master's sons laughed at him and said "Mind you don't drop them or let a mouse eat. them."

Kora said nothing but when the time for sowing maize came he took his grain of maize and sowed it by the dung heap, and he called them to see where he sowed it; and at the time of sowing rice he sowed his grain separately, and when the time for transplanting came he planted his rice seedling in a hollow and bade them note it. When the maize ripened it was found that his plant had two big cobs and one small one on it, and his rice seedling sent up a number of ears; and when it ripened he cut it and threshed it and got one pai of rice, and he kept the maize and rice for seed. And the next year also he sowed this seed separately and it produced a big basket of rice and another one of maize, and he kept this also for seed; and in the course of five or six years he had taken all their high lands to sow his seed in and in a few years more he had taken all their rice lands too. Then his master was very miserable but he saw that it was useless to make any complaint and the master became so poor that he had to worker as a servant to Kora. At last the miser called the heads of the village together and wept before them, and they had pity on him and interceded for him; but Kora said "It is God who has punished him and not I; he made poor men work for nothing for long and now he has to suffer; "but they asked him to be merciful and give him some land, and he agreed and said "Cut off his little finger and I will let him 'off his bargain; and call all the servants whom he has defrauded and I will pay them" but the miser would not have his finger cut off; then Kora said; Let him keep his finger and I will give him back half his land." The miser agreed to this and promised to treat his servants well on future, and in order to lessen his shame he married his daughter to Kora; and he had to admit that it was by his own folly that this trouble had befallen him.

XVII. KUWAR AND THE RAJAH'S DAUGHTER

There was once a rich merchant who lived in a Raja's city; and the Raja founded a school in order that his own children might have some education, and the boys and the girls of the town used to go to the school as well as the Raja's sons and daughters and among them the rich merchant's son, whose name was Kuwar. In the course of time the children all learned to read and write. In the evenings all the boys used to mount their horses and go for a ride.

Now it happened that Kuwar and the Raja's daughter fell in love with each other and she wrote him a letter saying that if he did not marry her she would forcibly install herself in his house. He wrote back and begged her not to come to his house as this would be the ruin of his family; but he said that he would willingly run away with her to a distant country, and spend his whole life with her, if she would overlook the fact that they were of different castes; and if she agreed to this they must settle to what country to go. Somehow news of their intention got about, and the Raja was told that his daughter was in love with the merchant's son. Then the Raja gave orders that his daughter was not to be allowed to go outside the palace, and the merchant spoke severely to Kuwar and neither of them was allowed to go to the school any more. But one day the princess went to the place where the Raja's horses were tied up and among them was a mare named Piyari and she went up to the mare and said, you have eaten our salt for a long time, will you now requite me?" And Piyari said "Certainly I will!". "Then the princess asked" "If I mount you will you jump over all these horses and this wall and escape?" And the mare said "Yes, but you will have to hold on very tight." The princess said "That is my look-out: it is settled that on the day I want you 'you will jump over the wall and escape." Then she wrote a letter to Kuwar and gave it to her maid-servant to deliver into Kuwar's own hands, without letting anyone know: and in the letter she fixed a day for their elopement and told Kuwar to wait for her by a certain tree. So on the day fixed after everyone was asleep Kuwar went to the tree and almost at once the princess came to him riding on Piyari; he asked her how she had escaped and whether she had been seen and she told him how the mare had jumped over the wall without anyone knowing.: then they both mounted Piyari and drove her like the wind and in one night they passed through the territory of two or three Rajas and in the morning were in a far country.

Then they dismounted to cook their rice, and went to the house of an old woman to ask for a light with which to light their fire. Now this old woman had seven sons and they were all robbers and murderers; and six of them had killed travellers and carried off their wives and married them. When Kuwar and the princess came asking for a light the seven sons were away, hunting and when the old woman saw the princess she resolved to marry her to her youngest son and made a plan to delay them; so she asked them to cook their rice at her house and offered them cooking pots and water pots and firewood and everything necessary; they did not know that she meant to kill Kuwar and, unsuspiciously accepted her offer. When they had finished cooking Kuwar asked the old woman whether she lived alone and she told him that she was a widow but had seven sons and they were all away on a trading expedition. The old woman kept on looking out to see if her sons were returning, and she had made an arrangement with them that if she ever wanted them she would set fire to a small hut and they would come home at once when they saw the smoke rising. But before her sons came back Kuwar and the princess finished their meal and paid the old woman and mounted Piyari and gallopped off. Then the old woman set fire to the hut and her sons, seeing the smoke hurried home. She told them that a beautiful girl had just left who would make a suitable wife for the youngest of the brothers. Then the brothers tied on their swords and mounted their horses and went in pursuit. Kuwar and the princess knew nothing of their danger and rode on happily, but presently they heard horses neighing behind them and looking round, saw men riding after them with drawn swords. Then the princess said to Kuwar "Our enemies are upon us; do you sit in front and let me sit behind you, then they will kill us both together. If I am in front they may kill you alone and carry me off alive." But while they were thinking of this the seven brothers caught them up and began to abuse them and charge them with having set fire to the house in which they had eaten their rice, and told them to come back with them at once. Kuwar and the princess were too frightened to answer and they had no sword with which to defend themselves.Then the robbers surrounded them and killed Kuwar, and they said to the princess "You cannot stay here all alone; we will take you back and you shall marry one of us." The princess answered "Kill me here at once, never will I go with you." They said "We shall take away your horse and all your food, will not that make you go?" But the princess threw herself on the dead body of Kuwar and for all they could do they could not drag her off it. Then the murderers said to the youngest brother "She is to be your wife: you must pull heraway." But he refused saying, " No, if I take her away she will not stay with me, she will probably hang herself or drown herself; I do not want a wife like that, if any of you want her, yon can have her." But they said that it would not be right for one of them to take a second wife while their youngest brother was unmarried, and that their mother intended him to marry this girl; if he would not they would kill her there and then. But the youngest brother had pity on her and asked them to spare her life, so they took away her horse and her food and everything that she had and went away and left her there.

For a day and a night the princess lay there weeping and lamenting her dead Kuwar and never ceased for a moment. Then Chando said, " who is this who is weeping and what has happened to her?" And he sent Bidhi and Bisha to see what was the matter; they came and told him that a princess was weeping over the body of her dead husband and would not leave him though she had been robbed of everything she had.

Then Chando told them to go and frighten her, and if they could frighten her away from her husband's dead body he would do nothing, but if she would not leave him then they were to restore him to life. So they went and found her holding the dead body of her husband in her lap and weeping; and they first assumed the form of tigers and began to circle round her roaring, but she only went on weeping and sang:—

"You have come roaring, 'tigress:
First eat me, tigress:
Then only will I let you eat the body of my lord."

She would not quit the body nor run away from fear of the tigers, so they slunk away and came back in the form of two leopards, and prowled round her growling; but she only sang

"You have come roaring, leopardess
First eat me, leopardess
Then only will I let you eat the body of my lord."

and as she would not fly from them they slunk away and came back in the form of two bears, but the princess only sang the same song,; then they appeared as two elephants; and then as two huge snake which hissed terribly but still she only wept; and many forms they tried to frighten her away but she would not move nor leave the corpse of Kuwar, so in the end they saw that all the heart of the princess was with Kuwar and that even in death they could not be separated, so at last they drew near to her in the form of human beings and asked her why she was crying, as they had heard her weeping from a long way off and had been filled with pity for her lamentations. Then the princess said "Alas, this youth and I are from such and such a country and as we loved and our lives were bound up in each other we ran away together hither, and here on the road he has been killed and the murderers have left me without my horse or food and this is why I weep. Then Bidhi and Bidha said, " Daughter, rise up and we will take you to your home, or we will find you another husband;

this one is dead and cannot be restored to you; you will find another; come arise, you have but one life." But the princes answered "No I will not go and leave him here. I will not leave him while my life lasts; but I pray you if you know of any medicine that might restore him to life, to try it." Then they answered "We know something of medicine and in you wish we will try to cure him;" so saying, they ground up some simples and told the princess to spread out a cloth and lay the dead body on it and to put the head which had been cut off into position, and then to cover it with the cloth and hold the head in position; so she did as they bade, and they rubbed the medicine on the body and then they suddenly disappeared from her sight.

Then in a few moments she saw Kuwar's chest heave as if he were breathing; thereupon she shook him violently and he rose up and said "Oh, what a long time I have slept," but the princess said, " Do not talk of sleep; you were killed and two men appeared from somewhere and applied medicine and brought you to life again;" then Kuwar asked where they were and she told him how they had disappeared without her knowledge.

Then they rose up and went in search of food, to a village where there was a bazar, and they tried to get employment as servants; but the people advised them to go to the capital city where the Raja lived, and there if no one would take them as servants they could get employment as coolies on a big tank which the Raja was excavating. So they went there, and as they could not get employment as servants they went to work at the tank with the common coolies and were paid their wages at the end of the week and so managed to live. Kuwar's desire was to somehow save five or six rupees and then build a little house for themselves.

Now although the tank had been dug very deep there were no signs of any water. Then the Raja ordered the centre post to be planted in hopes that this would make the water rise; and he told the coolies not to run away as he would make a feast to celebrate, the making of the tank and would distribute presents among them, and at this the labourers were very pleased.

Now Kuwar's wife was very fair to see and the Raja saw her and fell in love with her and made a plot to get possession of her. So when the centre post had been planted and still no water came he said " We must see what sacrifice is required to make the water come. I have animals of all kinds; one by one they shall be offered and you shall sing and dedicate them." So first an elephant was led down into the bed of the tank and the people sang

"Tank, we will sacrifice to you an elephant
Let clear water bubble up, O tank,"

but no water came.

Then they led down a horse and sang a similar song, but no water came;

and then in succession a camel, a donkey, a cow, a buffalo, a goat and a sheep were offered but no water came, and so they stopped. Then the Raja asked why they stopped and they said that they had no more animals. Then the Raja bade them sing a song dedicating a man, to see if that would bring the water; so they sang and as they sang water bubbled up everywhere from the bottom of the tank and then the coolies were stricken with fear for they did not know which of them would be sacrificed.

But the Raja sent his soldiers and they seized Kuwar and bound him to the post in the middle of the tank; and then a song was sung dedicating him to the tank and as the water rose around him the princess wept bitterly; but the Raja said "Do not cry I will arrange for your support and will give you part of my kingdom and you shall live in my palace." The princess said " Yes : hereafter I may stay with you, but let me now watch Kuwar till he is drowned;"so Kuwar fixed his eyes on the princess and tears streamed down his face until the waters rose and covered him; and the princess also gazed, at him till he was drowned. Then the Raja's soldiers told her to come with them and she said, Yes, I am coming, but let me first offer a libation of water to my dead husband;" and on this pretext she went into the water and then she darted to the place where Kuwar had been bound and sank beneath the surface. The Raja bade men rescue her but all were afraid to enter the water and she was seen no more. Then the Raja gave all the coolies a feast and scattered money among the crowd and dismissed them. And this is the end of the story.

XVIII. THE LAUGHING FISH

There was once a merchant who prospered in his business and in the course of time became very rich. He had five sons but none of them was married. In the village where he lived was an old tank which was half silted up and he resolved to clean it out and deepen it, if the Raja would give it to him; so he went to the Raja and the Raja said that he could have the tank if he paid forty rupees. The merchant paid the money and then went home and called his family together and said that they would first improve the tank and then find wives for all his sons. The sons agreed and they collected coolies and drained off the water and began to dig out the silt. When they had drained off the water they found in the bed of the tank a number of big fish of unknown age: which they caught and two of them they sent to the Raja as a present. When the fish were carried into the presence of the Raja they both began to laugh: then the Raja said "What is the meaning of this? Here are two dead fish, why are they laughing?,' And he told the men who brought the fish to explain what was the matter or else to take them away again. But they could give no explanation. Then the Raja called all his officers and astrologers and asked them what they thought it meant: but no one could give him any answer. Then the Raja told the men to take the fish away again, and to tell the merchant that, if he could not explain why the fish laughed, he would kill him and all his descendants; and he wrote a letter to the same effect, and fixed a day by which the merchant was to explain the matter. When the merchant read the letter he fell into the greatest distress and for two or three days he could not make up his mind whether to go on with the work on the tank or no; but in the end he resolved to finish it so that his name might be held in remembrance. So they finished the work and then the merchant said to his sons:, "My sons I cannot arrange for your marriages, for the Raja has threatened to kill us all, if I cannot explain why the fish laughed; you must all escape from here so that our family may not die out;" but the younger sons all answered "We are not able to take care of ourselves, either you come with us to protect us or we will stay here." Then the merchant told his eldest son to escape alone so that their family might not become extinct.

So the eldest son took a supply of money and went away into a far country. After travelling a long time he came to a town where a Raja lived and decided to stay there; so he first went to a tank and bathed and sat down on the bank to eat some refreshment; and as he sat the daughter of the Raja came down to the tank to bathe and she saw the merchant's son and their eyes met. Then the princess sent her maidservants to ask him where he came from; and he told them where he came from and that he meant to make a stay in that town, and he promised them a rupee if they could persuade the princess to uncover my face. They went and told their mistress all this and she answered "Go and get your rupee from him, I will uncover my face; and ask him what he wants." And when they went, she drew aside the cloth from her face; then he gave them the rupee, and they asked him whether he had seen her and what his intention was; then he said that his wish was to marry the princess and live with her in her father's house! When the princess heard this she said, "Yes, my heart has gone out to him also;" So then she bathed and went home and lay down in her room and would not get up, and when her father asked her what was the matter, she made no answer. Then they asked her maidens what was the matter and they said that she had seen a stranger by the tank and wished to marry him. The Rani asked whether the stranger was still there and they said that they had left him by the tank. So two men were sent to fetch the stranger or to find out where he had gone. The two servants went and found the merchant's son just ready to continue his journey, and they asked him who he was and what he wanted. He said that he was looking for employment but would like best to marry and live in the house of his father-in-law. Then they told him not go away and they would arrange such a marriage for him, so they took him to a house in the town and left him there and went back to the Raja. They told the Raja that the stranger had gone away but that they could follow him and bring him back if he gave them some money for their journey. So the Raja gave them two rupees; then they went off but only ate their dinner at home, and then they brought the merchant's son to the Raja, pretending that they had overtaken him a long way off. He was questioned about himself and he told his whole history except that the Raja had threatened to cut off his family, and his account being satisfactory it was arranged that he should marry the princess. Musicians were sent for and the marriage took place at once. After his marriage the merchant's son was much depressed at the thought of his brothers' fate and in the middle of the night he used to rise up and weep till the bed was soaked with his tears; the princess noticed this and one night she pretended to go to sleep but really lay awake and watched her husband; and in the middle of the night saw him rise quietly and begin to sob. She was filled with sympathy and went to him and begged him to tell her what was the matter and whether he was sorry that he had married her; and he answered "I cry because I am in despair; in the daytime I restrain my tears before others with difficulty but in the night they cannot be kept back; but I am ashamed for you to see me and I wait will you are asleep before I give way to my feelings."

Then she asked what was the cause of his sorrow and he answered "My father and mother and brothers and sisters are all doomed to die; for our Raja has sworn to kill them by a certain day if he is not told why two fish, which my father sent to him as a present, laughed when they were brought before him. In consequence of this threat my father sent me from home that one of the family might survive and although I may be safe here the thought of them and their fate makes me weep." The princess asked him what was the day fixed for the mystery to be explained ; and he told her that it was at the full moon of a certain month Then the princess said, " Come take me to your father' house: I shall be able to explain why the fishes laughed.' The merchant's son joyfully agreed to start off the next day; so in the morning they told the Raja why they wished to go, and he said to his daughter "Go and do not be afraid; go in confidence, I promise you that you will be able to explain why the fishes laughed.' So they made ready and journeyed to the merchant's house; and when they arrived they told the merchant to go to the Raja and ask him to collect all the citizens a certain day to hear the reason why the fishes laughed. The merchant went to the Raja and the Raja gave him a letter fixing the day and all the citizens were assembled in an open plain; and the princess dressed herself as a man and went to the assembly and stood before the Raja.

Then the Raja bade her explain why the fishes laughed, and the princess answered, "if you wish to know the reason order all your Ranis to be brought here;" so the Ranis were summoned; then the princess said" The reason why the fishes laughed was because among all your wives it is only the eldest Rani who is a woman and all the others are men. What will you give me if this is not proved to be true?" Then the Raja wrote a bond promising to give the Merchant half his kingdom if this were proved to be true. When enquiry was made it was found that the wives had really become men, and the Raja was put to shame before all his people. Then the assembly broke up and the merchant received half the Raja's kingdom.

XIX. HOW THE COWHERD FOUND A BRIDE

There was once a Goala who was in charge of a herd of cattle and every day he used to bring the herd for their midday rest to the foot of a peepul tree. One day the peepul tree spoke and said to him, "If you pour milk every day at my roots I will grant you a boon." So thenceforward the Goala every day poured milk at the roots of the tree and after some days he saw a crack in the ground; he thought that the roots of the tree were cracking the earth but the fact was that a snake was buried there, and as it increased in size from drinking the milk it cracked the ground and one day it issued forth; at the sight of it the Goala was filled with fear and made sure that the snake would devour him. But the snake said, "Do not fear: I was shut up in the nether world, and you by your kindness have rescued me. I wish to show gratitude to you and will confer on you any boon for which you ask." The Goala answered that the snake should choose what he would give him; then the snake called him near, and breathed on his hair which was very long and it became glistening as gold, and the snake said that his hair would obtain for him a wife and that he would be very powerful; and that whatever he said would come to pass. The Goala asked what sort of things would come to pass. The snake answered, "If you say a man shall die he will die and if you say he shall come to life, he will come to life. But you must not tell this to anyone not even to your wife when you marry; if you do the power will vanish."

Some time afterwards it happened that the Goala was bathing in the river; and as he bathed one of his hair came out and the fancy took him to wrap it in a leaf and set it to float down the stream. Lower down the river a princess was bathing with her attendants and they saw the packet come floating down and tried to stop but it floated straight to the princess and she caught and opened it and found the hair inside. It shone like gold and when they measured it, it was twelve fathom long. So the princess tied it up in her cloth and went home and shut herself up in her room, and would neither eat nor drink nor speak. Her mother sent two of her companions to question her, and at last she told them that she would not rise and eat until they found the person to whom the golden hair belonged; if it were the hair of a man he should be her husband and if it came from a girl she would have that girl come and live with her.

When the Raja and Rani heard this and that the hair had come floating down the river they went to their daughter and told her that they would at once send messengers up the stream to find the owner of the hair. Then she was comforted and rose up and ate her rice. That very day the Raja ordered messengers to follow up the banks of the stream and enquire in all the villages and question every one they met to find trace of the owner of the golden hair; so the messengers set out on both banks of the stream and followed it to its source but their search was vain and they returned without news; then holy mendicants were sent out to search and they also returned unsuccessful. Then the princess said " If you cannot find the owner of the golden hair I hang myself I" At this a tame crow and a parrot which were chained to a perch, said, "You will never be able to find the man with the golden hair; he is in the depths of the forest; if he had lived in a village you would have found him, but as it is we alone can fetch him, unfasten our chains and we will go in search of him." So the Raja ordered them to be unfastened and gave them a good meal before starting, for they could not carry a bag of provisions with them like a man. Then the crow and the parrot mounted into the air and flew away up the river, and after long search they spied the Goala in the jungle resting his cattle under the peepul tree; so they flew down and perched on the peepul tree and consulted how they could lure him away. The parrot said that he was afraid to go near the cattle and proposed that the crow should fly down and carry off the Goala's flute, from where it was lying with his stick and wrapper at the foot of the tree. So the crow went flitting from one cow to another till it suddenly pounced on the flute and carried it off in its beak, when the Goala saw this he ran after the crow to recover the flute and the crow tempted him on by just fluttering from tree to tree and the Goala kept following; and when the crow was tired the parrot took the flute from him and so between them they drew the Goala all right to the Raja's city, and they flew into the place and the Goala followed them in, and they flew to the room in which the princess was and dropped the flute into the hand of the princess and the Goala, followed and the door was shut upon him. The Goala asked the princess to give him the flute and she said that she would give it to him if he promised to marry her and not otherwise. He asked how he could marry her all of a sudden when they had never been betrothed; but the princess said "We have been betrothed for a long me; do you remember one day tying a hair up in a leaf and setting to float downstream; well that hair has the go-between which arranged our berothal." Then the Goala remembered how the snake said told that his hair would find him a wife and he asked to see the hair which the princess had found, so she brought it out and they found that it was like his, as long and as bright; then he said, "We belong to each other" and the princess called for the door to be opened and brought the Goala to her father and mother and told them that her heart's desire was fulfilled and that if they did not allow the wedding to take place in the palace she would run away with the Goala. So, a day was fixed for the wedding and invitations were issued and it duly took place. The Goala soon became so much in love with his bride that he forgot all about his herd of cattle which he had left behind, without any one to look after them; but after some time he bethought himself of them and he told his bride that he must return to his cattle, whether she came with him or no. She said that she would take leave of her parents and go with him; then the Raja gave them a farewell feast and he made over to the Goala half his kingdom, and gave him a son's share of his elephants and horses and flocks and herds and said to him, "You are free to do as you like: you can stay here or to your own home; but if you elect to stay here, I shall never turn you out." The Goala considered and said that he would live with his father-in-law but that he must anyhow go and see the cattle which he had abandoned without any one to look after them. So the next day he and his wife set off and when they got to the jungle they found that all the cattle were lying dead. At this the Goala was filled with grief and began to weep; then he remembered the promise of the snake that he should be able to restore the dead to life and he resolved to put it to the test.

So he told his wife that he would give the dead cows medicine and he got some jungle roots and a blind and held them to the noses of the dead animals and as he did so, he said "Come to life and, behold, one by one the cows all got up and began lowing to their calves. Having thus proved the promises of the snake the Goala was loud in his gratitude and he filled a large vessel with milk and poured it all out at the foot of the peepul tree and the snake came and breathed on the hair of the princess and it too became bright as gold.

The next day they collected all the cows and drove them back to the princess' home and there the Coala and his wife lived happily, ruling half the kingdom. And some years after the Goala reflected that the snake was to him as his father and mother and yet he had come away in a hurry without taking a proper farewell, so he went to see whether it was still there; but he could not find it and he asked the peepul tree and no answer came so he had to return home disappointed.

XX. KARA AND GUJA

Once upon a time there were two brothers named Kara and Guja who were first class shots with the bow and arrow. In the country where they lived, a pair of kites were doing great damage: they had young ones in a nest in a tree and used to carry off children to feed their nestlings until the whole country was desolated. So the whole population went in a body to the Raja and told him that they would have to leave the country if he could not have the kites killed. Then the Raja made proclamation that any one who could kill the two kites should receive a large tract of land as reward, and thereupon many men tried to kill them; but the kites had made their nest of ploughs and clod-crushers so that the arrows could not hit them, and the shooters had to give up the attempt. At last Kara and Guja thought that they would try, so they made an ambush and waited till the birds came to the nest to feed their young and then shot them both through the hole in a clod-crusher into which the pole fits, and the two kites fell down dead, at the source of the Ganges and Jumna, and where they fell they made a great depression in the ground. Then Kara and Guja carried the bodies to the Raja and he gave them a grant of land; and their grateful neighbours made a large rice field of the depression which the kites had made in the earth and this was given to Kara and Guja as service land to their great delight.

Kara and Guja used to spend their time in the forest, living on what they could find there; they slept in a cave and at evening would cook their rice there or roast jungle roots. One day a tiger spied them out as they were roasting tubers and came up to them suddenly and said. "What are you cooking? Give me some or I will eat you." So while they went on eating the roasted tubers, they threw the coals from the fire to the tiger at the mouth of-the cave and he, crunched them up and every now and then they threw him a bit of something good to eat; the tiger would not go away but lay there expecting to be fed, and Kara and Guja debated how to get rid of him. Then Guja suddenly jumped up and dashed at the tiger and caught him by the tail and began to twist the tail and he went on twisting until he twisted it right off and tiger ran roaring away. Kara and Guja roasted the tail and ate it, and they found it so nice that they decided to hunt the tiger and eat the rest of him. So the two brothers searched for him everywhere and when they found him they chased him until they ran him down and killed him; then they lit a fire and singed the hair off and roasted the flesh and made a grand meal: but they did not eat the paunch, Kara wanted to eat it but Guja would not let him, so Kara carried it away on his shoulder.

Presently they sat down in the shade of a banyan tree by the side of a road and along the road came a Raja's wedding procession; when Kara and Guja saw this they climbed into the tree and took the tiger's paunch up with them. The wedding party came to a halt at the foot of the tree and some of them lay down to eat and the Raja got out of his palki and lay down to sleep in the shade. After a time Kara got tired of holding the tiger's paunch in his arms and, whispered to Guja that he could hold it no longer. Guja told him on no account to let it go but at last Kar got so tired that he let it fall right on the top of the Raja; then all the Raja's attendants raised a shout that the Raja's stomach had burst and all ran away in panic leaving everything they had under the tree; but after they had gone a little distance they thought of the 'goods they had left behind and how they could not continue the journey without them, so they made their way back to the banyan tree.

But meanwhile Kara and Guja had climbed down and gathered together all the fine clothes and everything valuable and taken them up into the tree. And "Kara took up a large drum which he found and in one end of the drum he made a number of little holes: and he caught a number of wild bees which had a nest in the tree and put -them one by one into the drum,. When the Raja's attendants came back and saw that there were two men in the tree, they called out: "Why have you dishonored our Raja? We will kill you." Kara and Guja answered " Come and see who will do the killing." So they began to fight and the Raja's men fired their guns at Kara and Guja till they were tired of shooting, and had used up all their powder and shot, but they never hit them. Then Kara and Guja called out, " Now it is our turn! " And when the Raja's men saw that Kara and Guja had nothing but a drum they said " Yes, it is your turn." So Kara and Guja beat the drum and called "At them, My dears: at them my dears." And the wild bees flew out of the drum and stung the Raja's men and drove them right away. Then Kara and Guja took all their belongings and went home and ever after were esteemed as great Rajas because of the wealth which they had acquired.

XXI. THE MAGIC COW

There was once a Raja who had an only son named Kara and in the course of time the Raja fell into poverty and was little better than a beggar. One day when Kara was old enough to work as a cowherd his father called him and, said "My son, I am now poor but once I was rich. I had a fine estate and herds of cattle and fine clothes; now that is all gone and you have scarcely enough to eat. I am old and likely to die and before I leave you I wish to give you this advice: there are many Rajas in the world, Raja above Raja; when I am dead do you seek the protection of some, a powerful Raja."

As there was not enough to eat at home Kara had to take service as goat-herd under a neighbouring Raja; by which he earned his food and clothes and two rupees a year. Some time afterwards his father died and Kara went to his master and asked for a loan of money with which to perform his father's funeral ceremonies, and promised to continue in his service until he had worked off the loan. So the Raja advanced him five rupees and five rupees worth of rice, and with this money Kara gave the funeral feast. Five or six days later his mother died, and he again went to the Raja and asked for ten rupees more; at first the Raja refused but Kara besought him and promised to serve him for his whole life if he could not repay the loan. So at last the Raja lent him ten rupees more, and he gave the funeral feast. But the Raja's seven sons were very angry with their father because he had lent twenty rupees to a man who had no chance of paying, and they used to threaten and worry Kara because he had taken the money. Then Kara remembered how his father had said that there were many Rajas in the world, Raja above Raja, and he resolved to run away and seek service with the greatest Raja in the world. So he ran away and after travelling some distance he met a Raja being carried in a palki and going with a large party to fetch a bride for his son; and when he heard who it was he decided to follow the Raja; so he went along behind the palki and at one place a she-jackal ran across the road; then the Raja got out of his palki .and made a salaam to the jackal. When Kara saw this he thought "This cannot be the greatest Raja in the world or why should the salaam to the jackal. The jackal must be more powerful than the Raja; I will follow the jackal." So he left the wedding party and went after the jackal; now the jackal was hunting for food for hard young ones, and as Kara followed her wherever she went she could find no opportunity of killing a goat or sheep; so at last she went back to the cave in which she lived. Then her cubs came whining to meet her and she told her husband that she had been able to catch nothing that day because a man had followed her wherever she went, and had come right up to their cave and was waiting outside.

Then the he-jackal told her to ask what the man wanted. So she went out to Kara and asked him and Kara said "I have come to place myself under your protection;" then she called the he-jackal and they said to him, "We are jackals and you are a man. How can you stay with us; what could we give you to eat and what work could we find for you to do?" Kara said that he would not leave them as all his hopes lay in them; and at last the jackals took pity on him and consulted together and agreed to make him a gift as he had come to them so full of hope; so they gave him a cow which was in the cave, and said to him: "As you have believed in us we have made up our minds to benefit you; take this cow, she will supply you with everything you want, if you address her as mother she will give you whatever you ask, but do not ask her before people for they would take her from you; And do not give her away whatever inducements are offered you."

Then Kara thanked them and called down blessings on their heads and took the cow and led it away homewards. When he came to a tank he thought he would bathe and eat; while he bathed he saw a woman washing clothes at the other side of the tank but he thought that she would not notice him, so he, went up to the cow and said "Mother, give me a change of clothes." Thereupon the cow vomited up some nice new clothes and he put them on and looked very fine. Then he asked the cow for some plates and dishes and she gave them; then he asked for some bread and some dried rice, and he ate all he wanted and then asked the cow to keep the plates and dishes for him; and the cow swallowed them up again.

Now the woman by the tank had seen all that had happened and ran home and told her husband what she had seen and begged him to get hold of the wonderful cow by some means or other. Her husband could not believe her but agreed to put it to the test, so they both went to Kara and asked where he was going and offered to give him supper, and put him up for the night and give grass for his cow. He accepted this invitation and went with them to their house and they gave him the guest-room to sleep in and asked what he would have to eat, but he said that he did not want any supper—for he intended to get a meal from the cow after every one was asleep. Then the man and his wife made a plot and pretended to have a violent quarrel and after abusing each other for some time the man flung out of the house in a passion and pretended to run away; but after going a short distance he crept back quietly to the guest-room. Hanging from the roof was the body of a cart and he climbed up into that and hid himself, without Kara knowing anything about it. When Kara thought that every one was asleep, he asked his cow for some food and having made a good meal went to sleep.

The man watching up above saw everything and found that his wife had spoken the truth ; so in the middle of the night he climbed down and led away Kara's magic cow and put in its place one of his own cows of the same colour. Early the next morning Kara got up and unfastened the cow and began to lead it away, but the cow would not follow him; then he saw that it had been changed and he called his host and charged him with the theft. The man denied it and told him to call any villagers who had seen him bring his cow the day before; now no one had seen him come but Kara insisted that the cow had been changed and went to summon the village headman and the villagers to decide the matter: but the thief managed to give a bribe of one hundred rupees to the headman and one hundred rupees to the villagers and made them promise to decide in his favour ; so when they met together they told Kara that he must take the cow which he had found tied up in the morning.

Kara protested and said that he would fetch the person from whom he had got the Cow and take whichever cow he pointed out. Telling them that they were responsible for his cow while he was away, he hastened off to the cave where the jackals lived. The jackals somehow knew that he had been swindled out of the cow, and they met him saying " Well, man, have you lost your cow?" And he answered that he had come to fetch them to judge between himself and the villagers: so the jackals went with him and he went straight to the headman and told him to collect all the villagers; meanwhile the jackals spread a mat under a peepul tree and sat on it chewing *pan* and when the villagers had assembled the jackal began to speak, and said: "If a judge takes a bribe his descendants for several generations shall eat filth in this world and the next; but if he make public confession, then he shall escape this punishment. This is what our forefathers have said; and the man who defrauds another shall be thrust down into hell: this also they have said. Now all of you make honest enquiry into this matter; we will swear before God to do justice and the complainant and the accused shall also take oath and we will decide fairly." Then the village headman was conscience stricken till and admitted that he had taken a bribe of one hundred rupees, and the villagers also confessed that they had been bribed; then the jackal asked the accused what he had to say to this: but he persisted that he had not changed the cow; the jackal asked him what penalty he would pay if he were proved guilty and he said that he would pay double. Then the jackal called the villagers to witness that the man had fixed his punishment, and he proposed that he and his wife should go to the herd of cattle, and if they could pick out the cow that Kara claimed it would be sure proof that it was his. So the jackals went and at once picked out the cow and the villagers were astonished and cried. "This is a just judgment! They have come from a distance and have recognised the cow at once." The man who had stolen it had no answer to give; then the jackal said: "You yourself promised to pay double; you gave a bribe of one hundred rupees to the headman and one hundred rupees to the villagers and the cow you stole is worth two hundred rupees that is four hundred rupees, therefore you must pay a fine of eight hundred rupees; and the man was made to produce eight hundred rupees and the jackal gave all the money to the villagers except ten rupees which he gave to Kara; and he kept nothing for himself.

Then Kara and the jackals went away with the cow, and after getting outside the village the jackals again warned Kara not to ask the cow for anything when anyone was by and took their leave of him and went home. Kara continued his journey and at evening arrived at a large mango orchard in which a number of carters were camping for the night. So Kara stopped under a tree at a little distance from the carters and tied his cow to the root. Soon a storm came up and the carters all took shelter underneath their carts and Kara asked his cow for a tent and he and the cow took shelter in it. It rained hard all night and in the morning the carters saw the tent and wondered where it came from, and came to the conclusion that the cow must have produced it; so they resolved to steal the cow.

Kara did not dare to make the cow swallow the tent in the day time while the carters were about, so he stayed there all the next day and at night the cow put away the tent. Then when Kara was asleep some carters came and took away the cow and put in its place a cow with a calf, and they hid the magic cow within a wall of packs from their pack bullocks. In the morning Kara at once saw what had happened and went to the carters and charged them with the theft; they denied all knowledge of the matter and told him he might look for his cow if he liked; so he searched the encampment but could not see it.

Then he called the village headman and chowkidar and they searched and could not find the cow and they advised Kara to keep the cow and calf as it must be better than his own barren cow; but he refused and said that he would complain to the magistrate and he made the headman promise not to let the carters go until he came back. So he went to a Mahommedan magistrate and it chanced that he was an honest man who gave just judgments and took no bribes, and made no distinction between the rich and the poor; he always listened to both sides carefully, not like some rascally magistrates who always believe the story that is first told them and pay no attention to what the other side say. So when Kara made his complaint this magistrate at once sent for the carters and the carters swore that they had not stolen the cow: and offered to forfeit all the property they had with them, if the cow were found in their possession.

Then the magistrate sent police to search the encampment and the police pulled down the pile of packs that had been put round the cow, and found the cow inside and took it to the magistrate. Then the magistrate ordered the carters to fulfil their promise and put them all in prison and gave all their property to Kara. So Kara loaded all the merchandise on the carts and pack bullocks and went home rejoicing. At first the villagers did not recognise who it was who had come with so much wealth but Kara made himself known to them and they were very astonished and helped him to build a grand house. Then Kara went to the Raja from whom he had borrowed the money for his parent' funerals and paid back what he owed. The Raja was so pleased with him that he gave him his daughter in marriage and afterwards Kara claimed his father-in-law's kingdom and got possession of it and lived prosperously ever after.

And the seven sons of his first master who used to scold him were excited by his success and thought that if they went to foreign parts they also could gain great wealth; so they took some money from their father and went off. But all they did was to squander their capital and in the end they had to come back penniless to their father.

XXII. LITA AND HIS ANIMALS

Once upon a time there was a man who had four sons: two of them were married and two were unmarried and the youngest was named Lita. One day Lita went to his father and asked fifty or sixty rupees that he might go on a trading expedition and he promised that if he lost the money he would not ask for any share in the paternal property. As he was very urgent his father at last gave him sixty rupees and he set out on his travels. After going some way he came to a village in which all the inhabitants were chasing a cat; he asked them what was the matter and they told him that the cat was always stealing their Raja's milk and the Raja had offered a reward of twenty rupees to anyone who would kill it. Then Lita said to them "Do not kill the cat; catch it alive and give it to me and I will pay you twenty rupees for it; than you can go to the Raja and say that you have killed it and ask for the reward; and if to Raja asks to see the body tell him that a stranger came and asked for the body, for he thought that a cat which had fed on milk should be good eating and so you gave it to him." The villagers thought that this would be an excellent plan and promised to bring him the cat alive. They soon managed to catch it hiding under a heap of firewood and brought it to Lita and he paid them twenty rupees and then they went to the Raja and got twenty rupees from him.

Then Lita went on, and by-and-bye came to a village where the villagers were hunting an otter in a tank; they had made a cut in the tank and had let out all the water. Lita went to them and asked what they were doing: they said that they were hunting for an otter which had been destroying the Raja's fish and the Raja had promised them a reward if they killed it; and they had driven it into the tank and were draining off the water in order to catch it. Then Lita offered to buy it of them if they brought it to him alive; so when they caught it they brought it to him and he gave them money for it and continued his journey with the cat and the otter. Presently he saw a crowd of men and he went up to them and asked what they were doing: and they told him that they were hunting a rat which was always gnawing the Raja's pens and papers and the Raja had offered a reward had for it, and they had driven it out of the palace, but it had taken refuge in a hole and they were going to dig it out. Then Lita offered to buy it from them as he had bought the other two animals and they dug it out and sold it to him.

He went on and in the same way found a crowd of men hunting a snake which had bitten many people: and he offered to buy it for twenty rupees and when they had chased it till it was exhausted, they caught it alive and sold it to

Lita. As his money was all spent, he then set off homewards; and on the way the snake began to speak and said: "Lita, you have saved my life; had you not come by, those men would certainly have had my life; come with me to my home, where my father and mother are, and I will give your anything you ask for; we have great possessions." But Lita was afraid and said: " When you get me there you will eat me, or if you don't, your father and mother will." But the snake protested that it could not be guilty of such ingratitude and at last Lita agreed to accompany it when he had left the other animals at his home.

This he did and set off alone with the snake, and after some days they reached the snake's home. The snake told Lita to wait outside while he went and apprized his parents and he told Lita that when he was asked to choose his reward he should name nothing but the ring which was on the father-snake's finger, for the ring had this property that if it were placed in a *seer* of milk and then asked to produce anything whatever, that thing would immediately appear. Then the snake went on to his home and when the father and mother saw him they fell on his neck and kissed him and wept over him saying that they had never expected to see him again; the snake told them how he had gone to the country of men and how a reward had been set on his head and he had been hunted, and how Lita had bought him from the men who would have killed him. The father snake asked why he had not brought Lita to be rewarded and the snake said that he was afraid that when they saw him they would eat him.

But the father and mother swore that they could not be guilty of such ingratitude, and when he heard this the snake went and brought in Lita, and they entertained him handsomely for two days; and on the third day the father snake asked Lita what he would take as his reward. Lita looked round at the shining palace in which they lived and at first was afraid to speak but at last he said: "I do not want money or anything but this ring on your finger: if you will not give me that, I will take nothing; I saved your son from peril and that you will remember all your lives, and if you give me the ring I will honour you for it as long as I live." Then the father and mother snake consulted together and the mother said "Give it to him as he asks for it" so the father snake drew it from his finger and grave it to Lita and they gave him also some money for his journey back; and he went home and found the other three animals safe and sound waiting for him.

After a time his father said that Lita must marry; so marriage go betweens were sent out to look for a bride and they found a very rich and beautiful girl whose parents were agreeable to the match. But the girl herself said that she would only marry a man who would build a covered passage from her house to his, so that she could walk to her new home in the shade. The go-betweens reported this, and Lita's father and brothers consulted and agreed that they could never make such a passage, but Lita said to his father: "Arrange the match; it shall be my charge to arrange for making the covered passage; I will not let you be put to shame over it." For Lita had already put the ring to the test: he had dropped it into a *seer* of milk and said " Let five *bharias* of parched rice and two *bharias* of curds appear" and immediately the parched rice and curds were before him; and thereupon he had called out, " The snake has worthily rewarded me for saving his life;" and the cat and the otter and the rat overheard what he said.

So the go between was told to arrange for the wedding to take place that very month, as Lita's birthday fell in the next month, which therefore was not suitable for his wedding. Then the bride's family sent him back to say that they were prepared to send a string of nine knots; and the next day the go between told this to Lita's family and they said that they were willing to accept it; so the go between brought a string of nine knots to signify that the wedding would take place in nine days. The days passed by and Lita's father and brothers became very anxious because they saw no sign of the covered passage; but on the very night before the wedding, Lita took his ring and ordered a covered passage to be made from the one house to the other with a good path down the middle; and the next morning they found it made; and the bridegroom's party passed along it to the bride's house and the bride was escorted home along it.

Now the bride had been deeply in love with another young man who lived in her village and had much wished to marry him but her wishes of course were not consulted in the matter. Some time after the marriage she one day in the course of conversation asked her husband Lita how much he had spent on making the covered passage to her house and how he had built it so quickly. He told her that he knew nothing about it; that his father and mother had arranged for it and no doubt had spent a large sum of money. So the next day she took an opportunity of asking her mother-in-law about it, but Lita's mother said that nothing had been spent at all somehow the passage had been made in one night, she knew not how.

Then Lita's wife saw that Lita was keeping a secret from her, and she began to reproach him for having any secrets from his wife: and at last when she had faithfully promised never to reveal the matter to any one he told her the secret of the ring. Now her former lover used still to visit her and one day she sent for him and said that she would no longer live with Lita, but wished to run away with him. The lover at first objected that they would be pursued and killed while if they escaped to a distance he would have nothing to support her with; but the faithless woman said that there need be no anxiety about that and she told him about the magic ring and how by means of it they could provide themselves with a house and everything they wanted. So they fixed a night for the elopement and on that night when Lita was asleep his wife quietly drew the ring off his finger and went out to her lover who was waiting outside and told him to get a goat from the pen; then they beheaded the goat and went inside and poured all its blood on the ground under the bed on which Lita was sleeping, and then having hid the body and head of the goat, they ran away.

Towards morning Lita woke up and missed his wife, so he lit a lamp to look for her and then said the pool of blood under the bed. At this sight he was terror stricken. Some enemy had killed and carried off his wife and he would be charged with the murder. So he lay there wondering what would happen to him. At last his mother came into the room to see why he and his wife had not got up as usual and when she saw the blood she raised a cry; the village headman and chowkidar were sent for and they questioned Lita, but he could only say that he knew nothing of what had happened; he did not know what the blood was, he did not know where his wife was. Thereupon they sent two men to the house of the wife's parents to see if by any chance she had run away there and in any case to bring her relations to be present at the enquiry into her disappearance. When her father and brothers heard what had happened they at once went to Lita's house in wrath and abused him as a murderer. They asked why, if his wife had not done her duty to him, he had not sent her back to them to be chastised and taught better, instead of murdering her and they went straight to the magistrate and complained: the magistrate sent police who arrested Lita and took him before the magistrate.

Meanwhile it had become known that not only was Lita's wife missing but also her lover; and Lita's father presented a petition to the magistrate bringing this to notice and asserting that the two must have run away together. Then the magistrate ordered every search to be made for the missing couple but said that Lita must remain in custody till they were found, so he was shut up in prison. From prison he made an application to the magistrate that his three tame animals, the cat and the otter and the rat might be brought to the place where he was; the magistrate kindly consented but the animals were not allowed into the prison. However at night the rat being small made its way inside and found out Lita, and asked what was to be done. Lita said that he wanted the three animals to save him from his great danger as he had saved them; he wanted them to trace his wife and her lover and recover the ring; they would doubtless find them living in some gorgeous palace, the gift of the ring.

The rat went out and gave the other two Lita's message and they readily undertook to do their best ; so the next morning the three animals set off in; vain they hunted all over the country, till one day they came to the bank of the Ganges and there on the other side they saw a palace shining like gold. At this their hopes revived, for this might be a palace made by the magic ring. But the cat and the rat objected that they could not cross the river. The otter said that he would easily manage that and he took the cat on his back and the rat climbed on to the back of the cat and so the otter ferried them both across the river; then they consulted and decided that it would be safest to wait till the evening before they went to the palace to see who lived in it. When they looked in the evening, they at once recognised Lita's wife and her lover; but these two were in constant terror of being pursued and when they had their evening meal they fastened and bolted every entrance so securely that no one could gain admittance. Then the cat and the otter told the rat that he must collect all the rats of the neighbourhood and they must burrow through the wall and find some way of abstracting the magic ring.

So the rat collected a crowd of his friends and in no time they bored a hole through the wall; then they all began to look for the ring; they hunted high and low but could not find it; however the cat sat at the entrance of the hole which they had made and vowed that they should not come out, unless they got the ring. Then the first rat climbed on to the bed in which the couple were sleeping and searched their clothes and examined their fingers and toes but in vain; then he thought that the woman might have if in her mouth so he climbed on to her chest and tickled her nose with the tip of his tail; this made her sneeze and behold she sneezed out the ring which she had hidden in her mouth. The rat seized it and ran off with it and when the cat was satisfied that he had really got it, she let him out and the three friends set off rejoicing on their homeward journey. The crossed the river in the same way as when they came with the cat riding on the otter and the rat on the cat: and the rat held the ring in its mouth. Unfortunately when they were half way across, a kite swooped down to try and carry off the rat. Twice it swooped and missed its grasp but the second time it struck the rat with its wing said the rat in terror let the ring fall into the river.

When they reached the bank the three friends consulted what they were to do in this fresh misfortune. As the otter was the only one who could swim it volunteered to look for the ring, so it plunged into the water and searched the bottom of the river in vain; then it guessed that a fish must have swallowed the ring and it set to work to catch every fish it saw and tore them open; at last in the stomach of a big fish it found the ring, so it brought the fish to the bank and while they were all rejoicing and eating a little of the fish a kite swooped down and carried off the fish, ring and all.

The three animals watched the kite flying away with the fish; but some women who were gathering firewood ran after the kite and took the fish from it and putting it in their basket went home. Then the otter and the rat said to the cat. "Now it is your turn: we have both recovered the ring once, but we cannot go into the house of these humans. They will let you go near them easily enough;

the ring is in the fish's stomach, you must watch whether they throw away the stomach or clean it, and find an opportunity for carrying off the ring.".

So the cat ran after the women and when they began to cut up the fish, it kept mewing round them. They threw one or two scraps to it, but it only sniffed at them and would not eat them; then they began to wonder what on earth the cat wanted, and at last they threw the stomach to it. This it seized or gladly and carried it off and tore it open and found the ring and ran off with it to where the otter and the rat were waiting. Then the three friends travelled hard for a day and a night and reached the prison in which Lita was confined.

When Lita got the ring he begged his jailer to get him a *seer* of milk and when it was brought he dropped the ring in it, and said " I wish the bed on which my faithless wife and her lover are sleeping to be brought here with them in it this very night" and before morning the bed was brought to the prison. Then the magistrate was called and when he saw that the wife was alive he released Lita, and the lover who had run away with her had to pay Lita double the expenditure which had been incurred on his marriage, and was fined beside.

But Lita married another wife and lived happily with her. And some time afterwards he called the otter and the cat and the rat to him and said that he purposed to let them go and before they parted he would give them anything they wished for. They said that he owed them nothing, and they made Lita promise to let them know if ever he lost the ring or fell into trouble, and he promised to help them if ever their lives were in danger, and one morning he took them to a bazar, near which was a tank full of fish, and he turned the otter into the tank and left the cat and the rat to support themselves in the bazar. The next day he went to see them and the otter came out of the tank and gave him a fish which it had caught, and the cat brought him some milk it had stolen, and that was the last he saw of them.

XXIII. THE BOY WHO FOUND HIS FATHER

There was once a boy who used always to cheat when playing *Kati* (pitch and toss) and for this the village boys with whom he played useed to quarrel with him, saying "Fatherless orphan, why do you cheat?" So one day he asked his mother why they called him that name and whether his father was really dead. "He is alive" said she "but a long time ago a rhinoceros carried him off on its horn." Then the boy vowed that he would go in search of his father and made his mother put him up provisions for the journey ; and he started off taking with him an iron bow and a big bundle of arrows.

He journeyed on all day and at nightfall he came to a village; there he went up to the house of an old woman to ask for a bed. He stood at the thresholds and called out to her "Grannie, grannie, open the door." "I have no son, and no grandchildren to call me grannie," grumbled the old woman and went to open the door to see who was there and when she opened the door and saw him, she said "Ho, you are my grandson." "Yes, answered he, I am your grandchild." So she called him inside and gave him a bed to sleep on. The old woman was called Hutibudi; and she and the boy sat up late talking together and then they lay down to sleep; but in the middle of the night he heard the old woman crunching away trying to bite his bow to pieces. He asked her what she was eating: " Some pulse 1 got from the village headman," "Give me little to try" he begged. "I am sorry my child, I have finished it all." But really she had none to give, how ever she only hurt her jaws biting so that she began to groan with pain: "What are you groaning for, Grannie?" said the boy; "Because I have toothache" she answered and in truth her cheeks were badly swollen. Then he told her that a good cure for toothache was to bite on a white stone and she believed him and the next morning got a piece of white quartz and began to bite on it but this only broke her teeth and made her mouth bleed so that the pain was worse than before: then the boy jeered at her and said, " Did you think, Grannie, that you could bite my iron bow and arrows?"

So saying he left her and continued the search for his father and his road led him to a dense jungle which seemed to have no end, and in the middle of the jungle he came to a lake and he sat down by it to eat, what was left of the provisions he had brought: as he sat, he suddenly saw some cow-bison coming down to the lake: at this he caught up his bow and arrows in a hurry and climbed up a tall *sal* tree: from the tree he watched the bison go down to the water to drink and then go back into the jungle. And after them tigers and bears came down to the water: the sight of them frightened him and he sang:—

"Drink your fill, tiger.
I shall not shoot you.
I shall shoot the giant rhinceros."

and they drank and went away. Then various kinds of birds came and after them a great herd of rhinceroses and among them was one which had the dried up body of the boy's father stuck on its horn. The boy was rather frightened and sang:-

"Drink your fill, rhinceroses,
I shall not shoot you
I shall shoot the giant rhinceros."

and when the giant rhinceros with the body of his father stooped its head to drink from the lake, he put an arrow through it and it turned a somersault and fell over dead : while all the other rhinceroses turned tail and ran away. Then the boy climbed down from the tree and pulled the dead body of his father off the horn of the dead animal and laid it down at the foot of a tree and began to weep over it. As he wept a man suddenly stood before him and asked what was the matter, and when he heard, said "Cry no more: take a cloth and wet it in the lake and cover your father's body with it: and then whip the body with a *meral* twig and he will come to life." So saying the stranger suddenly disappeared; and the boy obeyed his instruction,, and behold his fathers at up alive and rubbing, his eyes said "I must have been asleep a very long time." Then his son explained to him all that had happened and gave him some food and took him home.

XXIV. THE OILMAN'S BULLOCK

There was once a poor but Industrious oilman; he got a log of wood and carved out an oil mill and, borrowing some money as capital, he bought mustard and sesame seed and set to work to press it; as he had no bullock he had to turn the mill himself. He was so industrious that he soon began to prosper, and was able to buy a bullock for his mill. By and bye he got so rich that he was able to buy some land and a cart and pair of bullocks and was quite a considerable man in the village. One day one of his cart bullocks died and this loss was a sad blow to the oilman. However he tied up the surviving bullock in the stable along with the old oil mill bullock and fed them well, One night it chanced that one of the villagers passed by the stable and heard the two animals talking and this is what he heard.

The young bullock said, "You came to this house first, friend: what sort of treatment does one get here" Why do you ask me, said the other. "Oh, I see your shoulder is galled and your neck shows mark of the yoke." The old bullock answered, "Whether my master treats me well or ill I owe him money and have to stay here until I have paid him off. When I have paid him five hundred rupees I shall go" "How will you ever pay back such a sum ?" "If my master would only match me to fight the Raja's elephant for five hundred rupees I should win the fight and my debt would be cleared; and if he does not do that I shall probably have to work for him all my life. How long do you intend to stay?" "My debt will be cleared if I work for him two years" answered the new comer.

The man who overheard this conversation was much astonished and went off to the oilman and told him all about it. Next day the whole village had heard of it and they were all anxious for the oilman to match his bullock against the Raja's elephant; but the oilman was very frightened, for he feared that if he sent such a challenge, the Raja would be angry with him and drive him out of the country. But the leading villagers urged him and undertook to find the money if he lost, and to persuade the Raja that the oilman was mad, if he became angry with him. At last the oilman consented, provided that some of the villagers went to the Raja and proposed the match; he was too frightened to go himself. So two of the village elders went to the Raja and asked him to match his elephant against the oilman's bullock for five hundred rupees; the Raja was very much amused and at once fixed a day for the fight. So they returned and told the oilman to be ready and raised a subscription of five hundred rupees.

The evening before the contest the oilman gave the bullock a big feed of meal and oilcake; and on the eventful morning the villagers all collected and watched him oiling its horns and tying a bell round its neck. Then the oilman gave the bullock a slap on its back and said, "Take care: you are going to fight an elephant; if you owe me so much money you will win, and if not, then you will be defeated." When he said this the bullock pawed the ground and snorted and put down its head.

Then they all set out with the five hundred rupees to a level field near the Raja's palace; a great crowd collected to see the fun and the Raja went there expecting easily to win five hundred rupees. The elephant was brought forward with vermilion on its cheeks, and a pad on its back, and a big bell round its neck, and a mahout riding it. The crowd called out "Put down the stakes:" so each side produced the money and publicly, announced that the owner of the animal which should be victorious should take all the stakes. But the oilman objected to the mahout's riding the elephant; no one was going to ride his bullock. This was seen to be fair and the mahout had to get off; then the fight began. The bullock, snorted and blew through its nose, and ran at the elephant with its head lowered. Then the elephant also rushed forward but the bullock stood its ground and stamped; at this the elephant turned tail and ran away; the bullock ran after it and gored it from behind until it trumpeted with pain. The crowd shouted "The Raja's elephant is beaten." And the oilman took the five hundred rupees and they all went home. From that day the oilman no longer put the bullock to work the oil mill but fed it well and left it free to go where it liked. But the bullock only stayed on with him one month and then died.

XXV. HOW SABAI GRASS GREW

Once upon a time there were seven brothers who had an only sister. These brothers undertook the excavation of a large tank; but although they spent large sums and dug very deep they could not reach water and the tank remained dry.

One day as they were consulting what to do to get the tank to fill, they saw a Jogi coming towards them with a lota in his hand; they at once called to him to come and advise them, for they thought that as he spent his time wandering from country to country, he might somewhere have learned some thing which would be of use to them. All the Jogi said to them was, "You have a sister: if you sacrifice her, the tank will fill with water. "The brothers were fond of the girl, but in their despair at seeing their labour wasted their agreed to give the advice of the Jogi a trial. So they told their mother the next day that, when their sister brought them out their midday meal, she was to be dressed in her best and carry the rice in a new basket and must bring a new water pot to draw their water in. At midday the girl went down to her brothers with her best cloth and all her jewellry on; and when they saw their victim coming they could not keep from tears. She asked them what they were grieving for; they told her that nothing was the matter and sent her to draw water in her new water-pot from the dry tank. Directly the girl drew near to the bank the water began to bubble up from the bottom; and when she went down to the water's edge it rose to her instep. She bent down to fill her pot but the pot would not fill though the water rose higher and higher; then she sang:—

"The water has risen, brother,
And wetted my ankle, brother,
But still the lota in my hand
Will not sink below the surface."

But the water rose to her knees and the pot would not fill, and she sang:—

"The water has risen, brother,
And wetted my knees, brother,
But still the lota in my hand
Will not sink below the surface."

Then the water rose to her waist and the pot would not fill, and she sang:—

"The water has risen, brother,
And wetted my waist, brother,
But still the lota in my hard
Will not sink below the surface."

Then the water reached to her neck and the pot would not fill, and she sang:—

The water has risen, brother,
And wetted my neck, brother,
But still the lota in my hand
Will not sink below the surface."

At last it flowed over her head and the water-pot was filled, but the girl was drowned. The tank however remained brimful of sparkling water.

Now the unhappy girl had been betrothed and her wedding day was just at hand on the day fixed the marriage broker came to announce the approach of the bridegroom; who shortly afterwards arrived at the outskirts of the village in his palki. The seven brothers met him, and the usual dancing began.

The bridegroom's party however wished to know why the bride did not appear. The brothers put them off with various excuses, saying, that the girl had gone with her friends to gather firewood or to the river to draw water. At last the bridegroom's party got tired of waiting and turned to go home in great wrath at the way in which they had been treated. On their way they passed by the tank in which the girl had been sacrificed and growing in the middle of it, they saw a most beautiful flower. The bridegroom at once determined to possess this, and he told his drummers to pick it for him; but whenever one of them tried to pick it, the flower moved out of his reach and a voice came from the flower saying:—

"Take the flower, drummer,
But the branch you must not break."

and when they told him what the flower sang the bridegroom said that he would try and pick it himself; no sooner had he reached the bank than the flower of its own accord floated towards him and he pulled it up by the roots and took it with him into the palki. After they had gone a little way the palki bearers felt the palki strangely heavy: and when they looked in they found the bride also sitting in it, dressed in yellow garments; for the flower was really the girl who had been drowned.

So they joyfully took the happy couple with drumming and music to the bridegroom's house.

In a short time misfortune befell, the seven brothers; they fell into the deepest poverty and were forced to earn what they could by selling leaves and sticks which they gathered in the jungle. As they went about selling these, they one day came to the village where their sister was living and as they cried their wares through the streets they were told to go to the house where the marriage had taken place. They went there, and as they were selling their leaf plates their sister saw and recognised them; they had only ragged loincloths on, and their skins were black and cracked like a crocodile's.

At the sight their sister began to cry. Her friends asked what was the matter and she said a straw from the thatch had run into her eye, so they pulled down some of the thatch; she still went on crying and they again asked what was wrong; she said that she had knocked her foot against a stone in the ground; so they dug up the stone and threw it away. But she still went on weeping and at last confessed that the miserable-looking leaf-sellers were her brothers. Then her husband's parents told her to be comforted, and they gave the brothers oil and bade them go and bathe and oil their bodies: but the brothers were so hungry that when they got to the bathing place they drank the oil and ate the oil cake that had been given to them; and came back with their skins as rough as when they went. So then they were given more oil and some of the household went with them and made them bathe and oil themselves properly and there brought them to the house and gave them new clothes and made them a feast of meat and rice. According to the custom of the country they were made to sit down in order of age and were helped in that order; when they had all been helped and had eaten, their sister said to them "Now brothers you come running to me for food, and yet you sacrificed me in the tank." Then they were overwhelmed with shame: they looked up at the sky but there was no escape there; they looked down at the earth; and the earth split open and they all ran into the chasm. The sister tried to catch the youngest brother by the hair and pull him out, calling "Come back, brother, come back brother, you shall carry my baby about for me!" but his hair came off in her hand and the earth swallowed them all up. Their sister planted the hair in a corner of the garden and it is said that from that human hair, *sabai* grass originated.

XXVI. THE MERCHANT'S SON AND THE RAJA'S DAUGHTER

Once a merchants wife and a Raja's wife were both with child and one day as they bathed together they fell into conversation, and they agreed that if they both bore daughters then the girls should by " flower friends while if one had a son and one a daughter then the children should marry: and they committed the agreement to writing. A month or two later the Raja's wife bore a daughter and the merchant's life a son. When the children grew up a bit they were sent to school, and as they were both very intelligent they soon learnt to read and write. At the school the boys used to be taught in an upstairs room and the girls on the ground floor. One day the boy wrote out a copy of the agreement which their mothers had made and threw it down to the girl who was below.

She read it and from that day they began to correspond with each other; love soon followed and they decided to elope. They fixed a day and they arranged that the boy should wait for the girl under a *turu* tree outside the town. When the evening came the girl made haste to cook her parents' supper and then, when they went to bed, she had as usual to soothe them to sleep by rubbing 'their limbs; all this took a long time and the merchant's son soon got tired of waiting, so he sang to the tree:—

"Be witness be witness for me 'Turn tree'
When the Raja's daughter comes."

and so singing he tied his horse to the roots of the tree and himself climbed up into the branches, and sitting in the tree he pulled off and threw down a number of twigs. Late at night the Raja's daughter came; she saw the horse tied and the twigs scattered on the ground, but no other sign of her lover. And at last she got tired of waiting and called the, *Turu* tree to witness, singing:—

"Be witness be witness for, me 'Turu tree'
when the merchant's son comes."

As she finished her song the merchant's son threw down a large branch to her, so she looked up and saw him sitting, in the tree. Then she climbed up to him and began to scold him for putting her to the pain of waiting so long. He retorted " It was you who made me anxious by keeping me waiting." "That was not my fault: you know how much work a woman has to do. I had to cook the supper and put my parents to bed and rub them to sleep. Climb down and let us be off." So they climbed down from the tree and mounted the horse and rode off to a far country. On the road the girl became very thirsty but in the dense jungle they could find no water, at last the merchant's son threw a stone at hazard and they heard it splash in a pool; so they went in the direction of the sound and there they found water but it was foul and full of worms and the girl refused to drink it. She said that she would only drink water "which had a father and mother."

So they went on their way, and after a time they came to a number of crows holding a meeting and in the midst was an owl with its head nodding drowsily; it was seeing dreams for them; every now and then a crow would give it a shove and ask what it had dreamt but the owl only murmured that it had not finished and went off to sleep again. At last it said " I have seen a gander and a goose go down into a river and swim about in it."

The merchant's son and his companion went on and presently came to a river in full flood, which was quite uncrossable ; on the far bank was a cow lowing to a calf which had been left on the bank where they were. When she saw them the girl began to sing:—

"The cow lows for its calf
The calf bleats for its mother:
My father and mother
Are weeping for me at home."

When he heard her lament like this the merchant's son exclaimed
" You women are all alike, come let us go back,"

"How can we go back now? answered the girl "You of course can pretend that you have been hunting; but we women lose our character if we are hidden by a bush for a minute".

So as they could not cross the river by themselves, a goose and gander carried them across on their backs. As they went on the merchant's son asked the girl how far she would like to go a six days' journey or a six months' journey. He told her that in the six month' journey they would only have fruits and roots and such like to eat and water to drink, but the six days' journey was easy and free from hardship.

The girl chose the six days' journey, so they went in for six days and came to a stream on the banks of which stood a cottage in which lived an old woman. Before they went up to it the girl told her lover not to eat any rice given to him by the old woman but to throw it to the fowls; then they went and asked to be allowed to cook their food there; now the old woman had seven unmarried sons, who were away hunting at the time, and when she saw the Raja's daughter she wished to detain her and marry her to one of her sons. So in order to delay them she gave then a damp stove and green fire-wood to cook with; she also offered the merchant's son some poisoned rice but he threw it to the fowls, and when they ate it they fell down dead.

The girl could not make the fire burn with the green wood, so they hurried away as fast as they could without waiting to cook any food. Before they started however the old woman managed to tie up some mustard seed in a cloth and fasten it to their horse's tail, so that as they rode, the seed was spilt along the road they took. When the old woman's sons came back from hunting she greeted them by saying,: "Why did you not come back sooner I have just found a pretty wife for you; but I have tied mustard seed to their horse's tail, and it is being scattered along the road: in one place it is sprouting in another it is flowering; in another it is seeding and in another it is ripe; when you get to the place where it is ripe you will catch them." So the seven brothers pursued the two lovers and caught them up but the merchant's son cut down six of them with his sword; the seventh however hid under the horse's belly and begged for mercy and offered to serve them as groom to their horse. This man's name was Damagurguria; they spared his life and he followed them running behind the horse; but he watched his opportunity and caught the merchant's son unawares and killed him with his sword.

Then he told the girl that she belonged to him and she admitted it and asked that she might ride behind him on the horse, so Damagurguria mounted and took her up behind him and turned homewards. He could not see what the girl was doing and they had not gone far when she drew his sword and killed him with it.

Then she rode back to where the body of her lover lay and began to weep over it. As she sat there, a man in shining white clothing appeared and asked what was the matter; she told him Damagurguria had killed her lover. Then he had her stop crying and go and wet a *gamcha* he gave her and come straight back with it without looking behind her and then pick a *metal* twig and beat the corpse with it, So the girl took the *gamcha* and went and dipped it in a pool but, as she was bringing it back, she heard a loud roaring behind her and she looked back to see what it was; so the stranger sent her back again to the pool and this time she did not look round though she heard the same roaring. Then the stranger told her to join the severed head to the body and cover it with the wet *gamcha*; and then after waiting a little, to beat the body with the *metal* twig. So saying he disappeared. The girl carefully complied with these instructions and to her joy, saw merchant's son sit up and rub his eyes, remarking that he must have been asleep for a long time. Great was his astonishment when he heard how Damagurguria had killed him and how he had been restored to life by the help of the stranger in white. This was the end of the lovers' troubles and they lived happily ever after.

XXVII. THE FLYCATCHER'S EGG

One day a herd boy found a flycatcher's egg and he brought it home and asked his mother to cook it for him, but she put it on a shelf and forgot about it. His mother was a poor woman and had to go out all day to work; so before she started she used always to cook, her son's dinner and leave it covered all ready for him. No sooner had she gone to work than a *bonga* girl used to come out of the flycatcher's egg and first eat up the rice that had been left for the herd boy and then quickly put water on to boil and cook some rice with pulse; and, having eaten part of it, cover up the rest, ready for the herd boy on his return. Then she used to comb and dress her hair and go back into the egg. This happened everyday and at last, the boy asked his mother why she gave him rice cooked with pulse every day as he was tired of it. His mother was much astonished and said that some one must have been changing his food, because she always cooked his rice with vegetables. At this the boy resolved to watch and see who was touching his food; so one day he climbed up on to the rafters and lay in wait. Presently out of the egg came the *bonga* girl and cooked the food and combed her hair as usual. Just as she was going back into the egg, the herd boy sprang down and caught her. " Fi, Fi," cried she "is it a *Dome* or a *Hadi* who is clasping me?" "No *Dome* or *Hadi*," said he: "we are husband and wife:" so he took her to wife and they lived happily together.

He strictly forbade her ever to go outside the house and he said incantations over some mustard seed and gave it to her, and told her that if any beggars came, she was to give them alms through the window and, if they refused to take them in that way, then she was to throw the mustard seed at them; but on no account to go outside the house. One day when her husband was away a Jugi came begging; the *bonga* girl offered him alms through the window but the jugi flatly refused to take them; he insisted on her coming out of the house arid giving them. Then she threw the mustard seed at him and he turned into ashes. By superior magic however he at once recovered his own form and again insisted on her coming outside to give him alms, so she went Out to him and he saw how beautiful she was.

The jugi went away and one day he went to beg at the Raja's palace and, talking, to the Raja, he told him how he had seen a girl of more than human beauty. The Raja resolved to possess her, and one day he took the form of a fly and flew to the house and saw the beautiful *bonga*; a second day he came back in the same form and suddenly caught her up and flew off with her on his back to his palace, and in spite of her weeping shut her up in a beautifully furnished room on the roof of his palace. There she had to stay and her food was brought to her there. When the herd boy came home and found that his beautiful wife was missing he filled the air with lamentations and leaving his home he put on the garb of a jugi and went about begging. One day he came to the palace of the Raja who had carried off is wife; as he begged he heard his wife's voice, so he sang:—

Give me, oh give me, my flycatcher wife,
Give me my many-coloured wife."

Then they offered him a jar full of money to pacify him, but he threw the rupees away one by one and continued his lament. Then the Raja called for his two dogs Rauta and Paika and set them on the man and they tore him to death. At this his wife wept grievously and begged them to let her out since there was no one to carry her away, now that her husband was dead.

They prepared to take away the corpse to burn it and the *bonga* girl asked to be allowed to go with them as she had never seen the funeral rites of a jugi ; so they let her go.

Before starting she tied a little salt in the corner of her cloth. When she reached the burning place, she sang to the two dogs:—

"Build the pyre, Rauta and Paika !
Alas ! The dogs have bitten the jugi,
Alas! They have chased and killed the jugi."

So the two dogs built the pyre and lay the body on it. Then she ordered them to split more wood, singing:—

"Cut the wood, Rauta and Paika!
Alas ! The dogs have bitten the jogi,

Alas! They have chased and killed the jugi."

So they split more wood and then she told them to apply the fire, singing:—

"Light the fire, Rauta and Paika !
Alas ! The dogs have bitten the jugi,
Alas ! They have chased and killed the jugi."

When the pyre was in full blaze she suddenly said to the dogs "Look up, Rauta and paika, see the stars are shining in the day time." When the two dogs looked up, she threw the salt into their eyes, and, while they were blinded, she sprang into the flames and died as a *sati* on the body of her husband.

XXVIII. THE WIFE WHO WOULD NOT BE BEATEN

There was once a Raja's son who announced that he would marry no woman who would not allow him to beat her every morning and evening. The Raja's servants hunted high and low in vain for a bride who would consent to these terms, at long last, they found a maiden who agreed to be beaten morning and evening if the prince would marry her. So the wedding took place and for two or three days the prince hesitated to begin the beating; but one morning he got up and taking a stick from the corner, went to his bride and told her that she must have her beating. "Wait a minute" said she, there is one thing I want to point out to you before you beat me. It is only on the strength of your father's position that you play the fine gentleman like this: your wealth is all your father's and it is on his wealth that you are relying. When you have earned something for yourself, and made a position for yourself, then I am willing that you should beat me and not before."

The prince saw that what his bride said was true and held his hand. Then, in order to earn wealth for himself, he set out on a trading expedition, taking quantities of merchandise loaded in sacks; and he had a large band of retainers with him, mounted on horses and elephants, and altogether made a fine show. The princess sent one of own servant with the prince and gave him secret instructions to watch his opportunity and if ever, when the prince was bathing, he should throw away a loin cloth, to take possession of it without the prince knowing anything about it and bring it to her. The prince journeyed on till he came to the country called Lutia.

The Raja of Lutia was walking on the roof of his palace and he saw the cavalcade approaching, and he sent a *sipahi* to meet the prince and ask him this question. "Have you the secret of prosperity for ever or of prosperity for a day?" When this question was put to the prince he answered that he had the secret of prosperity for ever. When the Lutia Raja was told of this answer, he ordered his men to stop the prince's train; so they surrounded them and seized all the merchandise and the prince's retainers fled on their horse and elephants and left him alone and penniless. In his distress the prince was forced to take service with a rich Hindu, and he had nothing to live on but what his master chose to give him and all he had to wear was a loin cloth like the poorest labourer.

The only man who did not desert him was the servant whom the Princess had sent; and one day he saw that the prince had thrown away an old loin cloth while bathing ; this he picked up and took home to his mistress, who put it away. When she heard all that and happened to her husband, she set out in her turn to the Lutia country and all she took with her was a mouse and a shawl. When she reached the Lutia country the Raja as before sent a messenger to ask whether she knew the secret of prosperity for ever or of prosperity for a day.

She answered " prosperity for a day." Thereupon the Raja had her sent for and also all the retainers who had deserted the Prince and who had collected together in the neighbourhood. When they had all come the Raja said that he would now decide who should have all the wealth which had been taken from the prince: he produced a cat and said that the person toward whom the cat jumped should have all the wealth. So they all sat round the Raja and the Princess had her mouse hidden under her shawl and every now and then she kept uncovering its head and covering it up again. The cat soon caught sight of the mouse and, when the Raja let it go, it jumped straight to the Princess in hopes of catching the mouse. The Raja at once adjudged all the merchandise to her, and she loaded it on the horses and elephants and took it home accompanied by her husband's retainers.

A few days afterwards her husband came home, having got tired of working as a servant, and, putting a bold face on it, he went up to her and said that how he was going to beat her; all the retainers who had accompanied him when he set out to trade and also the servant whom the princess had sent with him were present. Then, before them all, the princess took up the old loin cloth and asked him if he knew to whom it had belonged; at this reminder of his poverty the prince was dumb with shame. "Ask your retainers" continued the princess " to whom all the merchandise with which you set out now rightfully belongs, ask them whether it is yours or mine, and then say whether you will beat me."

The prince had no answer to give her and after this lesson gave up all idea of beating his bride.

XXIX. SAHDE GOALA

Once a marriage was arranged between Sahde Goala and Princess Chandaini and on the wedding day when it began to get dusk Sahde Goala ordered the sun to stand still. "How," said he can the people see the wedding of a mighty man like myself in the dark?" So at his behest the sun delayed its setting for an hour, and the great crowd which had assembled saw all the grand ceremonies.

The next day Sahde and his bride set off home and it took them three days to reach the place where he lived. Before they left they had invited the princess's father to come and see them; accordingly a day or two later he set out, but it took him three months to accomplish the distance which Sahde Goala had traversed in three days. When the old Raja reached his son-in-law's house they welcomed him and washed his feet and offered him refreshments; and when he had eaten, he asked his son-in-law to take him out for a stroll. So they went out, Sahde Goala in front and the old Raja following behind him and as they walked Sahde Goala struck his foot against a stone, and the stone was shattered to pieces. When the Raja saw this proof of his son-in-law's superhuman strengths he became alarmed for his daughter's safety. If Sahde ever lost his temper with her he might clearly smash her to atoms so he made up his mind that he could not leave her in such keeping. When he told his daughter what he had seen she was as frightened as her father and begged him to take her home, so they agreed to escape together some time when Sahde Goala was out of the way.

One morning Sahde Goala went out to watch his men working in the fields and the old Raja and his daughter seized this opportunity to escape. Sahde Goala had a sister named Lorokini and she ran to the field to tell her brother that his wife was running away,. "Let her go" said Sahde Goala. The old Raja travelled faster than his daughter and left her behind and as she travelled along alone Sahde Goala made a flooded river flow across her path. It was quite unfordable so the Princess stood on the bank and sang:—

"My mother gave me birth,
My father gave me in marriage:
If the water upstream would stand still
And the water downstream would flow away
Then I could go and live in my own home."

But no such thing happened and she had to go back to her husband's house.

When she arrived her mother-in-law gave her a large basket of cooked rice and a pot of relish and told her to take them to the labourers in the field. Her mother-in-law helped her to lift the basket on to her head and she set off. When she reached the field she called to her sister-in-law :—

Come, Lorokini,
Lift down from my head

The basket of rice
And the pot of relish."

But Lorokini was angry with her for trying to run and refused to help, singing:—

"I will not come
I will not lift down the basket:
Prop it against a *murup* tree:
I will not lift it down."

Then Chandaini Rani propped it against the trunk of a murup tree, and so set it on the ground.

Then she sang to her husband:—

"Here, husband, is the lota of water:
Here, husband, is the tooth stick;
Come, and wash your hands:
If you are angry with me
Take me back to my father and mother."

But Sahde Goala was ploughing at the head of his men and paid no attention to her: then she sang again:—

"Seven hundred labourers
And twenty hundred women labourers,
you are causing to die of thirst"

But still sahde Goala paid no attention. Then Chandaini rani got angry and by leaning the basket against the *murup* tree managed to get it on to her head again and carried it home, and from that time murup trees, grow slanting. Directly she had taken the rice and relish to the house she set off again to run away to her mother. As before Sahde Goala caused a flooded river to flow across her path and as before she sang:—

"My mother gave me birth,
My father gave me in marriage:
If the water upstream would stand still
And the water down stream would flow away
Then I could go and live in my own home."

And this time the water did stand still and the water below all flowed away and she crossed over. As she crossed she said " If am really chaste no one will be able to touch me.' And as she reached the opposite bank she saw a young man sitting, waiting for her; his name was Bosomunda, he had been sitting waiting for her on the bank for days without moving. When he saw Chandaini Rani mount the bank he rose and said " Come: I have been waiting for you, you are to be my mistress." "Fie, fie!" answered she, " Am I to belong to any Dome or Hari?" Bosomunda swore that she should be his. " If so, then follow a little behind me so as not to tread on my shadow." So they went on, the Rani in front and Bosomunda behind. Presently they camse to a tamarind tree on which grew two enormous fruits; the Rani pointed to them saying "If I am to belong to you, you must pick me those fruits." So Bosomunda began to climb the tree, and as he climbed she prayed that the tree might grow and touch the sky; and in fact as fast as Bosomunda climbed so the tree grew and he got no nearer to the fruit.

Then the Chandaini Rani picked up the weapons which he had laid on the ground and threw them away one to the north and one to the south, one to the east and one to the west, and ran off as fast as she could Bosomunda at first did not see her because his eyes, were fixed on the tamarind fruit, but after she had gone a long way he caught sight of her and came down as fast as he could and, gathering up his weapons, went in pursuit. But Chandaini Rani had a long start, and as she hurried along she passed a thorn tree standing by the side of the road and she called to it, " Thorn tree, Bosomunda is coming after me, do your best to detain aim for a little." As she spoke it seemed as if a weight descended on the tree and swayed it to and fro so that its branches swept the ground, and it answered her " I will do like this to him." Then she went on and met a goat on the road, and she asked it to do its best to delay Bosomunda, and the goat pawed the ground and dug its horns into the earth and said that it would so the same to Bosomunda. Then she went on and met a ram and made the same request; the ram charged a tree and butted it right over and promised to treat Bosomunda in the same way. Afterwards she came to the bull and the bull drove its horns into a bank and brought down a quantity of earth and said that, that was the way he would treat Basomunda. Next she came to a buffalo and the buffalo charged a bank of earth to show what he would do to Basomunda. Then she came to an elephant and the elephant trampled a clod of earth to dust and said that he would treat Bosomunda so. Then she went on and saw a paddy bird feeding by the roadside and the asked it to do its best to delay Bosomunda; the paddy bird drove its bill into the earth and said that it would treat Basomunda in the same way.

Meanwhile Bosomunda was in hot pursuit. When he came to the thorn tree, the tree swayed its branches and caught him with its thorns, but he cut down the tree and freed himself; he went on a little way and met the goat which ran at him with its horns, but Bosomunda sang:—

"Do not fight with me, goat,
I will cut off your legs and cut off your head
And take them to the shrine of Mahadeo."

So saying, he killed the goat and cut off its head and tied it to his waist and went on. Next the ram charged him but he sang:—

"Do not fight with me, Ram,
I will cut off your legs and cut off your head
And take them to the shrine of Mahadeo."

So saying he killed the Ram and took its head. Then in succession he was attacked by the bull and the buffalo and the elephant, but he killed them all and cut off their heads. Then he came to the paddy bird, which pretended to be busily engaged in picking up insects and gradually worked its way nearer and nearer. Bosomunda let it get quite close and then suddenly seized it and gave its neck a pull which lengthened it out considerably; "Thank you said the paddy bird, as he put it down, now I shall be able to catch all the fish in a pool without moving." Thereupon Bosomunda caught it again and gave its neck a jerk and that is why paddy birds have necks shaped like a letter S.

Bosomunda continued his pursuit and caught up Chandaini Rani just as she was entering her father's house; he seized her by her hair and managed to cut off the edge of her cloth and pull off one of her golden anklets, and then had to let her go.

He took up his abode at the *ghat* of a tank and began to kill every one who came down to the water. The citizens complained to the Raja of the destruction he was causing and the Raja ordered some valiant man to be searched for, fit to do battle with the murderer; so they sent for a Birbanta (giant) and the Raja promised to give him half his kingdom and his daughter in marriage if he could slay Bosomunda. So the Birbanta made ready for the fight and advanced brandishing his weapons against Bosomunda. Three days and three nights they fought, and in the end the Birbanta was defeated and killed.

Then the Raja ordered his subjects to find another champion and a Birburi was found willing to undertake the fight in hope of the promised reward; and as he was being taken to the field of battle his mother met him with a ladle full of curds and told him to do a war dance, and as he was dancing round she threw the curds at him; he caught the whole of it on his shield except one drop which fell on his thigh; from this his mother foresaw that he would bleed to death in the fight, so she took some rice and ran on ahead and again met her son and told him to do the war dance and show how he was going to fight; and as he danced his sword shivered to atoms. His mother said, Is this the way in which you intended to fight, of a surety you would have met your death." Then she made him gather together the pieces of his sword and cover them with a wet cloth, and in a few minutes the pieces joined together; then she allowed him to go to the fight.

When the battle began the Birburi's mother kept calling out " Well, Bosomunda, have you killed my son?" This enraged Bosomunda and he kept running after the old woman to drive her away, and this gave the opportunity to the Birburi to get in a good blow.In this way they fought for seven days and nights and at the end Bosomunda was defeated and killed. Then the Raja gave half his kingdom to the Birburi and married him to his daughter Chandaini Rani.

After their marriage they set out for their new home and on the way they met Sahde Goala who had come in search of his missing wife. "Hulloa" cried Sahde Goala "where are you taking my wife to?" "I know nothing about your wife" said the Birburi "this is the Raja's daughter whom I have married as a reward for killing Bosomunda; he has given me half his kingdom from Sir Sikar to the field of the cotton tree." Then Sahde Goala told him to go his way, so the Birburi and the Rani went on and Sahde Goala caused a flooded river with the water flowing bank high to cross their path. As they waited on the bank Sahde Goala made the Birburi an offer that if he could carry the woman across the river without getting the sole of her foot wet, then she should belong to him and if not Sahde Goala should take her. The Birburi agreed and tried and tried again to get the Rani across without wetting her, but the flood was too strong, so at last he gave in, and Sahde Goala took her back with him to their former home. There they lived and in the course of time Chandaini Rani bore a son and she named him Dhonontori, and after the birth of their son the family became so wealthy (dhon) that the Hindus revered Dhonontori as a god, And so ends the story.

XXX. THE RAJA'S SON AND THE MERCHANT'S SON

Once upon a time the son of a Raja and the son of a merchant were great friends; they neither of them had any taste for lessons but would play truant from school and waste their time running about the town. The Raja was much vexed at his son's behavior ; he wished him to grow up a worthy successor to himself, and with this object did all he could to break off his friendship with the merchant's son, as the two boys only led each other into mischief; but all his efforts failed and at last he offered a reward of one hundred rupees to any one who could separate them. One of the Raja's concubines made up her mind to earn the reward, and one day she met the two boys as they were going out to bathe. The Raja's son was walking ahead and the merchant's son a little way behind; the woman ran after the merchant's son and threw her arms round him and putting her lips to his ear pretended to whisper to him and then ran away. When they met at the river the Prince asked the merchant's son what the woman had told him, his friend denied that she had said anything but for all his protestations the Prince would not believe this. They quarrelled about it for a long time and at last the Prince went home in a rage and shut himself up in his room and refused to eat or be comforted. His father sent to enquire what was the matter with him and the Prince replied that food should not pass his lips until the merchant's son had been put to death.

Thereupon the Raja sent for some soldiers and told them to devise some means of killing the merchant's son. So they bound the youth and showed him to the Prince and said that they would take him to the jungle and kill and bury him there. They then led him off, but on the road they caught a lamb and when they got to the jungle they killed the lamb and steeped the clothes of the merchant's son in the blood that they might have something to show to the Prince and then went back leaving the boy in the jungle. They took the bloody cloth to the Prince and told him to rise and eat, but when he saw the blood, all his old friendship revived and he was filled with remorse and could not eat for sorrow. Then the Raja told his soldiers to find out some friend to comfort the Prince, and they told him that they would soon set things straight and going off to the jungle brought back the merchant's son and took him to the Prince; and the two youths forgot their differences and were as friendly as before.

Time passed and one day the Prince proposed to his friend that they should run away and seek their fortunes in the world. So they fixed a day and stole away without telling anyone, and, as they had not taken any money, they soon had to look about for employment. They found work and the arrangement their masters made with them was this: their wages were to be as much rice each day as would go on leaf; and if they threw up their work they were to forfeit one hand and one ear; on the other hand if their masters discharged them so long as they were willing to work for this wage the master was to lose one hand and one ear. The merchant's son was cunning enough to turn this agreement to his advantage, for every day he brought a large lotus leaf to be filled with rice; this gave him more than he could eat and he soon grew fat and flourishing, but the Raja's son only took an ordinary *sal* leaf to his master and the rice that he got on this was not enough to keep him alive, so he soon wasted away and died.

Now the merchant's son had told his master that his name was *Ujar*: one day his master said, *Ujar*, go and hoe that sugar cane and look sharp about it." So *Ujar* went and instead of hoeing the ground dug up all the sugar cane and piled it in a heap. When the master saw his fine crop destroyed he was very angry and called the villagers to punish *Ujar*, but when they questioned him, *Ujar* protested that he was bound to obey his master's orders; he had been ordered to hoe the sugar cane, not the ground, and he had done as he was told, and so they had to let him off.

Another day a Hindu neighbour came to *Ujar's* master and asked him to lend him his servant for a day. So *Ujar* went to the *Hindu's* house and there was told to scrape and spin some hemp, but *Ujar* did not understand the Hindu language and when he got the knife to scrape the hemp with, he proceeded to chop it all up into little pieces; when the Hindu saw what had happened he was very angry and called in the neighbour, but *Ujar* protested that he had been told to cut the hemp and had done so; and so lie got off.

Ujar's master had an only child and one day he told Ujar to take the child to a tank and give him a good washing, so *Ujar* took the child to a tank and there proceeded to dash the child against a stone in the way that washermen wash clothes; he knocked the child about until he knocked the life out of his and then carefully washed him in the tank and brought the body home and put it on the bed. Next morning the father was surprised not to hear the child running about and going to look, found the dead body. The villagers assembled but *Ujar* protested that his master had told him to wash the child thoroughly and he had only obeyed orders; so they had to let him off again.

After this the master made up his mind to get rid of *Ujar*, but he was in a fix: he could not dismiss him because of the agreement that if he did not continue to employ him so long as he was willing to serve for one leaf full of rice a day he was to lose a hand and an ear. So he decided to kill him, but he was afraid to do so himself for fear of being found out; so he decided to send *Ujar* to his father-in-law's house and get them to do the job. He wrote a letter to his father-in-law asking him to kill the bearer directly he arrived before many people knew of his coming and this letter he gave to *Ujar* to deliver.

On the way however *Ujar* had some misgivings and he opened the letter and read it; thereupon he tore it in pieces and instead of it wrote a letter to his master's father-in-law in which his master was made to say that *Ujar* was a most valuable servant and they should give him their youngest daughter in marriage as soon as possible. The fraud was not found out and directly *Ujar* arrived he was married to the youngest daughter of his master's father-in-law. A few days later the master went to see how his plan had worked and was disgusted to find *Ujar* not only alive but happily married.

So he thought that he would entice him into the jungle and kill him there; with this object he one day invited *Ujar* to come out hunting with him, but *Ujar* suspected what was up and took a hatchet with him; and directly they got to the jungle he fell behind his master and cut him down with his hatchet and then went home and told his wife's relations that his master had got tired of hunting and had gone back to his own home; no doubts were raised about his story and he lived on happily with his wife till he died at a ripe old age.

XXXI. THE POOR WIDOW

Once there was a poor widow who had two children; she lived by daily labour and if she got no work any day, then that day they had to go without food. One morning she went out to look for work and a rich woman called her and asked if she wanted a job; she said "Yes, that is what I am looking for," then the rich woman said "Stay here and pick the lice out of my hair, and I will pay you your usual wages and give you your dinner as well." So the poor widow agreed and spent the day picking out the lice and at evening the rich woman brought out a measure of rice to give her as her wages and, as she was measuring it, she felt her head itch and she put up her hand and scratched and pulled out a large louse.

Then she got very angry and scolded the widow and said that she would pay her nothing as she had not done her work properly and she turned her out. Then the widow was very unhappy for she had nothing to give her starving children and she wished that she had stuck to her usual work. When she got home and her children began to cry for food, she remembered that she had seen some wild *saru* (vegetable) growing in a certain place; so she took a basket and a sickle and telling her children not to cry went out to gather it. It was dark and lonely and she felt frightened but then she thought of her children and went on and gathered the *saru*, and returned home crying because she has nothing better to give her offspring. On the way she met an old man who asked her why she was crying and she told him all her story. Then he told her to take the herbs home and chop them all up and to put some in every basket and pot she had and to cook the rest for supper. So when she got home she did as she had been directed and when she came to take the herbs which she had cooked out of the pot, she found that they had turned into rice, and she and her children ate it with joy. The next morning, she found that every pot and basket into which she had put the herbs was full of rice; and from that time she prospered and bought goats and pigs and cattle and lived happily ever after.

But no one knew where the old man came from, as she had forgotten to ask him.

XXXII. THE MONKEY AND THE GIRL

Once upon a time the boys and girls of a village used to watch the crops of *but* growing by a river, and there was a Hanuman monkey who wished to eat the *but*, but they drove him away. So he made a plan: he used to make a garland of flowers and go with it to the field and, when he was driven away, he would leave the flowers behind; and the children were pleased with the flowers and ended by making friends with the monkey and did not drive him away. There was one of the young girls who was fascinated by the monkey and promised to marry him. Some of the other children told this in the village and the girl's father and mother came to hear of it and were angry and the father took some of the villagers and went and shot the monkey. Then they decided not to throw away the body, but to burn it like the corpse of a man. So they made a pyre and put the body on it and set fire to it; just then the girl came and they told her to go away, but she said that she wished to see whether they really burned him like a man. So she stood by and when the pyre was in full blaze, she called out "Oh look, what is happening to the stars in the sky !" at this every one looked up at the sky; then she took some sand which she had in the fold of her cloth and threw it into the air and it fell into their eyes and blinded them.

While they were rubbing the sand out of their eyes the girl leapt on to the pyre, and was burned along with the monkey and died a *sati*. Her father and brothers were very angry at this and said that the girl must have had a monkey's soul and so she was fascinated by him; and so saying they bathed and went home.

XXXIII. RAMAI AND THE ANIMALS

Once there was a blacksmith who had five sons and the sons were always quarrelling. Their father used to scold them, but they paid no heed; so he got angry and one day he sent for them and said" You waste your time quarrelling. I have brought you up and have amassed wealth; I should like to see what you are worth. I will put it to the test: I will give you each one hundred rupees, and I will see how you employ the money; if any of you puts it to profitable use, I will call him my son; but if any of you squander it, I shall call him a girl." So they went forth with the money and one bought buffaloes and one bought horses and another cattle, each according to his judgement, and brought them home. But the youngest son, who was named Ramai, soon after he started, found some men killing a cat and he begged them not to kill the cat, but let him have it and he bought it of them, and going on he found some men killing a dog which they had caught stealing and he bought it of them to save its life. By and bye he came to some men hunting an otter and he asked what they were doing, and they said that the otter ate the fish in a Raja's tank and so they were going to kill it; and he asked them to catch it and sell it to him, and promised to take it away where it could do no harm; and they did so. Then he went on and came to some men who were killing a young black snake and he saved that also, and then returned home with his four animals, and he tethered the cat and the dog and the otter in the yard and he put the snake into a pot with a lid on and hung it in the cow shed.

When his father saw Ramai's animals, he was very angry and jeered at him and said that he had no more mind than a woman; and especially he told him to throw away the snake at once, if he did not want it killed. So Ramai took down the pot with the snake in it, and the snake said: "Take me to my father and mother and they will reward you, and when they ask what you would like, take nothing but the ring which is on my father's hand: it is a magic ring and has the property that it will give you whatever you ask."

So Ramai took the young snake to its home and its father and mother were very grateful and asked what reward he would accept: and he said he would take nothing but the ring, so they gave it to him. On the way home he thought that he would test its virtues: so he bathed and spread out a cloth and then prayed: "Oh ring, give me some luncheon," and behold he saw a nice lunch heaped up in the middle of the cloth. He ate it joyfully and went back home, and there he found that his father had killed the other animals and he reproached him; but his father said: "They were useless and were only eating their heads off, why should not I kill them?" Ramai answered:, These were not useless, they were most valuable animals, much better than those my brothers bought; if you asked my brothers for a gold palace they could not make you one, but I could do so at once, thanks to the snake, and I could marry a princess and get anything else I want."

His father said that he would like to see him try: so Ramai asked the ring for a gold palace and immediately one appeared in their garden. Then his father was very repentant about having killed the other animals. But Ramai's boast that he could marry a princess got abroad and the Raja heard of it and as he was glad to have so rich a son-in-law, he gave him his daughter in marriage. And with his daughter the Raja sent elephants and horses, but Ramai sent them back again, lest it should be said that he had become rich through the bounty of the Raja; and by virtue of the ring they lived in wealthy and prosperity.

XXXIV. THE MAGIC BEDSTEAD

Once upon a time a carpenter made a bedstead, and when it was ready he put it in his verandah. At night he heard the four legs of the bedstead talking together and saying: "We will save the life of anyone who sleeps on this bedstead and protect him from his enemies." When the carpenter heard this, he decided not to part with the bed for less than a hundred rupees. So next day he went out to try and get this price for the bed, but people laughed at him and said that no one could pay such a price but the Raja; so he went to the Raja and the Raja asked why he wanted one hundred rupees for a bedstead that was apparently worth only five or six annas. The carpenter answered that the bed would protect its owner from all enemies; the Raja doubted at first but as the man persisted in his story he agreed to buy the bed, but he stipulated that if he found the story about it not to be true, he should take back his money.

One night the king lay awake on the bed and he heard the legs of the bed talking, so he lay still and listened: and they said that the Raja was in danger and that they must try to save him. So one leg loosened itself from the bed and went away outside and it found a tiger which had come to eat the Raja, and it beat the tiger to death, and then came back and fixed itself into its place again. Soon a second leg said that it would go outside; so it went and that leg met a leopard and a bear and it beat them to death and returned. Then the third leg said there was its turn and it went outside and it found four burglars digging a hole through the wall of the palace, and it set upon them and broke their legs and left them lying there. When this one returned, the fourth leg went out. and it heard a voice in the sky saying: "The Raja is very cunning, I will send a snake which shall hide in his shoe and when he puts the shoe on in the morning, it will bite him and he will die." When this leg came back, each one told the others what it had seen and done, and the Raja heard them and lay awake till morning, and at dawn he called his servants and sent them outside the palace and there they found the tiger and leopard and bear lying dead, and the four thieves with their legs broken. Then the Raja believed what the legs had said and he would not get up but first ordered his servants to make a fire in the courtyard and he had all his shoes thrown into the fire and then he got up.

After this the Raja ordered that great care was to be taken of the bedstead and that anyone who sat on it should be put to death; and he himself used not to sleep in it anymore but he kept it in his bedroom that it might protect him.

XXXV. THE GHORMUHAS

Ghormuhas have heads like horses and bodies and arms like men and their legs are shaped like men's but they have only one leg each, and they eat human beings.

One day a young man named Somai was hunting a deer and the deer run away to the country of the Ghormuhas and Somai pursued it, and the Ghormuhas caught him and took him home to eat. First they smoked him for two or three days so that all the vermin were driven out of his body and clothes and then they proceeded to fatten him; they fed him well every day on rice cooked with turmeric.

Somai saw how they dealt with their other victims: they tied them hand and foot and threw them alive into, a pot of boiling oil and when they were cooked they hung the bodies up in the doorway and would take a bite as they passed in and out; the liver and heart and brains they cooked separately. They used to eat their own parents also: for when a father or mother grew old they would throw them on to the roof of the house and when they rolled down and were killed they would say to their friends, "The pumpkin growing on our roof has got ripe and fallen off and burst, let us come and eat it;" and then they had a least.

Somai saw all this and was very frightened. The Ghormuhas could run very fast and they made Somai run a race with them every day and their plan was that they would eat him when he was strong enough to beat them in the race. In the course of time he came to beat them in running on the road; then they said that they would make him run in the fields and, if he beat them there, they meant to eat him.

Somai found out their plan and he decided to try and run away; if he stayed he would be eaten, so if they caught him when he tried to run away he would be no worse off. So the first day they raced in the fields Somai was winning but he remembered and stopped himself and let himself be beaten that day. But he resolved to try and escape the next day and the Ghormuhas had decided to eat him that day whatever happened. So when the race began, Somai set off towards the lower lanos where the rice fields were embanked and he jumped the embankments, but the Ghormuhas who pursued him could not jump well and tumbled and fell; and thus he ran away to his own country and made good his escape. And it was he who told men what Ghormuhas are like and how they live.

XXXVI. THE BOY WHO LEARNT MAGIC

Once upon a time there was a Raja who had seven wives and they were all childless, and he was very unhappy at having no heir. One day a Jogi came to this palace begging, and the Raja and his Ranis asked him whether he could say what should be done in order that they might have children; the Jogi asked what they would give him if he told them and they said that they would give him anything that he asked for and gave him a written bond to this effect. Then the Jogi said "I will not take elephants or horses or money, but you shall give me the child which is born first and any born afterwards shall be yours, do you agree?" And the Ranis consulted together and agreed. "Then," said the Jogi, "this is what you must do: you must all go and bathe, and after bathing you must go to a mango orchard and the Raja must choose a bunch of seven mangoes and knock it down with his left hand and catch it in a cloth, without letting it touch the ground; then you must go home and the Ranis must sit in a row according to their seniority and the Raja must give them each one of the mangoes to eat, and he must himself eat the rinds which the Ranis throw away; and then you will have children." And so saying the Jogi went away promising to return the next year.

A few days later the Raja decided to give a trial to the jogi's prescription and he and the Ranis did as they had been told; but the Raja did not eat the rind of the youngest Rani's mango; he did not love her very much. However five or six months after it was seen that the youngest Rani was with child and then she became the Raja's favourite; but the other Ranis were jealous of her and reminded the Raja that he would not be able to keep her child. But when her time was full she gave birth to twin sons, and the Raja was delighted to think that he would be able to keep the younger of the two and he loved it much.

When the year was up the jogi came and saw the boys and he said that he would return when they could walk; and when they could run about, he came again, and asked whether the Raja would fulfil his promise.

The Raja said that he would not break his bond. Then the Jogi said that he would take the two boys and when the Raja objected that he was only entitled to one, he said that he claimed both as they were born at the same time; but he promised that if he took both he would teach them magic and then let one come back; and he promised also that all the Ranis should have children. So the Raja agreed and sent away the boys with the Jogi and with them he sent goats and sheep and donkeys and horses and camels and elephants and furniture of all sorts.

The Jogi was called Sitari Jogi and he was a Raja in his own country. But before they reached his country all the animals died, first the goats, then the sheep and the donkeys and the horses and the camels and the elephants. And when the goats died the boys lamented:

" The goats have died, father,
How far, father,
Is it to the country of the Sitari Jogi?"

and so they sang when the other animals died.

At last they reached the Jogi's palace, and every day he taught them incantations and spells. He bought them each a water pot and sent them every morning to fill it with dew, but before they collected enough, the sun came out and dried up the dew; one day they got a cupful, another day half a cupful, but they never were able to fill the pots. In the course of time they learnt all the spells the Jogi knew and one day when they went out to gather dew, the younger boy secretly took with him a rag and he soaked this in the dew and then squeezed it into the pot and so he soon filled it; and the elder boy seeing his brother's pot full, filled his pot at a pool of water and they took them to the Jogi; but the jogi was not deceived by the elder boy and told him that he would never learn magic thoroughly; but the younger boy having learned all that the Jogi knew, learnt more still from his friends, for all the people of that country knew magic.

Then one day the Jogi took the two boys back to their home and he told the Raja that he would leave the elder boy at home. The Raja wanted to keep the younger one, but the jogi insisted and the younger boy whispered to his mother not to mind as he would soon come back by himself; so they let him go.

The Jogi and the boy used to practise magic: the Jogi would take the form of a young man and the boy would turn into a bullock and the Jogi would go to a village and sell the bullock for a good price; but he would not give up the tethering rope and then he would go away and do something with the tethering rope and the boy would resume his shape again and run off to the Jogi and when the purchasers looked for their bullock they found nothing, and when they went to look for the seller the jogi would change his shape again so that he could not be recognised, and in this way they deceived many people and amassed wealth.

Then the Jogi taught the boy the spell he used with the rope, and when he had learnt this, he asked to be taught the spell by which he could change his own shape without having a second person to work the spell with the rope. The Jogi said that he would teach him that later but he must wait. Then the boy reproached the Jogi and said that he did not love him; and he went away to his friends in the town and learnt the spell he wanted from them, so that he was able to change his shape at will.

Two or three days after the boy again went to the Jogi and said, "Teach me the spell about which I spoke to you the other day," and the Jogi refused. "Then, said the boy," I shall go back to my father, for I see that you do not love me."

At this the Jogi grew wrathful and said that if the away he would kill him, so the boy at this ran away in terror, and the Jogi became a leopard and pursued him: then the boy turned himself into a pigeon and the Jogi became a hawk and pursued him; so the boy turned himself into a fly and the Jogi became paddy bird and pursued him; the fly alighted on the plate of a Rani who was eating rice and the Jogi tok on his natural shape and told the Rani to scatter the rice which she was eating on the ground and she did so; but the boy turned himself into a bead of coral on the necklace which the Rani was wearing; and the Jogi did not notice this but became a pigeon and ate the rice which the Rani had thrown down. When he did not find the boy among the rice he turned him into a Jogi again and saw him in the necklace; then he told the Rani to break her necklace and scatter beads on the ground and she did so; then the Jogi again became a pigeon and began to pick up the beads, but the boy turned himself into a cat and hid under the verandah and when the pigeon came near, he pounced it and, ran outside with it. Then he became a boy again and twisted off the bird's head and wrapped it in his cloth and went off home; and looking behind he saw the Jogi's head come rolling after him, so when he came to a blacksmith's fire by the side of the road he threw the pigeon's head into it, and then the Jogi's head also ran into the fire and was consumed.

And the boy went home to his parents.

XXXVII. THE CHARITABLE JOGI

Once there was a very poor man with a large family; and when his eldest son grew, up he tried to arrange a marriage for him. He selected a bride and arranged matters with her relations but then he found that he had no money to pay for the performance of the marriage ceremonies. So he tried to borrow from his friends and from money lenders, but no one would lend him anything. So he proposed to the bride's relatives to only have the betrothal that year and the marriage the year after, but they would not agree and said that the marriage must be then or never.

Just then a Jogi came to his house to beg and he told the Jogi all about his difficulties and asked for help; the Jogi took pity on him and gave him twenty rupees which was all that he had collected by begging.

Now this Jogi had two wives at home and he thought that he would get a poor reception from them it he returned empty handed, so he picked up two stones and wrapped them up in two pieces of cloth. And when he reached home his wives welcomed him and brought out a bed for him to sit on and asked about his adventures and when they saw the bundles they wished to know what was inside and they opened them before him and behold the stones had turned into gold. When the Jogi saw this he wished that he had picked up three or four stones instead of only two and he understood that Chando had given him the gold because he helped the poor man.

This is why no money lender will refuse a loan if one is asked for the performance of a marriage and money borrowed is always paid back punctually. When the Jogi came back the next year the poor man paid him the twenty rupees.

XXXVIII. CHOTE AND MOTE

Once upon a time there were two brothers Chote and Mote; they were poor but very industrious and they got tired of working as hired labourers in their own village so they decided to try their luck elsewhere. They went to a distant village and Chote took service with an oilman and Mote with a potter on a yearly agreement. Chote had to drive the oil mill in the morning and then after having his dinner to feed the mill bullock and take it out to graze. But the bullock having had a good meal of oilcake would not settle down to graze alone but kept running after all the herds of cattle it saw, and Chote had to spend his whole time running after it till he was worn out and he was very soon sorry that he had taken up such hard. service; and was quite resolved not to stay on after his year was up.

Mote was no better off; the potter overworked him, making him carry water and dig earth from morn to night and for all he did he got nothing but abuse.

One day the brothers met and Mote asked Chote how he was getting on. Chote answered "Oh I have got a capital place; all the morning I sit at my ease on the oil mill, then I have a good dinner and take the bullock out to graze and as it has had a good meal of oilcake it lies down without giving any trouble and I sit in the shade and enjoy myself." Then Mote said "I am pretty lucky too. I have to fetch three or four pots of water, then I have my dinner and a rest and then I have to dig earth and knead it. Still I cannot say that I have so little work as you; will you change with me for three or four days, so that I may have a rest?"

Chote gladly agreed and each brother thought that he had got the better of the other. In the morning while Mote was driving the oil mill he was very pleased with his new job and when he had to take the bullock out to graze he took a bedstead with him to lie on. But directly the bullock got outside the village it rushed off, bellowing towards some other cattle and Mote had to run after it with his bedstead on his head, and all the afternoon the bullock kept him running about till he was worn out.

Meanwhile Chote was no better off; his unaccustomed shoulders were quite bruised with constantly carrying water. At the potter's house was a custard apple tree and it was believed that there was money buried at the foot of the tree; so as Chote was a stranger, the potter told him to water the earth by the tree to soften it, as it was to be used for pottery. Chote softened the earth and dug it and as he dug he uncovered pots of rupees; so he covered them up again and dug the earth elsewhere. And at evening he went and proposed to Mote to run away with the money. So at midnight, they went and dug it up and ran off home. As they were not pursued, they felt safe after a month or two, so they spent the money in buying land and cattle, and their cultivation prospered and they became quickly rich.

XXXIX. THE DAYDREAMER

Once an oil man was going to market with his pots of oil arranged on a flat basket and he engaged a Santal for two annas to carry the basket; and as he went along, the Santal thought "With one anna I will buy food and with the other I will buy chickens, and the chickens will grow up and multiply and then I will sell some of the fowls and eggs and with the money 1 will buy goats; and when the goats increase I will sell some and buy cows, and then I will exchange some of the calves for she-buffaloes, and when the buffaloes breed, I will sell some and buy land and start cultivation and then I will marry and have children and I will hurry back from my work in the fields and my wife will bring me water and I will have a rest and my children will say to me "Father, be quick and wash you hands for dinner," but I will shake my head and say "No, no, not yet!"—and as he thought about it he really shook his head and the basket fell to the ground and all the pots of oil were smashed.

Then the oilman abused him and said that he must pay two rupees for the oil and one anna for the pots but the Santal said that he had lost much more then that and the oilman asked him how that could be: and the Santal explained how with his wages he was going to get fowls and then goats and then oxen and buffaloes and land and how he came to spill the basket and at that the oilman roared with laughter and said "Well I have made up the account and I find that our losses are equal, so we will cry quits;" and so saying the went their ways laughing.

XL. THE EXTORTIONATE SENTRY

There was once a sentry outside a Raja's palace who would let no one go in to sell anything to the Raja until they first promised to give him half the price they received from the Raja, and the poor traders had to promise, for their livelihood depended on selling their goods. One day a fisherman caught an enormous fish and he thought that if he took it to the Raja he would get a big price for it.

So he went off to the palace, but when he came to the gate the sentry stopped him and would not let him go in, until he promised to give him half of what he got, and after some argument he had to promise. So he was admitted to the Raja's presence and when the Raja asked what was the price of the fish, the fisherman said, a hundred blows with a stick."

The Raja was very astonished and asked the meaning of such a request, Then the fisherman said that the sentry had extorted a promise that he should get half the price and he wanted him to get fifty blows. At this the Raja was very angry and he had the sentry beaten with one hundred stripes and dismissed him.

XLI. THE BROKEN FRIENDSHIP

Once upon a time there was a Raja and his Dewan and they each had one son, and the two boys were great friends, and, when they grew old enough, they took to hunting and when they became young men they were so devoted to the sport that they spent their whole time in pursuit of game; they followed every animal they could find until they killed it, and they shot every bird in the town.

Their parents were much distressed at this, for they thought that if their boys spent all their time together hunting they would grow up unruly and ignorant; so they made up their minds that they must separate the young men so that they would not be tempted to spend so much time in sport, but would be able to learn something useful; they scolded the youths and told them to give up their friendship and their hunting, but this had no effect. Then the Raja told the villagers that he would reward any one who would break up the friendship, and the villagers tried their best but effected nothing.

There was however an old woman in the village who one day said, "If the Raja gave me ten rupees I would soon put a stop to their friendship." This came to the ears of the Raja and he exclaimed" What is ten rupees to me! bring the old woman to me and I will give her ten rupees, if she can put an end to this friendship." So the old woman was brought trembling before the Raja and on being questioned undertook to break up the friendship if she were properly rewarded; and when this was promised she asked for two men to be given to her and she took them to her house and there she made them sling a bed on a pole, such as is used for carrying a man on a journey and she hung curtains all round it and drew them close and inside, on an old winnowing fan, they put some rotten manure from a dung hill.

Then she made the two men take up the bed and she fetched a drum and she paraded all through the bazar beating the drum with the bed following behind her. She told the two carriers not to answer any questions as to what was in the bed. Thus they passed out of the town and went in the direction in which the two young men had gone hunting. When these heard the sound of the drum and saw the two men carrying the bed they ran up to see what it was and told the carriers to put it down that they might look inside; so the bed was put on the ground and the Raja's son peeped inside the curtain, but as he caught the smell he jumped back and the Dewan's son asked what was the matter and he said "it stinks: it is dung." The Dewan's son would not believe him and also looked to convince himself; then they both asked what the meaning of this was: the old woman said that she would explain the meaning of it but only to one of them, and the one who had heard could tell the other.

So she made the carriers take away the bed and she called the Raja's son aside saying "Come I will tell you what it means" then she put her arms round the neck of the Raja's son and put her lips to his ear and pretended to whisper to him, but really she said nothing; then she let him go and followed the carriers. The Dewan's son at once ran to his friend and asked what the old woman had told him; the Raja's son answered, "She told me nothing at all, she only pretended to whisper." The Dewan's son would not believe this and pressed him to tell, saying" We have been friends for so long and have had no secrets from each other, why won't you tell me this? If you refuse to tell me there is an end of our friendship," but the Raja's son persisted that he had been told nothing and proposed that they should go and ask the old woman if it were not so; but the Dewan's son said that that was no good because the old woman and the Raja's son had plainly made a plot to keep him in the dark." The quarrel grew hotter and hotter, till at last they parted in anger and each went to his own home and from that time their friendship was broken off.

And being separated they gave up hunting and took to useful pursuits. Thus the old woman earned her reward from the Raja.

XLII. A STORY TOLD BY A HINDU

Once upon a time there was a Raja who had two sons and after their father's death they divided the kingdom between them. The two brothers were inveterate gamblers and spent their time playing cards with each other; for a long time fortune was equal, but one day it turned against the elder brother and he lost and lost until his money and his jewelry, his horses and his elephants and every thing that he had, had been won by his younger brother. Then in desperation he staked his share in the kingdom and that too he lost.

Then the younger brother sent drummers through the city to proclaim that the whole kingdom was his; the shame of this was more than the elder prince could bear, so he resolved to quit the country and he told his wife of his intention and bade her stay behind. But his faithful wife refused to be parted from him; she vowed that he had married her not for one day nor for two but for good and all, and that where he went, there she would go, and whatever troubles he met, she would share. So he allowed her to come with him and the two set off to foreign parts. After sometime their path led them through an extensive jungle and after travelling through it for two days they at last lost their way completely; their food gave out, they were faint with starvation and torn with briars.

The prince urged his wife to return but she would not hear of it, so they pushed on, supporting life on jungle fruits; sometimes the prince would go far ahead, for his faithful wife could only travel slowly, and then he would return and wait for her; at last he got tired of leading her on and made up his mind to abandon her. At night they lay down at the foot of a tree and the prince thought "If wild animals would come and eat us it would be the best that could happen. I cannot bear to see my wife suffer any more; although her flesh is torn with thorns, she will not leave me. I will leave her here; may wild beasts kill both her and me, but I cannot see her die before my eyes." So thinking he got up quietly and went off as quickly as he could.

When the princess woke and found that she had been abandoned, she began to weep and wept from dawn to noon without ceasing; at noon a being in the guise of an old woman appeared and asked her why she wept, and comforted her and promised to lead her out of the wood and told her that Chando had had compassion on her and would allow her to find her husband again if they both lived.

So saying the old woman led the princess from the forest and showed her the way to a great city where a Raja lived. The princess went begging her way through the city to the Raja's palace and there they engaged her as a servant.

Now her husband had also escaped from the jungle and sought employment as a labourer but no one would give him work for more than a day or two, and at last his search for work brought him to the city in which the princess was; and there he was engaged as a groom in the palace stables. The prince had changed his name and he had no chance of knowing that his wife was in the palace, because she was confined to the women's apartments ; so some years passed without their having news of each other.

At last one day the princess happened to go on to the roof and looking down at the stables saw and thought she recognised her husband; then she leaned over and listened till she heard his voice and at that she was sure that it was he, so she hastened to the Raja and begged to be allowed to meet her husband, and the Raja sent to call the syce with the name which the princess had given but no one came, for the prince would not reveal himself. Then the princess told their story and how her husband had gambled away his half of the kingdom. The Raja ordered any one with such a history to come forward, as his wife was in the palace; but the prince did not reveal himself.

Then the princess said "Let all the syces cook rice and bring me a bit of each man's cooking to taste." They did so, and when she tasted the rice cooked by her husband, she at once said that it was his; her husband was unable to deny it and admitted everything. Then they took him away from his work in the stables and let him live with his wife.

After a time the Raja wrote to the younger brother asking whether he would restore the half of the kingdom which he had won; and the younger brother answered that he would gladly do so, if his brother would sign an agreement never to gamble any more; it was with this object in view and to teach him the folly of his ways that he had dispossessed him, The elder brother gladly gave the required promise and returned to his kingdom with his faithful wife and lived happily ever afterwards.

XLIII. THE RAIBAR AND THE LEOPARD

Once upon a time a *Raibar* was going backwards and forwards between two families arranging a marriage and part of the road which he used to travel ran through a forest.

One day as he was going to the bride's house he took a sack with him intending to try and get the loan of some Indian corn from the bride's relations; but as he was passing through the piece of jungle he suddenly met a leopard; he was terribly frightened but collecting his wits he addressed the animal thus "Leopard; I beg you not to eat me; I am engaged on a work of great merit, I am making two men out of one." This address amazed the leopard and he after once asked the *raibar* whether he could make him into two, and promised that if he could his life should be spared. The raibar answered readily "Seeing, that in pursuit of my profession I have made two men out of one all over the country, of course I can make you into two leopards if I try; all you have to do is to get into this sack and keep quiet, if you utter a sound you will spoil the charm."

"Well," said the leopard, "I will try and see; I undertake to keep quite quiet, and if you are successful I promise to tell the whole race of leopards to spare the lives of *raibars*." So saying the leopard jumped into the sack and allowed the man to tie him up tightly in it. No sooner was this done than tie raibar took the sack on his head and carried it to the bank of a river and having given it two or three hearty whacks with his stick threw it into the water. The sack went floating down the stream and it happened that lower down a leopardess sat watching the water and when she saw the sack coming along she thought that it was a dead cow floating down. So when it came near she jumped into the water and pulled it ashore.

She then proceeded to tear open the sack, when out jumped the first leopard; he soon explained how he came to be in the sack, and declared that the raibar's promise had been fulfilled and that she was his destined mate. The leopardess agreed and the two set to work to tell all the other leopards what had happened and what a kindness the raibar had done them; and so it came to pass that to the present day leopards never interfere with *raibars* when they are going about arranging a marriage; no one ever heard of one being injured.

Meanwhile the *raibar* went on his way rejoicing at having rid himself of the leopard. But the next year, while engaged on the business of another marriage, the raibar was passing through the same jungle when he came face to face with the very leopard that he thought he had safely disposed of; he at once took to his heels, but the leopard called out to him not to be afraid and to wait, as he had something to say to him. So the *raibar* stopped and the leopard asked whether he did not recognise him ; the *raibar* stoutly denied all knowledge of him. "Well," said the leopard "I am the leopard of whom you made two out of one, and to show my gratitude I will give you any reward you like; would you like a cow or a deer or any other animal? I will kill you one and bring it to you."

When the *raibar* saw the turn that things had taken he thought that he had better take advantage of it, so he asked for a good large nilgai. The leopard told him to come to a certain tree at noon the next day and he would find the animal there. So they separated and the next day at noon the *raibar* went to the tree and found a fine nilgai wating for him, which he and his friends took home and ate with joy.

XLIV. THE UNGRATEFUL SNAKE

There was once a Raja and his dewan and they each had one son; these sons were married in infancy but as they grew up they never heard anything about their having been married. When the boys reached manhood and found no arrangements being made for their weddings they began to wonder at the delay and often talked about it, and in the end they agreed to run away to another country. Soon after this resolve of theirs some horse dealers came to their home with horses to sell; the two youths at once saw that if they could each have a horse and learn to ride it, it would be easy for them to run away from home. So they hurried to their fathers and begged them to buy them each one of the beautiful horses which the dealers had brought. The Raja and the dewan did not like to disappoint their sons so they bought the horses, to the great delight of the boys, who used to ride them every day.

One day the Raja's son was out riding by himself and he passed by a tank where a number of women and girls were bathing and drawing water; as he came galloping along the women ran back in a fright; and as they could not draw their water while he was there, an old woman came up to him and told him to go away and not stay making eyes at the girls as if he had no wife of his own: "What wife have I ? said the prince, I know nothing of having been married." "You were married sure enough when you were an infant," replied the old woman: "your wife is still in her father's house, but now that you have grown up they will probably bring her home to you this year."

Then the prince asked where his wife lived and having learnt the name of the village he galloped off home and at once began to question his mother about his marriage; his mother told him that they intended to have the bride brought home that year, but the prince was impatient and proposed that he should go off at once to his father-in-law's and see his wife, and try to persuade them to let her come back with him without any ceremony; his mother made no objection, so he got ready for the journey and started off on horseback. He had not gone far when he saw a field of thatching grass on fire, and in the middle, surrounded by the flames, was a huge poisonous snake, unable to escape.

As the prince rode by, the snake called out to him" Prince, you are going joyously to bring home your bride, and here am I in danger of being burned alive; will you not have pity on me and save me. If you do I will confer a boon on you. "But if I save you, objected the prince. "you will only eat me: snakes do not know what gratitude is." "I am not of that kind," answered the snake:" here I am in danger of death, I beseech you to have pity on me." These pleadings prevailed and the prince got off his horse and beat out the fire and then spread a cloth over the embers so that the snake could crawl out. When the snake was safe the prince asked for the boon that had been promised him. "No boon will you get" said the snake: you did a foolhardy thing in saving, me, for now I am going to eat you, and you cannot escape from me."

The prince saw that there was little hope for him but he begged the snake to allow two or three judges to decide whether it was fair that he should be killed, after what he had done. The snake agreed to this provided that the judges were not human beings; he was willing to be bound by the opinions of any one else.

They set out together to look for judges and soon saw a herd of cattle resting, under a banyan tree by a pool of water, so they agreed to make: these their judges; then the prince explained to one of the cows and the banyan tree and the water what they were to decide, whether it was fair for the snake, whose life he had saved, now to want to kill him. The banyan tree was the first to answer: it said "You did good to the snake and your wages for doing good are evil; you saved his life and he will now kill you, this is fair, this is the justice we have learnt from human beings; you enjoy the shade of us trees and in return you lop off our branches and sit on them, and do us all manner of injury; it is right that the snake should eat you."

Then the prince turned to the cow: "He may eat you, answered the cow": 'the tree is right, see how men treat cattle; you drive away our calves from us, take our milk and you beat us and make us work hard; for all this illtreatment the snake shall eat you."

Then the prince asked the water what is had to say: "I agree with the other two" said the water: "to return evil for good is the justice of mankind, it is by drinking water that your very lives are preserved; yet you spit into it and wash dirty things in it; shall not the snake return you evil for good?" So judgment was delivered and the snake wanted to eat the prince; but the prince asked the tree and the cow and the water to listen while he made one prayer; he told them how he had been married when he was too young to know anything about it, and how he was going for the first time to see his wife, when this misfortune befell him; so he begged that he might be allowed to go and see his bride and then be eaten on his way back; the banyan tree asked what the snake thought about this proposal and the snake said that it would make no objection if the tree and the cow and the water would be sureties for the return of the prince within three days. So the prince promised them faithfully that he would return and they let him go.

The prince rode on to his father-in-law's house, and when he arrived, a bed was brought out for him to sit on and he was asked where he came from. When he explained who he was, they at once brought water and washed his feet and then gave him oil and a tooth stick and took him to bathe; then they brought him curds and dried rice to eat and afterwards killed a goat and made a feast and showed him every honour.

That evening as his wife was rubbing his arms and legs, the prince remained silent and downcast and showed none of the joy of a bridegroom; and when his bride asked what was the matter, he told her that he had only come to see her for one day and that afterwards she must try and forget all about him At first he would not tell her more, but when she urged him, he told her how he had to go and surrender himself to the snake on the next day. When she heard this she vowed that she would go with him and die with him.

The next morning came and the prince said that he must return, and his wife said that she was going with him; so they made everything ready and set out on their way. When they came within sight of the banyan tree where the prince was to be killed, he tried to turn his wife back but though he used force she refused to leave him and said that she would first see him killed and then go home; so at last he let her accompany him.

When they reached the tree she asked to be allowed to go in front and be the first to meet the snake; to this the prince assented. They had not gone far when they saw the snake awaiting them in the path with its crest raised, and when they drew near, the prince's bride begged the snake to eat her first, as she had nowhere to live if she survived her husband. The snake refused and bade her go home to her parents; she said that that was impossible; they had sold her and the prince had bought her, in life and in death, bones and ashes. But the snake would not listen and made for the prince to eat him. His wife however kept in front of the snake and would not let it pass; she called the banyan tree to witness that the snake should not eat her husband without first killing her; without her husband she would have no one to support her.

Then the snake promised to teach her an incantation by means of which she could support herself, so saying, the snake conferred some magic power upon and taught her an incantation; and promised her that if she took some dust in her hand and repeated the incantation and then blew on the dust, any person on whom she sprinkled the dust would at once be burnt to ashes. Then the prince's wife asked how she should restore the people to life and the snake taught her that also, but she was not satisfied and said that she must try at once to see whether the snake was deceiving her or no; so the snake bade her experiment on a *tarop* tree which grew near. Thereupon she gathered up some dust and repeated the incantation and blew on it and suddenly threw it over the snake, which at once turned to ashes, and that was the end of the snake.

Then the prince and his wife went on their way rejoicing, and he was filled with wonder at the way in which his bride had saved him by persisting in going with him.

XLV. THE TIGER'S BRIDE

One day a woman went to cut thatching grass and she cut such a quantity that when she tied it up, the bundle was too big for her to lift on to her head; so she stood and called for some one to help her, but no one was within hearing and no one came. She called and called and at last began to promise that she would give her daughter in marriage to any one who would help her.

After she had called out this a few times, a tiger suddenly appeared and asked what she wanted; she explained her difficulty and the tiger undertook to lift the load on to her head, if she would really give him her daughter in marriage. She promised and with the help of the tiger took up the bundle and went home.

Two or three days after, the tiger presented himself at her house and was duly married to the daughter. After the wedding the couple started for the tiger's home; all the way the unhappy bride wept and sang:—

"How far off is our home, big head?"

"You can just see the mouth of the cave" answered the tiger and in a short time they came to a large cave, Then the tiger told her to set to work and cook a feast while he went off and invited his friends to come and share it. But the bride when left alone caught a cat and killed it and hung it over the fire, so that its blood dropped slowly into the pan and made a fizzling noise, as if cooking were going on; and then she ran off to her mother's house and climbed a tree which grew near it and began to sing:—

"You married me to a ti-ti-tiger;
You threw me to a bear;
Take back the necklace you gave me
Take back the bracket and the diamonds and the coral."

Meanwhile the tiger returned with his friend and sat down outside the cave and told his wife to be quick with the cooking of the cakes for he heard the hissing over the fire and thought that she was cooking. At last as she did not come out, he got tired of waiting and went in to fetch her: then he saw that she had disappeared and had to go and tell his friends. They were very angry at being cheated out of a feast, and fell upon the tiger and beat him, till he ran away and was seen no more : but his bride was left to flit from tree to tree singing :—

"You married me to a ti-ti-tiger:
You threw me to a bear:
Take back the necklace you gave me
Take back the bracelet and the diamonds and the coral."

XLVI. THE KILLING OF THE TIGER

They say that there was a time when all living things had a common speech and animals and men could understand each other, and in those days there was a man-eating tiger which infested a jungle through which a highroad ran; it preyed on people passing along the road till no one ventured to travel, and as the counter was so unsafe, the people went in a body to the Raja and told him of the ravages of the tiger and asked him to send a force of soldiers to hunt and shoot it.

So the Raja called together all his soldiers and promised to give half his kingdom to any one of them who would kill the tiger, but not one of them was brave enough to make the attempt; they said that their business was to fight men and not tigers and leopards; then the Raja extended his offer to all his subjects and the petitioners went home to consult about it; and the news was published that the Raja would give half his kingdom to the slayer of the tiger.

Now there was a poor man who was a very brave shikari of big game and cunning into the bargain, and he offered to go and kill the tiger. They questioned him carefully, and when they saw that he was in earnest they took him to the Raja to hear from the Raja's lips what his reward should be; and the Raja promised him half his kingdom, and wrote a bond to that effect, for he thought that the tiger would surely kill the man. Then the shikari said that he would start the next morning and return the next day either with the dead tiger or with bits of its ears and claws to shows that he had killed it. The Raja told the people to watch carefully and see that the shikari did not chear by taking the claws and ears of a tiger with him.

The next morning the shikari started off and all he took with him was a looking-glass and three pictures of a tiger drawn on three pieces of paper and a hatchet; he went to the road which the tiger frequented and climbed a banyan tree and spent the night in it. The tiger did not pass by at all that night but in the morning it appeared and called out. " Who is up in the tree?" The shikari said "It is I." "Come down quickly", said the tiger, "I have been looking for you." Wait a minute," answered the shikari, "I have been looking for you also."

"What for ?" said the tiger: "Tell me first why you are looking for me," said the man: "To eat you," answered the tiger, then the man said. "Well I have been hunting for you to catch you and take you away. I have caught three or four like you and if you don't believe me, let me get down and I will show you". The tiger got into a fright and said: "Come down and show me." So the shikari climbed down and uncovered his looking glass and told the tiger to look and he reflected in the glass the pictures of the tigers which he had brought and said, "Now I am going to catch you and put you in here also." The tiger asked why he was to be caught and the shikari said that it was because he had made the road unsafe by killing travellers; then the tiger begged and prayed to be let off and promised that he would never kill any travellers again. At last she shikari said that he would let him go, if he would allow him to cut off his claws and the tips of his ears and the tip of his tongue as a pledge of his good faith. The tiger said," Well, you may cut off one claw from each foot and the very tip of my cars and tongue," So the shikari cut them off with his hatchet and, after again warning the tiger, went back home; and then presented himself with all his friends before the Raja and the Raja gave him the promised reward. But the tiger's tongue festered and, after roaring with pain for a whole day, it died.

XLVII. THE DREAM

One night as a man and his wife lay talking in bed, the woman told her husband that she had dreamt that in a certain place she had dug up a pot full of rupees, and she proposed that they should go and look for it and see whether the dream was true. While they talked, it chanced that some thieves, who had climbed on to the roof, overheard the conversation and at once decided to forestall the others. So they went off to the place which the woman had described and began to dig, and after digging a little they were delighted to come on a pot with a lid on. But when they took off the lid an enormous snake raised its head and hissed at them. At this the thieves cursed the woman who had misled them and agreed to take the snake and drop it through the roof on to the man and his wife as they lay in bed. so they shut the snake up again and carried it off to the house, and, making a hole in the thatch, dropped it through. But as it fell the snake changed into a stream of money, which came rattling down on the couple below; the thieves found a snake, but it was not real snake, it was Thakur; and it was his will to give the money to the man and his wife. When those two had recovered from their astonishment, they gathered up the money, and lived in wealth ever afterwards.

XLVIII. THE KING OF THE BHUYANS

There was once a king of the Bhuyans and near his palace was a village of Santals; he was a kind ruler and both Santals and Bhuyans were very happy under his sway. But when he died, he was succeeded by his son, who was a very severe master and soon fell out with the Santals. If he found any cattle or buffaloes grazing anywhere near his crops, he had the cowherds beaten severely: so that no one dared to take the cattle in that direction.

The Santals were very angry at this and longed to get even with the Raja; they planned to turn the cattle into the Raja's crops at night when no one could see them or catch them, but in the end their courage failed them.

One year after the rice had been cut, but before the millet crop was gathered, the youths and maidens of the Santal village had a dance and danced all night till nearly morning; then they agreed that it was not worth while to go to bed and they had better take the cattle out to graze at once.

After grazing their fill, the cattle all collected at the midday resting place and the cowherds were so sleepy after their night's dancing, that they fell fast asleep on the bare ground. After a time the buffaloes began to move again and seeing a nice field of millet belonging to the Raja soon made their way to it and grazed the whole field down. The Raja happened to pass that way and, was filled with wrath at the sight; he at once ordered his *sipahis* to go and beat the cowherds within an inch of their lives and so the *sipahis* ran to the place with sticks. Their approach roused the sleeping cowherds who jumped up and ran off home as hard as they could; all but the servant of the village *paramanik* (assistant headman) he did not run away but went to drive the cattle out of the field; he knew that this was his duty to his master and he was resolved to do his duty even at the cost of his life.

As all the other boys had got away the *sipahis* turned their attention to him, but as they aimed blows at him with the sticks, he caught the blows on his arms and the sticks shivered to atoms without harming him; so, then they went to kick him but a great *cibei* snake came rustling up behind them; so they saw it was no use to contend with him and desisted: whereupon he drove all the village cattle home in triumph.

The *sipahis* reported to the Raja how the cowherds had all made good their escape, and how the *paramanik*'s herd boy had driven off the cattle. Then the Raja told them to go that afternoon at the time the cattle were brought home for the night and wait at the end of the village street and then give the cowherds the thrashing they deserved. The *sipahis* did as they were ordered and that evening waited for the returning herd boys; and caught them as they came home and thrashed them within an inch of their lives. The others were all left senseless on the ground: but the *sipahis* did not dare to lay hands on the paramanik's herd boy, he drove the cattle back into the villagers, and told the villagers what had been done to their sons. So the villagers went out with beds and carried the wounded boys home; then they assembled and resolved to go and punish the Raja, so they went to him and asked what he meant by killing their children. "Dear me," said the Raja," are they really dead?" Well, if not quite dead, they are very ill," was the answer." "I am sorry," said the Raja :, I admit that I have done wrong, but if you will forgive me this time, I will undertake to cure them in a minute and make them as well as ever; go and fetch them here."

So the Santals went off to fetch the wounded cowherds and carried them to the Raja, all lying senseless on beds and put them down before him. While they were away the Raja had told his sipahis to grind some good hot *chilis* ; and when the cowherds were brought to him he told the sipahis to thrust the chili paste up their noses; this was done and the smarting soon made the cowherds jump up and run away in a very lively fashion, and that was the way the Raja kept his word and cured them.

XLIX. THE FOOLISH SONS

There was once a man of the blacksmith caste who had six sons; the sons were all married and the whole family lived together. But the sons' wives took to quarrelling and at last the sons went to their parents and proposed that they should set up separate households, as the women folk could not live in peace.

The blacksmith and his wife did not like the idea at all and pointed out that it would be most inadvisable; while, so far, there was plenty of food and clothing for all, they would find it much more expensive to have seven separate households and split up what was quite enough so long as they lived together, and what was to become of their old parents who were now too old to work? The sons protested that they would support their father and mother as long as they lived, even though the family separated.

At last the old man said that he would put them to the test and see whether they were clever enough to manage their own affairs and smart enough to cheat people into giving them what they wanted. "I will see," said he, "how you would manage to support the family in time of famine or if we fell into poverty. I and your mother have managed to bring up a large family, and you know nothing of the anxiety that it has cost us; you have merely had to enjoy yourselves and eat your meals; if you insist on it, I will let you separate, but don't blame me afterwards. However tomorrow, I will take you on a journey and find some means of testing your cleverness."

So the next morning they made ready for the journey; their father only allowed them to take one meal of rice tied up in their cloths and he gave each of them one pice, which he said was their inheritance. They set off and after travelling some way they sat down and ate up their rice and then went on again. By the middle of the afternoon they began to feel hungry, so the father proposed their going to a bazar which was in sight; but between them and the bazar was a channel of stagnant water, very deep, and with its surface covered by a coating of weeds. They tried to cross, but directly they set foot on it they sank through the weeds, and it was too deep for wading. So their father said they would all camp on the bank and he would see whether they were clever enough to get across the channel and bring food for a meal; if they could do that he would believe that they could support their families in time of famine.

So the old man spread his cloth on the ground and set down and watched them try their luck one by one. The eldest brother first jumped up to try but he could not cross the channel; everytime he tried, he sank through the weeds, at last he gave up in despair and admitted that he could not feed the party. Then the other brothers all tried in turn and failed. At last it came to the turn of the youngest; he modestly said that he was not likely to succeed where his elders had failed but he would have a try, so he went to the edge of the water and spreading out his cloth on the weeds lay down on it so that his weight was distributed; in this position, the weeds supported him and he managed to wriggle himself across on his face to the other side.

Once across, he went to the bazar, and going to a shop began to talk with the shopkeeper; after a little he asked for the loan of an anna; the shopkeeper said that he could not lend to a stranger; the blacksmith's son gave the name of some village as his home and pressed for the loan, promising to pay him one anna as interest within a week and pulling out his pice he said "See here, I will pay you this pice as part of the interest in advance." At this the shopkeeper suffered himself to be persuaded and lent him the anna.

With this the blacksmith's son went off to a second shop and begged for the loan of four annas, as he had pressing need of it; he promised to pay an anna a week, interest, and to pay down at once the interest for the first week. After some hesitation the shopkeeper was deceived into lending the four annas. Then he went off to another shop and borrowed a rupee by promising to pay eight annas a month as interest and putting down four annas as advance.

Then he went to a Marwari's shop and asked for the loan of ten rupees; the Marwari asked for interest at the rate of one rupee a day; the blacksmith's son protested that was too high but offered to pay one rupee every two days and to pay one rupee of interest in advance; the Marwari hesitated, but after being given a name and address—which were however false—he gave way and took his signature to a bond and lent him the ten rupees. At this the blacksmith's son set off in triumph to rejoin his brothers; he crossed the water in the same way as before and took the ten rupees to his father.

Then they all went on to another bazar and bought dried rice and sweetmeats and curds and had a grand feast. Then their father proceeded to point out to his sons how, except the youngest, they were all useless; they had been unable to cross the channel or to make anything of their own pice of capital; they had nothing to answer, and all went home and from that day nothing was heard of any proposal to divide the family until the old father and mother died.

L. KORA AND HIS SISTER

There were once seven brothers and they had one sister who was the youngest of the family. The six eldest brothers were married but no wife had been found for the youngest; for three years enquiries were made to try and find a suitable bride for him, but all in vain. At last the young man, whose name was Kora, told his parents and brothers not to trouble any more, as he would find a wife for himself; he intended to bring a flowering plant from the forest and plant it by the stand on which the watering pots were kept, And then he would marry any maiden who picked one of the flowers and put it in her hair.

His father and mother approved of this proposal, so the next day he brought some sort of flowering plant and planted it by the water-pot stand. He charged all his family to be most careful that no one of his own relations picked the flower and also to warn any of the village girls who wanted to pick it, that if she did so and put it in her hair, she would thereby become his wife; but if, knowing this, anyone wished to do so, they were not to prevent her.

The neighbours soon got to hear what the plant meant and used often to come and look at it, and Kora watched it growing, till after a time it produced a bud and then a beautiful and sweet-scented flower. All the village girls came to see the beautiful flower; and one day Kora's sister when she went to the water-stand to get some water to drink, caught hold of it and longed to, pick it, it looked so pretty. Her mother saw what she was doing and scolded her for touching the forbidden flower, but the girl begged to see what it would look like in her hair, there could be no harm done if she pulled the whole plant up by its roots and put it in her hair and then replanted it; no one would know what had happened. In spite of her mother's remonstrances she insisted on doing this and having seen how the flower looked in her hair carefully replanted it.

Soon afterwards Kora came home and went to see his flower; he knew at once that some one had worn it and called to his mother and asked who it was. She protested that she knew nothing about the matter, but Kora said that he could tell by the smell that it had been worn and then he showed that there was also, a hair sticking to the flower. Then his mother admitted that in spite of all she could say, his sister had worn the flower and planted it again in the ground.

When she saw that she was found out, the girl began to cry, but her father said that it was clearly fated that she and Kora should marry and this was the reason why they had been unable to find any other bride; so they must now arrange for the wedding. Accordingly rice was got ready and all the usual preparations made for a marriage. The unfortunate girl saw that flight was her only means of escape from such a fate, so one day she ran away; all she took with her was a pet parrot.

For many days she travelled on and one day she stopped by a pool to bathe and as she rubbed her limbs she collected the scurf that she rubbed off her skin and put in on the ground in one place; then she went on with her bathing; but at the place where she had put the scurf of her skin, a palm tree sprang up and grew so rapidly, that, by the time she came out of the water, it had become a large tree.

The girl was struck by this strange sight and at once thought that the tree would afford her a safe refuge; so she climbed up it with her parrot in her hand and when safely seated among the leaves she begged the palm tree to grow so tall that no one would be able to find her, and the tree grew till it reached an unusual height. So the girl stayed in the tree top and the parrot used to go every day and bring her food. Meanwhile her parents and brothers searched high and low for her for two or three days, for the wedding day was close at hand, but their search was of course in vain; and they concluded that the girl must have drowned herself in some river.

Time passed and one day at noon a Mohuli girl, who was taking her basket-ware to market, stopped to rest in the shade of the palm tree: and as she sat there, Kora's sister called to her from the top of the tree and asked her to give her a small winnowing fan in exchange for a bracelet. The Mahuli girl told her to throw the bracelet down first. Kora's sister made no objection to this, and when she had got the bracelet, the Mahuli girl threw up a winnowing fan which soared right up to where Kora's sister was sitting. Before the Mahuli girl went on her way, Kora's sister made her promise never to let anyone see the bracelet when she went out selling her baskets as otherwise it would be stolen from her; and secondly on no account to let it be know that there was anyone in the palm tree, on pain of death. The Mahuli girl kept her promise and whenever she went out selling baskets she used to keep her bracelet covered with her cloth.

One day it chanced that she went to the house where Kora lived to sell her wares and they asked her why it was that she kept her arm covered; she told them that she had a sore on it; they wanted to see how big the sore was, but she refused to show it, saying that if she showed it she would die. They laughed at such a ridiculous story and at last forced her to show her arm, which of course was quite well; but they at once, recognised the bracelet and asked where she had got it from. The Mahuli girl refused to tell them and said that if she did, she would die "What a foolish girl you are" they objected "first you say you will die if you show us your arm and then if you tell us where you got this bracelet from; it belonged to our daughter whom we have lost, and so you must tell us ! Come, we will give you a basket full of rice if you tell us." The Mahuli girl could not resist this offer, and when the basket of rice was produced, she told them where the palm tree was, in which Kora's sister was hiding. In all haste the father and mother went to the tree and found that it was much too high for them to climb: so they begged their daughter to come down and promised not to marry her to her brother; but she would not come down: then they sang:—

"You have made a palm tree from the scrapings of your skin And have climbed up into it, daughter!

Come daughter, come down."

But she only answered:—

"Father and mother, why do you cry?
I must spend my life here:
"Do you return home."

So they went home in despair.

Then her sisters-in-law came in their turn and sang:—

"Palm tree, palm tree, give us back our sister:
The brother and sister have got to be married."

But she would not answer them nor come down from the tree, so they had to go home without her.

Then all her other relations came and besought her to come down, but she would not listen to them. So they went away and invoked a storm to come to their aid. And a storm arose and cold rain fell, till the girl in the palm tree was soaked and shivering, and the wind blew and swayed the palm tree so that its top kept touching the ground. At last she could bear the cold and wet no more and, seizing an opportunity when the tree touched the ground, she slipped off. Her relations had made all the villagers promise on no account to let her into their houses; so when she went into the village and called out at house after house no one answered her or opened to her. Then she went to her own home and there also they refused to open to her.

But Kora had lit a big fire in the cow house and sat by it warming himself, knowing that the girl would have to come to him; and as she could find no shelter elsewhere she had to go to his fire, and then she sat and warmed herself and thought " I fled for fear of this man and now I have come back to him; this is the end, I can no longer stay in this world; the people will not even let me into their houses. I have no wish to see them again."

So she sat and thought, and when she was warmed, she lay down by the side of Kora; and he wore tied to his waist a nail-cutter; she unfastened this and cut her throat with it as she lay. Her death struggles aroused Kora, and we got up and saw the ground covered with her blood and he saw that she had killed herself with his nail-cutter; then he took counsel with himself and also cut his throat in the same way. In the morning the two corpses were found lying side by side, and it was seen that their blood refused to mingle but had flowed in opposite directions.

So they took the bodies away to burn them and laid them on one pyre; and when the fire was lit, it was seen that the smoke from the two bodies rose separately into the air. Then all who saw it, said , "we wished to marry brother and sister but Chando would not approve of it; see how their blood would not mingle though spilt on the same floor, and how the smoke from the pyre rises in two separate columns; it is plain that the marriage of brother and sister is wrong." From that time such mariages have been discontinued.

LI. A STORY ON CASTE

There was once a village inhabited only by Musahars. Among them was one girl who was so beautiful that she seemed more than human. Her father and mother were so proud of her looks that they determined not to marry her to a man of their own caste. They were constantly discussing whom they should choose as a son-in-law; one day they began to consider who were the greatest persons in the world. The old woman was of opinion that there was no one greater than Chando, the Sun God, and suggested that they should marry the girl to him. Her husband agreed and off they set and presented themselves before Chando. Chando asked why they had come. "O Chando, we understand that you are the greatest being in the world and we have come to marry our daughter to you." Chando answered "I fancy there is some one greater than I," "Who is he?" asked the parents. "The cloud is greater than I, for it can hide my face and quench my rays,"

At this the father and mother hurried off with their daughter in search of the Cloud, and when they found him, told him that they had brought their daughter to give him to wife, as he was the greatest being in the world. " I may, be great," said the Cloud, " but there is a greater than I, the Wind. The Wind rises and blows me away in a minute." So they went in search of the Wind and when they found him, explained to him why they had brought him their daughter. The Wind said " I am strong but there are stronger than I: the Mountains are stronger. I can blow things down or whirl them away, but I cannot move the mountains."

So on they went to the Mountain and explained their errand. The Mountain said "I am great but there are more powerful than I: The ground-rat is more powerful for however high I may be the ground-rats burrow holes in me and I cannot resist them."

The poor parents by this time began to feel rather discouraged, but still they made up their minds to persevere and went on to look for the ground-rat. They found him and offered him their daughter in marriage, but the ground-rat denied that he was the most powerful being on earth, the Musahars were more powerful for they lived by digging our ground-rats and eating them.

The hopless couple went home very dejectedly, reflecting that they had begun by despising their own caste and had gone in search, of something greater and had ended where they began. So they arranged to marry their daughter to a man of their own caste after all.

Moral. You should not despise your own caste or race; you cannot help what caste you are born into. A Santal may learn to read and write and associate with men of good position and thereby his mind may be perverted. He may wish to change his caste and become a Sadhu, or a Kherwar, or a Boistab, or a Mussulman, or a Christian or anything else; but people will still know him for a beef-eating Santal. If he becomes a Christian, no one will think him the equal of a Saheb or a Brahman; no Saheb will marry his daughter or give him his daughter in marriage. Remember what happened to the Musahar, who despised his own caste. God caused you to be born in a certain caste. He and not we made the different castes and He knows what is good and bad for us.

LII. TIPI AND TEPA

Tipi and Tepa dwelt together and lived on baked cakes. One day they met a bear in the jungle. "Now I will eat you" growled the bear. "Spare us," said Tipi and Tepa "and to-morrow we will beg some food and bake it into cakes and give it to you." So the bear let them go away to beg; but when they came back they ate the food which they had procured and then hid themselves inside a hollow gourd. The bear came and looked about for them but could not find them and went away.

The next day Tipi and Tepa again went out begging and as luck would have it again met the bear. "Now I will eat you" said the bear. " No " said they " let us go and beg some food,, for you." So they went off begging and came back and baked cakes and ate them and then hid inside the gourd. The bear came and carried off the gourd on its shoulder and began to pick plums and other fruit and put them into the gourd. As fast as the fruit was put in Tipi and Tepa ate it up. "It is a very funny thing that the gourd does not become full" thought the bear. But Tepa ate so much that at last he burst, with such a noise that the bear threw down the gourd and ran away.

LIII. THE CHILD WITH THE EARS OF AN OX

Once upon a time a son was born to a certain Raja and the child had the ears of an ox. The Raja was very much ashamed and let no one know. But the secret could not be kept from the barber who had to perform the ceremony of shaving the child's head. However the Raja made the barber vow not to tell anyone of what he had seen.

So the barber went away, but the secret which he might not tell had an unfortunate effect; it made his stomach swell to an enormous size. As the barber went along in this unhappy condition he met a Dom who asked why his stomach was so swollen. The barber said that it was because he had shaved the Raja's child and had seen that it had the ears of an ox. Directly he had broken his vow and blurted out the secret, his stomach returned to its usual size.

The Dom went his way and cut down a tree and made a drum out of the wood, and went about playing on the drum and begging. He came to the Raja's palace and there he drummed and sang:—

"The son of the Raja
Has the ears of an ox."

When the Raja heard this, he was very angry, and swore to punish the barber who must have broken his vow. But the Dom assured the Raja that he knew nothing about the matter; that it was the drum that sang the words and not he and that he had no idea what they meant. So the Raja was pacified and gave the Dom a present and sent him away and the barber was not punished.

LIV. THE CHILD WHO KNEW HIS FATHER

Once upon a time there was a girl whose parents took the greatest care that she should not be familiar with any of the young men of the village. But in spite of their precautions she formed an intimacy with a young man and was presently found to be with child. When this became known the villagers held a panchayat to enquire into the matter, but the girl flatly declined to give any information and her father and brothers were unable to point out the offender. So the village elders decided to let the matter stand over till the child was born.

When the birth took place the question arose in whose name its head should be shaved; as its father was still unknown, the villagers decided that this should be settled when the child was old enough to talk. So when the child was two or three years old and could prattle a little, the girl's father went to the headman and *paranic* and asked them what was to be done. They said that he must pay a fine to them and another to the villagers, because he had made the village unclean for so long, and give a feast to the villagers and then they would find out the father of the child and make him marry the girl; and if he refused to do this, he would be outcasted. The unfortunate man agreed and then the *jog manjhi* and *godet* were sent to call all the men of the neighbourhood to a meeting.

They assembled in their best clothes and pagris and sat down in rows, and in the middle a circle was drawn on the ground; then prayers were offered to Chando and the child was set in the circle and told to find its father. The child began to walk slowly along the lines of men but it did not stop till it came to its real father, who was sitting a little apart, and then it threw itself into his arms. Thus the truth was discovered and the man married the girl and, as he was very poor, went to live in his father-in-law's house.

LV. JOGESHWAR'S MARRIAGE

Once upon a time there was a young man of the weaver caste, named Jogeshwar. He was an orphan and lived all alone. One summer he planted a field of pumpkins on the sandy bed of a river. The plants grew well and bore plenty of fruit: but when the pumpkins were ripe, a jackal found them out and went every night and feasted on them. Jogeshwar soon found out from the foot-marks who was doing the damage; so he set a snare and a few days later found the jackal caught in it. He took a stick to beat its life out, but the jackal cried: "Spare me and I will find you a wife." So Jogeshwar stayed his hand and released the jackal who promised at once to set off about the business.

The jackal kept his word and went to a city where a Raja lived. There he sat down on the bank of one of the Raja's tanks. To this tank the servants from th palace brought the pots and dishes to be washed, and to this tank also came the Rani and princesses to bathe. Whenever the servants came to wash their dishes, the jackal kept on repeating: "What sort of a Raja is this whose plates are washed in water in which people have bathed? There is no Raja like Raja Jogeshwar: he eats of golden plates and yet he never uses them second time but throws them away directly he has eaten off them once."

The servants soon carried word to the Raja of the jackal who sat by the tank and of his story of Raja Jogeshwar. Then the Raja sent for the jackal and asked why he had come: the jackal answered that he was looking for a bride for Raja jogeshwar. Now the Raja had three or four daughters and he thought that he saw his way to a fine match for one of them. So he sent for the young women and asked the jackal to say whether one of them would be a suitable bride for Raja jogeshwar. The jackal chose the second sister and said that he would go and get the consent of Raja Jogeshwar.

The jackal hurried back and told the astonished weaver that he had found a Raja's daughter for him to marry. Jogeshwar had nothing to delay him and only asked that an early day might be fixed for the wedding. So the jackal went back to the Raja and received from him the knotted string that fixed the date of the wedding.

The jackal had now to devise some means by which Jogeshwar could go through the wedding ceremonies without his poverty being found out. He first went to the Raja and asked how many attendants Raja Jogeshwar should bring with him, as he did not want to bring more than the bride's father could entertain. The Raja was too proud to fix any number and said they could bring as many as they liked.

Jogeshwar having no relations and no money, was quite unable to arrange for a grand procession to escort him; he could only just afford to hire a palki in which to be carried to the bride's house; so the jackal sent word to all the jackals and paddy birds of the neighbourhood to come to a feast at the palace of the bride, an invitation which was eagerly accepted. At the time fixed they started off, with all the paddy birds riding on the backs of the jackals. When they came within sight of the palace, the jackal ran on ahead and invited the Raja to come out and look at the procession as there was still time to send them back, if they were too many, but it would be a great disgrace if they were allowed to arrive and find no entertainment. The Raja went out to look and when he saw the procession stretching away for a distance of two miles or more with all the paddy birds looking like white horsemen as they rode on the backs of the jackals, his heart failed him and he begged the jackal to send then away, as he could not entertain such a host.

So then the jackal hurried back and turned them all away and Jogeshwar reached the palace, accompanied only by his palki bearers.

Before the wedding feast, the jackal gave Jogeshwar some hints as to his behaviour. He warned him that three or four kinds of meat and vegetables would be handed round with the rice, and bade him to be sure to help himself from each dish—of course in his own house the poor weaver had never had more than one dish to eat with his rice—and when *pan* was handed to him after the feast he was not to take any until he had a handful of money given him; by such behaviour he would lead every one to think that he was really prince. Jogeshwar did exactly as he was told and was thought a very grand personage.

The next evening Jogeshwar set off homewards with his bride, the bride's brothers and attendants accompanying them. They travelled on and on till the bride' party began to grow tired and kept asking the jackal how much further they had to go. The jackal kept on putting them off, till at last they came in sight of a grove of palm trees, and he told them that Raja Jogeshwar's palace stood among the palm trees but was so old and weather worn that it could not be seen from a distance.

When they reached the palm grove and found nothing but Jogeshwar's humble hut, the bride's brothers turned on the jackal and asked what he meant by deceiving them. The jackal protested that he had told no lies: the weaver ate every day off plates made of dry leaves and threw them away when done with and that was all he meant when he talked of golden plates. At this excuse they turned on him and wanted to beat him but he ran away and escaped.

The bride's friends went back and told the Raja how things had turned out and as divorce was not lawful for them, the Raja could only send for his daughter and her husband and give them an estate to live on.

LVI. THE STRONG MAN

There was once a Strong man but no one knew of his strength. He was in the service of a farmer who made him headman over all his laboures. In those days much of the country was still covered with jungle. One day the farmer chose a piece of forest land which he thought suitable for cultivation and told his labourers to set to work and clear it, and as usual after giving his orders he troubled himself no more about the matter as he could fully rely on the Strong man.

The next morning, the Strong man set the other labourers to work ploughing a field and then said that he would go and have a look at the jungle which his master wanted cleared. So he went off alone with only a stick in his hand. When he reached the place, he walked all round it, and saw how much could be made into good arable land, and then he began to clear it. He pulled up the trees by the roots and piled them into a heap and he took the rocks and threw them to one side and made the ground quite clear and smooth, and then went back to the house. On being asked why he had been so long away, he answered that he had been pulling up a few bushes at the place which was to be cleared.

The following morning the Strong man told the farm labourers to take their ploughs to the clearing and begin to plough it. When the farmer heard this, he was puzzled to think how the land could be ready for ploughing so soon, and went to see it and to his amazement found the whole land cleared, every tree pulled up by the roots and all the rocks removed.

Then he asked the Strong man whether he had done the work by himself. The Strong man aswered "no," a number of people had volunteered to help him and so the work had been finished in a day.

The farmer said nothing but he did not believe the story and saw that his servant must really be a man of marvellous strength. Neither he nor the farm labourers let any one else know what had happened, they kept it to themselves.

Now the Strong man's wages were twelve measures of rice a year. After working for four years he made up his mind to leave his master and start farming on his own account. So he told the farmer that he wished to leave but offered to finish any work there was to do before he went, that no one might be able to say that he had gone away, leaving his work half done. The farmer assured him that there was nothing for him to do and gave him rice equal to his four years' wages. The rice made two big *bandis*, each more than an ordinary man could lift, but the Strong man slung them on to a bamboo and carried them off over his shoulder.

After he had gone a little way, it struck the farmer that it would not do to let him display his strength in this way and that it would be better if he took the rice away at night. So he had the Strong man called back and told him that there was one job which he had forgotten to finish; he had put two bundles of *sabai* grass into the trough to steep and had forgotten to twist it into string. Without a word the Strong man went and picked the *sabai* out of the water and began to twist it, but he could tell at once by the feel that the sabai had only just been placed in the water and he charged the farmer with playing a trick on him. The farmer swore that there was no trick and, rather than quarrel, the Strong man went on with the work.

While he was so engaged the farmer offered him some tobacco, and the Strong man took it without washing and wiping his hands. Now no one should prepare or chew tobacco while twisting sabai ; if one does not first wash and dry one's hands one's strength will go. The Strong man knew this, but he was so angry at being called back on false pretences that he forgot all about it.

But when he had finished the string and the farmer said that he might go, he essayed to take up the two bandis of rice as before. To his sorrow he found that he could not lift them. Then he saw the mistake that he had made. He had to leave one *bandi* behind and divide the other into two halves and sling them on the bamboo and carry them off with him.

The Strong man's cultivation did not prosper, and after three or four years he found himself at the end of his means and had again to take service with a farmer.

One day when field work was in full swing the Strong man had a quarrel with his new master. So when he had finished the morning's ploughing he pulled the iron point of the ploughshare out of its socket and snapped it in two. Then he took the pieces to his master and explained that it had caught on the stump of a tree and got broken. The master took the broken share to the blacksmith and had it mended. The next day the Strong man went through the same performance and his master had again to go the blacksmith. The same thing happened several days running, till at last the farmer decided to keep watch and see what really happened. So he hid himself and saw the Strong man snap the ploughshare in two; but in view of such a display of strength he was much too frightened to let his servant know that he had found out the trick that was being played on him. He took the pieces to the blacksmith as usual and at the smithy he found some of his friends and told them what had happened. They advised him to set the Strong man to twisting sabai string and then by some pretext induce him to take tobacco. the farmer did as they advised and in about a fortnight the Strong man lost all his strength and became as other men. Then his master dismissed him and he had to go back to his house and his strength never returned to him.

LVII. THE RAJA'S ADVICE

Once upon a time an aged Raja lay dying. Before he breathed his last he sent for his only son and gave him the following advice. "My son," he said, "never go on a journey alone; do not associate with low people, for if you do no one will respect you; never confide a secret to your wife; do not tell outsiders the affairs of your house; do not let village affairs go beyond the village street, and never get into a rage."

The son succeeded to the Raja and shortly afterwards set out to pay a visit to his wife's relations. He started alone and after going some distance he his father's injunctions never to go on a journey alone. He had gone too far to go back and he saw no one within call so he looked about and presently found a crab hole. He set to work and dug out the crab and fixing it in his *pagri* continued his journey.

By-and-bye, he came to a river. Now in this river lived a crocodile, which had leagued with a crow to destroy travellers crossing the river. Whenever the crow saw anyone coming, it gave warning to the crocodile, and the crocodile then seized the traveller as he entered the river, while the crow pecked out his eyes. In this way they had been the death of many travellers. So when the crow saw the young Raja coming, it cawed to the crocodile, which hastened to the ford and seized the Raja as he stepped into the water, while the crow flew at his head. But the crab caught the crow by the leg and nipped it so hard that the crow, in agony, called out to the crocodile to let the man go, as it was being killed. So the crocodile released its hold and the Raja struggled to the bank, and then caught the crow which was held fast by the crab and wrung its neck. Then he went back home with the crab, reflecting on the wisdom of his father's advice.

Later on, the Raja thought that he would put another of his father's maxims to the proof and see what would happen if he told his wife a secret. So he took a spade and buried an old earthen pot in the corner of his garden. He let his wife see him and she promptly asked what he was burying; he put her off, but that night she insisted so much on knowing, that, after swearing her to secrecy, he told her that a child had come straying to his house and he had killed it to obtain good luck and had buried the body.

Time passed, and one day the Raja had a quarrel with his wife, he began to beat her and she in return abused him and kept on calling out that he was a murderer, who had buried a child in his garden. Their next door neighbour heard all this and, directly she found the Raja's wife alone, asked whether what she said was true. The Raja's wife, being still in a passion, asserted that it was quite true. The story was soon all over the town, and the townspeople rose and seized the Raja and charged him with the murder. Then he took them to the garden and made them dig up what he had buried and they found only an old pot.

So they had to pay him compensation for making a false charge, and the Raja valued more than ever the advice given him by his father.

LVIII. THE FOUR JOGIS

Once four Jogis were out on a begging expedition and came to a city where a Raja lived. As they went along they discussed how they should beg of the Raja; and while they were discussing the point, they saw a field rat and one of them exclaimed "I know how I shall beg of him ! I shall say,' See, he throws up the earth, scrapety scrape" This did not help the other three, but, further on, some frogs jumped into a pond as they passed by, and one of the others at once said "I know what I shall say! I shall say plumpety plump!, down he has sat." A little later, they saw pig wallowing in the mud, and the third Jogi called out, I have it! I shall say ,Rub away, rub away! Now some more water! "Rub away, rub away! I know, my boys, what you are going to do." The fourth Jogi was still in perplexity but, when they came in sight of the Raja's city, he exclaimed "I know what I shall say "Highways and byeways, what a big city ! The kotwal is going his rounds, his rounds."

Then they got a man to write down these four forms of address on a sheet of paper and presented it to the Raja. The Raja took it, and read it, and could not make head or tail of it. And when the four Jogis saw him looking so puzzled, they got frightened and took to their heels, for they could not read themselves and were not sure of what the paper really contained.

Now the Raja's chief officer was a Tehsildar, and he had also a Barber, who shaved him every day. And that evening after the Jogis had run away, the Tehsildar proposed to the Barber that, when shaving the Raja the next morning, he should cut the Raja's throat and they could then divide the kingdom between them, and the Barber consented. Not content with this, the Tehsildar and the palace chowkidar that same night tried to break into the Raja's palace and steal his money and jewelry. They began to cut a hole through the mud wall of the Raja's room, but it chanced that the Raja was so puzzled by the paper which the Jogis had put into his hand, that he kept on reading it over and over again, and just as the Tehsildar and chowkidar had half cut their way through the wall, they heard the Raja saying "See, he throws up the earth, scrapety, scrape !" At once they concluded that they had been heard and they crouched down; the Raja went on "Plumpety, plump! down he has sat." This made them think that they had been seen and the chowkidar crept to the door to listen: he heard the Raja saying "Highways and byeways, what a big city! The kotwal is going his rounds, his rounds ! " Then the chowkidar felt sure that he was discovered and he ran off with the Tehsildar, without completing their burglary.

The next morning the Barber went to shave the Raja, and, while he was sharpening the razor, the Raja again began to study the mysterious paper, murmuring "Rub away, rub away, now some more water: Rub away, rub away ! I know my boy what you are going to do." The Barber thought that the Raja referred to his rubbing water over his face for shaving, and concluded that the Tehsildar had revealed the plot; so he threw himself at the Raja's feet and confessed everything, swearing that the Tehsildar and not he was to blame. The Raja at once sent for the chowkidar to take the Tehsildar and Barber to prison. When the chowkidar came in he found the Raja repeating "See he throws up the earth, scrapety, scrape ! " He at once concluded that the Raja was referring to the burglary and he fell on his knees and confessed all that had happened. This was news to the Raja, but he went and saw the place where the wall had been partly cut through, and then he sent all the guilty men to prison and despatched messengers to look for the Jogis who had been the means of saving his life and property; but the Jogis had been so frightened and had run away so far, that they were never found.

LIX. THE CHARITABLE RAJA

There was once a Raja who was very charitable; he used to give a new cloth and a good meal to every one who came and begged of him. But one day a Jogi came and refused to take what was offered to him: he demanded that the Raja should give him his kingdom and everything that he had. The Raja thought it wrong to refuse the request, and went out into the world with his wife and his two young children, a beggar. For a long time they wandered about living on charity, till their clothes were worn to rags, and then they chanced to hear of a rich merchant who gave a cloth to any beggar who asked it of him; so they resolved to go to him for help. When they reached the village where the merchant lived, the Rani left the Raja with the two children to cook some dinner and went to the merchant's house to beg for some clothes; but when the merchant saw her he fell in love with her and shut her up and would not let her go. To be saved from the merchant's designs the Rani prayed that she might be smitten with disease and at once she became very ill.

After waiting in vain for her return the Raja set off with his two sons to look for her and presently came to a flooded river. He carried one child across first but, as he was returning for the other, he was swept away by the current and the children were left alone. A Goala woman, going to the river for water, found them, and as she was childless took them home with her and brought them up.

Meanwhile the Raja was carried down stream by the flood and was washed ashore, bruised and wounded, a long way down. At the place where he landed a large crowd was collected; for the Raja of the country had lately died leaving no heir, and the widow had ordered all the people to assemble in order that two elephants, belonging to the late Raja, might choose his successor. The half-drowned Raja joined the crowd and as he sat looking on, one elephant, passing by all its own people, came to him and put the golden necklace on his neck and the other elephant lifted him on to its back and carried him off and seated him on the Raja' s throne; and as he sat on the throne all his wounds and bruises were healed.

Years passed and the Raja's two sons grew up, and as the Goala woman who had adopted them was very poor, they went out into the world to earn their living. As it chanced, they took service as sipahis with the Raja, their father, whom of course they did not recognise. Just after their arrival the Raja arranged a great festival at which people from all parts assembled; and among others the merchant went there with the Raja's wife, in hopes that among the crowd he might find some physician able to cure the woman. When he arrived, he went to the Raja and asked that two sipahis might be deputed to keep watch over the woman he had brought. The Raja sent his two newly enlisted sipahis, and thus the sons were set to guard their own mother, and it was not long before they found out their relationship. The Rani was delighted to recover her long lost children, but when she heard that her husband had been washed away by the river and drowned, she began to weep and wail. The merchant went to the Raja and complained that the sipahis who had been sent, had thrown the woman into great distress and the Raja thereupon sent for all the parties in order that he might enquire into the matter. When he heard their story, he at once recognised that it was his own wife and sons who stood before him and thus the whole family was happily united. Then his wife prayed to Thakur that if she were really the wife he had lost and had been faithful to him, she might be restored to health; water was poured over her and she was at once cured of her disease, and they all lived happily ever afterwards.

LX. A VARIANT—THE WANDERING RAJA

Once there was a Raja who was very prosperous; but his wife found their life of wealth and ease monotonous, and she continually urged him to travel into other countries and to see whether other modes of life were pleasant or distressful; she pestered her husband so much that at last he gave way. He put his kingdom in charge of his father's sister and her husband and set off with his wife and his two sons as an ordinary traveller.

After travelling some days they got tired of eating the parched rice which they had brought with them and thought they would boil some rice for their dinner. So the Rani went into a bazar to get cooking pots, and a light for the fire.

She went to the house of a rich merchant for these, but he was attracted by her beauty and seized her and shut her up and would not let her go back, but kept her as his wife. The Raja and his sons soon got tired of waiting for her ; he concluded that the journey was merely a pretext of his wife's to escape from him, as she had disappeared the first time that he let her out of his sight.

So he turned to go home and soon came to a river which had to be crossed, he left his sons on the bank and went into the water to see how deep it was and as he was wading in, a large fish came and swallowed him The fish swam away down stream and was caught in the net of some fishermen. When they saw how big a fish they had caught, they decided to take it to the Raja of that country. The Raja bought it at a high price, but when it was cut open at the palace the man it had swallowed was found alive inside; so the Raja of the country appointed him one of his retainers.

Meanwhile the two boys had been found abandoned on the bank of the river by a cowherd, who was too poor to bring them up, so he took them also to the Raja; and they rejoiced to meet their father and when they grew up, were also appointed retainers.

They had to travel all over the country on the Raja's business and it happened that they one day came to the village where their mother was and they met and recognised her; she told them how she had been seized and confined and begged them to bring her husband to her. So the sons fetched their father and the Rani told her husband how unhappy she was and begged him to get her released, and he promised to ask the help of his master. When the Raja of the country heard the story he took pity on them and went with a body of soldiers and seized the wicked merchant and ordered him to give up all his wealth and as the merchant tried to conceal where some of his money was buried, the Raja cut him down with his sword. He also laid a heavy fine on the villagers, because they had not sent word to him of the capture of the Rani.

Then he took home the Raja who had been swallowed by the fish and his wife and sons, and entertained them for some days, and then gave them elephants and horses and men and all the merchant's property and sent them to their own country. The uncle and aunt who had been appointed Regents came out to meet them and escorted them home.

Two or three days after the aunt asked the Raja how he had got his elephants and horses and money, and he said "They are the profits of my wife's sin ; I will not tell you the whole story for if you heard it you also might be led astray; my wife induced me to travel by false pretences. It is not good to follow the advice of a woman; it is by mere chance that you see me alive to-day." His wife heard what he said, and she went out and cut her throat from remorse; and they went and burned her body.

LXI. THE TWO WIVES

There were once a Raja and his Dewan who had each one son, and the two boys were great friends. Both had been married in their infancy and when they grew up and heard that they had wives, they agreed to go together and visit them. So they set out, and they arranged that on account of the superior rank of the Raja's son they would go first and visit his wife; and they also agreed that, as they were going to a strange place, they would keep together day and night.

When they reached the house of the Prince's father-in-law they were received with great honour and when night came they lay down with their beds side by side. Presently the Prince's wife came to him and began to rub his arms and legs, until she had soothed him off to sleep. The Dewan's son pretended also to go fast asleep, but really he was careful to keep awake, for he thought it safer to be on the watch in a strange place.

His prudence was rewarded, for after a time he saw the Prince's wife leave her sleeping husband and go out of the house.

The Dewan's son followed her and saw her enter the house of a Gosain who lived on the outskirts of the village. He went near and listened at the door. He heard the Gosain ask the young woman why she was so late in coming, and her answer that she had been detained by the visit of her husband. The Gosain reproached her for not having told him that she was married, and she protested that she had known nothing about it until her husband appeared. The Gosain said that she must choose between him and her husband, and she answered that she would never give him up. "Then" said the Gosain " if you really mean it, go and bring me your husband's head." At this the Dewan's son hurried back and lay down on his bed. Presently he saw the woman come with a sword and cut off her husband's head. But when she took it to the Gosain, he rose and beat her with his iron pincers and drove her out, swearing that he would have nothing more to do with a woman who was so heartless as to kill her own husband. Then the woman returned and placed the severed head by her husband's body and raised a great outcry, that her husband had been murdered. The people of the house came and at first they charged the Dewan's son with the crime and were about to put him to death; but he called the Gosain as a witness and the real facts were proved by his evidence, and the murderess was hanged.

The Dewan's son would not allow the Prince's body to be burnt but insisted on taking it with him, that it might be cremated at his own home. So he took it on his back and carried it off.

He thought that, as he had come so far, it would be better to visit his own wife before going home. So, when he reached the village where his wife lived, he hid the Prince's body in a hollow tree and went to his father-in-law's house.

That night when they had gone to bed, the Dewan's son saw that his wife had something on her mind, so he resolved to watch her.

When she thought that he was asleep, he saw her rise and go out of the house. He followed her to a shrine of Mahadeb; there she smeared the ground with cowdung and worshipped the god and said "O Siva !I have worshipped you for many days; now my husband has come to take me to his house, and you must find another worshipper." The Mahadeb answered "You have served me for many days; call hither your husband; as you have worshipped me for so long, I will confer a boon on you." So she went and called her husband and as he knew what had happened, he had no hesitation in going with her to the shrine. There the Siv bade him ask a boon, and he prayed that the Raja's son might be restored to life. The Siv bade them bring the body and cover it with a wet cloth; and when hey had done so, the body began to breathe and presently the Prince rose up alive and well. The Dewan's son told him all that had happened and the next day they went home taking with them the wife of the Dewan's son, through whose virtue and piety the Prince had been restored to life.

LXII. SPANLING AND HIS UNCLES

There was once a little man named Spanling (Bita) because he was only a span (*Bita*) high; and he had a beard one span and four finger-breadths long. His father was dead, and he lived alone with his mother and he was as cunning as anyone in the world. He had one cow-buffalo and this he always grazed at night, for fear that the sun might melt it. Once it happened that as he was following his buffalo he got buried in its droppings and he was so small that he could not get out.

However, next morning, some girls, who were gathering cowdung for fuel, found him and set him free. Spanling decided to get rid of the buffalo after this; so he killed it and flayed it and when the skin was dry, took it away to sell. Before he found a purchaser night came on, so he climbed a tree with his hide to be out of danger. During the night a gang of thieves came to the tree, and began to divide their booty. While there were busy over this, Spanling let the hide fall with a clatter into their midst, and they all ran away in a fright, leaving all their stolen goods behind.

When day dawned, Spanling climbed down and found piles of gold waiting for him. He took it home and sent his mother to borrow a wooden measure from his uncles to measure it with. When he returned the measure, one of the gold pieces was left sticking in a crack. His uncles at once hastened to enquire how he came to be measuring gold. Spanling told them that he had sold his buffalo skin at a town which he named, for an enormous price and no doubt they could find the same market, if they chose to kill their buffaloes. The uncles hurried home and killed all their buffaloes and took the hides to the city, which Spanling had named, but they were only laughed at when they asked more than the price which was paid every day for hides. The uncles came home very angry at the way in which they had been tricked by Spanling, and in revenge they burnt his house down. Finding himself homeless, Spanling gathered the ashes of his house into sacks, loaded them on a cart and drove away. When evening came he camped by the roadside in company with some other carters and, in the middle of the night, he quietly changed his sacks of ashes for some of the sacks in the other carts, When he got home he found that the sacks which he had stolen were full of gold coins. He again sent to his uncles for a measure and when the measure was returned a gold coin was again left sticking in crack. The uncles at once came to enquire how Spanling had got the money. He told them that he had sold the ashes of his house for gold and, as their houses were bigger than his, they would doubtless make their fortunes if they burnt them down and sold the ashes. The uncles took his advice but when they tried to sell the ashes they were only laughed at for their pains.

LXIII. THE SILENT WIFE

There was once a madcap of a fellow, whose wife got on very well with him and did all the house work very nicely, but she would never speak a single word to him. As nothing he tried would make her speak, the madcap at last hit on a plan of taking her on a long journey. But even when he told his wife that she must come with him to a far country, she did not utter a word. When all was ready for a start the madcap bathed his feet and took a *lota* of water isto the house and pouring it out, prayed to the spirit of his grandfather thus "Grandfather, grant that my wife may speak; if you do not fail me in this, I will make offerings to you on my return; grant that we may come back together happily; teach her to speak to me soon."

Then he set out with his wife and they travelled on until they entered a dense forest, where there was no sign of human habitation. As they went on, the tailor birds and babblers began to chatter and scream at them. The madcap got angry at this and called out to the birds that if they did not stop, he would chase them and go on chasing them for a day and a night. Then he sat down and watched them. His wife stood waiting by his side, and soon she began to wonder what she would do and where she would go, if her husband really went in chase of the birds. So at last she spoke to him and said "Come, get up;

we must make haste out of this jungle." Directly the words were out of her mouth, the madcap knelt down and bowing to the ground said "I thank you, Grandfather". Then he rose and went on with his wife.

Presently they met a bear; the madcap called out "You brute of a bear, what do you mean by coming to meet us like this? I will chase you and go on chasing you till to-morrow morning. "But his wife besought him to come along and not leave her. Directly she spoke, the madcap cried "Bravo" and kneeling down thanked his grandfather. They went out and presently a jackal crossed their path; the madcap cursed it and vowed that he would chase it all the night. Again his wife urged him to come on and again the madcap knelt down and thanked his grandfather; but his wife did not know why he did so, nor did she trouble to ask.

Just as they reached the edge of the forest they saw a leopard and this also the madcap threatened to chase. "Then go and chase it, said his wife, who now felt safe. So he went in pursuit of the leopard, but after going a little way he lost sight of it And went back to where his wife was. "What has become of all your boasting?" said she "You have not chased it till tomorrow morning." "No," said the madcap "I have killed it; if you don't believe me, come and see." But she did not want to go back into the jungle and said no more about it. As his wife had broken her silence the madcap saw no use in going further and they turned homewards; all the way his wife went on chatting and singing along with him. When he reached home he sacrificed a number of goats to his grandfather, and lived happily with his wife ever after.

LXIV. THE DUMB SHEPHERD

There was once a very rich and powerful Raja and in his heart he thought that there was no one so powerful in the world as himself; thus he thought but he told no one of his thought. One day he made up his mind to see whether others could guess what he was thinking, so he called together his officers and servants and dependants and bade them tell him what thought was in his heart. Many of them made guesses, but not one gave an answer which satisfied the Raja.

Then the Raja told his dewan that he must without fail find some one who would guess his thought, and he gave the dewan exactly one month's time in which to search. The dewan searched high and low but all in vain, and as the time drew near he grew more and more anxious, for he feared that he would fall into disgrace. But he had a daughter and she consoled him and told him to cheer up, as she would find a man on the day fixed to read the Raja's thoughts. The dewan had to take what comfort he could from this promise, and when the appointed day arrived, his daughter brought a dumb shepherd whom they employed and bade her father take him to the Raja. The dewan thought it very unlikely that the dumb shepherd would succeed where others had failed, but he saw no alternative to following his daughter's advice.

So the dewan presented himself before the Raja with the dumb shepherd and found a large company assembled to see what happened. The two stood before the Raja and the dumb man looked at the Raja. Then the Raja held up one finger, at this the dumb shepherd held up two fingers. Then the Raja held up three fingers, but at this the dumb man made signs of dissent and ran away as fast as he could. Then the Raja laughed and seemed very pleased and praised the dewan for having brought him such a clever man, and gave the dewan a rich reward.

The dewan was still at a loss to know what had happened, and begged the Raja to explain what had passed between him and the shepherd. "When I held up one finger," said the Raja "I asked him whether I alone was Raja, and he by holding up two reminded me that there was God, who was as powerful as I am. Then I asked him whether there was any third and he vehemently denied that there was. Thus he has read my thoughts, for I have always been thinking that I alone am powerful, but he has reminded me that there is God as well, but no third."

Then they all went their ways, and that night the dewan questioned the dumb shepherd as to how he had been able to understand the Raja: and the dumb man explained "I have only three sheep of my own, and when I appeared before the Raja ht help up one finger, meaning that he wanted me to give him one of my sheep, and as he is a great Raja I offered to give him two; but when he held up three fingers to show that he wanted to take all three from me, I thought that he was going too far and so I ran away.

By this lucky chance the dewan earned his reward from the Raja.

LXV. THE GOOD DAUGHTER-IN-LAW

There was once a very rich man who had seven sons and the sons were all married and lived with their father. The father was a miser: he lived in the poorest manner in spite of all his wealth and hoarded all his money. His eldest daughter-in-law managed the household and she alone of the family, did pot approve of the miserly way in which the family affairs were conducted.

One day a Jugi came to the house and asked for alms. The eldest daughter-in-law happened to be away at the time, fetching water from the stream. Those of the family who were at home flatly declined to give the poor beggar anything and turned him away from the house so the Jugi went away, cursing them for their miserliness. On his way he met the eldest daughter-in-law coming back with her jar of water and she asked the Jugi why he seemed so angry.

When she heard how he had been treated, she at once besought him to return to the house and explained that she was the housekeeper and that that was the reason why none of others had ventured to give him alms.

The Jugi returned with her and she gave him a *seer* of rice to put in his bag. At first the Jugi refuse to take it, on the ground that she was only giving it for fear of his curses but she assured him that she never refused alms to anyone who begged. So the Jugi took the rice and then asked what boon she would accept in return. The woman at first said that she was in want of nothing, but, on the Jugi pressing her, she said that she would like to be able to understand the language of birds and beasts and to see the disembodied souls of men. Then the Jugi took a feather from his bag and draw it across her eyes and blew into her eyes and ears and she found herself possessed of the powers for which she had asked. But before he left, the Jugi told her that she must never reveal to any human being the boon he had conferred on her, for if she did she would die.

Years passed and nothing happened but then it chanced that a Chamar who lived at the end of the village died, and as he had been a good and kind man his family wept bitterly at their loss. The woman saw the spirit of the Chamar being taken away in a grand chariot and she also wept for the death of so good a man. Her family became very suspicious at her showing sorrow for the death of a stranger of another caste.

A few days later the miserly father-in-law died and the woman saw three beings dragging him out of the house by his heels, and she laughed to see him treated so for his sins. But the family were shocked by her laughter and concluded that she was a witch and had killed her father-in-law by her witchcraft; so after the funeral they held a family council and called on the woman to explain why she had laughed. She assured them that if she told she would die but they Insisted and at last she told them of the boon conferred on her by the Jugi, and what she had seen, and then she lay down upon her bed and died.

LXVI. THE RAJA'S DREAM

Once upon a time there was a Raja who had no children. So he and his wife agreed that he should marry again. His second wife bore him two sons, and they were very pleased that the Raja should have heirs and all lived happily together. But after the two sons had been born, the elder Rani also gave birth to a son. This caused discord in the family, for the younger Rani had counted on her sons succeeding to the Raja, but now she feared that the son of the elder Rani would be preferred. So she went to the Raja and besought him to send away the elder Rani and her son. The Raja listened to her and gave the first wife a separate estate and a separate house and sent them away.

Time passed and one night the Raja had a dream, the meaning of which he could not understand; he dreamt that he saw a golden leopard and a golden snake and a golden monkey dancing together. The Raja could not rest until he had found out the meaning of the dream, so he sent for this younger wife and her two sons and consulted them. They could give no explanation, but the younger son said that he had a presentiment that his brother, the son of the elder Rani, could interpret the dream. So that son was sent for, and when he appeared before his father and heard the story of the dream, he said "This is the interpretation: the three golden animals represent us three brothers, for we are like gold to you. Thakur has sent this dream in order that we may not fight hereafter; we cannot all three succeed to the Raja and we shall assuredly fight if one is not chosen as the heir. It is intended that whichever of us can find a golden leopard, and a golden snake and a golden monkey and make them dance before the people he is your principal son and shall be your heir." The Raja was pleased with this interpretation and told his three sons that he would give the Raj to whichever of them could find the three animals by that day year.

The sons of the younger Rani went away, feeling that it was useless for them to make any attempt to fulfil the conditions; even if they got a goldsmith to make the animals, they would never be able to make them dance.

But the other brother went to his mother and told her all that had happened, and she bade him be of good courage and he would find the animals; if he went to a Gosain who lived in the jungle, he would be told what to do.

So the Raja's son set out, and after travelling for some days he found himself benighted in a dense jungle. Wandering about, he at last saw a fire burning in the distance, so he went to it and sat down by it and began to smoke. Now the Gosain was sleeping nearby and the smell of the smoke awoke him, and he rose and asked who was there.

"O uncle, it is I."

"Really, is it you my nephew? Where have you come from so late at night?"

"From home, uncle."

"What has brought me to your memory now? You have never paid me a visit before. I am afraid that something has happened."

"You need not fear that, I have come to you because my mother tells me that you can help me to find the golden leopard and the golden snake and the golden monkey."

At this the Gosain promised to help the Raja's son to find the animals and then put the cooking-pot on the fire to the boil ; and in it he put only three grains of rice, but when it was cooked, they found that there was enough to make a meal of. When they had eaten, the Gosain said "Nephew, I cannot tell you what you have to do; but further in the jungle lives my younger brother, go to him and he will tell you."

So when it was morning the Raja's son set out, and in two days he reached the second Gosain and told him of his quest. The Gosain listened to his story and put the cooking-pot on to boil and in it threw two grains of rice, and this, when cooked, was sufficient for a good meal. After they had eaten, the Gosain said that he could not tell how the animals were to be found, but that he had a still younger brother who could tell. So the next morning the Raja's son continued his journey, and in two or three days he came to the third Gosain and there he learnt what was to be done. This Gosain also put the pot on to boil but in the pot he only put one grain of rice and a bit of a grain, yet when cooked it was enough for a meal.

In the morning the Gosain told the Raja's son to go to a blacksmith and have a shield made of twelve maunds of iron and with its edge so sharp that a leaf falling on it would be cut in two. So he went to the blacksmith and had a shield made, and took it to the Gosain. The Gosain said that they must test it, and he set it edgewise in the ground under a tree and told the Raja's son to climb the tree and shake some leaves down. The Raja's son climbed the tree and shook the branches, but not a leaf fell. Then the Gosain climbed up and gave the tree a shake and the leaves fell in showers and every leaf that touched the edge of the shield was cut in two. Then the Gosain was satisfied that the shield was rightly made.

Then the Gosain told the Raja's son that further on in the jungle he would find a pair of snakes living in a bamboo house; and they had a daughter whom they never allowed to come out of the house; he must fix the sharp shield in the door of the house and bide himself in a tree, and when the snakes came out they would be cut to pieces; then, when the snakes were dead, he was to go to their daughter and she would show him where to find the golden animals. So the Raja's son set out and about noon he came to the home of the snakes, and he set the shield in the doorway as the Gosain had said, and at evening, when the snakes tried to come out of the house, they were cut to pieces. When her father and mother were dead, the daughter came out to see what had happened, and the Raja's son saw that she was very beautiful. He went to her and began to talk and it did not take them long to fall in love with each other. The snake maiden soon forgot her father and mother, and she and the Raja's son lived together in the bamboo house many days.

The snake maiden strictly forebade him to go anywhere to the west or south of the house, but one day he disobeyed her and wandered away to the west. After going a short distance he saw golden leopards dancing, and directly he set eyes on them, he himself was changed into a golden leopard and began to dance with the others. The snake maiden soon knew what had happened, and she followed him and led him back and restored him to his own shape.

A few days later, the Raja's son went away to the south and there he found golden snakes dancing on the bank of a tank and directly he saw them, he too became a golden snake and joined the dance. Again the snake maiden fetched him back and restored him to his own form. But again the Raja's son went out to the southwest and there he saw golden monkeys dancing under a banyan tree, and when he saw them he became a golden monkey; again the snake maiden brought him back and restored him to human shape.

After this the Raja's son said that it was time for him to go back home. The snake maiden asked why he had come there at all, and then he told her all about the Raja's dream and said that as he had found the animals he would now go home.

"Kill me first" said the snake maiden; "you have killed my parents and I cannot live alone here." "No, I will not kill you, I will take you with me" answered the Raja's son, and the snake maiden gladly agreed. Then the Raja's son asked how he was to take the golden animals with him, for so far he had only seen where they were. The snake maiden said that if he faithfully promised never to desert her, nor take another wife, she would produce the animals for him when the time came. So he swore never to leave her and they set out for his home.

When they reached the place where the third Gosain lived, the Raja's son said that he had promised to visit the Gosain on his homeward journey and show him the golden animals; but he did not know what to do, as he had not got the animals with him. Then the snake maiden tied three knots in his cloth and bade him untie them when the Gosain asked to see the animals. So the Raja's son went to see the Gosain, and the Gosain asked whether he had brought the golden leopard and snake and monkey.

"I am not sure answered the other, "but I have something tied up in my cloth," and he untied the three knots and found in them a clod of earth, a potsherd and a piece of charcoal. He threw them away and went back to the snake maiden, and asked why she had put worthless rubbish in his cloth,, "You had no faith " said she " if you had believed, the animals would not have turned into the clod and the potsherd and the charcoal." So they journeyed on, till they came to the second Gosain, and he also asked to see the golden animals and this time the Raja's son set his mind hard to believe and, when he untied the knots, there were a golden leopard and a golden snake and a golden monkey. Then they went on and showed the animals to the first Gosain, and then went to the house where his mother lived.

When the appointed day came, the Raja's son sent word to his father to have a number of booths and shelters erected in a spacious plain, and to have covered way made from his mother's house to the plain, and then he would show the dancing animals. So the Raja gave the necessary orders, and on the day fixed all the people assembled to see the fun. Then the Raja's son set the three animals on the ground and his wife remained hidden in the covered way and caused the animals to dance. The people stayed watching all day till evening and then dispersed, That night all the booths and shelters which had been erected were changed into houses of gold; and when he saw this, the Raja left his younger wife and her children and went and lived with his first wife.

LXVII. THE MONGOOSE BOY

Once upon a time there was a Raja who had two wives. By his first wife he had six sons, but the second wife bore only one son and he was born as a mongoose. When the six sons of the elder wife grew up, they used to jeer at their mongoose brother and his mother, so the Raja sent his second wife to live in a separate house. The Mongoose boy could talk like any man but he never grew bigger than an ordinary mongoose and his name was Lelsing,

One day the Raja called all his sons to him and said that he wished, before he died, to divide his property among them. But the sons said that they had rather he did not do so then; they wished to go abroad and see the world, and if he would give each of them some capital to start with, they would go abroad and trade and even if they did not make much profit they would have the advantage of seeing the world.

So the Raja gave his six sons twenty rupees each to start business with; but when Lelsing also asked for some money, his brothers jeered at him and declared that he certainly could not go with them, for he would only get eaten up by some dog. Lelsing made no answer at the time but afterwards he went to his father alone and begged again for some money. At last the Raja, though he scarcely believed that Lelsing would really go out trading, gave him ten rupees.

The six brothers made everything ready and one morning set out on their travels, without saying anything to Lelsing. But Lelsing saw them start and followed after them, and as the brothers were resting in the middle the day they looked back and saw Lelsing galloping along to overtake them. So they all travelled together for three or four days, till they came to a great jungle and camped on its outskirts. There they debated how long they should stay away from home and they decided that they would trade for six months and then go back.

The next morning they entered the jungle, and as they travelled through it, the six brothers managed to give Lelsing the slip, so that when they came out of the forest they found themselves at Nilam bazar, but Lelsing after wandering about for some time came out at Sujan bazar.

The six brothers bought sun-horses at Nilam bazar, and began to trade. But Lelsing at Sujan bazar looked about for someone who would engage him as a servant. No one would employ a mongoose, and Lelsing was in despair, for he had very little money. At last he began to enquire whether anyone would sell him a cheap horse, and learnt that the horse market was at Nilam bazar; so he went to Nilam bazar and there found his brothers trading, but he did not make himself known to them. He tried to buy a horse but they were all to highly priced for him, so at last he had to be content with buying a donkey for three rupees and some articles to trade with.

When the six months expired, the brothers went home; and a little after them came Lelsing, leading his donkey, his brothers laughed at him but the Raja did not laugh; and Lelsing showed his father and mother what profits he had made by his trading, which his brothers declined to do. The Raja was pleased with Lelsing for this and declared that, in spite of his shape, he was a man and a Raja. It only made his brothers more angry with him to hear Lelsing praised.

Two or three years later there was a famine in the land. Lelsing foresaw it and he dug a large hole in the floor of his house and buried in it all the grain on which he could lay his hand. The famine grew severe, but Lelsing and his mother always had enough to eat from their private store. But his brothers were starving and their children cried from want of food. Lelsing had pity on them and sent his mother with some rice for them to eat. The Raja and his sons were amazed that Lelsing should have rice to give away, and they went to his house to see how much he had; but they found the house apparently empty, for they did not know of the store buried in the ground. Puzzled and jealous the brothers made up their minds to burn down Lelsing's house. So one night they set fire to it, and it was burnt to ashes: the store buried in the ground was however uninjured.

Lelsing put the ashes of his house into sacks and, loading them on his donkey, set out to sell them. As he found no buyers he rested for the night under a tree by the road side. Presently a band of merchants with well loaded pack-bullocks came to the place. "You must not camp here" called out Lelsing to them " I have two sacks of gold coin here and you may take an opportunity to steal them. If you are honest men, you will go to a distance." So the merchants camped a little way off, but in the middle of the night they came and carried off Lelsing's sacks, leaving two of their own in their place, and hurried on their way. In the morning Lelsing made haste to carry home the sacks which had been changed, and when he came to open them he found them full of rice and rupees. He sent his mother to borrow a measure from his brothers with which to measure the rupees; and when he returned it, he sent it to them full of rupees.

His brothers came running to know where he had found so much money. "I got it by selling the ashes of my house" said Lelsing ,and it is a pity that I had only one house; if I had had more houses, I should have got more ashes, and should have got more money, still." On hearing this the brothers of once made up their mind to burn their own houses, and take the ashes for sale. But when they did so and took the ashes for sale from village to village they were only laughed at for their pains, and in the end had to throw away the ashes and come back empty handed. They were very angry at the trick which Lelsing had played on them and decided to kill him and his mother; but when they went to the house to do the murder, Lelsing happened to be away from home and so they were only able to kill his mother.

When Lelsing came home he found his mother lying dead. He placed the body on his donkey and carried it off to burn it on the banks of the Ganges. As he went, he saw a large herd of pack bullocks coming along the road. He quickly propped the body of his mother against a tree which grew by the road and himself climbed into its branches, and when the bullocks came up he began to call out "Take care, take care: you will have my sick mother trampled to death." But the drivers were too far behind to hear what he said. When they came up, he climbed down from the tree and charged them with having allowed their bullocks to kill his mother. The drivers had no wish to face, a charge of murder; and in the end, to secure their release, they made over to Lelsing all their bullocks, with the merchandize which they were carrying.

Lelsing threw his mother's corpse into some bushes, and drove the laden bullocks home. Naturally his brothers wanted to know where his had got such wealth from, and he explained that it was by selling the dead body of his mother and he was sorry that he had only one to dispose of. At once his brothers went and killed all their wives, and took the corpses away to sell; but no one would buy and they had to return disappointed.

Another trick that Lelsing played his brothers was this: he used to mix rupees in the food he gave his donkey, and these passed out in the droppings; and Lelsing took care that his brothers should know of it. They found no rupees in the dung of their horses, and consulted Lelsing as to the reason why. He told them that if they gave their horses a blow with an axe while they ate their grain, they would find rupees in the dung. The brothers did as they were advised, but the only result was that they killed all their horses.

More and more angry, the brothers resolved to kill Lelsing by guile. So they went to him and said that they had found a wife for him, and would take him to be married. When the, procession was ready, Lelsing got into a palki. His brothers made the doors of the palki fast and carried him off towards a deep river, into which they meant to throw him, palki and all.

When they reached the river, they put the palki down and went to look for a suitably deep pool. Lelsing found that he was outwitted, and began to weep and wail. Just then a shepherd came by, driving a flock of sheep and asked what was the matter. Lelsings cried out that they were going to marry him against his will, but that anyone who would take his place in the palki could marry his bride. The shepherd thought that this would be a great opportunity to get a wife without spending any money on the marriage, and readily changed places with Lelsing, who drove away the flock of sheep. The brothers soon came back and, picking up the palki, threw it into the river and went home, thinking that they had at last got rid of Lelsing.

But four or five days later Lelsing appeared, driving a large flock of sheep. His brothers asked him, in amazement where he had come from "you threw me" said Lelsing" into a shallow pool of the river where there were only sheep, but in the deeper parts there are cattle and buffaloes as well. I can take you to fetch some of them if you like. You take your palkis to the bank of the river,—for I cannot carry you all—and then shut yourselves inside and I will push you into the water." So the brothers took their palkis to the river side and shut themselves in, and each called out "Let me have the deepest place, brother." Then Lelsing pushed them in one by one and they were all drowned. Then he went home rejoining at the revenge which he had taken for their ill treatment of him.

LXVIII. THE STOLEN TREASURE

Once upon a time three jars full of money were stolen from a Raja's palace. As all search was fruitless the Raja at last gave notice that, whoever could find them, should receive one half of the money. The offer brought all the *jans* and *ojhas* in the country to try their hand, but not one of them could find the treasurer

The fact was that the money had been stolen by two of the Raja's own servants and it fell to the duty of these same two men to entertain the *ojhas* who came to try and find the money. Thus they were able to keep watch and see whether any of them got on the right track.

Not far from the Raja's city lived a certain tricky fellow. From his boyhood he had always been up to strange pranks, and he had married the daughter of a rich village headman. At the time that the Raja's money was stolen his wife was on a visit to her father, and after she had been some time away, he went to fetch her home. However, on his way, he stopped to have a flirtation with a girl he knew in the village and the result was that he did not get to his father-in-law's house till long after dark. As he stood outside he heard his wife's relations talking inside, and from their conversation he learnt that they had killed a capon for supper, and that there was enough for each of them to have. three slices of capon and five pieces of the vegetable which was cooked with it.

Having learnt this he opened the door and went in. The household was amazed at his arriving so late at night but he explained that he had dreamt that they had killed a capon and were having a feast: and that there was enough for them each to have three slices of capon and five pieces of vegetable, so he had come to have a share. At this his father-in-law could do nothing but have another fowl killed and give him supper; he was naturally astonished at the Trickster's powers of dreaming and insisted that he must certainly go and try his luck at finding the Raja's stolen money.

The Trickster was taken aback, at this, but there was no getting out of it; so the next morning he set out with his-father-in-law to the Raja's palace. When they arrived they were placed in charge of the two guilty servants, who offered them refreshments of curds and parched rice. As he was washing his hands after eating, the Trickster ejaculated, "Find or fail I have at any rate had a square meal." Now the two servants were named Find and Fail and when they heard what the Trickster said, they thought he was speaking of them, and had by some magic already found out that they were the thieves.

This threw them into consternation and they took the Trickster aside and begged him not to tell the Raja that they were the thieves. He asked where they had put the money, and they told him that they had hidden it in the sand by the river. Then he promised not to reveal their guilt, if they would show him where to find the money when the time came. They gladly promised and took him to the Raja. The Trickster pretended to read an incantation over some mustard seed, and then taking a bamboo went along tapping, the ground with it. He refused to have a crowd with him, because they would spoil the spell, but Find and Fail followed behind him and showed him where to go. So he soon found the jars of money and took them to the Raja, who according to his promise gave him half their contents.

LXIX. DUKHU AND HIS BONGA WIFE

Once upon a time there was a man named Bhagrit who had two sons named Lukhu and Dukhu; and Lukhu used to work in the fields, while Dukhu herded the buffaloes. In summer Dukhu used to take his buffaloes to drink and rest at a pool in the bed of a dry river.

Now in the pool lived a *bonga* girl and she fell in love with Dukhu. So one day as he was sitting on the bank she appeared to. him in the guise of a human maiden. She went up to him and began to talk, and soon they become great friends and agreed to meet at the same place every day. As the girl was beautiful Dukhu fell deeply in love with her and resolved to marry her, not knowing that she was a *bonga*. One day the bonga girl asked Dukhu to come home with her to dinner, as he had stayed too late to go to his own house; but he said he was too shy to do so, as her parents knew nothing about him. The *bonga* girl said "Oh no, I have told my people all about our love, but if you won't come with me, stay here till I fetch you some rice; it is too late for you to go home now; by the time you come back, the buffaloes will have wandered off for their afternoon grazing." So Dukhu agreed to wait while she brought the rice, and she got up and moved away and disappeared behind some bushes, but a minute later Dukhu saw her come smiling towards him with a pot of rice on her head; though how she had fetched it so quickly he could not make out. She came to him and put it down and told him to wash his hands and come and eat his dinner. Dukhu asked her whether she had had her own dinner and she said that she would go back and have that later. Then he proposed that she should eat part of what she had brought ; and she said that she would do so, if he did not want it all. Dukhu resolved to test her, for it would be a proof of true love, if she ate what he left over. So after eating half the rice he said that he was satisfied and when she found that Dukhu would eat no more she took what was left; then he was satisfied that she really loved him and they began to talk of getting married, and he told her that there would be no difficulty about it, as his elder brother Lukhu was already married.

Then Dukhu asked the *bonga* to take him to her house to see her parents, so one day she led him into the pool and as he went in, the water never came above his ankles; and somehow they passed along a broad road until they came to the *bonga* girl's house, and this was full of tigers and leopards and snakes. At the sight of them Dukhu was too frightened to speak; the *bonga* said that she would not let them touch him and offered him a large coiled-up snake to sit on; but he would not sit down till she came and sat by his side. Then the *bonga* father and mother asked their daughter whether this was her husband, and when she said "yes" they came and made obeisance to him.

After they had had their dinner she took him back and he knew that she was a *bonga*; but still he could not give her up. After this the *bonga* girl brought Dukhu his dinner every day on the bank of the river, and he never went home for his midday-meal at all. His brother's wife asked him why he did not come home and he said that he did not get hungry and was content with some buffalo's milk; but she did not believe him and resolved to watch and see who brought him his dinner, but though she went and watched every day she only saw him sitting alone, and the *bonga* girl was invisible to her. But one day she saw him disappear into the pool, and come out again.

When she told this at home, Dukhu's father, Bhagrit, got very angry and decided to find out who made Dukhu disappear into the pool. He resolved to bale out the water and find out what was at the bottom. So he sent for men with baling basket and began to divide off the water with dams, but out of the water a voice was heard, singing:—

"Do not dam the water, father,
Do not dam the water, father,
Your daughter-in-law, the Ginduri fish is dying."

At this sound the workmen were frightened and stopped; but Bhagrit made them go on, saying that whatever happened should be on his head. And when the dams were finished, they began to bale out the water thereupon a voice sang:—

"Do not bale the water, father,
Do not bale the water, father,
Your daughter-in-law, the Ginduri fish is dying."

But they paid no attention and baled the water dry, and at the bottom of the pool they found an enormous fish, for the bonga girl had turned into a fish. And they went to kill it, but the fish sang:—

Do not hit me, father,
Do not hit me, father,
Your daughter-in-law, the Ginduri fish is dying."

Nevertheless they killed it and dragged it on to the bank. Then they began to cut it up, and as they did so, it sang—

"Do not cut me, father,
Do not cut me, father,
Your daughter-in-law, the Ginduri fish, is dying."

Nevertheless they cut it up, and Bhagrit divided the pieces among the workmen, but they were too frightened to take any and preferred to take the smaller fishes as their share. So he told Lukhu's wife to take up the pieces and wash them: and as she did so the song was heard: —

"Do not wash me, sister,
Do not wash me, sister,
The Ginduri fish is dying."

And she was very frightened, but her father made her wash them and then they took home the pieces and lit a fire and ground spices and turmeric and heated oil and made ready to cook the fish. Then the fish sang again:—

"Do not cook me, sister,
Do not cook me, sister,
The Ginduri fish, sister, is dying."

But she nevertheless put the pieces into the pot to boil, when lo and behold, out of the pot jumped the pretty *bonga* girl. Then Bhagrit said to his neighbours. "You see by my persistence I have got a daughter-in-law"—and she was duly married to Dukhu. At the wedding the *bonga* girl said "Listen, Father and all of you: I tell you and I tell my husband—however much we quarrel let not my husband strike me on the head, let him beat me on the body, I shall not mind; but on the day that he hits me on the head: I shall depart for good."

After the marriage the family became very prosperous and their crops flourished and every one liked the *bonga* girl; but between her and her husband there were constant quarrels and their friends could not stop them. One day it happened that Dukhu smacked her on the head. Then the *bonga* girl began to cry and called her father-in-law and mother-in-law and said "Father, listen, the father of your grandson has turned me out, you must do your work yourselves today;" then she took her child on her hip and left the house; and they ran after her and begged her to return, but she would not heed; and they tried to snatch the child from her but she would not give it up! and went away and was seen no more.

LXX. THE MONKEY HUSBAND

One very hot day some children were bathing in a pool, when a Hanuman monkey snatched up the cloth which one of the girls had left on the bank and ran up a tree with it. When the children came out of the water and went to take up their clothes, they found one missing, and looking about, they saw the monkey in the tree with it. They begged the Hanuman to give it back, but the monkey only said—"I will not give it unless its owner consents to marry me."—Then they began to throw sticks and stones at him but he climbed to the top of the tree out of the way,

Then they ran and told the parents of the girl whose cloth had been stolen; and they called their neighbours and went with bows and arrows and threatened to shoot the monkey if he did not give up the cloth, but he still said that he would not, unless the girl would marry him. Then they shot all their arrows at him but not one of them hit him; then the neighbours said. "This child is fated to belong to the monkey and that is why we cannot hit him." Then the girl's father and mother began to cry and sang:—

"Give the girl her cloth,
Her silk cloth, monkey boy,"

and he answered

"If she consents to marry me I will give it:
If she consents I will put it in her hand."

And as he did not listen to the father and mother, her father's younger brother and his wife sang the same song, but in vain; and then the girl herself begged for it, and thereupon the monkey let down one end of the cloth to her; and when she caught hold of it, he pulled her up into the tree, and there made her put on her cloth and ran off with her on his back.

The girl was quite willing to go with him and called out as she was carried away: "Never mind, father and mother I am going away." The Hanuman took her to a cave in the mountains and they lived on fruit,—mangoes or jack or whatever fruit was in season. The monkey climbed the trees and shook the fruit down; but if the girl saw by the marks of teeth that the monkey had bitten off any fruit, instead of only shaking it down, she would not eat it, and pretended that she had had enough; for she would not eat the leavings of the monkey.

At last the girl got tired of having only fruit to eat ; and demanded rice. So the monkey took her to a bazar, and leaving her on the outskirts of the village under a tree, he went and stole some pots from a potter and rice and salt and turmeric and pulse and sweetmeats from other shops, and brought them to the girl. Then she collected sticks and lit a fire and cooked a meal; and the monkey liked the cooked food, and asked her to cook for him every day. So they stayed there several days. Then the girl asked for more clothes and the monkey tried to steal them too, but the shopkeepers were on the watch and drove him away:

The girl soon got tired of sleeping under a tree so they went back to the cave and the monkey gathered mangoes and jackfruit and told her to go and sell them in the market and then she would be able to buy cloth. But when she had sold the fruit, she stayed in the village and took service with a well-to-do shopkeeper, and never returned to the monkey. The monkey watched for her and searched for her in vain, and returned sorrowfully to his hill; but the girl stayed on in the village and eventually married one of the villagers.

LXXI. LAKHAN AND THE WILD BUFFALOES

Once upon a time there was the only son of a widow, who used to tend the sheep and goats of a Raja and his name was Lakhan. One day he harnessed one of the goats to a plough and ploughed up a piece of high land and sowed hemp there. The crop grew finely, but one night a herd of wild buffaloes came and ate it all up; at this Lakhan resolved to pursue the buffaloes and shoot them.

His mother did all she could to dissuade him but he made up a bundle of provisions, and set off on his journey with a stick, and a bow and arrows, and a flute made of the castor oil plant. He tracked the buffaloes for some days and one evening he came to the house of an old witch (hutibudhi) and he went up to it and asked the witch if he might sleep there. She answered "My house is rough and dirty, but you can choose a corner to sleep in; I can give you nothing more, as I have not a morsel of food in the house." "Then," said he, 'I must go to bed hungry" and he lay down supperless.

In the middle of the night the witch began to gnaw at Lakhan's bow and he heard her gnawing and called out " What are you munching? Give me a bit, but she answered that it was only a little pulse which she had gleaned from the fields and she had finished it. So Lakhan said no more; but during the night the witch bit his bow to pieces and when he saw this in the morning, he was very unhappy; for it was useless to find the bison, if he had nothing to shoot them with.

So he went home and had an iron bow and arrow made by a blacksmith, and then started off again. As before he came to the witch's house and arranged to sleep there; and in the night the witch tried to bite the bow to pieces, and Lakhan heard her crunching it an asked her what she was eating: she said it was only a little grain which she had gleaned. In the morning he found the bow all right, but the witch's jaws were badly swollen. Lakhan laughed at her and asked what was the matter and she said that she had toothache.

So Lakhan went on his way rejoicing and at last reached the place where the wild buffaloes rested at night; he waited there and while he waited he swept away all the droppings and made the place clean, and then climbed up into a tree. At evening great herds of buffaloes came to the place and they were so many that Lakhan was afraid to shoot. So he stayed there, and every day he used to sweep the place clean while the buffaloes were away, and at night time hid himself in the tree.

The buffaloes determined to find out who their benefactor was, and they chose an old cow to stay behind and watch. The next day the old cow pretended that she was too weak to rise, and was left behind when the herd went out to graze. Lakhan thought that she was too old to do him any harm, so although she was there, he got down from the tree and cleaned up the place as usual, and even swept quite close up to the old cow buffalo. In the evening the other buffaloes came back and the old cow told them that it was a human being who swept their resting place clean; and when they promised not to hurt him, she pointed out the tree where Lakhan was. Then the buffaloes told him to come down and swore not to kill him but to support him and keep him as their sevant. They told him to make a leaf bowl and they filled this with their milk, as much as he could drink, and they arranged that he should stay at the sleeping place and keep it clean and when he wanted milk he was to play on his flute and they would came at the sound.

So every noon he used to blow the flute and the cows came, running and gave him more milk than he wanted so that he used even to bathe himself in milk, and this made his hair grow very long.

One day a parrot belonging to a Raja saw him drying his long hair in the sun and the parrot went to the Raja and told him that he had found a husband for the Raja's daughter, with beautiful long hair; but that no one could go near where he lived because of the wild buffaloes; however the parrot undertook to bring him with the help of a tame crow of the Raja's; so the crow and the parrot flew off to the jungle, and they decided that the best way to entice Lakhan away, was to carry off his flute. So when the cows gave him milk at noon and he put down his flute, the crow seized it in his beak and flew away to the top of a tree. When Lakhan missed the flute and saw the crow with it, he began to throw stones but the crow flew off with it, keeping just out of range; the crow flew from tree to tree and seemed to be always just about to drop the flute and in this way enticed Lakhan on, till they came to the Raja's palace and Lakhan followed the crow right inside and they shut the door on him and made him marry the princess.

After some time his wife's brothers began to talk rudely about him saying "I suppose this fellow is some poor orphan, without any relations" and when Lakhan heard this he said that if they wanted to see his cattle and buffaloes they must make a yard for them. So the Raja gave orders for a large cattle yard to be made, and when it was ready Lakhan took his flute and put his wife on the roof of the palace and he himself climbed a tree and blew on the flute. Then the wild buffaloes came running at the sound and gored to death every one they met, and Lakhan and his wife became Raja and Rani.

LXXII. THE BOY WITH THE STAG

Once all the men of a village went out to hunt in the hills and a certain orphan boy wanted to go with them, and although they told him that there was no water in the hills and he would die of thirst, he insisted on starting. The first day they found no water, but the orphan boy managed to endure it; but the second day he suffered so much, that he begged the hunters to take him to water; they told him that there was no water and they could not take him to any. So he set off alone in the direction in which he understood there might be water, but he soon lost his way in the jungle; so in despair he climbed a *meral* tree and picked the fruit and threw it in all directions and to his joy he heard one fruit splash as it fell into water; so he climbed down and sure enough close to the tree he found a pool and drank his fill.

And then he saw a fawn stuck fast in the mud at the edge of the pool, so he fixed an arrow to his bow and crept towards it, resolved to catch it alive if he could, but if it ran away, to shoot it. The fawn did not move and he managed to seize it and pulling it out of the mud, he rubbed it clean and put his bow string round its neck and took it home. The fawn grew up into a stag and he trained it to fight and one day he matched it to fight with a goat. The agreement was that the owner of the winner should take both the animals; in the fight the stag was victorious, so the boy won the goat. Then he matched his stag with a ram and a bullock and even with a buffalo, and the stag was always victorious and in this way he soon grew rich. Seeing him so rich one of the villagers gave him his daughter in marriage and took him to live in his house, and so he lived happily ever afterwards.

LXXIII. THE SEVEN BROTHERS AND THE BONGA GIRL

Once upon a time there were seven brothers who lived all alone in the jungle, far from human habitations. None of them was married and they lived on the game they killed. It chanced that a *bonga* maiden saw the youngest brother and fell deeply in love with him. So one day when all the brothers were away hunting, she placed in their house seven nicely cooked plates of rice.

When the brothers returned in the evening from the chase, they were astonished to find the rice waiting for them; all but the youngest said that it must be some plot to kill them and refused to touch the food but the youngest wished to eat it. His brothers would not let him and told him to throw the rice away; so he took it outside the house, but instead of throwing it away, he ate up the whole seven plates full, without letting his brothers know. But when they went to bed that night, the youngest brother snored loudly, because he had eaten so much, and thereby his brothers guessed that he had eaten the rice, and they were very unhappy for they were sure that he was about to die. However in the morning he was none the worse; so they went out hunting as usual but the youngest brother suffered continually from thirst, the result of overeating, and this convinced his brothers that he had eaten the rice, though he denied it.

When they reached home that evening, they again found seven dishes of rice placed ready for then. And that day the youngest brother and the youngest but one ate; and the day after there was the rice again, and the three youngest ate it. Then the eldest brother said: "Tomorrow I will stay behind and watch, and see who it is who brings the rice; we have no servant, If I can catch the person who is so kind to us, I will engage him as a cook for us, and we need have no more of this mystery. Do you bring back my share of the game you shoot."

So the next morning the eldest brother stayed behind and hid himself and watched. But he could not see the *bonga*, though she brought the rice as usual; an when he told his brothers this, it was decided that the second brother should stay behind the next day, and see if he had better luck ; and that day they all ate the rice, except the eldest brother, who said that he would never eat it, until he knew who brought it; so the next day the second brother watched but he also could not see the *bonga*.

One by one all the brothers watched in vain, until only the youngest one was left. Then they said to the youngest brother: " Now it is your turn and if our friend does not show himself to you, we will eat no more of his rice." So the next day the other brothers went off to hunt and the youngest stayed at home; he did not trouble to hide himself, but sat in the house making a bow. At noon he saw the *bonga* girl coming with the rice on her head, but he took no notice and pretended to be looking down at something. Then the *bonga* came into the courtyard and put down the rice and looked about and said: " I saw something like a man here, where has he got to?" and she looked into the house and still the youngest brother kept silent; then she spoke to him and asked whether he was ill, that he had not gone hunting. He answered her that he was not ill, but had been left to watch for the person who brought them rice every day. Thereupon the *bonga* went outside and brought in the rice and putting it down, said: "It is I who do it. Come, wash your hands and I will give you your dinner," but he said: "First tell me what all this means," and she said: "It means that I want to live with you." He objected. "How can I marry you when my brothers are not married?' She answered that if he married her, they would soon find wives for his brothers. Then she urged him to eat, but he said that if he ate one plateful, his brothers would question him, so the *bonga* girl went and brought, an extra dish and he ate that. And as they talked together, he soon fell deeply in love with her, and promised to consult his brothers about her living with them; but he saw a difficulty wnich would arise if she married him, for his elder brothers would not care even to ask her for water, and thus she would be really of very little use in the house: so with some hesitation he proposed that she should marry the eldest brother and then they could all talk freely to her; but the girl would not agree to this and said that there would be no harm at all in their talking to her, provided that they did not touch her, and she would not mind giving his elder brother water. So they plighted their troth to each other, subject to the consent of the brothers, and towards evening the *bonga* girl left, promising, to return on the tomorrow. When the brothers returned they discussed the matter and agreed that the youngest should marry the girl, provided that she promised to keep house for them, So the next day the girl came back and stayed with them; and they found wives for the other brothers, and got cattle and buffaloes and broke up land for cultivation and though the brothers did not altogether give up hunting, they became rich.

A certain Jogi found out where they lived and once every year he came to ask for alms; one year he came just after the bonga girl had borne a child, so as she was doing no work, it was her sisters-in-law who brought out food for the Jogi. But at this he was displeased, and said that he would only eat at the hands of the girl, who had given him food the year before. They told him that she was in child-bed and could not come out. Then he said: "Go and tell her that the Jhades Jogi has come and wants her arm tassel." So she sent out her arm tassel to him and he put it in his bag and got up and went away. Thereupon the bonga girl arose and left her baby, and followed him, and never came back. At evening the brothers returned from hunting, and heard what had happered. They were very distressed and told their wives to look after the bady while they went in pursuit. They followed as hard as they could and caught up the Jogi on the banks of a river; then they tried to shoot him, but their arrows were powerless against him, and he by magic turned the seven brothers into stones.

So the Jogi carried off the woman to his home. He was a Raja in his own country and he had a big garden; and an old woman who looked after it used to make garlands every day and bring them to the Rani, and the Rani used to pay their weight in silver for them. In the course of time the child who was left behind grew up and when he used to play with his fellows at pitch and toss and there was any dispute about the game his playmates would say "Fatherless boy, you want to cheat!" So he asked his aunts whether it was true that he had no father and they told him that the Jhades Jogi had carried off his mother, and how his father and uncles had gone in pursuit and had never returned. So the boy decided to go in search of his mother and he set off, and first he met some goatherds and he sang to them:—

"Ho, ho, goatherds
Have you seen the Jhades Jogi
On this road?"

But they could tell him nothing. And then he met some shepherd boys, and he sang to them:—

"Ho, ho, shepherds,
Have you seen the Jhades Jogi
On this road?"

But they could tell him nothing. Then he met some boys tending buffaloes and he sang:—

"Ho, ho, buffalo herds,
Have you seen the Jhades Jogi
On this road?"

But they could tell him nothing. Then he came to a thorn bush, with a number of rags fluttering on it, and he sang:—

"Ho, ho, plum bush,
Have you seen the Jhades Jogi
On this road?"

And the plum tree said. "The Jhades Jogi brought your mother this way, and I did my best to stop them. If you don't believe me see the rags as a proof." And he put his hand on the tree and went on. And then he came to a squirrel which was chattering in a banyan tree, and he sang:—

"Ho, ho, squirrel,
Have you seen the Jhades Jogi
On this road?"

And the squirrel said "I have been calling you since yesterday. The Jogi brought your mother this way, go on and you will overtake them. And your father and uncles also came this road." The boy was cheered by this news and he put his hand on the squirrel's back and said "You are a fine fellow to give me this clue" and the marks of his fingers were imprinted on the squirrel and that is why squirrels have striped backs to the present day.

Then he went on and came to a river and he decided to sit and have his lunch there; he did not know that his father and uncles had been turned into stones in that very place, but as he sat and ate, his eyes were opened and he saw the stones weeping, and he recognised them, and he dropt a little food on each that they might eat, and pursued his way, until he came to the Jhades Jogi's kingdom, and he went to the old woman who kept the Jogi's garden and asked to be allowed to stay with her and help her to make the garlands.

One day when he had made a garland, he tied to it a ring which had belonged to his mother. So when the old woman took the garland to the Rani, the Rani wondered why it weighed so heavy, and when she examined it she saw her own ring. Then she asked the old woman who had tied the ring there, and when she heard that a strange boy had come, she at once ran to him and recognised her own son.

Then they planned how they could kill the Jhades Jogi and escape! The mother agreed to find out in what lay the life of the Jogi. So she questioned him and worried him till he told her that his life lay in a certain pumpkin vine. Then the boy went and cut down the pumpkin vine, but the Jogi did not die; then the Rani worried and worried the Jogi till he told her that his life lay in his sword; then the boy stole the sword and burnt it in a fire of cowdung, but still the Jogi did not die; then his mother again worried and plagued the Jogi till at last he told her the truth and said" In the middle of the sea is a cotton tree, and on the tree are two Bohmae birds; if they are killed I shall die."

So the boy set off to the sea and on the road he met three old women and one had a stool stuck to her back, and one had a bundle of thatching grass stuck on her head, and the third had her foot stuck fast to a rice-pounder, and they asked him where he was going, and he told them, "to visit the shrine of the Bohmae bird : then they asked him to consult the oracle and find out how they could be freed from the things which were stuck fast to them, and he promsed to do so.

By-and-bye he came to the sea and, was puzzled as to how he was to cross it. As he walked up and down the shore he saw an alligator rolling about : In pain with a swollen stomach; and when it saw the boy it said. "I am like to die with this pain in my stomach, how can I be cured?" and the boy proposed that it should take him to the cotton tree in the midst of the sea and there they might learn a remedy from the Bohmae birds. The alligator agreed, so the boy got on its back and was taken across the water. Then the boy sat at the foot of the cotton tree and sang:—

"Come down, Bohmae birds,
I wish to consult the oracle."

But the birds were frightened and flew to the top of the tree. But as he went on singing, they became curious and came down and asked what was the matter, and he said "There are three old woman and one has a stool stuck to her and one a bundle of grass and one a rice pounder; how are they to be freed?" And they said "The first old woman never asked visitors to her house to take a seat; if she does so in future she will get rid of the stool,"—and as they said this they came nearer— "and the second old woman, if she saw anyone with straws sticking in their hair never offered to take them out. If she does so in future she will be freed," and as they said this they came nearer still—"and the third old woman would not allow widows and orphans to use her rice pounder : if she does so she will be freed:" and as they said this they came quite near, and the boy seized them and broke their wings, and as he did so the Jogi's arms were broken; then he snapped off their legs, and as he did so the Jogi's legs were broken; and the birds screamed and the Jogi howled.

Then the alligator carried the boy back, and by the time it reached the shore it was cured of its pain. On his way back the boy told the three old women of what the birds had said; and when he got to the Jogi's palace he twisted off the heads of the Bohmae birds and then the Jogi's head fell to the ground.

Then he started homewards with his mother, carrying the birds and their heads; and the jogi's head came rolling after them. But he saw a blacksmith's fire burning by the side of the road and he threw the birds into the fire and the Jogi's head rolled into the fire and was burnt, and that was the end of him. When they came to the river where his father and uncles were turned into stones, he bathed in the river, and then put a cloth over the stones and they were restored to human shape; and they rubbed their eyes and said "We must have slept a long time" and were astonished when they heard how the Jogi had turned them into stones. Then they all went home and lived happily ever after.

LXXIV. THE TIGER'S FOSTER CHILD

Once upon a time a Potter woman went to dig earth, for making pots, and while she was working she was prematurely delivered of a boy. And she considered whether she should carry the child home, or the basket of clay, but in the end decided to take the clay which was urgently wanted, while she would doubtless have plenty more children in the course of time. So she went away, leaving the baby in the pit. At evening a tiger came by and heard the child crying and he took pity on it and carried it away and he and his wife reared it.

As the child grew up they used to take him to the tigers' assembly. He was not at all afraid of the tigers and understood all they said and one day he heard them saying that the Pargana (tribal chief) tiger was a great man-eater. At this he was very angry and set off to look for the man-eater, without telling his foster parents. When the Pargana tiger saw the boy coming he had just finished cleaning his teeth, and he thought "This is lucky here is my breakfast coming;" but just as he was about to spring on the boy, the boy caught hold of him and tore him to pieces.

The news of this exploit soon spread, and the tigers called a meeting to consider the matter, and they told the foster father that he must take steps to prevent the boy doing any such thing again. So the tiger and tigress went home and told the boy that it was time that he went back to his own people, as he had brought shame upon them; the boy objected that men would not receive him, but they told him to go as an orphan boy and beg in the villages till he found his mother.

So he went away and when he came to a village he sang:—

"My mother went to dig earth
And left me in the pit;
The tiger and the tigress of the jungle
Reared me–give me alms."

And thus he went begging from village to village and one day he came to the village where his father and mother lived. His mother heard him a long way off and running to him knew him for her son. Then she brought water and oil and turmeric and bathed him and anointed him, and gave him new clothes and fed him on curds and parched rice. And the villagers collected, and when they heard the stories of the mother and son, they believed them and gave a feast in honour of the boy, and took him into the village.

LXXV. THE CATERPILLAR BOY

Once there was an old woman who lived on the grain she could collect from other people's threshing floors. One day as she swept up a threshing floor she found a caterpillar among the paddy; she threw it away but it came crawling back again; she threw it away again, but it said "Do not throw me away, take me home with you and you will prosper." So she let it stay and that day she found that she collected a whole basketful of rice; at this she was delighted, and put the caterpillar on the top of her basket and took it home. There she asked the caterpillar what work it would do, and it said that it would watch the paddy, when it was spread out to dry after being boiled, and prevent the fowls and pigs from eating it.

So the caterpillar used to watch the paddy while the old woman went out looking for food; and every day she brought back a full basket of rice, and so she soon became rich. It got whispered about that the old woman was so prosperous, because she had a caterpillar boy in her house.

One day the caterpillar said that he wanted to go and bathe, so he went to the river and took off his caterpillar skin, and bathed, and as he rubbed his head, one or two hairs came out, and these he wrapped up in a leaf and set the packet to float down the stream. Lower down the stream a princess was bathing and when she saw the packet come floating down, she had it fished out, and when she opened it she saw the hairs inside and she measured them and found them to be twelve fathoms long; then the princess vowed that she would not eat rice, till she found the man to whom the hair belonged. And she went home and shut herself in her room and refused to eat.

At this her father and mother were much distressed, and when they heard what had happenpd the Raja said "Well she wants a husband, I will find him for her." And he sent a notice throughout his kingdom saying that he would give his daughter and half his kingdom to the man who had hair twelve fathoms long. Everyone who heard this came with his sons and the princess was told to look at them and choose whom she liked; but none had hair twelve fathoms long, and she would take none of them. Then the Raja asked whether everyone in the kingdom had come, and he was told that there was a caterpillar boy, who lived with an old woman, who had not come, so the Raja sent to fetch him, but he said that he had no arms or legs and could not go; so they sent a palki for him and he was brought in that. And when the palki was set on the ground, the caterpillar boys rolled out and the princess said that he should be her husband.

At this her father and mother were much ashamed and remonstrated with her, but she persisted in her fancy, so the marriage took place. They sent the newly married pair to live in a house at the outskirts of the village and only one maidservant accompanied the princess. Every night the caterpillar boy used to take off his skin and go out to dance, and one night the maidservant saw him and told her mistress. And they agreed to watch him, so the next night they pretended to go to sleep, but when the caterpillar boy went out, they took his skin and burnt it on the fire; and when he came back, he looked for it, but could not find it. Then the princess got up and caught him in her arms, and he retained his human form, and he was as handsome as a god.

In the morning the caterpillar boy and his wife stayed inside the house, and the Raja sent some children to see what had happened, and the children brought back word that there was a being in the house, but whether human or divine they could not say. Then the Raja went and fetched his son-in-law to the palace, but the caterpillar was not pleased and said to his wife; "They treat me very well now that they see that I am a man, but what did they do before?" However he stayed in his father-in-law's palace.

Presently the Raja said that his kingdom was too small to give half of it to his son-in-law so he proposed that they should go and conquer fresh territory, and carve out a kingdom for the caterpillar boy. So they went to war and attacked another Raja, but they were defeated and their army cut to pieces. Then the son-in-law said that he would fight himself; so he drew his sword and brandished it and it flashed like lightning and dazzled the eyes of the enemy and his shield clanged on his thigh with a noise like thunder; and he defeated the other Raja and took his kingdom and carried off all his wealth.

But the Raja thought that as his son-in-law was so strong, he would one day kill him also and take his kingdom: so he resolved to find a means to kill him. On their way back from the war they found no water on the road and were distressed with thirst. One day they came to a large tank and found it dry. So they made a sacrifice in the hopes that water would flow. First they sacrificed goats and sang:—

"Tank, we are giving goats
Trickle out water!
Tank, we are giving goats
Flow, water !"

But no water came. Then in succession they sacrificed sheep, and oxen and buffaloes, and horses and elephants, but all in vain: and after each failure the Raja said "Son-in-law, it is your turn," and at last his son-in-law said, "Well, let it be me;" and he armed himself and mounted his horse and went and stood in the middle of the tank, and he sang:—

"Up to my knees the water, father,
The water, father, has oozed out."

And the Raja answered:—

"Do you, my son, remain standing there."

And as he sang the water welled out up to his horse's knee and then to its belly; and he still sang and the water rose to the horse's back and then to his own waist, and to his chest, and he still sang, and it reached his mouth and then he was completely submered and the tank was full. Then they all drank their fill and the Raja said to his men. "We have sacrificed this Saru prince. I will kill any of you who tells my daughter what has happened" and they promised not to tell, but they forgot that there were two dogs with them. And when they got home each man's wife brought out water and welcomed him and the princess asked where her husband, the Saru prince, was, and no one answered; then she sang:—

"Oh Father, my father; How far away
Is the Saru Prince, the Gindu Raja?"

and the Raja answered

"My daughter, my darling, the Saru Prince, the Gindu Raja
Is very far away, amusing himself with hunting."

And she sang to them all, but no one told her anything, and then she sang to the two dogs, who were named Chaura and Bhaura:—

"Oh Chaura, oh Bhaura,
How far away
Is the Saru Prince, the Gindu Raja?"

and they answered

"Oh sister, oh Rani!
Your father has sacrificed him
In the big tank."

Thereupon she began to cry, and every day she sat and cried on the bank of the tank.

Now the two daughters of the Snake King and Queen had received the Saru Prince as he disappeared under the water, and when they heard the princess crying every day they had pity on her; she used to sing:—

"Oh husband! Oh Raja!
My father has sacrificed you
In the big tank.
Oh hasband! Oh Raja,
Take me with you too."

So the daughters of the Snake King and Queen took pity on her and told their frog chowkidar to restore the Saru Prince to his wife; and the Prince and his wife went home together. When the Raja and his wife saw their son-in-law again, they were terrified, but he said nothing to reproach them. The princess however could not forgive them for trying to kill her husband and always looked angrily at them; then the Raja and the Rani took counsel together and agreed that they had done wrong to the prince, and that he must be a magician; and they thought that their daughter must also be a magician, as she had recognised the prince when he was a caterpillar, and she could not even see his long hair; so they were afraid and thought it best to make over the kingdom to their son-in-law, and they abdicated in his favour, and he took the kingdom.

LXXVI. THE MONKEY NURSEMAID

Once upon a time there were seven brothers who were all married and each had one child and the brothers arranged to engage a boy to carry the children about; so they sent for a boy and to see if he was strong enough, they made a loaf as big as a door and they told the boy to take it away and eat it; but he was not strong enough to lift it; so they told him that he could not carry their children. Now a Hanuman monkey was looking on from the top of a tree, and he came down and carried off the loaf and ate it. Thereupon the mothers engaged him to carry the children, and he used to carry the whole seven about on his back.

One day the children were running about the house and kept interfering with their mothers' work, and the mothers scolded the monkey for not keeping them out of the way. Then the monkey got sulky and carried off the children to a distant hill and did not bring them back at evening. So the mothers got very anxious, but the villagers laughed at them for engaging a monkey, instead of a human being, to look after the children.

When the mothers heard that the monkey had taken the children to the hill, they were still more unhappy for in the hill lived a *rakhas* (ogre) but it was too late to go in search of them that night. Meanwhile the monkey for fear of the *rakhas* had carried the children up to the top of a palm tree and when the *rakhas* spied them out he tried to climb the free, but the monkey drove him away by throwing the palm fruit at him.

However the monkey was really in a fix, for he was sure that the Rakhas would return, and he knew that if he let the children be eaten, their parents would make him pay for it with his life. So he went off to a blacksmith and bought sharp knives and tied them on to the trunk of the palm tree: and when the Rakhas came back and tried to climb the tree, he was so badly cut by the knives, that he fell down to the ground with a thud and lay there groaning. Then the monkey cautiously descended and the Rakhas begged him to cure his wounds; the monkey answered that he would cure him if he gave him complete outfits for the children. The Rakhas said that he would give them directly he was cured. So the monkey applied some medicines and recited the following spells:—

"Rustling, rustling sesamum,
Slender sesamum :
Tell your grandfather,
Tell him of seven waist strings.

Rustling, rustling, sesamum,
Slender sesamum:
Tell your grandfather,
Tell him of seven dhotis."

And in succeeding verses, he mentioned seven coats, seven pair of shoes, seven hats, seven swords, seven horses, and seven hogs; and as he repeated the incantation he blew on the Rakhas, and he was healed.

The Rakhas was to give the things mentioned in the incantation, but when seven hogs were mentioned he objected and wished only to give one, and in the end the monkey agreed to be content with two; so the Rakhas departed and the next day appeared with seven waist strings, seven dhoties, seven coats, seven hats, seven pairs of shoes, seven swords, seven horses and two hogs. Then the monkey rigged the children out in this apparel and mounted them on the horses; and the monkey and the Rakhas mounted on the two hogs,—the Rakhas having faithfully promised not to eat the children or their parents,—and they all set out for the children's home. When the mothers saw the cavalcade come jingling along, they were frightened at first; but when they recognised their children they were delighted, and they gave the monkey and Rakhas a good dinner. Then the monkey made over the children to their parents and gave up his post as nurse, and left amid the good wishes of all.

LXXVII. THE WIFE WHO COULD NOT KEEP A SECRET

Once there was a man of the Goala caste, who looked after the cattle of a rich farmer. One day a cow dropped a calf in the jungle without the Goala knowing, and at evening the cow came running to join the others, without the calf. When they got home the cow kept on lowing and the master asked whether she had had a calf; the Goala had to confess that the calf had been left in the jungle; the master scolded him well, so he took a rope and stick and went out into the night.

But when he got to the jungle he could not hear the calf, so he decided to wait where he was till the morning; he was too frightened of wild animals to stay on the ground, so he climbed a tree leaving the stick and rope at the foot of it. Soon a tiger smelt him out and came to the place. Then the stick and the rope took council together as to how they could save their master; the stick saw that it could not see in the dark and so was powerless; so the rope agreed to fight first, and it whirled itself round in the air with a whistling noise, and the tiger hearing the noise and seeing no one, got frightened, and thought that there was an evil spirit there; so it did not dare to come very near and in the morning it took itself off.

Then the Goala saw the cow come to look for her calf, so he took up the stick and rope and followed her. The cow soon found her calf and asked it whether it had not been a very cold and uncomfortable all night; but the calf said "No mother, I put my foot in these four pots of rupees and they kept me warm." The Goala heard this and resolved to see if it were true; so he dug up the earth where the calf had been lying and soon uncovered the rims of four pots full of money.

But the Goala did not care to take the money home for fear his wife should talk about it; he resolved to see first whether his wife could keep a secret.

So he went home and told her to cook him some food quickly; she asked why, and he said "The Raja has a tortoise inside him and I am going to look at him." Then his wife said that she must fetch some water, and she went off with the water pot. On the way she met several women of the village, who asked her why she was fetching water so early, and she said, "Because the

Raja has a tortoise inside him and my husband is going off to see it " In less than an hour the village was full of the news, and the rumour spread until it reached the ears of the Raja. The Raja was very angry and said that he would kill the man who started the report, unless he could prove it to be true. So he sent messengers throughout the country to trace back the rumour to its source.

One messenger found out that it was the Goala who had started the story and told him that the Raja wanted to give him a present; so he gladly put on his best clothes and went off to the Raja's palace. But the Raja had him bound with ropes, and then questioned him as to why he had told a false story. The Goala admitted that his story was false, but explained that he had only told it to his wife, in order to see whether she could keep a secret, because he had found four pots of money. The Raja asked where the money was and the Goala said that he would show it, but he wanted to know first how much of it he was to have for himself. The Raja promised him half; so the Goala led men to the place and they dug up the money, and the Goala kept half and became a rich man.

Moral. However friendly you are with a man do not tell him what is in your heart, and never tell your wife the real truth, for one day she will lose her temper and let the matter out.

LXXVIII. SIT AND LAKHAN

Once upon a time there was a Raja who had two wives and a concubine, but after giving birth to her second son, the first Rani died, and the name of her elder boy was Sit and that of the younger was Lakhan. The two children used to cry for their mother but the second Rani never comforted them, for she hated them; it was the concubine who used to bathe them and care for them, and their father loved them much. They used to go to the place where their father sat administering justice and Sit would sit behind his father and Lakhan in front. The second Rani hated to see them with their father and would tell the concubine to drive them away; but she refused and said that it was natural for a father to love his motherless children; so the Rani kept silent, but anger remained in her heart.

At last the Rani feigned to be ill and kept her bed: the Raja sent for doctors and *ojhas*, and they came and saw that she could not rise and they wanted to feel her pulse, but she would not let them touch her; all she would do was to make the concubine tie a string to her wrist and let the doctors hold the other end of the string; so the doctors diagnosed the disease as best they could in this way and gave her medicines, but she got no better.

After some days the Rani sent for the Raja and said "I am dying and you don't care; these doctors' medicines do me no good; there is one medicine only which will cure me." The Raja asked "What is it ? I will get it for you." Then the Rani made him swear by Kali that he would give her the medicine she wanted, and he swore blindly. Then the Rani said "If I eat the livers of Sit and Lakhan I shall get well, and if not I shall die." At this request the Raja was struck dumb.

Now the concubine and a sipahi had overheard the conversation, and when they heard what the Rani said, they withdrew and the concubine went and told Sit and Lakhan of what was in store for them, and Sit began to cry :—but Lakhan said "Do not cry brother, our father gave us life, and it is for him to take it away if he will." So the Raja came out from the Rani's room and when he saw the boys he wept and he went to them and told them to eat their rice quickly, but they would not eat; then he had their best clothes brought for them and told them to put them on, but they refused. Then the Raja called for *sipahis* and the *sipahi* who had been with the concubine, and two others, came and the Raja told them with tears in his voice to take the two boys away and let him never see them again, and he added so that the boys should not hear "Bring me their livers." So the sipahis took away the boys, and as they passed through the bazar they bought them some sweetmeats. After walking for a time they came to a jungle; then Sit said to the sipahis "How far are we to go? Do here what is in your minds."

But the sipahis went on further; then Sit again told them to do what they had to do. But the sipahis said "Do not be frightened, we shall not kill you; we shall not obey your father; you must go away and never come back here."

Now two dogs had followed them, attracted by the smell of the sweetmeats, and the *sipahis* caught and killed them and cut out their livers, and they put them on a plate and took them to the Raja. The Rani was delighted and had the livers cooked, and ate them and the next day she rose from her bed.

Meanwhile Sit and Lakhan travelled on, and in a few days they had eaten all their food and were very tired, and one evening they sat down at the foot of a tree in the jungle intending to spend the night there. In that tree a pair of birds had their nest. Every year they hatched their eggs and reared the young: but every year when the young were half grown, a snake came and devoured them. That year also there were two young in the nest, and on the day that the boys rested at the foot of the tree the snake had resolved to eat them. But when it came, the boys heard it moving in the leaves and killed it.

At evening the old birds returned and the nestlings said that the boys had saved their lives, and asked the old birds to give them some of the food that they had brought. So they threw down two bits of food, and it was ordained that whoever ate the first piece, should marry the daughter of a Raja, and whoever ate the second piece, should spit gold; and it chanced that Sit ate the first piece, and Lakhan the second. The next morning the boys went on their way, and the Raja of the country was looking for a husband for his daughter and he had sent an elephant out with a flower in its trunk and it was arranged that the princess should marry the man to whom the elephant gave the flower. The elephant came upon Sit sitting by the side of the road, while Lakhan was at a distance; and when the elephant saw Sit, it went up and gave him the flower and the attendants mounted him on the elephant and took him to the Raja and he married the princess.

A few days after the wedding Sit sat outside the palace with his wife, and did not come in though it was evening, and the Raja asked him why he was sitting outside in the dew. Then Sit began to cry and lament his brother, singing:—

"O Brother Lakhan, where have you gone?
"O younger brother, where have you gone?"

Then the Raja heard how he had been separated from his brother, and he promised to send men in search of Lakhan, and they found him in the house of a potter; but the potter refused to give him up until he had been paid for the days that he had entertained him; but really the Potter had become wealthy, because whenever Lakhan opened his mouth he spat gold, and he did not wish to lose such a valuable guest. Then Sit mounted his horse and took five rupees and gave them to the Potter in payment for his entertainment, and brought Lakhan home with him. When they found that Lakhan spat gold they were very glad to keep him and the Raja gave him his second daughter in marriage; and Lakhan made the whole family rich.

Meanwhile Sit and Lakhan's father had fallen into poverty; his country had been conquered and his army destroyed and he and his wife wandered about begging; when the boys heard this, they sent for the concubine who had been good to them, and she came and lived with them, but they did not forgive their father and step-mother.

Moral. There is no controlling a second wife and they are hard to get on with. First wives are the best, they are obedient and agree with the opinions of their husband.

LXXIX. THE RAJA WHO WENT TO HEAVEN

Once upon a time there was a Raja, who had many water reservoirs and tanks, and round the edges he planted trees, mangoes, pipals, palms and banyans; and the banyan trees were bigger than any. Every day after bathing the Raja used to walk about and look at his trees, and one morning, as he did so, he saw a maiden go up to a banyan tree and climb it, and the tree was then carried up to the sky, but when he went in the evening he saw the tree in its place again; the same thing happened three or four days running. The Raja told no one, but one morning he climbed the banyan tree before the maiden appeared, and when she came, he was carried up to the sky along with the tree. Then he saw the maiden descend and go and dance with a crowd of Gupinis (Divine milk maids) and the Raja also got down and joined in the dance.

He was so absorbed in the dance that he took no note of time; so when at last he tore himself away, he found that the banyan tree had disappeared. There was nothing to be done, but stay where he was; so he began to wander about and he soon came to some men building a palace as hard as they could. He asked them for whom the palace was being built, and they named his own name. He asked why it was being built for him, and they said that Thakur intended to bring him 'there, because he was a good ruler, who did not oppress his subjects and gave alms to the poor and to widows and orphans.

There was no difference between night and day up in the sky, but when the Raja came back, he found that the banyan tree was there, and he climbed up it and was carried back to earth by it. Then he went home and told his people that he had been on a visit to a friend. After that the Raja used to visit the banyan tree every day and when he found that it did not wither although it had been taken up by the roots, he concluded that what he had seen was true and he began to prepare for death. So he distributed all his wealth among his friends and among the poor and when his officers remonstrated he made them no answer. A few days later he died, and was taken to the palace which he had seen being built.

It is said that you give away in this world, you will get back in the next; there you will get good wages for what you have done in this life.

LXXX. SEVEN-TRICKS AND SINGLE-TRICK

Seven-Tricks and Single-Trick were great friends, but some one told Seven-Tricks that Single-Trick was the cleverer man of the two. Seven-Tricks pondered over this but felt sure that his very name showed that he was the cleverer; so one day he went to pay a visit to Single-Trick, and put the matter to the test. When Single-Trick saw him coming, he called a pretty girl and hid her inside the house and told his wife to put the rice on to boil. Seven-Tricks arrived and was pressed to stay for the midday meal ; he accepted. and Single-Trick's wife brought them water to wash their hands and when they sat down, helped them to the rice.

As they ate, Single-Trick pretended to get very angry and began to abuse his wife "You lazy slartern, why have you put no salt in the rice? I will beat you for this, I will beat you into a girl again." So saying he caught up a club and gave her a blow with it, and pushed her into the house and pretended to continue the beating inside; and then came out dragging with him the pretty girl whom he had hidden. When Seven-Tricks saw this transformation he made up his mind to steal the club, and try whether he could beat his own wife into a girl again. So when he went home he secretly took away the club, and the next day when his wife was giving him his dinner he pretended to get angry with her for not putting salt in the rice, and snatching up the club gave her a good pounding with it, and drove her into the house and then pulled her forth again; but to his dismay she did not look a day younger than before. Seven-Tricks was puzzled but could only opine that he had not beaten the woman hard enough, so he beat her till her bones cracked; but still there was no result and he had to give up in despair.

After a time Seven-Tricks paid another visit to SingleTrick, and Single-Trick invited him to come hunting in the forest; before they started Single-Trick told his wife to go and buy a hare and keep it in the house. The two friends set off, and after a time they put up a hare; Single-Trick had brought with him his dog, which was shocking coward and no good at hunting; when they saw the hare Single-Trick loosed the dog calling "After it, after it, drive it right home." And the coward of a dog, directly it was free, put its tail between its legs and ran straight home. "Come along home now; that is a splendid sporting dog, it is sure to have taken the hare home;" so saying Single-Trick set off back, and when they arrived he asked his wife wheather the dog had brought home a hare. "Yes", said she, "I have put it in that room" and promptly produced the hare that she had bought. Seven-Tricks at once resolved to possess himself of a dog that brought the game home by itself, and the next night he came and stole it, and in the morning took it out hunting. He soon started a hare and loosed the dog after it; the dog ran straight away in the direction of the house, and Seven-Tricks followed at his leisure, and asked his wife where the dog had put the hare. "Hare," said she "there is no hare, the dog came running back alone." "Perhaps I was too slow and gave him time to eat the hare," thought Seven-Tricks; so he took it out again and when he loosed it after a hare, he ran after it as fast as he could to see what it did. Everyone laughed to see the hunter chasing his dog, instead of his game. When he got to the house of course there was no hare, and so he gave up trying to hunt.

Another day he paid a visit to Single-Trick and Single-Trick asked him to come out fishing. Before they started Single-Trick told his wife to buy some live *codgo* fish and keep them ready in the house. When they came to a pool, Single-Trick at once let down his line and soon got a bite from a *codgo* fish; as he pulled it out he threw it, rod and all, behind him in the direction of his home and said to Seven-Tricks "Come along home, I expect that all the fish in the pool will have reached home by now." Directly they got to the house Single-Trick asked his wife whether the fish had come. "Yes", said she, "I have put them all in this basket" and brought out a basket of lives *codgo* fish. SevenTricks at once made up his mind to steal the wonderful fishing rod, so he came back that evening and managed to abstract it, and next morning went fishing with it. Directly he had caught a *codgo* fish, he threw it over his shoulder and went off home and asked whether the fish had arrived, but he only got laughed at for his folly. Then he was convinced that Single-Trick was more than a match for him, and he would have nothing more to do with him.

LXXXI. FULJHARI RAJA

There was once a Raja named Fuljhari and he was childless; and he and his wife made Pilgrimages to many shrines but all in vain, the wished-for son never arrived. One day a Jugi came to the palace begging and the Raja asked the holy man to tell him how he could have a son; then the Jugi examined the palms of their hands but having done so remained silent. The Raja urged him to speak but the Jugi said that he feared that the reply would be distasteful to the Raja and make him angry. But the Raja and his wife begged for his advice and promised to do him no harm whatever he said. At last the Jugi explained that they could never have a child unless they separated, and the Raja went right away and the Rani lived with another man; with this he took his departure.

Then the Raja and his wife consulted together and the Raja proposed to take the Jugi's advise, as he felt that he could not leave his kingdom without an heir; so he said that he would go away to a far country, on pretence of visiting a distant shrine; but the Rani feared that if, on his return, he found that she had borne a child, he would kill her or at least turn her and the child out to beg their bread; but the Raja assured her that he would never treat her in that way and after making his final arrangements he went off to a far country.

There he stayed some years and in the meanwhile the Rani had five sons; at last she wrote to her husband to come home and directly he reached the palace he bade the Rani to bring the boys to him, that he might embrace and acknowledge them; so they were brought and he took them one by one in his arrms and kissed them, and he saw that they were all the images of himself. But when.he kissed the youngest child he was suddenly struck with blindness. Then he rose in wrath and ordered the child to be taken away and killed; but the mother had pity on it and persuaded the soldiers not to kill it but to convey it away to a far country.

The child's name was Lita and he grew up and was married to the daughter of the Raja of the land and lived in his father-in-law's house. But Lita was always tormented by the thought that he had been the cause of his father's blindness; although he would not tell anyone of his sorrow, he used to get up when every one was asleep and spend the night in tears. One night his wife surprised him weeping and begged him to tell her what was the matter. She pressed him until he told her how immediately his father kissed him, he had gone blind and how his mother had smuggled him out of the country and saved his life, but how the recollection of the harm he had done tormented him and how he longed to be able to return to his own country and restore his father's sight. His wife on hearing this at once began to comfort him and assured him that he would help him to obtain a medicine which would restore his father's sight. In a range of mountains was a Rakhas who had a daughter who was buried in a heap of Fuljhari flowers; if Lita went and could persuade the Rakhas to let him marry his daughter, he could then get a Fuljhari flower and if that were rubbed on his father's eyes his sight would be restored.

So Lita set out towards the mountains and sat down by the road side at their foot. Presently the Rakhas and his wife came by; the wife asked him what he was sitting there for; he said that he was looking out for some one who would have him to come and live in his house as a son-in-law. The Rakhas paid no heed to this and proposed to eat up Lita at once, but his wife begged him to spare the young man and take him home and marry him to their daughter, who was very lonely. The Rakhas gave way and they took Lita to the cavern in which they lived and there was their daughter buried under a heap of flowers. They made her get up, and told her that they had brought a husband for her.

Lita and his bride lived happily together and were soon deeply in love with each other, and after a time he told her about his father's blindness and how he wished to try to cure it with one of her flowers. She readily agreed to help him; so the next day she went to her father and said that she wished to pay a short visit to her husband's home; the Rakhas consented and she and Lita took their leave. She told Lita that when the Rakhas offered him a farewell gift, he should take nothing but a hair from the Rakhas' head; this he did and they tied the flower and the hair up carefully and set off to the home, where Lita's first wife was awaiting them. She told her parents that Lita had come back with one of his sisters, and that she now wished to go back with them on a visit to their home. Her parents assented and the three of them set out and one evening reached the outskirts of the village in which Lita had been born.

They camped under a roadside tree, but in the middle of the night they took out the Rakhas' hair and said to it "Make us a golden palace" and at once a golden palace sprang up. Next morning all the residents of the village collected to see the wonderful new palace, and Lita told them to bring their Raja and he would cure him of his blindness. So they went and fetched the old blind Raja and directly Lita touched his eyes with the flower his sight was restored. Then they wept over each other and told all that had happened. And the old Raja and his wife came and lived with Lita and his wives and the other brothers stayed on at their old home; and they all lived happily ever after.

LXXXII. THE CORPSE OF THE RAJA'S SON

There was once a blacksmith named Chitru who had a very pretty wife; and the woman attracted the attention of the son of the Raja. Chitru suspected that his wife was unfaithful to him, and one night he pretended to go away from home, but really he lay in wait and surprised the prince visiting his wife; then he sprang out upon him and strangled him.

But when he found himself with the corpse of the prince on his hands, he began to wonder what he should do to avoid being convicted of the murder. At last he took up the corpse and carried it to the house of two dancing girls who lived in the village, and laid it down inside. Soon after the dancing girls woke up and saw the corpse lying in their room; they at once aroused their parents, and when they found that it was the corpse of the Prince, they were filled with consternation.

Now Chitru had a reputation for cunning, so they decided to send for him quietly and take his advice. When he came they begged him to save them; he pretended to be much surprised and puzzled and at last undertook to get them out of their difficulty, if they paid him one hundred rupees; they gladly paid him the money, and then he took up the corpse and carried it off and laid it down on the verandah of the house of a *mahajan* who lived near. Soon after some one came out of the house and found the corpse; at once they were all in consternation and sent for the clever Chitru to help them out of their difficulty.

Chitru refused to lift a finger unless he were paid two hundred rupees, and when he had got the money he took up the corpse and put it in a sitting position in a little patch of *brinjals* which a Koeri had planted by his front door. At dawn the Koeri came out and saw what he thought was a thief stealing his brinjals, and promptly threw a stone at the man. The corpse fell over, and when the Koeri went to see who it was he found the dead body of the Raja's son. As it was daylight, he had no opportunity of making away with the body, so he was arrested and sent for trial. He was acquitted, because he had acted unwittingly,but he was too frightened of the Raja to stay any longer in the village and absconded as soon as he could.

Chitru, who was the real murderer, made his wife promise to keep silence by threats and was three hundred rupees the better for the business.

LXXXIII. THE SHAM CHILD

There was once a Raja who had two wives and each Rani had a maidservant who was the Raja's concubine; but none of them had any children. In the course of time the ladies began to quarrel and when they appealed to the Raja, he found that the elder Rani was to blame and turned her out of the palace, and sent her to live in a palm leaf hut on the outskirts of the town. Her faithful maidservant followed her, and the two supported themselves by begging. But they barely got enought to keep body and soul together.

After a few days the maidservant asked permission of her mistress to play a trick on the Raja, by which they should at least get sufficient food. The Rani assented and the maidservant went off to the Raja and told him that the wife whom he had turned out was five months with child, and that it was a disgrace that one who was to be the mother of his heir should have to beg her bread. On hearing this the Raja somewhat relented towards the Rani, and he ordered money to be sent her sufficient to provide her with food, and had a proper house prepared for her. When the proper time arrived, the maidservant went to the Raja and told him that a son had been born; at this joyful news the Raja became still more generous and told the maidservant that she was free to take whatever was wanted for the child.

This suited the maid and her mistress excellently; so long as they could keep up the deception they lived in comfort; when the child was supposed to have grown old enough to run about, they asked for the price of some anklets with bells on them and bought a pair, and whenever the Raja passed by the house in which the Rani lived, the maidservant made her mistress rattle the Raja to anklets, and then went outside and told the listen to the anklets tinkling as his son ran about the house. The Raja would tell the maidservant not to let the boy run about too much, lest he should fall and hurt himself; then she would hurry inside and tell the Rani to stop the jingling, and then come and tell the Raja that the boy was resting in his mother's lap; but for all this the Raja was never given an opportunity of seeing his son.

However as time went on the Raja chose a bride and arranged for his son's wedding; the bride's friends did not come to inspect the bridegroom; a day was fixed right off for the wedding. As this day drew negar, the Rani, became more and more frightened, for it seemed that her deception most at last be discovered, and she would probably be put to death. But the maidservant encouraged her and promised to devise a plan; so when the day came for them to start for the bride's house she made a paste of ground mowah flowers and out of this fashioned an image of a child; and when the procession started off, with the Raja in a palki, and drummers, and palki-bearers, the maidservant was also carried in a palki and pretended that she was holding the child. Off they started and as it was too far to go in one day, they stopped for the night at a bazar, where there was the shrine of a saint. At midnight the maidservant arose and went to the shrine and called to the spirit (bonga) which dwelt there, and said that he must grant her a boon, and if not it would be the worse for him; the spirit asked what she wanted and she showed the paste image and said that she was going with the procession to marry her son, and somehow on the way he had been turned into paste; if the spirit would not give her another son, she would spit on him and curse him. The spirit saw that she meant what she said, and for fear of being spat upon, he produced a boy from somewhere and gave him to her. The maidservant was delighted at her success and bowed down three times in reverence to the spirit and took away the boy and put him in her palki.

The next morning they rose and reached the bride's house and the wedding took place in due form. As they were returning, the maidservant sent on two men to warn her mistress of what had happened and to tell her to get ready a feast. So when they reached home there was a feast ready and the bride's friends were duly entatained and dismissed. Afterwards the Raja fell out with his second wife and left the palace where she lived and came and stayed with the elder Rani, whom he had formerly turned out.

LXXXIV. THE SONS OF THE KHEROHURI RAJA

The Kherohuri Raja had five sons, and he made up his mind that he would only marry them to five sisters. So he sent out Brahmans and Jugis to search the world to find a Raja with five unmarried daughters. And at the same time the Chandmuni Raja had five marriageable daughters, and he made up his mind that he would marry them to five brothers; he did not care what their rank in life was, but he was determined to find a family of five brothers to marry his daughters. And he also told all the Brahmans and Jugis who wandered about begging, to look out for a family of five unmarried brothers.

One day it chanced that the emissaries of the Kherohuri Raja and those of the Chandmuni Raja met at a river; both parties were resting after taking their midday meal and as they smoked they fell into conversation, and soon found that their meeting war most fortunate; each party had found the very thing they wanted, so they all set off to the palace of the Kherohuri Raja in order that the Chandmuni Raja's messengers might see the young men.

The Kherohuri Raja ordered them to be hospitably entertained and food to be set before them; they however refused to eat anything till they had seen the five bridegrooms. The five young men were then introduced and as they appeared to be sound in wind and limb and in all respects satisfactory, there was no further obstacle to the entertainment. The next day the Kherohuri Raja sent out officials to visit and inspect the daughters of the Chandmuni Raja, and as their report was satisfactory, nothing remained but to fix the day for the wedding.

When the time came for the bridegrooms and their retinue to set off to the country of the Chandmani Raja, they and their servants and followers all started, so that no one was left at home but their mother. After they had gone a little way the eldest prince stopped them and said that they could not leave their mother all alone, what would she do supposing some sudden danger arose?" The others agreed that this was so, but the difficulty was to decide who should stay; not one of the other brothers would consent to do so. So at last the eldest brother said that he would stay, and he gave them his shield and sword and told them to perform his marriage for him by putting the vermilion on the bride's forehead with his sword.

When they reached the home of the Chandmuni Raja they proceeded at once to perform the vermilion ceremony, beginning with the eldest daughter; but when the sword was produced and she was told that she must go through the ceremony with the sword, as her bridegroom had not come, she began to cry and make a great to-do "Nothing would induce her to consent." Why was her husband the only one who had not come in person? he must be blind or lame or married;" this resistance put all the others into a difficulty, for the younger sisters could not be married before the elder. At last after much talking her father and mother persuaded the eldest daughter to go through the ceremony; the women put vermilion on the sword and with the sword the mark was made on the bride's forehead; and then the younger sisters were married and after a grand feast the whole party set out for the palace of the Kherohuri Raja.

On the way they were benighted in the midst of a great jungle twelve *kos* wide, and the palki bearers declined to go any further in the dark, so they had all to camp where they were. In the middle of the night, suddenly sixteen hundred Rakhases descended on them and swallowed up the whole cavalcade, elephants and horses and palkis and men. In this danger the eldest princess who had been married to the sword prayed to Chando saying "O Chando ! I have never yet set eyes on my husband; he is not with one here. I pray they carry my palki in safety up into the sky." And Chando heard her prayer and lifted her palki up into the air and preserved her, but all those who were left on the ground were swallowed up by the Rakhases; when the day dawned not one was to be seen.

As the princess from mid air gazed on this melancholy spectacle, a parrot came flying over and she called to it and begged it to take a letter for her to her husband in the palace of the Kherohuri Raja. The parrot obeyed her behest, and when the eldest prince read the letter and learned what had happened, he made a hasty meal and saddled his horse and was ready to start; but : as it was nearly evening he thought it better to wait till the next day.

Very early the following morning he set out and when his bride saw him come riding along she prayed to Chando that if it were really her husband the palki might descend to the ground; it immediately sank, and the bride and bridegroom met; then she told him all that had happened and gave him the shield and sword that he had sent to represent him at the marriage; with these in his hands he waited and when at night-fall the Rakhases returned, the Prince slew everyone of them with his sword; and as he killed them the Rakhases vomited up the elephants, horses and men that they had eaten. Then his wife told the prince to dip a cloth in water and ring it out over the dead and as the water fell on them they all became alive again, elephants, horses and men.

But his brothers far from being grateful to him for having restored them to life, took counsel together saying "Now that he has delivered us from this danger, he will think that he has a claim on us and will treat us as his servants; let us cut open his stomach and then the Rakhas will eat him. So they turned on him, cut open his stomach, and went their ways. Then the wounded prince told the palki-bearers to carry his bride back to her father house.

When they appeared before the Chandmuni Raja, he upbraided them for not having brought the prince too, to try if he could not have been healed. Meanwhile the prince lay in the jungle groaning for a whole day and night; then Chando and his wife heard his cries and came down and told him to push in his entrails; and when he had done so, they gave him a slap on his stomach and he became whole again. Then as he was afraid to return to his home where his brothers were, he went begging to his father-in-law's house; as he came to it, his wife said to her sister-in-law that the beggar seemed to be like her husband, so she went to him and they recognised each other and he was taken in and well treated and lived there many years. In the end he was seized with a desire to go and see his old mother, and, his wife consenting to go with him, they set off to his father's home, when his brothers saw him come, they were filled with fear and made him Raja over them and they became his servants and. he lived in prosperity for the rest of his life.

LXXXV. THE DOG BRIDE

Once upon a time there was a youth who used to herd buffaloes; and as he watched his animals graze he noticed that exactly at noon every day a she-dog used to make its way to a ravine, in which there were some pools of water. This made him curious and he wondered to whom it belonged and what it did in the ravine; so he decided to watch, and one day when the dog came he hid himself and saw that when it got to the water, it shed its dog skin and out stepped a beautiful maiden and began to bathe; and when she had finished bathing she put on the skin and became a dog again, and went off to the village; the herdboy followed her and watched into what house she entered, and he enquired to whom the house belonged. Having found out all about it, he went back to his work.

That year the herdboy's father and mother decided that it was time for him to marry and began to look about for a wife for him; but he announced that he had made up his mind to have a dog for his wife and, he would never marry a human girl.

Everyone laughed at him for such an extraordinary idea, but he could not be moved; so at last they concluded that he must really have the soul of a dog in him, and that it was best to let him have his own way. So his father and mother asked him whether there was any particular dog he would like to have for his bride, and then he gave the name of the man into whose house he had tracked the dog that he had seen going to the ravine. The master of the dog laughed at the idea that anyone should wish to marry her, and gladly accepted a bride's price for her; so a day was fixed for the wedding and the booth built for the ceremony and the bridegroom's party went to the bride's house and the marriage took place in due form and the bride was escorted to her husband's house.

Every night when her husband was asleep, the bride used to come out of the dog's skin and go out of the house; and when her husband found out this, he one night only pretended to go to sleep and lay watching her, and when she was about to leave the room he jumped up and caught hold of her and seizing the dog skin, threw it into the fire, where it was burnt to ashes, so his bride remained a woman, but she was of more than human beanty. This soon became known in the village and everyone congratulated the herdboy on his wisdom in marrying a dog.

Now the herdboy had a friend named Jitu and when Jitu saw what a prize his friend had got, he thought that he could not do better than marry a dog himself. His relations made no objection and a bride was selected and the marriage took place, but when they were putting vermilion on the bride's forehead she began to growl; but in spite of her growling they dragged her to the bridegroom's house, and forcibly anointed her with oil and turmeric; but when the bride's party set off home, the dog broke loose and ran after them; then everyone. shouted to Jitu to run after his bride and bring her back, but she only growled and bit at him, so that he had at last, to give it up. Then everyone laughed at him so much that he was too ashamed to speak, and two or three days later he hanged himself.

LXXXVI. WEALTH OR WISDOM

Once upon a time there were a Raja and a rich merchant, and they each had one son. The two boys went to the same school and in the course of time became great friends; they were always together out of school hours; the merchant's son would take his meals at the Raja's palace or the Raja's son would eat with his friend at the merchant's house.One day the two youths began a discussion as to whether wealth or wisdom were the more powerful: the Raja's son said that wealth was most important, while the merchant's son declared for wisdom, the discussion waxed hot and would neither yield his opinion. At last the merchant's son declared; "It is of no use for us to argue like this, let us put it to the test: let us both go to some far country and take service with some master for a year, and try whether wealth or wisdom is the more successful." The Prince agreed to this plan and they fixed a day for starting.

Then they both went home and collected what money they could lay hands on and, when the time arrived, started off early one morning. After they had travelled some distance the Prince began to think of how his parents must be searching for him, for he had said nothing about his going away; but the merchant's son comforted him by saying that he had left word of their intentions at his home, and his relations would tell the Raja; so they continued on their way, and after a time they came to a certain country where the merchant's son proposed that they should look for employment. But now that it had come to the point, the prince did not like the idea of becoming a servant and he said that he would live on the money which he had brought with him, and which would last for a year or two. "You may do as you like" answered his friend, but for my part I must look for work." So he went to a village and found employment as a teacher in a school; his pupils gave him his food and also some small wages, so that he had enough to live on, without spending any of the money he had brought with him.

Meanwhile the Raja's son hired a house in the village and began to lead a riotous life; in a very short time he had wasted all his money on his evil companions and was reduced to absolute starvation; for when his money came to an end, all his so-called friends deserted him. Thin and wretched, he went to the merchant's son and asked him either to take him back to his father's home or to find him work. His friend agreed to find him some employment, and after a little enquiry heard of a farmer who wanted a servant to take a bullock out to graze and to fill a trough with water once a day. The prince thought that he could easily manage that amount of work, so he went to the farmer and engaged himself as his servant.

The terms of service were these:—If the prince threw up his work one of his little fingers was to be cut off, but if the farmer dismissed him while he was working well then the farmer was to lose a little finger; and if the prince grazed the bullock and filled the trough with water regularly, he was to get as much cooked rice as would cover a plantain leaf, but if he did not do the work he was to get only what would go on a tamarind leaf. The prince readily agreed to these terms, for he thought that the work would not take him more than an hour or two. But unhappily for him, things did not turn out as he expected. On the first morning he took the bullock out to graze, but the animal would not eat; whenever it saw any other cattle passing, it would gallop off to join them, and when the prince had run after it and brought it back, nothing would make it graze quietly; it kept running away in one direction or another with the prince in pursuit. So at last he had to bring it home and shut it up in the cow-shed and even that he found difficult.

Then they set him to filling the trough, and he found that he could not do that either, for the trough had a hole in the bottom and had been set over the mouth of an old well; and as fast as the prince poured the water in, it ran away, but he was too stupid to see what was the matter and went on pouring till he was quite tired out; so as he had not completed the tasks set him, he only got a tamarind leaf full of rice for his supper; this went on every day and the prince began to starve, but he was afraid to run away and tell his troubles to the merchant's son, lest he should have his little finger cut off.

But the merchant's son had not forgotten his friend and began to wonder why the Prince kept away from him. So one day he went to pay him a visit and was horrified to find him looking so ill and starved; when he heard how the prince was only getting a tamarind leaf full of rice every day, because he could not perform the task set him, he offered to change places with the Prince and sent him off to teach in the school while he himself stayed with the farmer. The next morning the merchant's son took the bullock out to graze and he also found that the animal would not graze quietly but spent its time in chasing the other cattle, so at noon he brought it home and set to work to fill the trough; he soon found the hole in the bottom through which the water escaped and stopped it up with a lump of clay and then he easily filled the trough to that brim. Then in the afternoon he took the bullock out again to graze and when he brought it back at sunset he was given a plantain leaf full of rice; this meant more food than he could possibly eat in a day.

He was determined that the bullock should not give him any more trouble, so the next morning when he took it out to graze, he took with him a thick rope and tethered the animal to a tree; this saved him all the trouble of running after it, but it was clear that it would not get enough to eat in that way, so he made up his mind to get rid of it altogether, and when he took it out in the afternoon, he took with him a small axe and drove the bullock to a place where a herd of cattle were grazing and then knocked it on the head with the axe and threw the body into a ravine near by. Then he hid the axe and ran off to his master and told him that the bullock had started fighting with another animal in the herd and had been pushed over the edge of the ravine and killed by the fall. The farmer went out to see for himself and when he found the dead body lying in the ravine he could not but believe the story, and had no fault to find with his cunning servant.

A few days later, as the rice crop was ripe, the farmer told the merchant's son to go to the fields to reap the rice. "How shall I reap it?" asked he "With a sickle," replied the farmer. "Then it will be the the sickle and not I, that reaps it." "As you like," a said the farmer, " you go along with the sickle, no doubt it knows all about it;" so they got him a sickle and he went off to the fields. When he got there, he noticed how bright the sickle looked, and when he touched it, he found it quite hot from being carried in the sun. "Dear, dear," said he, "I cannot let this sickle reap the rice: it is so hot that it must have very bad fever; I will let it rest in the shade until it gets better," so he laid it down in a shady spot and began to stroll about. Presently up came the farmer, and was very angry to find no work going on. "Did I send you out to stroll about, or to start cutting the rice?" roared he. " To cut the rice," answered the merchant's son, "but the sickle has fallen ill with high fever and is resting in the shade; come and feel how hot it is." "You are nothing but an idiot," answered the farmer. "You are no good here; go back home and start a fire in the big house and boil some water by the time I get back." The merchant's son was only on the lookout for an excuse to annoy the farmer and the words used by the farmer were ambiguous; so he went straight back to the farm and set the biggest house on fire. The farmer saw the conflagration and came rushing home and asked the merchant's son what on earth he meant by doing such mischief. "I am only doing exactly what you told me, nothing would induce me to disobey any order of yours my worthy master." The farmer had nothing more to say; his words would bear the construction put upon them by the merchant's son, and he was afraid to dismiss him lest he should have to lose his little finger; so he made up his mind to get rid of this inconvenient servant in another way, and the next day he called him and told him that he must send word to his father-in-law of the unfortunate burning of the house, and the merchant's son must carry the letter.

The latter accordingly set off with the letter, but on the road he thought that it would be just as well to see what the letter was really about; so he opened it and found that it contained a request from the farmer to his father-in-law to kill the bearer of the letter immediately on his arrival. The merchant's son at once tore this up and wrote another letter in the farmer's name: saying that the bearer of the letter was a most excellent servant and he wished him to marry into the family; but that as he himself had no daughters he hoped that his father-in-law would give him one of his daughters of wife. Armed with this he proceeded on his journey. The father-in-law was rather surprised at the contents of the letter and asked the merchant's son if he knew what it was about; he protested complete ignorance: the farmer had told him nothing, and as he was only a poor cowherd, of course he could not read. This set suspicion at rest; the wedding was at once arranged and duly took place, and the merchant's son settled down to live with his wife's family.

After a time the farmer got news of what had happened, and when he saw how the merchant's son had always been sharp enough to get the better of him, he began to fear that in the end he would be made to cut off his finger; so he sought safety in flight. He ran away from his house and home and was never heard of more. .

When news of this came to the ears of the merchant's son, he set out to visit his old friend the Prince and found him still teaching in the little village school. "What do you think now," he asked him, "is wisdom or money the better. By my cleverness, I got the better of that farmer; he had to give me more rice than I could eat, I killed his bullock, I set fire to his house, and I got a wife without expending a pice on my marriage; while you–you have spent all the money you brought with you from home, and have met with nothing but starvation and trouble; what good has your money done you?" The Prince had not a word to answer.

Two or three days later the Prinpe proposed that they should go back to their parents; his friend agreed but said that he must first inform his wife's relations, so they went back to the village where the merchant's son had married, and while they were staying there the Prince caught sight of a Raja's daughter and fell violently in love with her.

Learning of the Prince's state of mind the merchant's son undertook to arrange the match; so he sent his wife to the Raja's daughter with orders to talk of nothing, but the virtues and graces of the Prince who was staying at their house. Her words had their due effect and the Raja"s daughter became so well disposed towards the Prince, that when one day she met him, she also fell violently in love with him and felt that she could not be happy unless she became his wife. So the wedding duly took place, and then the Prince and the merchant's son with their respective wives returned to their fathers' houses.

LXXXVII. THE GOALA AND THE COW

Once upon a time a young man of the Goala caste was going to his wedding; he was riding along in a palki, with all his friends, to the bride's house and as he was passing by a pool of water he heard a voice saying, "Stop you happy bridegroom; you are happy, going to fetch your bride ; spare a thought for my misfortune and stay and pull me out of this quagmire." Looking out he saw a cow stuck fast in the mud at the edge of the pool, but he had no pity for it and harshly refused to go to its help, for fear lest he should make his clothes muddy.

Then the cow cursed the Goala, saying, "Because you have refused to help me in my extremity, this curse shall light on you, directly you touch your bride you shall turn into a donkey." At these words the Goala was filled with fear and telling the bearers to put down the palki he alighted and ran and pulled the cow out of the mud; this done, he begged her to withdraw the curse, but the cow declared that this was impossible, what she had said was bound to come to pass. At these words the Goala began to lament and threw himself at the feet of the cow, beseeching her; at length the cow relented, and promised that though the curse could not be withdrawn it should be mitigated and it would be possible for his wife to restore him to human shape. So the Goala had to take what comfort he could from this and returning to the palki he told his friends what had passed. Much downcast the procession continued its way, wondering what would be the upshot of this adventure.

Arrived at the bride's house, they proceeded to celebrate the wedding; but as the Goala touched the bride with his finger to apply the vermilion mark to her forehead, he suddenly became a donkey. The company were filled with dismay and the bride's parents declared that they would never let their daughter go away with such a husband, but the bride herself spoke up and said that as Thakur for some reason had given her such a husband she would cleave to him, and nothing that her relations said could shake her purpose; so when the bridal party set out homewards, she went with them to her husband's house. But there everyone laughed at her so much for having married a donkey that she made up her mind to run away to another country; so one day she packed up some provisions for the journey and set out, driving the donkey before her.

She journeyed on and on till one day she happened to come to a tank with a large well near it; she turned the donkey loose to graze on the banks of the tank and sat down by the well to eat some of the food which she had with her. In the fields below the tank were some twenty ploughmen in the service of the Raja of that country, driving their ploughs; and when it got past noon these men began to grumble, because no one had brought them their dinner; as it got later and, later they became more and more violent, and vowed that when anyone did come they would give him a good beating for his laziness. At last one of the maid-servants of the Raja was seen coming along, carrying their food in a basket on her head and with her child running by her side. The sight pacified the ploughmen and the maidservant hastened to set down the basket near them and then went off to the well to draw some water for them.

Just as she was ready to let down the water-pot, a wedding procession passed along the road with drums and music, making a fine show. The maid could not keep her eyes off this, but at the same time did not wish to keep the ploughmen waiting any longer; so, with her eyes on the procession, she tied the well-rope, as she thought round the neck of the water-pot, but really, without knowing it, she tied the rope round the neck of her own little child and proceeded to lower him into the well. When she pulled up the rope she found that she had strangled her own child.

She was of course much distressed at this, but she was even more afraid of what might be done to her and at once hit on a device to save herself from the charge of murder. Taking the dead child in her arms she ran to the ploughmen and scattered all the food she had brought about the ground; then with the child still in her arms, she ran to the Raja and complained to him that his ploughmen had assaulted her, because she was late in taking them their dinner, had knocked the basket of food all about the ground and had beaten her child to death; she added that a strange woman was grazing a donkey near the place and must have seen all that passed.

The Raja at once sent a sipahi to fetch the ploughmen and when they came before him he asked them what had happened, and bade them swear before *Sing bonga* whether they were guilty of the murder. The ploughmen solemnly swore to speak the truth, and then told the Raja exactly what had happened, how the woman had killed her child by mistake and then falsely charged them with the murder. Then the Raja asked them whether they had any witnesses, and they said that there was no one of their own village present at the time, but that a strange woman was grazing an ass on the banks of the tank, who must have seen all that happened. Then the Raja sent two sipahis to fetch the woman, telling them to treat her well and bring her along gently. So the sipahis went to the woman and told her that the Raja wanted her on very important business; she made no demur and went to fetch her donkey. The sipahis advised her to leave it behind to graze, but she said that wherever she went the donkey must go and drove it along with her.

When she appeared before the Raja he explained to her what had happened, and how the maid-servant told one story about the death of the child and the plough men another, and he charged her to speak the truth as to what she had seen. The Goala's bride answered that she was ready to take an oath and to swear by her donkey: if she spoke the truth the donkey would turn into a man, and if she lied it would retain its shape. "If you take that oath," said the Raja, "the case shall be decided accordingly." Then the Goala's wife began to tell all that she had seen and how the ploughmen were angry because their dinner was late, and how the maid-servant had gone to the well to draw water and had strangled her child by mistake and had then knocked over the basket and charged the ploughmen with the murder. "If I have lied may Chando punish me and if I have spoken the truth may this ass become a man;" so saying she laid her hand on the back of the animal and it at once resumed its human shape.

This was sufficient to convince the Raja, who turned to the maid-servant and reproached her with trying to ruin the ploughmen by her false charge. She had no answer to make but took up the dead body of the child and went out without a word.

Thus the Goala was restored to his original shape, but he and his faithful wife did not return to their own relations; they took service with a farmer of that country and after a time they saved money and took some land and lived prosperously and well. From that time men of the Goala caste have always been very careful to treat cattle well.

LXXXVIII. THE TELLTALE WIFE

Once upon a time a man was setting out in his best clothes to attend a village meeting. As he was passing at the back of the house his maid-servant happened to throw a basket of cow-dung on the manure heap and some of it accidentally splashed his clothes. He thought that he would be laughed at if he went to the meeting in dirty clothes so he went back to change them; and he put the dirty cloth he took off in an earthen pot and covered the mouth with leaves and hung it to the roof of the room in which he and his wife slept.

Two or three days later his wife began to question him as to what was in the pot hanging from the roof. At first he refused to tell her; but every time she set eyes on it she renewed her questioning; for a time he refused to gratify her curiosity, saying that no woman could keep a secret, but she protested that she would tell no one ; her husband's secrets were her own; at last he pretended that his patience was worn out and having made her promise never to tell a soul, he said "I have killed a man, and to prevent the murder being traced I cut off his head and hid it in that pot; mind you do not say a word or my life will be forfeit."

For a time nothing more was said, but one day husband and wife had a quarrel; high words and blows passed between them and at last the woman ran out of the house, crying: "You have struck me, I shall let it be known that you are a murderer." She went to the village headman and told him what was hidden in the pot; the villagers assembled and bound the supposed murderer with ropes and took him to the police. The police officer came and took down the pot and found in it nothing but a stained cloth. So he fined the readman for troubling him with false information and went away. Then the man addressed his fellow villagers in these words " Listen to me: never tell a secret to a woman and be careful in your conversation with them; they are sure to let out a secret and one day will turn your accusers."

From that time we have learnt the lesson that anything which you tell to a woman will become known.

LXXXIX. THE BRIDEGROOM WHO SPOKE IN RIDDLES

Once upon a time there were two brothers; the elder was named Bhagrai and was married, but the younger, named Kora, was still a bachelor. One day Bhagrai's wife asked her husband when he intended to look out for a wife for Kora, for people would think it very mean of them if they did not provide for his marriage. But to his wife's astonishment Bhagrai flatly refused to have anything to do with the matter. He said that Kora must find a wife for himself. His wife potested that that was impossible as Kora had no money of his own, but Bhagrai would not listen to her and refused even to give Kora his share in the family property.

Bhagrai's cruel conduct was very distressing to his wife; and one day as she was sitting picking the lice out of Kora's head, she began to cry and Kora felt her tears dropping on to his back; he turned round and asked his sister-in-law why she was crying. She said that she could not tell him, as it would only make him unhappy, but he would not be put off and said that she had no right to have any secrets from him and at last she told him that Bhagrai had said that he must arrange his own marriage without any help from them. At this cruel news Kora began to cry too and falling on his sister-in-law's neck he wept bitterly. Then he went and fetched his clothes and bow and arrows and flute and what other little property he had, and told his sister-in-law that he must go out into the world and seek his fortune, for he would never get a wife by staying at home. So she tied up some dried rice for him to eat by the way and let him go.

Kora set out and had not travelled far, before he fell in with an old man who was travelling in the same direction as himself and they agreed to continue their way together. After walking some miles, Kora said, "I have a proposal to make: let us take it in turns to carry each other: then we shall neither of us get tired and shall do the journey comfortably." The old man refused to have anything to do with such an extraordinary arrangement: so on they went and by and bye came to a tank which seemed a good place to rest and eat some food by. The old man sat down at the steps leading down to the water, but Kora went and sat on the bank where it was covered with rough grass. Presently he called out, "Friend, I do not like the look of this tank: to whom does it belong?" The old man told him the name of the owner, "Then why has he put no post in the middle of it?" This question amazed his companion for there was the usual post sticking up in the middle of the tank in front of them: he began to think that he had fallen in with a lunatic: however he said nothing and they went on together: and presently they passed a large herd of cow-buffaloes: looking at them Kora said "Whose are these: why have. they no horns? But they have got horns: what on earth do you mean by saying that they have not? " replied his companion, Kora however persisted "No, there is not a horn among them." The old man began to lose his temper but they went on and presently passed by a herd of cows, most of them with bells tied round their necks. No sooner did Kora catch sight of them than he began again "Whose can these cows be? Why have they not got bells on?" "Look at the bells," said the old man " cannot you use your eyes? "No," said Kora, "I cannot see a bell among them." The old man did not think it worth while to argue with him and at evening they reached the village where he lived: and Kora asked to be allowed to stay with him for the night.

So they went to his house and sat down on a string bed in the cow-shed while the women folk brought them out water to wash their feet. After sitting awhile, Kora suddenly said "Father, why did you not put up a king post when you were making this cow-shed?" Now at that very moment he was leaning against the king post and the old man was too puzzled and angry at his idiotic question to say anything: So, he got up and went into the house to tell his wife to put some extra rice into the pot for their visitor. His wife and. daughter at once began asking him who their guest was: he said that he knew nothing about him except that he was an absolute idiot. "What is the matter with him," asked the daughter: "he looks quite sensible" : then her father began to tell her all the extraordinary things that Kora had said: how he had proposed that they should carry each other in turn: and had declared that there was no post in the middle of the tank: and that the buffaloes had no horns and the cows no bells: and that there was no king post to the cow house. His daughter listened attentively and then said "I think it is you, father, who have been stupid and not our guest: I understand quite well what he meant. I suppose that when he proposed that you should carry each other, you had not been doing much talking as you went along?" "That is so," said her father,"we had not spoken for a long time:" "Then all he meant was that you should chat as you went along and so make the way seem shorter: and as to the tank, were there any trees on its banks?" "No, they were quite bare." "Then that is what he meant when he talked about the post: he meant that the tank should have had trees planted round it: and as to the buffaloes and cows, there was doubtless no but with either herd." "I certainly did not notice one," said her father. "Then that is what he was talking about: I think that it was very stupid of you not to understand him." Then what does he mean by the king post in the cow house" asked the old man. "he meant that there was no cross beam from wall to wall." "Then you don't think him a fool at all?" "No, he seems to me very sensible." "Then perhaps you would like to have him for your husband?" "That is for you and my mother to decide."

So the old man went off to his wife and asked her what she thought about the match and they both agreed that it would be very suitable: the girl understood Kora's riddles so well that they seemed made for each other. So the next morning when Kora proposed to start off on his journey again, the old man asked whether he would care to stay with them and marry his daughter. Kora was delighted to find a wife so soon, and readily agreed to work for five years in his father-in-law's house to win his bride: so a day was fixed for the betrothal ceremony, and thus Kora succeeded in arranging his own marriage.

XC. THE LAZY MAN

Once upon a time three brothers lived together: the youngest of them was named Kora and he was the laziest man alive: he was never willing to do any work but at meal times he was always first on the spot. His laziness began to drag the family down in the world, for they could not afford to feed a man who did no work. His two elder brothers were always scolding him but he would not mend his ways: however the scolding annoyed him and one day he ran away. from home.

He had become so poor that he had nothing on but a loin cloth: it was the middle of winter and when the evening drew on he began to shiver with cold: so he was very glad when he came to a village to see a group of herdboys sitting round a fire in the village street, roasting field rats. He went up to them and sat down by the fire to warm himself. The herd boys gave him some of the rats to eat and when they had finished their feast went off to their homes to sleep. It was nice and warm by the fire and Kora was too lazy to go round the village looking for some one who would take him in for the night: so he made up his mind to go to sleep by the fire. He curled himself up beside it and was about to take off his waist cloth to spread over himself as a sheet when he found a bit of thread which he had tied up in one of the corners of the cloth."Why!" thought he "cloth is made of thread: so this thread must be cloth! I will use it as a sheet." So he tied one end of the thread round his big toe and wound the other end round his ear and stretching himself out at full length soon fell asleep.

During the night the fire died down and a village dog which was on the prowl came and coiled itself up on the warm ashes and also went to sleep alongside Kora.

Now the headman of that village was a well-to-do man with much land under cultivation and a number of servants, and as it was the time where the paddy was being threshed he got up very early in the morning to start the work betimes. As he walked up the village street he came on the man and dog lying fast asleep side by side. he roused up Kora and asked him who he was and whether he did not find it very cold, lying out in the open. 'No" answered Kori I don't find it cold: this is my dog and he has eaten up all my cold: he will eat up the cold of a lakh of people." The headman at once thought that a dog that could do this would be a very useful animal to possess: he had to spend a lot of money in providing clothes for his farm labourers and yet they all suffered from the cold, while if he could get hold of the dog he and all his household would be permanently warm: so he asked. Kora what price he set on the dog. Kora said that he would sell it for fifty lakhs of rupees and no less: he would not bargain about the matter: the headman might take it or leave it as he liked. The headman agreed to the terms and taking Kora to his house paid him over the money. Kora made no delay in setting off homewards and when he arrived the first thing he did was to tell his brothers to find him a wife as he had now enough money to pay all the expenses of his marriage. When his brothers found that the lazy one of the family had come home with such a fortune they gave him a very different reception from what they used to before, and set to work to arrange his marriage and the three brothers all lived happily ever after.

Meanwhile the headman who had bought the dog sent for his labourers and told them of his luck in finding such a valuable animal. He bade them tie it up at the door of the hut on the threshing floor in which they slept: and in the morning to lead it round with them as they drove the oxen that trod out the grain, and then they would none of them feel cold. That night the labourers put the matter to the test but although the dog was tied up by the door the men in the hut shivered all night long as usual. Then in the morning they one after the other tried leading the dog as they drove the oxen round the threshing floor but it did not make them any warmer, so they soon got tired and tied the dog up again. Presently their master came along and asked what they had done with the dog and was told that the animal would not eat up the cold at all. The headman would not believe that he had been duped and began to lead the dog round to try for himself. Only too soon he had to admit that it made no diffence. So, in a race he caught up a stick and beat the poor dog to death. Thus he lost his money and got well laughed at by all the village for his folly.

XCI. ANOTHER LAZY MAN

Once upon a time there was a man named Kora who was so lazy that his brothers turned him out of the house and he had to go out into the world to seek his fortune. At first he tried to get some other young man of the village to keep him company on his travels but they all refused to have anything to do with such a lazy fellow, so he had to set out alone. However, he was resolved to have a companion of some sort, so when he came to a place where a crab has been burrowing he set to work and dug it out of the ground and took it along with him, tied up in his cloth.

He travelled on for days and weeks until he came to a country which was being devastated by a Rakhas who preyed on human beings, and the Raja of the country had proclaimed that any one who could kill the Rakhas should have one of his sisters in marriage and a large grant of land. Kora however knew nothing of all this and that evening he camped for the night under a tree on the outskirts of a village. Presently the villagers came out and begged him to come and spend the night in one of their houses, as it was impossible for a man to sleep safely in the open by himself. "Do not trouble about me," said Kora, " I am not alone: I have a companion and we two shall be quite safe together." The villagers saw no one with him and could not understand what he was talking about, but as he would not listen to them they had to leave him to his fate.

Night came on and as usual Kora untied the crab from his cloth and soon fell asleep. About midnight the Rakhas came prowling along and seeing Kora sleeping alone made towards him. But the crab rushed at the Rakhas and climbing up his body seized his neck with its claws and slit the windpipe. Down fell the Rakhas and lay kicking on the ground. The noise awoke Kora, who seized a big stone and dashed out the brains of the Rakhas. He then cut off the tips of the ears and tongue and claws and wrapped them up in his cloth and lay down to sleep again with the crab in his bosom.

At dawn the chowkidar of the village, who was a Dome, came on his rounds and found the Rakhas lying dead. He thought that it would be easy for him to obtain the credit of having killed it: so he cut off one of the legs and hurrying home told his wife and children to clear out of the house at once : he had nothing more to do with them, as he was going to marry the Raja's sister and become a great landowner. Then he rushed out into the village, shouting out that he had killed the Rakhas. The villagers all went to see the dead body and found it lying near the tree under which they had left Kora to spend the night. They were not quite convinced that the Dome's story was true and asked Kora who had really killed the Rakhas. He declined to answer but asked that he and the Dome might both be taken to the Raja, and then proof would be forth coming as to who was really entitled to the reward.

So the villagers took up the dead body and carried it off to the Raja, taking Kora and the Dome with them. The Raja asked what proof there was as to who had killed the Rakhas: and first the Dome produced the leg which he had cut off; but Kora unrolled his cloth and showed the ears and tongue and claws of the Rakhas. It was at once seen that the leg which the Dome had brought wanted the claws, so his fraud was clearly proved and he was driven from the assembly with derision and had to go and humbly make his peace with the wife whom he had turned out of his house. But the nuptials of Kora and the Raja's sister took place at once and they were given a fine palace to live in and a large tract of country for their own.

Kora never allowed himself to be separated from his faithful crab and this led to his life being saved a second time. A few nights after he was married, Kora was lying asleep with the crab upon his breast, when two snakes began to issue from the nostrils of his bride: their purpose was to kill Kora but when they saw the watchful crab they drew in their heads again. A few minutes later they again looked out: then the crab went and hid under the chin of the Princess and when the snakes put out their heads far enough it seized both of them with its claws: the snakes wriggled and struggled until they came entirely out of the nose of the princess and were dragged to the floor where the crab strangled them. In the morning Kora awoke and saw what the crab had done: he asked what he could do to show his gratitude to his faithful friend, and the crab asked to be set free in some pond which never dried up and that Kora would rescue it if any one ever succeeded in catching it. So Kora chose a tank and set the crab free and every day he used to go and bathe in that tank and the crab used to come and meet him.

After living in luxury for a time Kora went with a grand procession of horses and elephants to visit his industrious brothers who had turned him out of their home for laziness, and he showed them that he had chosen the better part, for they would never be able to keep horses and elephants for all their industry: so he invited them to come and live with him on his estate and when they had reaped that year's crops they went with him.

XCII. THE WIDOW'S SON

Once upon a time there was a poor woman whose husband died suddenly from snake bite, leaving her with one little girl. At the time she was expecting another child and every day she lamented the loss of her husband and prayed to Chando that the child she should bear might be a son: but fresh troubles came upon her, for when her husband's brothers saw that she was with child they declared that she had been unfaithful to her husband and had murdered him to conceal her shame: and although they had no proof of this, they seized on all their dead brother's property and land and left the widow nothing but the bare house to live in.

But Chando had pity on her and when her time was full a boy was born to her. She gave thanks to Chando and devoted herself to bringing up the child. The boy grew up and learned to walk and talk and one day he asked his mother where his father was. She told him that a snake had bitten his father before he was born. There upon the boy embraced her and told her not to cry as he would support her and take the place of his father. The mother was filled with wonder and gratitude at the boy's intelligence.

In answer to her daily prayers she met with kindness at all hands: when she went not working her employers gave her extra wages: when she went gleaning something extra was left for her, and if she had to beg no one refused to give her alms, so in time she was able to get together some household requisites and start keeping fowls and pigs. By selling these she saved enough money to buy goats and sheep: and in course of time was able to think of buying a cow.

By that time her son—whom she called Bhagraihad grown up to be a boy and took an interest in all that went on : so he asked his mother how he could tell when to buy a heifer. She said that if when the seller was showing a cow to an intending purchaser the animal dropped dung, it should be bought without hesitation, as such a cow was sure to take kindly to its new home and to have plenty of calves; another equally good sign was if the cow had nine teeth. Thereupon Bhagrai declared that he would set out to buy a cow and be guided in his choice by these signs and not come back till he found one. His mother thought that he was too young to undertake such a business but at last yielded to his entreaties. Then he tried to get some one in the village to go with him to his expedition but no one of his own friends of relations would go, so he had to arrange with a man of the blacksmith caste to keep him company.

Early one morning they set out, enquiring as they went along whether any one had a cow for sale. For a long time they were unsuccessful but after passing right through the territories of one Raja, they at length came to a village where they heard of a heifer for sale. As they were examining it, it dropped dung, and on inspection its mouth showed nine teeth. Bhagari at once declard that he must buy it and would not lisen to the blacksmith who tried to dissuade him because, although the animal was full grown, it had no calf and was probably barren. Bhagrai however preferred to be guided by the signs of which his mother had told him, and after a certain amouint of haggling bought the animal for five rupees. The money was paid and he and the blacksmith set off homewards with the cow.

Night overtook them and they turned into a village and asked to be allowed to sleep in the verandah of one of the houses: and permission being given they tied the cow to a post and went to sleep. In the middle of the night the owner of the house came and took away their cow and tied an old and worthless one of his own in its place. On waking in the morning Bhagrai and the blacksmith saw at once what had happened and charged the owner of the house with the theft. He vehemently denied all knowledge of the matter and after they had quarreled for a long time went to call the villagers to arbitrate between them. But he took care to promise the headman and leading villagers a bribe of five rupees if they decided the case in his favour: so the result was a foregone conclusion and the arbitrators told Bhagrai to take away the old worthless cow.

He however refused to accept the decision and said that he would go and find two people to represent him on the panchayat. The villagers raised no objection for they knew that he was a stranger, and thought that they could easily convince any persons he might pick up. Bhagrai set off towards a village he saw in the distance but lost his way in the jungle, and as he was wandering about he came on two jackals. On seeing him they started to run but he called to them to stop and telling them all that had happened asked them to come to the panchayat. The jackals answered that it was clear that the villagers had been bribed, but they would come and do what was possible. They told him to bring the villagers with both the cows to a big banyan tree outside the village. All the villagers went out to meet the jackals and Bhagrai stood up in the midst and began to explain his grievance.

Meanwhile the jackals sat quite still, seeming to take no interest in what was going on. "A fine pair these are to have on a panchayat" said the villagers to each other, "they are nearly asleep: they have been up all night catching crabs and grasshoppers and now are too tired to keep awake." "No," said one jackal, "we are not as sleepy as you think we are quite willing to take a part in deciding this dispute; but the fact is that I and my wife have a quarrel and we want yiou first to decide that for us and then we will take up the question of the cow, if you villagers can settle our differnce satisfactorily we shall be able to conclude that you have given a fair judgement on the complaint of this orphan boy."

The villagers told him to continue and he explained "I and my wife always go about together: we eat at the same time and drink at the same time and yet she drops dung twice a day while I do so only once: what is the reason of this?" The villagers could think of no answer and the jackal bade them ask his wife: so they laughed and asked whether it was true that she dropped dung twice to the he-jackal's once. But the jackal reproved them for their levity, wise men of old had said that it was wrong to jest when men of weight met to decide a dispute; so they became serious and the she-jackal answered "it is true that I drop dung twice to his once: there is an order laid on me to do so: I drop dung once at the same time that he does: that excrement falls to the ground and stays there: but the second time the excrement falls into the mouths of the ancestors of those men who take bribes and do injustice to the widow and orphan and when such bribetakers reach the next world they will also have to eat it. If however they confess their sin and ask pardon of me they will be let off the punishment: this is the reason why I have been ordered to drop dung twice." "Now you have heard what she has to say" put in the he-jackal "what do you think of the explanation? I hope that there are no such bribetakers among you: if there are they had better confess at once."

Then all the villagers who had agreed to take a share of the bribe and had helped to rob the boy of his cow confessed what they had done and declared that the boy should have his cow again, and they fined the thief five rupees. So Bhagrai and the blacksmith went gladly on their way and the blacksmith soon told his neighbours of the two wonderful jackals who talked like men and had compelled the villagers to restore the stolen cow. "Ah" said the boy's mother, they were not jackals, they were Chando." When Bhagrai's uncles heard all this and saw how he and his mother had prospered in spite of the loss of all their property, they became frightened and gave back the land and cattle which they had taken, without waiting for them to be claimed.

XCIII. THE BOY WHO WAS CHANGED INTO A DOG

Once upon a time there were seven brothers: the six eldest were married, but the youngest was only a youth and looked after the cattle. The six married brothers spent their life in hunting and used often to be away from home for one or two months at a time. Now all their six wives were witches and directly their husbands left home the six women used to climb a peepul tree and ride away on it, to eat men or do some other devilry. The youngest brother saw them disappear every day and made up his mind to find out what they did. So one morning he hid in a hollow in the trunk of the peepul tree and waited till his sisters-in-law came and climbed up into the branches: then the tree rose up and was carried through the air to the banks of a large river, where the women climbed down and disapeared. After a time they came back and climbed into the tree and rode on it back to the place where it came from. But as they descended they saw their brother-in-law hiding in the trunk and at first the tried to make him promise not to tell what he had seen, but he swore that he would let his brothers know all about it, so then they thought of killing him, but in the end the eldest said that this was not necessary and she fetched two iron nails and drove them into the soles of his feet whereupon he at once became a dog.

He could understand all that was said but of course could not speak, He followed them home and they treated him well and always gave him a regular helping at meals as if he were a human being and did not merely throw him the scraps as if he were a dog: nor would he have eaten them if they had.

A month afterwards the other brothers came home and asked if all had gone well in their absence. Their wives said that all was well except that the youngest brother had unfortunately disappeared without leaving any trace. While they were talking the dog came up and fawned on the brothers, so they asked where it had come from and the women said that it had followed them home on the day that they were looking for the missing boy: and they had kept it ever since. So matters rested: the brothers searched high and low but could not find the missing boy and so gave up the quest.

Now the Raja of that country had three daughters whom he had tried in vain to get married: whenever a bridegroom was proposed to them they declared that he was not to their liking and they would have nothing to do with him. At last their father said that as they would not let him choose husbands for them, they must make the choice themselves: he proposed to assemble all the men in his kingdom on a certain day and there and then they must take to themselves husbands.

So proclamation was made that all the men were to assemble outside the palace and that three of them would receive the Raja's daughters in marriage without having to pay any brideprice. On the fixed day a great crowd collected and among others went the six brothers: and, the dog followed them. Then the three princesses were brought out and three flies were caught: round one fly was tied a piece of white thread for the eldest princess and round the second fly a red thread for the second princess:and roun the last fly blue thread for the youngest princess. Then the three princess solemnly promised that each would marry the man on whom the fly marked with her colour settled and the flies were let loose. The red fly and the blue fly soon settled on two of the men sitting in the crowd but the white fly flew high in the air and circled round and at last settled on the dog which was sitting beside the six brothers.

At this the crowd laughed and jeered but the eldest princess said that she must accept what fate had decreed and that she would marry the dog. So the betrothal ceremony of the three princesses took place at once soon followed by their weddings. The husbands of the two youngest princesses took their brides home, but the eldest princess stayed in her father's house with her dog.

One day after its dinner the dog was lying on its side asleep and the princess chanced to see the heads of the iron nails in its feet: "Ah", thought she," that is why the poor dog limps." So she ran and fetched a pair of pincers and pulled out the nails: no sooner had she done so than the dog was restored to its human shape and the princess was delighted to find that not only was he a man but also very handsome: and they settled down to live happily together..

Some months later the six brothers resolved to go and visit the Raja, so that the princess might not feel that the dog she had married had no friends in the world. Off they set and when they reached the Raja's palace they were amazed to find their younger brother and still more so when they heard the story of all that had happened to him.

They immediately decided to take vengeance on their wives and when they reached home gave orders for a large well to be dug: when it was ready they told their wives to join in the consecration ceremony which was to ensure a pure and plentiful supply of water: so the six witches went to the well and while their attention was occupied, their husbands pushed them all into the well and filled it up with earth and that was the end of the witches.

XCIV. BIRLURI AND BIRBANTA

Birluri was of the Goala caste and Birbanta of the oilman's caste. And this is the story of their fight.

Birluri was very rich, with great herds of cattle and buffaloes but Birbanta's wealth consisted in tanks and ponds. Birluri used every day to water his cattle at Birbanta's ponds: and this made Birbanta very angry: he felt it an injustice that though Birluri was so rich he would not dig his own ponds: so he sent word that Birluri must stop watering his cattle or he would be killed. Birluri answered the messengers that he was quite ready to fight Birbanta: for though Birbanta had made the tanks, it was God who had made the water in them and so he considered that his cattle had a perfect right to drink the water. When Birbanta heard this he fell into a rage and vowed that he would not let the cattle drink, but would kill evrery living thing that went down to the water. From that day he let no one drink from his tanks: when women went to draw water he used to smash their water pots and put the rims round their necks like necklaces: all wild birds and animals he shot: and the cattle and buffaloes he cut down with his axe: and at last he proceeded to kill any human beings who went there.

When the Raja of the country heard this he was very angry and bade his *sipahis* search for some one strong enough to overcome and kill Birbanta: and he promised as a reward the hand of one of his daughters and half his kingdom. So the *sipahis* made proclamation all through the country and at last Birluri heard of it and volunteered to fight Birbanta. Then the Raja fixed a day for the fight, so that all the country might know and Birbanta also have due warning.

Both the combatants made ready for the fray: Birbanta was armed with a sword and a shield like a cart wheel and was skilful at sword play, while Birluri's weapon was the quarter-staff. The day arrived and Birluri girded up his loins and set out, twirling his staff round his head. Now his father and mother were both dead; but on the road his mother met him in the guise of an old woman, so that he did not recognise her. She greeted him and asked where he was going and when she heard that it was to fight Birbanta she said "My son, you are very strong: but if he asks for water do not give it him, for if you do, he will assuredly kill you: but when he throws away his sword, do you make haste and take it and slay him with it." So saying she went on her way and when Birluri came within a *kos* of the fighting place he began to twirl his staff and he made such a cloud of dust that it became dark as night and in the darkness the staff gleamed like lightning.

When Birbanta saw this he rose up and shouted "Here comes my enemy: I will fight my best and we will see who will conquer" and when he saw Birluri armed only with a quarter-staff he felt sure that he would not be overcome by such a weapon: so he grasped his sword and took his shield on his arm and went out to the fight. The fray was fast and furious: Birbanta hacked and hacked with his sword but Birluri caught all the blows on his quarterstaff and took no injury. At last the end of the staff was hacked off leaving a sharp point: then Birluri transfixed Birbanta with the pointed end and Birbanta faltered: again he thrust him through and Birbanta acknowledged himself defeated, saying "My life is yours: let me drink some water at your hands before you kill me." So Birluri agreed to a truce and they stopped fighting. Then Birluri cut down a palm tree and dipped it into Birbanta's tank and holding out the end to Birbanta told him to suck it. Birbanta refused to take it and asked him to give him water in his hands: but Birluri remembered his mother's warning and refused. Then Birbanta in despair threw away his sword and shield and Birluri snatched up the sword and smote off his head: and this is the song of victory which Birluri sang.—

"Birbanta stopped the *ghat* for the golden oxen—
The dust is raised up to heaven!
Birbanta sat by the *ghat* of the oxen—
The lighting is flashing in the sky!
He has made an embankment: he has made a tank:
But the water he collected in it, has become his enemy!"

Then Birluri was taken to the Raja and married to one of the Raja's daughters and given one half of the Raja's kingdom.

After a time Birluri told his wife that they must go back to his home to look after the large herds of cattle which he had left behind him. But his wife laughed at him and would not believe that he owned so much property: then Birluri said that if she would not go with him he would call the cattle to come to him: so he called them all by name and the great herd came running to the Raja's palace and filled the whole barn yard and as there was no room for them to stay there, they went away into the jungle and became wild cattle.

XCV. THE KILLING OF THE RAKHAS

Once upon a time a certain country was ravaged by a Rakhas to such an extent that there were only the Raja and a few ryots left. When things came to this pass, the Raja saw that something must be done: for he could not be left alone in the land. Ryots need a Raja and a Raja needs ryots: if he had no ryots where was he to get money for his support: and he repeated verse of the poet Kalidas:

"When the jungle is destroyed, the deer are in trouble,
without jungle:
When the Raja is destroyed, the ryots are in trouble
without their Raja:
When the good wife of the house is destroyed,
good fortune flees away."

So thinking the Raja made a proclamation throughout all the land that if any one could kill the Rakhas he would reward him with the hand of one of his daughters and half his kingdom. This proclamation was read out by the headman of a certain village to the assembled villagers and among the crowd was a mischievous youth, named Jhalka, who when he heard the proclamation called out that he could kill the Rakhas in ten minutes. The villagers turned on him "Why don't you go and do so: then you would marry the Raja's daughter and we should all bow down to you." At the thought of this Jhalka began to skip about crying "I will finish him off in no time." The headman heard him and took him at his word and wrote to the Raja that in his village there was a man who undertook to kill the Rakhas. When Jhalka heard this he hurried to the headman and explained that he had only been joking. "I can not treat such things as a joke" answered the headman: "Don't you know that this is a Raja's matter: to deal with Rajas is the same as to deal with *bongas*: You may make a promise to the *bongas* in jest, but they will not let you off it on that plea. You are much too fond of playing the fool."

Ten or twelve days later sipahis came from the Raja to fetch Jhalka: he told them that he had only spoken in jest and did not want to go to the Raja, but they took him away all the same.

Before he started he picked out a well-tempered battle axe and begged his father to propitiate the *bongas* and pray that he might be saved from the Rakhas. When he was produced before the Raja, Jhalka again tried to explain that there had been a mistake, but the Raja told him that he would be taken at his word and must go and kill the Rakhas. Then he saw that there was nothing left for him but to put his trust in God: so he asked that he might be given two mirrors and a large box and when these were brought he had the box taken to the foot of a large banyan tree which grew by a ford in the river which flowed by the hill in which the Rakhas lived: it was at this ford that the Rakhas used to lie in wait for prey.

Left alone there Jhalka put one of the mirrors into the box and then tightened his cloth and climbed the banyan tree with his battle axe and the other mirror. He was not at all happy as he waited for the Rahkas, thinking of all the people who had killed as they passed along the road below the tree: however he was determined to outwit the Rakhas if he could. All night long he watched in vain but just at dawn the Rakhas appeared. At the sight of him Jhalka shook so much with fright that the branches of the tree swayed. The Rakhas smelt that there was a human being about and holding up into the tree saw the branches waving. "Ha" said he, "here is my breakfast." Jhalka retorted "Ha! here is another Rakhas to match those I have got." "What are you talking about?" asked the Rakhas: "I am glad to have met you at last" returned Jhalka. "Why?" asked the Rakhas, "and what are you trembling for?" "I am trembling with rage: we shall now see whether I am to eat you or you are to eat me."

"Come down and try."

"No, you come up here and try."

Jhalka would not leave the tree and the Rakhas would not climb it: so they waited. At last the Rakhas asked "who are you? I have seen a thousands men like you" And Jhalka answered "Who are you ? I have seen a thousands like you," At his the Rakhas began to hesitate and wonder whether Jhalka was really his equal in strength, so he changed the subject and asked what the big box was. "That is the box into which I put Rakhases like you when I catch them; I have got plenty more at home." "How many are there in the box ?" "Two or three"

The Rakhas asked to see them, but Jhalka would not leave the tree until the Rakhas had sworn an oath to do him no harm; then he came down and opened the box and made the Rakhas look into the mirror insde the box; and he also held up the second mirror saying that there was another Rakhas. The Rakhas was fascinated at the sight of his own reflection; when he grinned or opened his mouth the reflection did the same; and while he was amusing himself with making different grimaces Jhalka suddenly cut him down with the battle axe, and he fell down dead. Then Jhalka cut off the ears and tongue and toes and hastened with them to the Raja. When it was found that the Rakhas was really dead the Raja assembled all his subjects and in their presence married Jhalka to his daughter and made over to him half the kingdom and gave him horses and elephants and half of everything in his palace.

XCVI. THE CHILDREN AND THE VULTURES

Once upon a time all the women of a village went to the jungle to gather *karla* fruit; and one of them was pregnant. In the jungle she felt that her time was come and she went aside without telling any of her friends and gave birth to twin boys. The other women went on gathering fruit and when they had filled their baskets and were on their way home they noticed that one of their number was missing, but as it was late they were afraid to go back and look for her, and besides they felt sure that she must have been devoured by some wild animal.

Meanwhile the mother of the twins began to call to her friends, but they were far out of hearing; so she debated whether she should carry home the two babes or her basket of *karla* fruit; she did not feel strong enough to carry both the infants in her arms and so she decided to take the basket of fruit, especially as she would probably have plenty more children, while the *karla* fruit could not be replaced. She covered the twins with leaves of the Asan tree and went home.

But when her husband heard what had happened he was very angry and scolded her well; she could easily have thrown away the fruit and carried home the children in the basket insead of taking so much trouble about the *karla* fruit, as if no one had ever seen any before. He wanted to take a few friends and go and look for the children at once; but his father and mother begged him not to risk his life in the jungle at night; the woman had been a fool but that could not be remedied; people must learn by experience; as the Hindu proverb says "When your caste goes, wisdom comes." They could not allow the breadwinner of the family to risk his life; though the roof and doors of the house had gone, the walls remained; as long as the tree stood new branches would grow; but if the tree fell there was no more hope; so in the end the children were left where they were.

No sooner had the mother gone than a pair of king vultures swooped down to make a meal of the children but they cried so pitifully that the vultures had not the heart to kill them but instead carried them up to their nest and brought them food: and nurtured them.

And when the children began to walk they carried them down to the ground and when they were big enough to take care of themselves they told them to go into the neighboring villages and beg; but they forbade them to go towards the village in which their real parents lived. So every day the two boys went out begging, and as they went from house to house, they sang :—

"Our mother took away the *karla* fruit
She covered us up with Asan leaves.
The pair of King vultures

Reared us.—Give us alms."

And people had pity on them and gave them enough to live on. One day the two boys thought that they would go and see what the country was like in the direction which had been forbidden to them; so they set out singing their usual song, and when they came to the house where their mother lived she heard them sing and knew that they must be her children; so she called them and bathed them and oiled their bodies and told them that she was their mother and they were very glad to stay with her.

But when the children did not return, the vultures flew in search of them and circled round and round in the air looking for them. The mother saw them and knew what they wanted, so she took the children into the house and hid them under a large basket. But the vultures flew down to the house and tore a hole in the thatch and entered through it and overturned the basket and seized the children. Then the father and mother also caught hold of them and the vultures pulled and the parents pulled until the children were torn in two and the vultures flew away with the portions they had secured. The father and mother sorrowfully burnt on a pyre the remains of the children that were left to them.

The vultures when they reached their nest were unwilling to eat the flesh of the children they had reared, so they set fire to their nest; but as the flames rose high, some juice spirted out from the burning flesh on to the vultures and they tasted it and found it so good that they pulled the rest of the flesh out of the flames and ate it, and from that time vultures feed on human bodies.

XCVII. THE FERRYMAN

There was once a ferryman who plied a ferry across a big river, and he had two wives. By the elder wife he had five sons and by the younger only one. When he grew old he gave up work himself and left his sons to manage the boats; but the step-brothers could not agree and were always quarrelling. So the father gave one boat to the son of the younger wife and told him to work it by himself at a separate crossing higher up the river, while the five other brothers plied to old ferry.

It turned out that most passengers used to cross at the youngest brother's ferry and as he had no one to share the profits with him, his earnings were very large. Because of this he used to jeer at his other brothers who were not so well off. This made them hate him more than ever, and they resolved to be revenged; so one day when he was alone in the boat they sat it adrift down the river without any oars.

As he drifted helplessly down the river he saw a river snake, as long as the river was broad, waiting for him with open mouth. He thought that his last hour had come, but he seized a knife which was in the boat and waited. When the stream brought him within reach, the snake swallowed him, boat and all, and swam to the bank. When he felt the snake climbing up the bank he began to cut his way out of its stomach with his knife, and soon made a wound which killed the snake and enabled him to make his way out and pull out the boat. Then he looked about him and saw a large village near by; so he went towards it to tell the villagers how he had killed the great snake. But when he reached it he found it deserted; he went from house to house but found no one. At last he came to a house in which there was one girl, who told him that she was the only inhabitant left, as the great river snake had eaten up all the other people. Then he told her how he had killed the snake and took her to see its dead body. The village was full of the wealth left by its former inhabitants; so he and the girl decided to stay there, and there were such riches that they lived like a Raja and Rani.

One morning his wife told him that she had had a dream, in which she was warned that he must on no account go out towards the south of the village; but he laughed at her, because he had up to that time moved about wherever he liked without any harm. She begged him to listen to her advice, because it was by her wisdom that she had saved her life when every one else in the village had been killed, so for a few days he obeyed her, but one morning he took a sword and went off towards the south. He had not gone far when he came to a cow, which had fallen into a pit, and it called to him. "Oh Brother, I have fallen into great trouble; help me out and one day I will do the same to you, if you ask my aid." So he took pity on the cow and pulled it out. Going on a little further he came to a buffalo which had stuck fast in a bog and it also called to him for help and promised to do the like for him in case of need. So he pulled it out of the mud and went on his way. Presently he came to a well and from the depths of the well a man who had fallen into it cried to him for help; so he went and pulled him up; but no sooner had the man reached the surface than he turned and pushed his rescuer down the well and ran away.

His wife waited and waited for his return and when he did not come, she divined that he had gone towards the south in spite of her warning. So she went to look for him and presently found him at the bottom of the well. So she let down a rope and pulled him up and gave him a scolding for his folly.

After this they thought it best to leave that country, so they embarked on the boat and travelled back to his father's house.

XCVIII. CATCHING A THIEF

There was once a rich Raja; and in order to frighten away thieves whenever he woke up at night he used to call out —

"What are you people saying? I know all about it:

You are digging the earth and throwing the earth away:
I know all about it: you are skulking there scraping a hole."

One night a gang of thieves really came and began to dig a hole through the mud wall of the Raja's house. And while they were at work the Raja woke up and called out as usual. The thieves thought that they were discovered and bolted. The next morning the hole they had been making was found, and the Raja ordered his sipahies to catch the thieves. The head of all the thieves was a Bhuyan by caste and for five rupees he would catch any thief you wanted. So the sipahies were told to bring this Bhuyan and they went to a potter and asked. "Ho, maker of pots, he who makes whole paddy into *China*: where does he live?" And the potter answered. "He who heats pewter; his house is over there." Following his direction they found the Bhuyan and he caught the thieves for them.

XCIX. THE GRASPING RAJA

There was once a Raja who was very rich. He was a stern man and overbearing and would brook no contradiction. Not one of his servants or his subjects dared to question his orders; if they did so they got nothing but abuse and blows. He was a grasping man too; if a cow or a goat strayed into his herds he would return the animal if its owner claimed in the same day; but he would not listen to any claim made later. He was so proud that he thought that there was no one in the world wiser than himself.

It happened that a certain man living in the kingdom of this Raja lost a cow; one evening it did not come back to its stall from the grazing-ground; so the next day he set out to search for it and questioned every one he met. He soon got news that a cow like his had been seen in the Raja's herd. So he went to look, and there, among the Raja's cattle, he saw his own cow. He asked the cowherd to let him take it away; but the cowherd refused to do so without a written order from the Raja.But the Raja would not listen and gave him only abuse and turned him out. Then he went to his friends and asked them to help him but they were afraid to do anything and advised him to regard the cow as lost for good.

So the unfortunate man took his way homeward very unhappily; on the way he sat down by the bank of a stream and began to bewail his loss. As he cried, Thakur took pity on him and sent a jackal to him. The jackal came and asked why he was crying, and when it had heard the story of the loss of the cow, it said "Cheer up! go back to the Raja and tell him that you want a panchayat to settle the matter about the cow; and that you intend to call one whether he agrees to abide by its decision or no. If he agrees, come back quickly to me and I will arrange to get back your cow for you." So off went the owner of the cow to the Raja and told him that he wanted to call a panchayat. The Raja made no objection and bade him call the neighbours together. The poor man did so and then hurried off to the jackal and told it how things had turned out. The jackal returned with him to the outskirts of the city and then sent him to the Raja to say that the panchayat must be held on the plain outside the city—for the jackal was afraid of the dogs in the city.

When the Raja received this message it made him very angry, however he went outside the city and met the panchayat and ordered them to get to business quickly. Then the owner of the cow stood up and told his story and the neighbours who had assembled called to him encouragingly, but the jackal sat in the background and pretended to be asleep. When the tale was finished, the Raja told the people who had assembled to give their decision, but they were all so afraid of the Raja that not one ventured to speak. As they kept silence the Raja turned to the owner of the cow. "Well, where are the people who are going to judge the case? No one here will say a word." "That is my judge," said the man pointing to the jackal. "Why it is fast asleep; what sort of a judge is that?" But just then the jackal shook itself and said. "I have had a most remarkable dream." "There, he has been dreaming, instead of listening to the case." exclaimed the Raja.

"O Raja'don't be so scornful" said the jackal, "I am a cleverer judge than you." "You, who are you? I have grown old in judging cases and finding out the truth; and you dare to talk to me like that!" "Well," retorted the jackal, "if you are so clever guess the meaning of my dream; and if you cannot give the man back his cow; if you can say what it means, I will acknowledge that you are fit to be a Raja. This is what I dreamt.—I saw three die in one place; One from sleepiness; one from anger and one from greed. Tell me what were the three and how did they come to be in one place."

This riddle puzzled every one, but the friends of the man who had lost his cow saw their opportunity and began to call out to the Raja to be quick and give the answer. The Raja made several guesses, but the jackal each time said that he was wrong, and asserted that the real answer would strike every one present as satisfactory. The Raja was completely puzzled and then suggested that there was no coherency in dreams: if the jackal had had some meaningless dream, no one could guess it. "No," said the jackal, "you just now laughed at the idea that any one should come to a panchayat and go to sleep; and what you said was true; I would not really go to sleep on an occasion like this; and I did not really dream. Now show that you are cleverer than I; if you can, you keep the cow."

The Raja thought and thought in vain, and at last asked to be told the answer to the puzzle. First the jackal made him write out a promise to restore the cow and to pay twenty-five rupees to the panchayat; and then it began:—"In a forest lived a wild elephant and every night it wandered about grazing and in the day it returned to its retreat in a certain hill. One dawn as it was on its way back after a night's, feeding, it felt so sleepy that it lay down where it was; and it happened that its body blocked the entrance to a hole in which was a poisonous snake. When the snake wanted to come out and found the way blocked, it got angry and in its rage bit the elephant and the elephant died then and there. Presently a jackal came prowling by and saw the elephant lying dead; it could not restrain itself from such a feast and choosing a place where the skin was soft began to tear at the flesh. Soon it made such a large hole that it got quite inside the elephant and still went on eating. But when the sun grew strong, the elephant's skin shrunk and closed the hole and the jackal could not get out again and died miserably inside the elephant. The snake too in its hole soon died from want of food and air. So the elephant met its death through sleepiness and the snake through anger and the jackal through greed. This is the answer to the puzzle, but Chando prevented your guessing it, because you unjustly took the poor man's cow and as a lesson to you that he is lord of all, of the poor and weak as well as of Rajas and Princes."

When the jackal concluded all present cried out that the answer was a perfect one; but the Raja said "I don't think much of that; I know a lot of stories like that myself." However he had to give back the cow and pay twenty-five rupees to the panchayat. In gratitude to the jackal the owner of the cow bought a goat and gave it to the jackal and then the jackal went away and was seen no more.

C. THE PRINCE WHO WOULD NOT MARRY

There was once a Raja who in spite of having many wives was childless; and his great desire was to have a son. He made many vows and performed every ceremony that was recommended to him, but in vain. At last a Jogi came to his kingdom and hearing of his case told him that if he would pray to Thakur and give away to the poor one-fourth of all his wealth, he should have a son.

The Raja followed the Jogi's advice, and in due time his youngest wife bore him a son so fair and so beautiful that there was no one on earth to match him. When the boy grew up, they began to think about his marriage and the Raja said that he would only marry him to a bride as fair and as beautiful as himself. It did not matter whether she were poor or rich, all that was needful was that she should be a match for his son in looks. So messengers were sent out to all the surrounding kingdoms to look for such a bride. They searched for years; nine years, ten years passed and still no bride was found to match in looks the Prince. After ten years had passed the Prince heard of this search and he went to his father and announced that he did not wish to marry; and that if he ever should wish to do so, he would find a wife for himself.

The Raja was very angry at this and said that the Prince wished to bring him to shame, every one would say that the Raja was too mean to arrange a marriage for his only son. But the Prince was obstinate and persisted that he did not wish the Raja to take any steps in the matter. At this the Raja grew more and more angry, until at last he ordered the Prince to be taken to prison and kept there, until he promised to marry any one whom his father chose.

Every day the warders asked whether he would yield and every day he refused; and it is impossible to say how long he would have languished in prison, had not the wife of the Parganna of the Bongas come one night to the prison with two other bongas. They began to talk about the Prince's hard case. The warders heard them talking, but could see no one. The Bonga Parganna's wife proposed that they should provide a *bonga* bride for the Prince, for it was certain that no human bride could be his match for beauty. The two bongas agreed that it was a good idea but the Prince had declared that he would not marry and that was a difficulty. "Let him see the bride I offer him and see what happens" answered the old *Bonga's* wife. So the next night when the Prince was asleep a beautiful bonga maiden was brought to the prison and when he awoke he saw her sitting by his side. He fell in love with her at first sight and exchanging rings with her promised that she should be his wife.

Then the warders, who had been watching, ran to the Raja and told him that the Prince had agreed to marry. The Raja came and took the Prince and his bride out of the prison, and the wedding was celebrated with great rejoicings throughout the kingdom.

CI. THE PRINCE WHO FOUND TWO WIVES

There was once a Raja who had an only son. When the Prince grew up the courtiers proposed to the Raja that he should arrange for his son's marriage; the Raja however wished to postpone it for it a time. So the courtiers used to laugh and say to the Prince "Wait a little and we will find you a couple of wives;" the young man would answer, "What is that? I can find them for myself. If you offered to find me ten or twelve wives there would be something in it." The Raja heard of his boasting like this and was very angry and said, "Well if he is so sure that he can find a wife for himself, let him do it;" and he took no further steps to arrange for his son's marriage.

Now the Prince had a most beautiful voice and used also to play on the one-stringed lute. He used often to sit up half the night singing and playing to himself. One night as he sat singing, he heard a laugh and looking round saw a beautiful *bonga* girl. He asked who she was and how she had come there, and she told him that she lived close by and could not help coming to see who it was, who was singing so beautifully. After that she used to visit the Prince every night, but always disappeared before dawn. This went on for some weeks and then the Prince asked her to stay and be his wife. She agreed, provided he would first go to her home and see her relations. So the next night he went with her; and found that her father was also a Raja and very rich. He stayed there three or four days; while his mysterious disappearance caused the greatest consternation at his own home. However he returned quietly by night and was found sleeping as usual in his bed one morning. Then he told his parents all that had happened and how he had left his wife behind at her father's house.

Two or three days later the Prince fell very ill: every sort of remedy was tried in vain. As he grew worse and worse, one day a messenger came from his father-in-law and offered to cure him if he were removed to his wife's house. So he was carried thither and when he arrived he found that his wife was also very ill; but directly he was brought to where she lay, at the mere sight of each other they both became well again.

After some months the Prince and his wife set out to return to their own home. They were benighted on the way; so they tied their horses to a tree and prepared to camp under it. The Prince went to a bazar to buy provisions and while there, was arrested on a false charge and was sent to prison. The Princess waited and waited and at last felt sure that something must have detained him against his will. She would not leave the spot, and to make it less likely that she should be molested, she dressed herself as a man.

Some days passed and the Prince did not return; then one morning an old woman passing by came and asked for a light for her hookah, and stayed talking for some time. The old woman was struck by the sweet face and gentle voice of the stranger, and on her return told the daughter of the Raja of that country that there was a strange young man, who looked and talked very differently from any of the young men of that neighborhood. The Raja's daughter was curious to see him, and the next morning she went with the old woman and talked with the disguised Princess. Before she left she was deeply in love with him, and directly she reached home she sent word to her father that she had seen the man whom she must marry. "It is of no use to thwart one's children," said the Raja and at once sent messengers to bring the stranger to marry his daughter.

When the disguised Princess was brought before the Raja, she said that she had no objection to being married provided that it was done according to the custom of her own country, and that was that the vermilion should be applied to the bride's forehead with a sword. The Raja made no objection; so the Princess took her husband's sword and put vermilion on it and then applied it to the bride's forehead; and so the marriage was complete. But when the Princess was left alone with her bride, she confessed that she was a woman and told her all her history and how her husband had disappeared in the bazar.

Then the Raja's daughter went to her father and told him what had happened and had enquiries made and speedily had the Prince released from prison. Then the prince himself again put vermilion on the forehead of the Raja's-daughter, and a few days later set off home with both his wives. This was the way in which he found two wives for himself, as he had boasted that he would.

CII. THE UNFAITHFUL WIFE

Once upon a time there were two brothers and as their wives did not get on well together, they lived separately. After a time it came to the ears of the elder brother that the younger brother's wife was carrying on an intrigue with a certain jugi; so he made up his mind to watch her movements. One night he saw a white figure leave his brother's house and, following it quietly, he saw it go into the Jugi's house, and creeping nearer, he heard his sister-in-law's voice talking inside. He was much grieved at what he had seen, but could not make up his mind to tell his brother.

One day the elder brother found that he had no milk in the house, as all his cows had run dry; so he sent a servant to his brother's house to ask for some milk; but the younger brother's wife declined to give any, and sent word that her brother-in-law was quite rich enough to buy milch cows if he wanted milk. The elder brother said nothing at this rebuff, but after a time it happened that the younger brother's cows all became dry, and he in his turn sent to his elder brother for milk. The elder brother's wife was not disposed to give it, but her husband bade her not bear malice and to send the milk.

After this the elder brother sent for the other and advised him to watch his wife and see where she went to at night. So that night the younger brother lay awake and watched; and in the middle of the night saw his wife get up very quietly and leave the house. He followed her; as the woman passed down the village street, some Mahommedans, who had been sitting up smoking ganja, saw her and emboldened by the drug set out to see who it was, who was wandering about so late at night. The woman took refuge in a clump of bamboos and pulled down one of the bamboos to conceal herself. The Mahommedans surrounded the clump but when they saw the one bamboo which the woman held shaking, while all the rest were still-for it was a windless night they concluded that it was an evil spirit that they were pursuing and ran away in a panic.

When they were gone, the woman came out from the bamboos and went on to the Jugi's house. Her husband who had been watching all that happened followed her: and having seen her enter the Jugi's house hastened home and bolted his door from inside. Presently his wife returned and found the door which she had left ajar, fastened; then she knew that she was discovered. She was however full of resource; she began to beg to be let her in, but her husband only showered abuse upon her and bade her go back to the friend she had left. Then she took a large stone and heaved it into a pool of water near the house.

Her husband heard the splash and concluded that she was drowning herself. He did not want to get into trouble with the police, as would surely be the case if his wife were found drowned, so he ran out of the house to the pool of water to try and save her. Seizing this opportunity his wife slipped into the house and in her turn locked the door from inside; so that her husband had to spend the rest of the night out-of-doors.

He could not be kept out of the house permanently and the next day he gave his wife a thrashing and turned her out. At evening however she came back and sat outside in the court-yard, weeping and wailing. The noise made her husband more angry than ever, and he shouted out to her that if she did not keep quiet he would come and cut off her nose. She kept on crying, and the Jugi heard her and sent an old woman to call her to him. She declared that if she went her husband would know and be the more angry with her, but she might go if the old woman would sit in her place and keep on crying, so that her husband might believe her to be still in the courtyard. The old woman agreed and began to weep and wail, while the other went off to the Jugi. She wept to such purpose that the husband at last could not restrain his anger, and rushing out into the darkness with a knife, cut off the nose, as he supposed of his wife.

Presently, the wife came back and found the old woman weeping in real earnest over the loss of her nose. "Never mind, I'll find it and fix it on for you," so saying she felt about for the nose till she found it, clapped it on to the old woman's face and told her to hold it tight and it would soon grow again. Then she sat down where she had sat before and began to lament the cruelty of her husband in bringing a false charge against her and challenged him to come out and see the miracle which had occurred to indicate her innocence. She repeated this so often that at last her husband began to wonder what she meant, and took a lamp and went out to see. When he found her sitting on the ground without a blemish on her face, although he had seen her with his own eyes go to the Jugi's house, he could not doubt her virtue and had to receive her back into the house.

Thus by her cunning the faithless wife escaped the punishment which she deserved.

CIII. THE INDUSTRIOUS BRIDE

Once upon a time a party of three or four men went to a village to see if a certain girl would make a suitable bride for the son of one of their friends; and while they were talking to her, another young woman came up. The visitors asked the first girl where her father was and she told them that he had gone to "meet water."

Then they asked where her mother was, and she said that she had gone "to make two men out of one." These answers puzzled the questioners, and they did not know what more to say; as they stood-silent the other girl got up and went away remarking, "While I have been waiting here, I might have carded a seer of cotton." The men who were looking for a girl who would make a good wife, at once concluded that they had found what they wanted: "How industrious she must be to talk like that" thought they "much better than this other girl who can only give us incomprehensible answers." And before they left the village they set everything in train for a match between their friend's son and the girl who seemed so industrious.

When they got home and told their wives what they had done they got well laughed at: their wives declared that it was quite easy to understand what the first girl had meant: of course she meant that her father had gone to reap thatching grass and her mother had gone to thresh *dal*. The poor men only gaped with astonishment at this explanation.

However the marriage they had arranged duly took place, but the fact was that the bride was entirely ignorant of how to clean and spin cotton. It was not long before this was found out, for, in the spring, when there was no work in the fields, her father-in-law set all the women of the household to spinning cotton; and told then that they and their husbands should have no new clothes until they had finished their task. The bride, who had been so carefully chosen, tried to learn how to spin by watching the others, but all in vain. The other women laughed at her efforts and she protested that it was the fault of the spinning wheel: it did not know her; her mother's spinning wheel knew her well and she could spin capitally with that. They jeered at the idea of a spinning wheel having eyes and being able to recognize its owner; however one day the young woman went and fetched her mother's spinning wheel and tried to spin with that. She got on no better than before, and could only explain it by saying that the spinning wheel had forgotten her.

Whatever the reason was, the other women all finished their spinning and received their new clothes, while she had nothing to show, Then her father-in-law scolded her and told her that it was too late to make other arrangements and as she could not get any new clothes the best thing for her to do would be to smear her body with *Gur* and stick raw cotton all over it. A *parrab* soon came round and all the other women got out their new clothes and went to see the fun. The clumsy bride had no new clothes and she took her father-in-law's advice and smeared her body with *gur* and covered herself with raw cotton and so went to the *parrab*.

Her husband was very angry that she should have taken her father-in-law's jest in earnest, and when she came home he gave her a good beating and turned her out of the house. And that was the end of the "industrious" bride.

CIV. THE BOY AND HIS FATE

There was once a Raja and Rani who had had three sons, but they had all died when only three or four months old. Then a fourth son was born, a fine handsome child and he did not die in infancy but grew up to boyhood. It was however fated that he should die when he was sixteen years old and his parents knew this and when they saw him coming happily home from his games of play, their eyes filled with tears at the thought of the fate that hung over him.

One day the boy asked his father and mother why it was that they were so sorrowful: and they told him how his three little brothers had died and how they feared that he had but little longer to live. On hearing this the boy proposed that he should be allowed to go away into a far country, as perhaps by this means he might avoid his fate. His father was glad to catch at the faintest hope and readily gave his consent: so they supplied him with money and mounted him on a horse, and off he set.

He travelled far and settled down in a place that pleased him. But in a short time the messengers of death came to the Raja's palace to take him away. When they did not find him, they followed in pursuit along the road which he had taken; they wore the likeness of men and soon traced out the Raja's son. They presented themselves to him and said that they had come to take him home again. The prince said that he was ready to go, but asked them to allow him to cook and eat his rice before starting. They told him that he might do this if he were quick about it: he promised to hurry, and set to his cooking: he put sufficient rice into the pot to feed them all and when it was ready he offered some to each of the messengers. They consulted together as to whether they should eat it, but their appetites got the better of their caution and they agreed to do so, and made a good meal. But directly they had finished they began to debate what they should do; they had eaten his rice and could no longer compass his death.

So they told him frankly that Chando had sent them to call him; he was to die that night and they were to take away his spirit; but they had made the mistake of eating at his hands and although they must take him away, they would give him advice as to how he might save his life: he was to take a thin piece of lamp-wick and when Chando questioned him, he was to put it up his nose and make himself sneeze. The prince promised to remember this, and that night they took his spirit away to Chando, but when Chando began to question him he made himself sneeze with the lamp-wick; thereupon Chando at once wrote that he should live for sixty years more and ordered the messengers to immediately restore his spirit to its body. Then the prince hastened back to his father and mother, and told them that he had broken through his fate and had a long life before him; and they had better make arrangements for his marriage at once. This they did and he lived to a ripe old age, as he had been promised.

CV. THE MESSENGERS OF DEATH

There was once a Brahman who had four sons born to him, but they all died young; a fifth son however was born to him, who grew up to boyhood. But it was fated that he too should die before reaching manhood. One day while his father was away from home, the messengers of death came to take him away. The Brahman's wife thought that they were three friends or relations of her husband, who had come to pay a visit, and gave them a hearty welcome. And when she asked who they were, they also told her that they were connections of her husband. Then she asked them to have some dinner and they said that they would eat, provided that she used no salt in the cooking. She promised not to do, but what she did was to scatter some salt over the bottom of the dish. Then she cooked the rice and turned it into the dish and gave it to them to eat. They ate but when they came to the bottom of the dish they tasted the salt which had been underneath. Then the three messengers said "She has got the better of us; we have eaten her salt and can no longer deceive her; we must tell her why we have come."

So they told her that her son was to die that night and that Chando had sent them to take away his spirit: all they could do was to let her come too, and see the place to which her son's spirit was going. The mother thought that this would be a consolation to her, so she went with them. When they arrived in the spirit world they told the Brahman's wife to wait for them by a certain house in which dwelt her son's wife; and they took the boy to Chando. Presently they brought him back to the house in which his wife dwelt and near which his mother was waiting and she over-heard the following conversation between the boy and his wife. The wife said "Have you come for good this time, or must you again go back to the world?"

"I have to go back once more."

"And how will you manage to return again here?"

"I shall ask for the dust of April and May and if it is not given to me I shall cry myself to death; and if that fails, I shall cry for a toy winnowing fan; and if they give me that, then I will cry for an elephant and if that fails then on my wedding day there will be two thorns in the rice they give me to eat and they will stick in my throat and kill me. And if that does not come to pass, then, when I return home after the wedding, a leopard will kill a cow and I shall run out to chase the leopard and I shall run after it till I run hither to you."

"When you come back," said his wife, "bring me some of the vermilion they use in the world" and the boy promised.

The messengers then took the Brahman's wife home, and shortly afterwards the boy was born again. His mother had carefully guarded the memory of all that she had heard in the other world; and when the child asked for the dust and the winnowing fan and the elephant, she at once gratified his desires. So the boy grew up, and his wedding day arrived. His mother insisted on accompanying him to the bride's house, and when the rice was brought for the bride and bridegroom to eat together, she asked to be allowed to look at it first, and on examining it pulled out the two thorns; and then her son ate it unharmed. But when the wedding party returned home and the ceremony of introducing the bride to the house was being performed, word was brought that a leopard had killed one of the cows; at once the bridegroom ran out in pursuit; but his mother followed him and called out, "My son, your wife told you to take her some of the vermilion of this world; here is some that I have brought, take it with you." At this her son stopped and asked her to explain what she meant; then she told him all and he went no more in pursuit of the leopard: so he stayed and grew up and lived to a good old age.

CVI. THE SPEAKING CRAB

There was once a farmer who kept a labourer and a field woman to do the work of the farm; and they were both very industrious and worked as if they were working on their own account and not for a master.

Once at the time of transplanting rice, they were so busy that they stayed in the fields all day and had their meals there and did not go home till the evening. During this time it happened that the man had unyoked his plough bullocks and taking his hoe began to dress the embankment of the field, and as he dug, he dug out a very large crab; so he plucked some leaves from the bushes and wrapped the crab in them and fetching the yoke rope from the plough, he tied the bundle up tightly with it and put it on the stump of a tree, intending to take it home in the evening; but when he went home he forgot about it.

Now the crab was alive and in the middle of the night it began to struggle to get out, but could not free itself. It happened that just then the farmer was walking in the field to see that no one came to steal his rice seedlings, and the crab began to sing:—

"This servant, this servant, father,
And this maidservant, this maidservant, father,
Caught me while digging the bank:

And in leaves, leaves, father,
With the yoke rope, yoke rope, father
Tied me and left me on the stump."

At this sound the farmer was very frightened, and puzzled also; for he thought, "If this were a human being crying, every one in the neighborhood would have heard and woke up, but it seems that I alone am able to hear the sound; who can it be who is talking about my servants ?" So he went back to bed and told no one. The next morning when the labourer looked for his yoke ropes, he missed one; and then he remembered that he had used it to tie up the crab; so he went to the place and found his rope. When his master brought them their breakfast that day and they had finished eating, the labourer began to tell how he had lost one of the yoke ropes and had found it again: and how he had used it for tying up the crab which he had found. The master asked whether the crab was alive or dead; and the labourer said that it was dead.

Then the master said "My man you have done a very foolish thing; why did you tie it up alive? Last night I could not sleep for its crying. Why did you imprison the innocent creature until it died?" And he told them the song it had sung, and forbade them ever to cause such pain to living creatures. He said "Kill them outright or you will bring disgrace on me; when I heard the lament I thought it was a man, but now I learn from you that it was a crab. I forbid you ever to do the like again." And at the time of the Sohrai festival the farmer called together all his household and sang them the song and explained its meaning to them, and the men who heard it remember it to this day.

CVII. THE LEOPARD OUTWITTED

There was once a man-eating leopard, whose depredations became so serious, that the whole neighboring population decided to have a great hunt and kill it. On the day fixed a great crowd of beaters collected, and their drums made a noise as if the world were being turned upside down.

When the leopard heard the shouting and the drumming, it started to escape to another jungle, and as it was crossing a road it came on a merchant driving a pack bullock. The merchant tried to run away, but the leopard stopped him and said "You must hide me or I will eat you." The merchant continued to run, thinking that if he helped the leopard it would surely eat him afterwards, but the leopard swore an oath not to eat him if he would only hide it. So the merchant stopped and took one of his sacks off the bullock and emptied it out and tied up the leopard in it, and put it on the bullock and then drove on.

When they got out of hearing of the hunters the leopard asked to be let out; but directly the sack was untied it said that it would devour the merchant. The merchant said "You can of course eat me, but let us consult an arbitrator as to whether it is fair." The leopard agreed and as they were near a stream, the man asked the water whether it was fair that he should be killed, after he had saved the leopard's life; the water answered "Yes; you men wash all manner of filthy things in me; let it eat you!" Then the leopard wanted to eat him, but the merchant asked leave to take two more opinions; so he asked a tree; but the tree said "Men cut me down; let the leopard eat you."

The merchant was very downcast to find everyone against him and the leopard said, "Well, whom will you consult next? You have so many friends;" so they went on and presently met a jackal and the merchant said that he would appeal to him. The jackal considered for some time and then said "I don't understand how you hid the leopard; let me see how it was done; and then I shall be able to decide." The merchant said "I hid him in this sack." "Really," said the jackal "show me exactly how you did it." So the leopard got into the sack to show how he was hidden; then the jackal asked to be shown how the leopard was carried out of danger; so the merchant tied up the sack and put it on the bullock. "Now," said the jackal, "drive on, and when we come to yonder ravine and I tell you to put the sack down, do you knock in the head of the leopard with a stone." And the merchant did so and when he had killed the leopard, he took it out of the sack and the jackal ate its body.

CVIII. THE WIND AND THE SUN

Once the Wind and the Sun disputed as to which was the more powerful. And while they were quarrelling a man came by wrapped in a shawl and wearing a big *pagri*. And they said "It is no good quarrelling; let us put our power to the test and see who can deprive this man of the shawl he has wrapped round him." Then the Wind asked to be allowed to try first and said "You will see that I will blow away the blanket in no time," and the Sun said, "All right, you go first." So the Wind began to blow hard; but the man only wrapped his shawl more tightly round him to prevent its being blown away and fastened it round himself with his *pagri*; and though the Wind blew fit to blow the man away, it could not snatch the shawl from him; so it gave up and the Sun had a try; he rose in the sky, and blazed with full force and soon the man began to drip with sweat; and he took off his shawl and hung it on the stick he carried over his shoulder and the Wind had to admit defeat.

CIX. THE COLDEST SEASON

Once winter day a bear and a tiger began to dispute as to which is the coldest season of the year; the bear said July and August, which is the rainy season, and the tiger said December and January, which is the winter season. They argued and argued but could not convince each other; for the bear with his long coat did not feel the cold of winter but when he got soaked through in the rain he felt chilly.

At last they saw a man coming that way and called on him to decide—"but have a care"—said the tiger—"if you give an opinion favorable to the bear, I will eat you;" and the bear said, "If you side with the tiger, I will eat you." At this the man was terror stricken but an idea struck him and he made the tiger and the bear promise not to eat him if he gave a fair decision and then he said "It is not the winter which is the coldest, nor the rainy season which is the coldest, but windy weather; if there is no wind no one feels the cold much either in the winter or in the rainy season." And the tiger and the bear said "You are right, we never thought of that" and they let him go.

PART II

To a people living in the jungles the wild animals are much more than animals are to us. To the man who makes clearing in the forest, life is largely a struggle against the beasts of prey and the animals who graze down the crops. It is but natural that he should credit them with feelings and intelligence similar to those of human beings, and that they should seem to him suitable characters around which to weave stories.

These storeis are likely to be particularly currrent among a people occupying a forest country, and for this reason are less likely to appear in collections made among the inhabitants of towns. It is a strange coincidence and presumably only a coincidence that Story 118, 'The Hyena outwitted' is known in a precisely similar form among the Kaffirs of South Africa.

CX. THE JACKAL AND THE CROW

Once upon a time a crow and a jackal became bosom friends and they agreed that the crow should support the jackal in the hot weather and the jackal support the crow in the rainy season. By-and-bye the jackal got discontented with the arrangement, and vowed that it would not go on supporting an animal of another species, but would take some opportunity of eating it up. But he did not let this appear, and one day he invited the crow to a feast and gave him as many frogs and grasshoppers as he could eat and treated him well and they parted very affectionately.

Then a few days later the crow invited the jackal to dinner in return; and when the jackal arrived the crow led him to an ant-hill and showed him a hollow gourd which he had filled with live mice and said "Here is your dinner" The jackal could not get his nose into the hole of the gourd so, to get at the mice. He had to break it. And the mice ran all over the plate and the jackal jumped about here and there trying to catch them. At this sight the crow stood and laughed; and the jackal said to himself "Very well, my friend, you invited me here to have a laugh at me; wait till I have finished with the mice; then it will be your turn."

So when he had caught all the mice he could, he declared that he had had as much as he could eat and would like to go and sleep off his meal. As they said farewell and were salaaming to each other, the jackal pounced on the crow and ate him up; not a bone or a claw was left. Then the jackal began to skip with joy and sang:—

"I ate a gourdful of mice
And by the side of the ant-hill
I ate the crow: Hurrah!"

And singing thus he went skipping homewards; and on the way he met a fowl and called to it to get out of the way or he would eat it,— singing:—

"I ate a gourdful of mice
And by the side of the ant-hill
I ate the crow:— Hurrah!"

And as the fowl did not move he ate it up; then he skipped on and came to a goat and he sang his verse and told it to get out of the way and as it did not, he ate it; and in the same way he met and killed a sheep and a cow and he ate the liver and lungs of the cow; and then he killed a buffalo and ate its liver and lungs; and by this time he was as full as he could hold. Then he came to a pool of water and he called to it to get out of the way or he would drink it up and as it did not move, he drank it dry. Then he came to a post and said "Get out of my way or I will jump over you"—

"I ate a gourdful of mice
And by the side of the anthill
I ate the crow - Hurrah!"

And so saying he tried to jump over it; but he was so full of what he had eaten and drunk that he leaped short and fell on the point of the stake and was, transfixed, so that he died.

CXI. THE TIGER CUB AND THE CALF.

A Tigress and a Cow used to graze in a dense jungle, and they were both with young. They became great friends and agreed that they would marry their children to each other. In the course of time the tigress gave birth to a she-cub and the cow to a bull-calf. They kept the young ones in the same place and used to go and graze together, and then return at the same time to suckle their young. On their way back they used to drink at a certain river, the tigress up the stream and the cow lower down. One day it happened that the cow got first to the river and drank at the upper drinking place, and the tigress drank lower down. And the froth from the cow's mouth-floated down the stream and the, tigress tasted it and found it nice, and this made her think that the flesh of the cow must also be good; so she resolved to eat the cow one day. The cow saw what was in the mind of the tigress and she left some of her milk in a bowl, and said to her calf: "The tigress has resolved to eat me; watch this milk and when you see it turn red like blood, you will know that I have been killed;" then she went off to graze with the tigress.

The two youngsters always used to play together very happily but that day the calf would not play but kept going to look at the bowl of milk; and the tigress cub asked the reason. The calf told her what his mother had said; then the tigress cub said that if this happened she would never suck from her mother again and it would be better for them both to run away. So the two kept going to look at the bowl of milk, and about midday they saw that it had changed to blood and they both began to weep. Shortly after, the tigress came back, and flies were clustered round her mouth because of the blood on it. The tigress told her daughter to come and suck, but, the said that she would wait the cow came and then she and the calf could have their meal together is usual; at this the tigress frowned terribly and the cub was frightened, so she said, "Very well, mother, I will suck, but first go and wash your mouth; why are the flies clustered round it?" So the tigress went off but she did not wash, she only ate some more of the cow. While she was away the calf and the cub ran off to another jungle, and when the tigress came back, she searched for them with horrid roarings and could not find them, and if she had found them she would have killed them.

CXII. THE JACKAL AND THE CHICKENS

Once upon a time a jackal and a hen were great friends and regarded each other as brother and sister; and they agreed to have a feast to celebrate their friendship; so they both brewed rice beer and they first drank at the jackal's house and then went to the hen's house; and there they drank so much that the hen got blind drunk, and while she lay intoxicated the jackal ate her up. The jackal found the flesh so nice that he made up his mind to eat the hen's chickens too; so the next day he went to their house and found them all crying "Cheep, cheep," and he asked what was the matter; they said that they had lost their mother; he told them to cheer up and asked where they slept; they told him 'on the shelf in the wall'.

Then he went away; but the chickens saw that he meant to come and eat them at night, so they did not go to sleep on the shelf but filled it with razors and knives and when the jackal came at night and felt about the shelf he got badly cut and ran away screaming.

But a few day later he paid another visit to the chickens, and condoled with them on the loss of their mother and again asked where they slept and they told him, 'in the fireplace.' Directly the jackal was gone, they filled the stove with live embers and covered them up with ashes; and went to sleep themselves inside a drum. At night the jackal came and put his paws into the fireplace; but he only scraped the hot embers up against his belly and got burnt; this made him scream and the chickens burst out laughing. The jackal heard them and said "You have got me burnt; now I am going to eat you." They said, "Yes, uncle, but please eat us outside the house; you did not eat our mother in her own house; take us to yonder flat rock."

So the jackal took up the drum but when he got to the rock he accidentally let it fall and it broke and the chickens ran away in all directions; but the chicken that had been at the bottom of the drum had got covered with the droppings of the others and could not fly away; so the jackal thought "Well it is the will of heaven that I should have only one chicken; it is doubtless for the best!" The chicken said to the jackal, "I see that you will eat me, but you cannot eat me in this state; wash me clean first."

So the jackal took the chicken to a pool and washed it; then the chicken asked to be allowed to get a little dry; but the jackal said that if it got dry it would fly away. "Then," said the chicken, "rub me dry with your snout and I will myself tell you when I am ready to be eaten;" so the jackal rubbed it dry and then proceeded to eat it; but directly the jackal got it in his mouth it voided there, so the jackal spat it out and it flew away.

The jackal thought that it had gone into a hole in a white ant-hill, but really it had hidden elsewhere; however the jackal felt for it in the hole and then tried in vain to scrape the hole larger; as he could not get into the hole he determined to sit and wait till hunger or suffocation forced the chicken to come out. So he sat and watched, and he sat so long that the white ants ate off his hind quarters; at last he gave up and went off to the rice fields to look for fish and crabs. There he saw an old woman catching fish, and he asked to be allowed to help her. So the old woman sat on the bank and the jackal jumped and twisted about in the water and presently he caught a *potha* fish which he ate; but as the jackal had no hind quarters the fish passed through him none the worse. Soon the jackal caught the same fish over again, and he laughed at the old woman because she had caught none. She told him that he was catching the same fish over and over again, and when he would not believe her she told him to mark with a thorn the next one which he caught; he did so and then found that he really was catching and eating the same fish over and over again.

At this he was much upset and asked what he should do. The old woman advised him to go to a cobbler and get patched up; so he went and killed a fowl and took it to a cobbler and offered it to him if he would put him to rights; so the cobbler sewed on a leather patch with a long leather tail which rapped on the ground as the jackal went along. Then the jackal went to a village to steal fowls and he danced along with his tail tapping, and sang:—

"Now the Moghul cavalry are coming
"And the Koenda Rajas.
"Run away or they will utterly destroy you."

And when the villagers heard this they all ran away and the jackal entered the village and killed as many fowls as he wanted.

A few days later he went again to the village and frightened away the villagers as before; but one old woman was too feeble to run away and she hid in a pig sty, and one fowl that the jackal chased, ran into this sty and the jackal followed it, and when he saw the old woman, he told her to catch the fowl for him or he would knock her teeth out; but she told him to catch it himself; so he caught and ate it. Then he said to the old woman. Say "Toyo" (jackal) and she said "Toyo;" then he took a curry pounder and knocked all her teeth out and told her again to say "Toyo ;" but as she had no teeth she said "Hoyo;" this amused the jackal immensely and he went away laughing.

When the villagers returned, the old woman told them that it was only a jackal who had attacked the village, so they decided to kill him; but one man said "You won't be able to catch him; let us make an image of this old woman and cover it with birdlime and set it up at the end of the village street; he will stop and abuse her, and we shall know where he is." So they did this, and the next morning, when the jackal came singing along the road, they hid inside their houses. When the jackal reached the village, he saw the figure of the old woman with its arms stretched out, and he said to it, "What are you blocking my road for? get out of the way; I knocked your teeth out yesterday: aren't you afraid? Get out of the way or I will kick you out."

As the figure did not move he gave it a kick and his leg was caught in the birdlime; then he said, "Let me go, you old hag, or I will give you a slap." Then he gave it a slap and his front paw was stuck fast; then he slapped at it with his other paw and that stuck; then he tried to bite the figure and his jaws got caught, also; and when he was thus helpless the villagers came out and beat him to death and that was the end of the jackal.

CXIII. THE JACKAL PUNISHED

Once a hen and a jackal were great friends and they decided to have a feast and each brewed beer for the occasion; the hen brewed with rice, and maize and millet and the jackal brewed with lizards, locusts, frogs and fish. And when the brew was ready, they first went to the jackal's house, but the hen could not touch his beer, it smelt so bad and the jackal drank it all; then they went to the hen's house and her beer was very nice and they both drank till the hen got very drunk and began to stagger about; and the jackal made up his mind that the hen must be very nice to eat, as her beer was so good to drink and when he saw her drunk he was delighted and sang :—

"Fowl, do not graze in the field!
The jackal laughs to see you.
Paddy bird, do not fish in the pond!
You pecked a piece of sedge thinking it was
a frog's leg !
Do not drink rice beer, O fowl!
The jackal laughs to see you.

And so saying he gobbled her up; and her chickens cried at the sight. Then the jackal resolved to eat the chickens also, so he came back the next day, and asked them where they slept and they said "In the hearth." But when the jackal had gone, the chickens planned how they should save their lives.

Their mother had laid an egg and as there was no one to hatch it now, they said. "Egg, you must lie in the fireplace and blind the jackal;" and they said to the paddy husker, "You must stand by the door and when the jackal runs out you must knock him down; and they told the paddy mortar to wait on the roof over the door and fall and crush the jackal. So they put the egg among the hot ashes in the fireplace and they themselves sat in a cupboard with axes ready; and when the jackal came he went to the fireplace and scratched out the ashes; and the egg burst and spirted into his eyes and blinded him and as he ran out of the door the paddy husker knocked him over; and as he crawled away the paddy mortar fell on him from the roof and crushed him; then he chickens ran out and chopped him to pieces with their axes and revenged the death of their mother.

CXIV. THE TIGERS AND THE CAT

In former days tigers and cats were friends and used to hunt together and share the game they caught; and they did not eat the game raw but used to cook it as men do.

One day some tigers and a cat had killed a deer and they had no fire with which to cook it; then the tigers said to the cat "You are small, go and beg a light from yonder village." But the cat said that he was afraid to go; however they urged him saying, "You have a thin tail and plump feet; you can bring it in a trice." So, as they all insisted on his going, he at last consented; and said "Well, I will go; but don't expect me to be very quick; if I get a good opportunity for fetching the fire, I will come back soon." They said "All right, go and run off with a small fire-brand and we will meet you outside the village."

So the cat went off and coming to a house, went inside to pull a firebrand from the hearth. On the fire some milk was boiling; and the cat thought "This smells very nice, I will have a taste of it" and he found it so nice that he made up his mind to drink it all, before her took away the fire-brand. But in order to lap the milk he had to put his feet on the fireplace, and it was so hot that he burnt his feet and had to get down; so then he sat down and waited till the fire went out and the hearth grew cool, and then he lapped up the milk and ran off with a piece of smouldering wood.

Meanwhile the tigers had got tired of waiting and had eaten the deer raw; and they were very angry at being made to eat raw flesh and swore that they would eat the cat too. When they saw that cat bringing the fire they ran to meet him and abused him and cried out "You have made us eat raw flesh; we will eat you too, dung and all." On hearing this threat the cat ran back to the village in fear of his life; and the tigers followed in pursuit; but when they got near the village, the village dogs all ran out barking and the tigers were frightened and turned back and the cat was saved. From that day tigers and leopards have eaten raw flesh; and cats bury their excrement, because of what the tigers had said.

Every day the tigers went to the village in search of the cat; but when the dogs barked they slunk away; for the tigers were very frightened at the sight of the dogs' curly tails; they thought that the tails were nooses and that they would be strangled by them. One day one of the tigers met a jackal and called to him "Nephew, listen to me; a cat made us eat raw flesh and has escaped into this village and I want to catch it, but the dogs come barking at me. I don't mind that, but I am very frightened of their nooses. Now, you are very like a dog, cannot you go and tell them not to use their nooses." The jackal answered, "Uncle, you are quite mistaken; what you see are their tails, not nooses; they will not strangle you with them." So the tiger took courage and the next day went to the village to hunt for the cat, but he could not find if. And when the dogs barked he got angry and caught and killed one of them; and from that time tigers and leopards eat dogs.

CXV. THE ELEPHANT AND THE ANTS

In the days of old there was a great deal more jungle than there is now, and wild elephants were very numerous; once upon a time a red ant and a black ant were burrowing in the ground, when a wild elephant appeared and said "Why are you burrowing here; I will trample all your work to pieces;" the ants answered "Why do you talk like this; do not despise us because we are small; perhaps we are better than you in some ways;" The elephant said "Do not talk nonsense: there is nothing at which you could beat me; I am in all ways the largest and most powerful animal on the face of the earth." Then the ants said, "Well, let us run a race and see who will win, unless you win we will not admit that you are supreme." At this the elephant got into a rage and shouted; "Well, come we will start at once," and it set off to run with all its might and when it got tired it looked down at the ground and there were two ants. So it started off again and when it stopped and looked down, there on the ground were two ants; so it ran on again, but wherever it stopped it saw the ants, and at last it ran so far that it dropped down dead from exhaustion.

Now it is a saying that ants are more numerous in this world than any other kind of living creature; and what happened was that the two ants never ran at all, but stayed where they were; but whenever the elephant looked at the ground, it saw some ants running about and thought that they were the first two, and so ran itself to death.

This story teaches us not to despise the poor man, because one day he may have an opportunity to put us to shame.

From this story of the elephant we should learn this lesson; the Creator knows why He made some animals big and some small and why He made some men fools; so we should neither bully nor cheat men who happen to be born stupid.

CXVI. A FOX AND HIS WIFE

Once upon a time there were a fox and his wife who lived in a hole with their five little ones. Every evening the two foxes used to make their way to a bazar to feed on the scraps thrown away by the bazar people; and every night on their way home the following conversation passed between them. 'The fox would say to his wife, "Come tell me how much wit you have," and she would answer him by, "Only so much as would fill a small vegetable basket." Then she in her turn would ask "And how much wit have you?" "As much as would load twelve buffaloes."

One night as they were on their way home as usual, the two suddenly found themselves face to face with a tiger, who greeted them by saying "At last my friends, I have got you."

At this the fox for all his wit, could not utter a word but crouched down and shook with fright. Mrs. Fox however was not at all inclined to give way to despair. She saluted the tiger and said "Ah, uncle, do not eat us up just now; I and my husband have a dispute and we want you to settle it for us." The tiger was mollified by being addressed by so respectful a name as uncle, and answered in a gentler voice, "Well, my niece, tell me what is the point and I will decide it for you."

"It is this," went on Mrs. Fox," we have five children and we wish to divide them between us but we cannot decide how to do so; I say that I will take three and leave him two; while he wants to take three and leave me two. We came out to look for some man to settle the dispute but have not met one: and now providentially you have appeared before us like a god; no doubt you will be able to make the division for us." The tiger reflected that if he managed things well, he would be able to eat not only the two foxes but their young ones as well, so he graciously agreed to make the division.

The foxes then invited him to come back with them to the hole in which they lived, and when they reached it, Mr. Fox bolted into it saying that he was going to bring out the children. As however he did not come out again, Mrs. Fox said that it was clear that he could not manage the children by himself, and she would go and help; and thereupon proceeded to back into the hole, keeping her face turned towards the tiger.

Seeing her disappearing the tiger thought to seize her, but as she kept her eyes on him he could only say "Hullo, what is the matter? Why are you going in backwards?" "Oh, uncle," replied Mrs. Fox, "how could I turn my back on so great a personage as you?" and with that she disappeared. Presently the tiger heard the two foxes calling out from inside "Goodbye, uncle, you can go away now; we have arranged how to divide the children ourselves." Then he saw how he had been fooled and flew into a terrible rage and tried to squeeze his way into the hole; but it was much too small and at last he had to go away baffled: and so the foxes were saved by Mrs. Fox's wit.

CXVII. THE JACKAL AND THE CROCODILES

Once upon a time there was a Raja who had an only son. As the boy grew up his father sent him to a school to learn to read and write. One day on his way back from school, the boy sat down by the road side to rest, and placed his school books on the ground by his side. Suddenly a jackal came along and snatched up the bundle of books and ran away with it; and though the boy ran after it, he failed to catch the jackal and had to go and tell his father how he had lost his school books. The Raja told him not to mind, as it was a very good omen and meant that he would grow up as clever as a jackal; and so the matter ended as far as the boy was concerned; and his father bought him a new set of books.

But the jackal ran off to the side of a tank and taking a book from the bundle sat down and. began to read it aloud. He kept on saying over and over again "Ibor, obor, iakoro sotro" "Ibor obor iakoro setro."

Hearing the noise a crocodile who lived in the tank poked his head out of the water and began "Well, nephew, what is that you are repeating?" "I am only reading a book, uncle."

"What, nephew, do you know how to read and write?" "Yes, certainly I do," answered the jackal.

"In that case," returned the crocodile "would you mind teaching my five children?" The jackal was quite willing to be their master, but a difficulty struck the crocodile; the jackal lived on high land, and the little crocodiles could not go so far from the water. The jackal at once suggested a way out of the difficulty: "Let the crocodile dig a little pool near where the jackal lived and put the children into it. Then the jackal could take the little crocodiles out of it when he was giving them their lessons and put them back again when they had finished. So it was arranged, and in two or three days the crocodile dug the pool and the jackal began the lessons.

Each morning the jackal took the five little crocodiles out of the water and told them to repeat after him what he said, and then he began "Ibor obor iakoro sotro" Ibor obor iakoro sotro." But try as they might the little crocodiles could not pronounce the words properly; then the jackal lost his temper and cuffed them soundly. In spite of this they still showed no signs of improvement, till at last the jackal made up his mind that he could not go on with such unsatisfactory pupils, and that the best thing he could do would be to eat them up one at a time. So the next morning he addressed the little crocodiles, "I see that you can't learn, when I take you in class all together: in future I will have you up one at a time and teach you like that." So he took one out of the water and began to teach it; but the little crocodile could not pronounce its words properly, so in a very short time the jackal got angry and gobbled it up. The next day he took out another, which soon met the same fate as its brother; and so things went on till the jackal has eaten four out of the five.

When there was only one left, the crocodile came to see how the lessons were getting on. The sight of him put the jackal in a terrible fright; but he answered the crocodile that the children were making very fair progress. "Well, I want to see them. Come along and let us have a look at them."

This was awkward for the jackal, but his wits did not desert him; he ran on ahead to the pool and going into the water, caught the one little crocodile which remained, and held it up, saying "See here is one." Then he popped it under the water and brought it up again and said "See, here's another, and this he did five times and persuaded the crocodile that he had seen his five children.

The crocodile pretended to be satisfied but he was not quite easy in his mind and would have preferred to see all the five little ones at once. However, he said nothing, but made up his mind to watch the jackal; so the next day he hid himself and waited to see what happened. He saw the jackal take the little crocodile out of the water and begin the lesson-"Ibor obor iakoro." Then when the unfortunate pupil still failed to pronounce the words, the jackal began to give it cuffs and blows. At this sight the crocodile ran forward and caught the jackal, crying out "Show me my other four little ones; is this the way you treat my children?" The jackal had no answer to give and the crocodile soon put an end to his life And took back his one remaining child to the tank where he lived.

CXVIII. THE BULLFROG AND THE CRAB

There was a Raja who had no head and there was a Tiger who had no tail. One day they met in a nullah. "Here's a fine dinner for me" said the Tiger. "Here's a fine dinner for me!" said the Raja. At this retort the Tiger's courage oozed away; and he did not dare to go any nearer; but he called out "Well, if I am to be your dinner, come and catch me." and the Raja called out "If I am to be your dinner, come and catch me." So they stood challenging each other, but neither took a step forward. Then the tiger became abusive and called out, "What have you done with your head?" The Raja retorted what is a tiger without a tail? You also are short of a member. I may have no head but I have more legs than you." The Tiger could think of no retort to make to this and so said "Come, don't let us quarrel any more; let us be friends; I live near here, where do you live?

"My home is also near here.

"Then we are neighbours: there is no reason why we should be enemies."

"Who knows what you are at?" answered the Raja: for you are pretending that you cannot see aright, but it is quite true that we are neighbours." "You are right," said the other, "I admit that I did wrong, and I bow down before you." So they saluted each other and the Tiger said "Let's have a song to show what good friends we are: and he sang (to the rice planting tune):

"The Frog King and the Frog Queen
Sat at their front door.
The Frog King's marriage is going on:
Look, my master!
The Frog King and the Frog Queen!
The Frog King's marriage is going on."

CXIX. THE HYAENA OUTWITTED

Once upon a time there was a great tiger who lived in a forest; and all the other animals that lived in the forest treated him as their Raja, down to the very birds. They all felt safe under his protection, because he was so much feared that no men dared hunt in that forest. One day it happened that this Raja tiger killed a man and made such a enormous meal on the flesh, that he got very bad indigestion. The pain grew worse and worse, till he felt sure that his last hour was come.

In his agony he sent for a hyaena and offered to make him his *dewan*, if only he would call all the other animals of the forest to come and pay a farewell visit to their lord. The hyaena readily agreed but thought it would be better to send another messenger, while he stayed by the tiger to see that all the animals duly presented themselves. Just then a crow flew overhead; so they called him and deputed him to summon all the animals.

The crow flew off and in a short time all the animals assembled before the tiger and paid their respects to him and expressed wishes for his speedy recovery;—all except the jackals. They had been summoned along with the others; but somehow they paid no attention and only remembered about it in the afternoon. Then they were very frightened as to what would be the consequence of their remissness; but one chief jackal stood up and told them not to fear, as he would contrive a way of getting the better of the hyaena. There was nothing else to be done, so they had to put what trust they could in their chief and follow him to the Tiger.

On his way the chief jackal picked up a few roots and took them with him. When they reached the place where the suffering monarch lay, the hyaena at once began to abuse them for being late, and the Tiger also angrily asked why they had not come before; then the chief jackal began humbly "O Maharaja, we were duly summoned; your messenger is not to blame; but we reflected that it was useless merely to go and look at you when you were so ill: that could do you no good; so we bestirred ourselves to try and find some medicine that would cure you. We have searched the length and breadth of the jungle and have found all that is necessary, except one thing and that we have failed to find." "Tell me what it is," said the hyaena," and I will at once despatch all these animals to look for it and it will surely be found." "Yes," echoed the tiger, "what is it?" "Maharaja," said the jackal, " when you take these medicines, you must lie down on the fresh skin of a hyaena, which has been flayed alive; but the only hyaena we can find in the forest is your *dewan.*" "The world can well bear the loss of one hyaena," said the Tiger: "take him and skin him." At these words all the animals set upon the hyaena and flayed him alive; and the tiger lay down on the skin and took the medicines brought by the jackal; and as he was not seriously ill, his pain soon began to pass away.

"That is a lesson to the hyaena not to scold us and get us into trouble," said the jackal, as he went home.

CXX. THE CROW AND THE EGRET

A crow and a white egret once made their nests in the same tree, and when the nestlings began to grow up the crow saw how pretty and white the young egrets were, and thought them much nicer than her own black young ones. So one day when the egre was away, the crow changed the nestlings and brought the little white egrets to her own nest. When the mother egret returned and found the ugly little black crows in her own nest, it did not take her long to see what had happened and she at once taxed the crow with the theft. The crow denied all knowledge of the matter and a fine quarrel ensued.

Quarrelling led to nothing and they agreed to refer the dispute to the decision of a money-lender, whose house stood by the tree in which the two nests were. The crow, as the less shy of the two, flew down and asked the money-lender to come out and settle their dispute. The first question the, money-lender asked was what they were going to give him. The egret promised to catch him a fine *rohu* fish, which was what she was accustomed to eat, but the crow said that she would give him a golden necklace. The money-lender said that the fees must be brought first before he heard the case, so the egret flew off and caught a big fish, but the crow went to where a Raja was bathing and carried off the gold chain which the Raja had left on the bank of the river. The money-lender then gave his decision, which was in favour of the party who had given him the most valuable present; he decided that the young birds must stay where they were. "But," protested the egret "how have my white nestlings become black?" "That is quite natural" answered the money-lender, "a white cow may have a black or brown calf: why should not you have black young ones?" And so saying he drove them away.

The poor egret was not at all content with this unjust decision, and was about to renew the quarrel, when a jackal came racing by; it had just made its escape from some hunters. "Where are you off to so fast, uncle?" called out the egret. "I am in arrears with my rent and am hurrying to pay it to the Raja," answered the jackal. "Stay and listen to my grievance," begged the egret, and she told the jackal all that had happened and how the money-lender had let himself be bribed by the gold necklace. The jackal was very indignant, "A man who could give a decision like that would call a buffalo, a bullock or a pig, a sheep. It is no decision at all; I cannot stop now, but I will come back to-morrow and decide the matter for you and before doing so, I will stuff the mouth of that unjust judge with filth." So saying the jackal hurried off.

The money-lender heard all that passed and was filled with shame at having earned the contempt of the jackal; he feared more disgrace on the morrow, so he at once called the crow and made her return the egret's nestlings, and the next morning when the jackal came back it found that everything had been settled to the satisfaction of the egret.

CXXI. THE JACKAL AND THE HARE

A Jackal and a hare were sworn friends. One day they planned to have a dinner of rice cooked with milk. So the hare crouched down under a bush which grew by the side of a road leading to a busy market; and the jackal stayed watching a little way off. Presently some men came along, taking rice to sell at the market. When they saw the hare by the side of the road, they put down their baskets of rice and ran to catch the hare. He led them a long chase, and then escaped. Meanwhile the jackal carried off as much of the unguarded rice as he wanted. By the same trick they got hold of milk, and firewood, and a cooking pot, and some leaf plates. Thus they had everything necessary for the meal except fire.

So the jackal ran off to a village and went to the house of a poor old woman who was pounding dried plum fruit into meal, and asked her for a light, "Go into the house and take a brand from the fire yourself" said the old woman: "No" said the jackal "you go and get it; and I will pound your meal for you, while you are away." So the old woman went into the house; and while she was away, the jackal put filth into the mortar and covered it up with meal. Then he took away the lighted brand, and after he had gone the old woman found that all her meal was spoilt.

Then the jackal cooked their rice and milk and when it was ready, they began to discuss which should first go and bathe, before they began to eat. At last the jackal went off; he hurried over his bath and came back as quickly as possible. Then the hare went, and he spent a long time having a thorough bath.

While the hare was away, the jackal ate as much of the rice as he wanted and then filled the pot with filth and covered it over with rice. When the hare came back, they debated which should help the rice. At last they agreed that the hare should do so; but when the hare had taken out a little rice he found the pot full of filth. "So it is for this that I took all the trouble to get the provisions for our meal" cried the hare; and threw the contents of the pot over the jackal and drove him away.

The jackal went off and made a drum, and every day he sat in the sun beneath a bank and played the drum. The hare heard the sound and one day he went to the jackal and asked to be allowed to play the drum. The jackal handed it over but the hare beat it and shook it so vigorously that at last it was smashed to pieces. Then the hare ran away.

CXXII. THE BRAVE JACKAL

Once upon a time a he-goat ran away for fear of being slaughtered and took refuge in a leopard's cave. When the leopard came back to the cave the goat called out "Hum Pakpak," and the leopard ran away in a fright. Presently it met a jackal and called out "Ah! my sister's son, some fearful animal has occupied my house !" "What is it like, uncle?" asked the jackal "It has a wisp of hemp tied to its chin," answered the leopard: "I am not afraid, uncle," boasted the jackal, "I have eaten many animals like that, bones and all." So they tied their tails together and went back to the Leopard's cave. When the two drew near the goat stood up: and the leopard said "This morning he called out something dreadful at me." At this they both fled, and in their struggles to separate all the hair on the jackal's tail was scraped off and the jackal called out "Alas, alas! Uncle, you have scraped off all my skin!"

CXXIII. THE JACKAL AND THE LEOPARDS

Once upon a time a leopard and a leopardess were living with their cubs; and when the parents were away a jackal used to go to the cubs and say "If you won't pay up the paddy you owe, give me something on account." And the cubs gave him all the meat which their parents had brought; and as this happened every day the cubs began to starve. The leopard asked why they looked so thin although he brought them lots of game and the cubs explained that they had to give up all their food to the jackal from whom he had borrowed paddy. So the leopard lay in wait and when the jackal came again to beg of the cubs he chased him. The jackal ran away and hid in a crack in the ground; the leopard tried to follow and got stuck in the crack and was squeezed to death. The jackal came out and kicked the dead body, crying "I see you lying in wait for me."

Now the jackal wore silk shoes and a silk dhoti and he went back to the leopard's family and asked who would look after them now the leopard was dead. They said that they would live with him; so the jackal stayed there and they all went hunting deer. The jackal lay in wait and the leopards drove the game to him. But when the deer came out, the jackal was too frightened to attack them and climbed to the top of an ant-hill to be out of the way. So when the leopards came up they found that the jackal had killed nothing. But the jackal only complained that they had not driven the deer in the right direction. So the next day the leopardess lay in wait and the jackal and the cubs beat the jungle; when they came up they found that the leopardess had killed a fine deer. "Now," said the jackal "let me first offer the game as a sacrifice to the spirit of our dead leopard; so saying he tried to bite a hole in the deer but the skin was too tough. So he made the leopardess tear the skin and then he pushed inside the carcase and ate up all the entrails. When he had had as much as he could eat he came out and let the leopards begin their meal.

Another day they wished to cross a flooded river. The young leopards offered to carry the jackal over on their shoulders but the jackal was too proud to allow this. So the leopards all jumped across the stream safely but when the jackal tried he fell into the middle of the water and was carried away down stream. Lower down a crocodile was lying on the bank sunning itself "Pull me out, pull me out!" called the jackal "and I will bring you some fat venison." So the crocodile pulled him out. "Now open your mouth and shut your eyes" said the jackal and when the crocodile obeyed he popped a large stone into its jaws and ran away. This made the crocodile very angry and it vowed to be revenged.

The jackal used to go every day to a certain tank to drink: and to reach the water he used to sit on the root of an *arjun* tree which projected from the bank. The crocodile observed this habit any one day lay in wait under the water, by the *arjun* tree and when the jackal came to drink caught him by the leg. The jackal did not lose his presence of mind but called out "What a fool of a crocodile to catch hold of the root of the tree instead of my leg." On hearing this the crocodile let go its hold and the jackal laughed and ran away.

Every day the jackal used to lie in the sun on the top of a stack of straw. The crocodile found this out and buried itself in the straw and waited for the jackal. That day it happened that the jackal found a sheep bell and tied it round his neck so that it tinkled as he ran. When it heard the bell the crocodile said "What a bother! I am waiting for the jackal and here comes a sheep tinkling its bell." The jackal heard the crocodile's exclamation and so detected the trick; he at once went and fetched a light and set fire to the heap of straw and the crocodile was burnt to death.

PART III

Some authorities are inclined to search too deep for the origin of folklore stories; every story is a sun myth or enshrines some forgotten historical event; they do not admit that stories are told from sheer love of story telling.

The anecdotes in this part do not lend themselves to any such abstruse theories. They are anecdotes for the most part of Santal social life. Some e. g. 123, 125, 127 turn on those verbal quibbles and metaphors of which the Santals are so fond. He will for instance call a mother a milk tree and enquiring of the sex of a new born child will ask whether it is a carrier on the shoulder (a boy) or on the head (a girl).

133 and I34 illustrate the misunderstandings which may occur owing to the custom that a wife may not mention her husband's names, nor a man speak familiarly to the wife of his younger brother.—Story 128 is found elsewhere in *Hidia.*

CXXIV. THE FOOL AND HIS DINNER

A man once went to visit his mother-in-law and for dinner they gave him rice with a relish made of young bamboo shoots. The man liked it extremely and thought that it was meat, but he saw no pieces of meat; so he asked his mother-in-law what it was made of; and behind him was a door made of bamboos: so the mother-in-law said, "I have cooked that which il behind you;" and he looked round and saw the door; so he resolved to carry off the door, as it made such good eating, and in the middle of the night he took it off the hinges and ran away with it. In the morning the door was missed and the mother-in-law guessed what had happened and had a hearty laugh.

Meanwhile the man went home with the door and chopped it up and gave the pieces to his wife to cook; the wife said that it was useless to cook dry chips but he insisted and said that her mother had made a beautiful dish of them. So they were cooked and the man sat down to eat; but they were all hard and tasteless; then he scolded his wife and she told him to cook them himself if he was not pleased; so he cooked some himself and the result was the same; and his wife laughed at him and when the villagers heard of it they nicknamed him "Silly", and used to call the name after him when they met him.

CXXV. THE STINGY DAUGHTER

Once a man went to visit his married daughter: he intended to arrive in time for dinner; so though he passed some edible herbs on the way he did not stop to eat them.

When he arrived he was duly welcomed and after some conversation he told his daughter that he must return the same day; she said "All right, but wait till it gets hot." (The father understood this to be a metaphorical way of saying "Wait till the dinner is cooked.) But the daughter was determined not to cook the rice while her father was there: so they sat talking and when the sun was high the daughter went into the yard and felt the ground with her foot and finding it scorching she said "Now father, it is time for you to be going: it has got hot." Then the old man understood that she was not going to give him his dinner. So he took his stick and got up to go.

Now the son-in-law was a great hunter and that day he had killed and brought home a peacock; as he was leaving, the father said "My daughter, if your husband ever brings home a peacock I advise you to cook it with mowah oil cake; that makes it taste very nice." So directly her father had gone, the woman set to work and cooked the peacock with mowah oil cake; but when her husband and children began to eat it they found it horribly bitter and she herself tasted it and found it uneatable; then she told them that her father had made fun of her and made her spoil all the meat. Her husband asked whether she had cooked rice for her father; and when she said "No" he said that this was the way in which he had punished her; he had had nothing to eat and so he had prevented their having any either; she should entertain all visitors and especially her father. So they threw away the meat and had no dinner.

CXXVI. THE BACKWARDS AND FORWARDS DANCE

There was once a Santal who owed money to a money-lender: the lender went to dun him every day but as he had nothing to pay with he used to hide in the jungle and as he had no warm clothes he used to light a fire to warm himself by; and when the fire was low he would sit near it and when it blazed up he would move back from it. When the money-lender asked the man's wife where he was, she always replied "He is dancing the "Backwards and Forwards" dance." The money-lender got curious about this; and said that he would like to learn the dance. So one evening the Santal met him and offered to teach him the dance but, he said he must be paid and what would the money-lender give? The money-lender said that he would give any thing that was asked; so the Santal called two witnesses and before them the moneylender promised that if the Santal taught him the dance he would let him off his debt.

The next morning the Santal took the moneylender to the jungle and told him to take off his clothes as they would dance with only loin cloths on; then he lit a heap of straw and they sat by it warming themselves; and he purposely made only a small fire at first. Then the money-lender asked when they were going to begin to dance but the Santal said "Let us warm ourselves first, I am very cold," so saying he piled oil more straw and as the fire blazed up they moved away from it; and when it sank they drew nearer again. While this was going on the two witnesses came up and the moneylender began to object that he was not being taught to dance; but the Santal said, "What more do you want; don't you keep moving backwards and forwards in front of the fire? This is the "Backwards and Forwards" dance." Seeing how he had been tricked the money-lender was much upset and he appealed to the witnesses, but they decided against him; and he went home crying and lost his money.

CXXVII. THE DEAF FAMILY

Formerly Santals were very stupid and much afraid of Hindus; and once a Santal was ploughing at a place where two roads met and a Hindu came along and asked him in Hindi, where the two roads went to; now the Santal did not understand Hindi and was also deaf and he thought that the Hindu said "These two bullocks are mine,"—and he answered "When did I take your bullocks?" The Hindu sat down and repeated his question; but the Santal did not understand and continued to assert that the bullocks were his and were named Rice eater and Jaituk *) and had formed part of his wife's dowry; the Hindu kept on asking about the roads and at last the Santal got frightened and thought "perhaps my father-in-law took the bullocks from this man and at any rate he will beat me and take them by force"; so he unyoked his bullocks and handed them over to the stranger; and the Hindu when he found out what was meant went off with them as fast as he could.

Soon after the Santal's mother brought him out his dinner and he told her what had happened about the bullocks and she also was deaf and thought that he was complaining that the rice had no salt in it; so she answered, "Your wife gave it to me like this; I cannot say whether she put salt into it; come, eat it up." After he had eaten his dinner the old woman took the dishes home; and she found her husband cutting out a rice pounder; and she told him how their son had scolded her because there was no salt in the rice; and the husband was also deaf and he thought that she wanted to know what he was making and he answered crossly "It may be a rice pounder and it may be a rice mortar." And as often as she repeated her story he made this answer and told her not to worry him. Then she went to her daughter-in-law who was also deaf and sat spinning in the verandah; and she scolded her for not putting salt in the rice; and she answered "Who knows what I am spinning; the thread may be all knotty, but still I reel it up." And this is the end of the story. Thus the man lost his bullocks through cross questions and crooked answers; and as the whole family talked like that they soon became poor.

CXXVIII. THE FATHER-IN-LAW'S VISIT

A man once went to visit his married daughter in the month of October and he went round the fields with his son-in-law to see how his crop was growing. At each rice field they came to, the father-in-law said "You have not dammed up the outlets" and the son-in-law said "Yes, I have; the water is standing in the fields all right," and could not understand what, the old man meant. The next day they both set off to visit some friends at a distance; and the son-in-law carried his shoes in his hand except when they came to a river when he always put them on; and when they were going along in the sun he carried his umbrella under his arm, but when they came to any shady trees he put it up; and he did the

*) Jaituk is a bullock given to a girl by her parents at the time of the marriage. same on

the way back. The old man was very astounded at this but made no remark. On reaching the house however he told his daughter that he was sorry that her husband was a mad man and told her what had happened. His daughter said "No, father, he is not mad: he has a very good reason, he does not wear his shoes on dry ground because he can see where he is going; but in a river you cannot see what is under-foot; there may be sharp stones or thorns and so he puts on his shoes then; and he puts up his umbrella under trees lest falling branches should hit him or the droppings of birds fall on him, but in the open he can see that there is nothing to hurt him."

Her father admitted that these were good reasons and he had been foolish not to understand them; he then took his leave.

And in the following January he visited them again; and when he saw their stock of rice he asked how much they had, and the son-in-law said that there was only what he saw. "But," said the old man, "When I saw your fields you had a very fine crop coming on." "The crop was good," answered the son-in-law "but I owed rice to the money-lender and I have had to pay that back and I have had to pay my rent and this is all that I have left." "Ah!" said the father-in-law, "when I saw your fields I told you that you had not dammed up the outlets; by outlets I meant these drains; as water flows away through an outlet so has your wealth flowed away to money-lenders and landlords; is not this so?" And the son-in-law admitted that he was right and that his words had had a meaning.

CXXIX. RAMAI AND SOMAI

Once two poor men named Ramai and Somai came to a village and took some waste land from the headman, and ploughed it and sowed millet; and their plough was only drawn by cows and their ploughshare was very small, what is called a "stumpy share;" and when they had sowed a little the rains came on; and Somai gave up cultivation and took to fishing and for a time he made very good profits by catching and selling fish; and he did not trouble even to reap the millet he had sown; he laughed at Ramai who was toiling away clearing more land and sowing maize and rice. He used to go and look at him and tell him that he would never get a crop while he had nothing better than a "stumpy" plough; it would probably break to pieces one day and then he would be helpless; he had much better take to fishing which gave quick and easy returns. Ramai made no answer, but when the rains were over there was no more fishing to be done; and Somai was left to starve and had to go from village to village begging. But Ramai reaped his millet and lived on that till his maize was ripe and then his maize supported him until his rice was ripe and he always had plenty to eat; and to show his despite for Somai, after he had had a good dinner, he would come out in front of his house and call out "What of the stumpy share now?" Every day after eating he would come out and say "At first I worked hard and suffered hunger but now I am eating in happiness; and you were happy then but now you are starving."

CXXX. THE TWO BROTHERS

There were once two brothers who were constantly quarrelling and one afternoon after a heated quarrel the younger brother asked the villagers to come and judge between them. The villagers agreed to meet the next morning. At cockcrow the next day the elder brother went to the other's house and woke him up and said "Brother, this is a bad business; you have called in the villagers and they will certainly fine us both for quarrelling; it would be much better for us; to save the money and spend it on a pig; then we and our families by could have a feast." "I quite agree," said the younger brother, "but now I have summoned the villagers, what can be done? If I merely tell them to go away, they will never come again when I summon them.'

The elder brother said, "I have a plan; when they come they will ask how the quarrel began and what abusive words I used; and then you must tell them that that is a point which they have to decide; and then they will be able to do nothing and will go away. "The younger brother agreed to this and when the villagers came and, asked what the quarrel was about he said, "Don't you know what the quarrel was? That was the very matter I wanted you to decide; if you don't know, how can you judge about it?" And this answer he repeated to all their questioning; then they got angry and said that he was mocking them; and they declined to give any decision, but said that the brothers must give them dinner as they had detained them so long; but the brothers flatly declined to do so as no decision had been given, and the villagers went away grumbling, while the brothers bought a pig with the money they had saved and had a jolly feast and as they ate the elder brother said: "See what a good plan mine was; but for it we should now have been feasting others at our expense."

CXXXI. THE THREE FOOLS

Once upon a time three men were sitting at the foot of a tamarind tree and a stranger came up to them with a bunch of plantains on his shoulder and he put the plantains on the ground in front of them and bowed and went away. Thereupon the three men began to quarrel as to who was to have the plantains; each said that they were his because it was to him that the man had bowed. So they started calling each other, "Fool" and after quarrelling for some time one said "Well, yes, I admit that I am a great fool" and the other two asked why he thought himself a fool and he said "Well one day my wife went to the jungle with the other village women to get firewood and left our baby in my charge; as she was a long time coming back the child became hungry and began to cry; I walked him about but he would not stop crying; I tried to feed him with rice and with rice water and with Gur and with cow's milk but he would not eat or stop crying; I was in despair when his mother came back and took him up and gave him the breast and the child was quiet at once.

Seeing this I said to my wife "Human milk must be sweeter than anything else." My wife said "Who can say whether it is nice; we all drink it when we are infants; but when we grow up we cannot say what it is like." Then I said that I would try what it was like and I sucked her breast and found that it was much sweeter than cow's milk; after that I formed the habit and used to drink her milk every day; And as I left none for the child it died soon afterwards of starvation; this shows what a fool I am."

Then one of the other men said "But I am a bigger fool than you." And they asked him in what way; and he said "I was married and was very much in love with my wife; once when she had gone on a visit to her father's I went to fetch her home; and she was got up in all her finery, with her hair well dressed and vermilion on her forehead and red *arta* on her feet. On our way home it began to rain and we took shelter in a village; and when the shower was over we went on; and we came to a river which was in flood from the rain; the water was up to a man's armpits and I decided to carry my wife across so that the arta on her feet might not get washed off. So I took her on my shoulder and to prevent her feet getting wet I held her feet uppermost and as her head was under water when I got across I found that she had been drowned; and if I had not been such a fool she would not have been killed."

Then the third man said "And I also am a fool. I had quarrelled with my own family so I lived with my wife in a house alone at the end of the village and we had no children. Now I was very fond of smoking; and one night I wanted a light for my hookah but there was none in the house; so I started to go and ask for a light from some neighbour; but as it was very dark I did not like to leave my wife all alone: nor did I like to send her out alone to ask for the light; so at last I took my hookah in my hand and set my wife astride on my shoulder and went round from house to house like that, asking for a light; and all the villagers laughed like anything; so I am a fool." Then they agreed that they were all three fools and had better divide the plantains equally among them and go home; and that is what they did.

CXXXII. THE CURE FOR LAZINESS

There was once a man who lived happily with his wife, but she was very lazy; when work in the fields was at its height she would pretend to be ill. In June and July, she would begin to moan as if in pain, and when every one else had gone off to work she would eat any rice that they had left over or if there were none, would cook some for herself. Her father-in-law decided to call in some *ojhas* to examine her and if they could not cure her, then to send her back to her father: so he called in two *ojhas* and told them to do their best, as he did not want the woman's relations to complain that she had not been properly treated.

So the first *ojha* felt her pulse and smiled and said nothing, and the second *ojha* felt her pulse and smiled and said nothing, and when the father-in-law asked them if they knew what was the matter, they answered that the illness was very serious and medicines must be applied; the father-in-law said "Yes; but you must get the medicines or tell me exactly what is wanted and I will arrange for it;" this conversation took place before the woman; the ojhas said "Very well, we will do what you want but before applying the medicine we shall have to do some incantations;" the father-in-law answered "Do whatever is necessary to make a good job of it. Don't spare anything; try and get everything ready by tomorrow: for we are in great difficulty; I do not like to leave the patient alone in the house and yet I cannot spare anyone to look after her;" the *ojhas* promised and got up and went out with the father-in-law, and in the village street they told him that laziness was all that was the matter with the woman, but that they knew a medicine which would cure her; so they went to the jungle and dug up two very big tubers of the *tirra* plant, as big as pumpkins, and in the evening they went to the man's house and told him that they had found the medicine, and that the whole household was to come to the cross roads at the end of the village very early the next morning with the patient and they would exorcise the disease and apply remedies.

At cockcrow the next morning the two *ojhas* brought the two tubers and put them down at the end of the village street, and then went to the house where the sick woman lived and awoke the inmates, and they borrowed a pot of water and some vermilion and an old winnowing fan and then they all went to the place where the tubers had been left, and the *ojhas* made the patient sit on the winnowing fan facing the east and painted her with vermilion; then they waved pig's dung round her head and tied the two tubers round her neck and told her to walk up and down the village street three times; and that would remove the spell that was on her. So the woman began to walk up the village street and every one laughed at her and the children ran after her and smacked her and jumped and shouted for joy and the *ojhas* called out to her "You must not take off the tubers until you are cured."

The woman walked up and down twice, but then she was so ashamed at being laughed at that she threw away the tubers and ran off home; then they all laughed the more; and followed her to the house, and the *ojhas* asked whether she was cured that she had taken off the remedies they had applied; she only smiled in answer and they told her to take care because if she ever got ill again they would apply the same remedy; but from that day the woman completely recovered and did her fair share of all the work.

CXXXIII. THE BRAHMAN'S POWERS

A long time ago a Brahman came from the west and did many wonders to the astonishment of those who saw him. He came to a certain village and at first put up in an old bamboo hut; there he sat motionless for three or four days and so far as anyone could see ate and drank nothing. The villagers said that he must eat during the night, so four men arranged to watch him continuously; two by day and two by night, but though they watched they could not detect him eating or drinking. Then the villagers collected and began to question him and as his answers seemed worthy of credit they began to bring him offerings of milk; one day he asked to be supplied with coolies that he might rebuild the hut in which he had taken up his abode; so coolies were brought and he made them collect bricks and prepare mortar and at the end of the day's work they asked to be paid; then the Brahman wrapped himself in his cloth and repeated some *mantras*, whereupon pice fell tinkling down from his body and with them he paid the coolies; and so it was every day until the house was finished. All this was a source of great wonder to those who saw it.

CXXXIV. RAM'S WIFE

It is a custom among us Santals that husband and wife do not mention each other's names; and even if a husband sometimes mentions his wife's name in a case of urgent necessity, the wife will never speak her husband's; in the same way a man may not mention the name of his younger brother's wife or of his wife's elder sister; women again may not use the name of their younger sister's husband or their husband's elder brother. Our forefathers have said that if any one breaks this rule his children will be born deaf or dumb; we believe this and fear to break through the custom.

There was once a man named Ram who was ploughing his field; when he got to the end he found that he had not brought the seed with him; so he called out to his wife, pretending however that he was speaking to his daughter "Seed, daughter, seed!" And she called back, "What do you want it for? Are you going to sow it? (eram = will you sow) and every time he called, she answered "Eram?" At this he lost his temper and ran up to the house and asked what she meant by speaking his name, when he told her to bring out the seed for sowing; and thereupon he proceeded to give her a good thrashing. His wife said to him "Your name is the same as the word for 'sow,' it is a very fine name you have got." At this Ram laughed and asked how he could help having the name which his father and mother had given him. At this she giggled. "Then why are you hurt by it? You read better in future take out the seed corn with you and then you won't have to call to me; if you do I shall answer you as I did today."

To the present day people do not use the forbidden words; or if compelled to they spit on the ground first; even Christian converts do not like to infringe the rule if many people are present and usually speak of a person with a forbidden name as the father, or mother of such and such a child.

CXXXV. PALO

There was once a man named Dhuju, and he had sons named Ret Mongla, Saru Sama and Chapat Champa; and their wives were named Chibo, Porbet and Palo.

One rainy season the family was busy with the ploughing: Ret Mongla used to take the plough cattle out to get some grazing before the sun rose; and his two brothers took the ploughs to the fields a little later and the old father used to look on and tell them what to do. It was their practice when they wanted to attract each other's attention to call out: "Ho!" and not "Ya!" or "Brother." One day it had been arranged that they should sow *gundli* in a field; but when the eldest brother arrived at the place with the bullocks ready to plough he found that his two brothers had not turned up with the ploughs; so he began to call "Pal, ho!" (Pal = plough share).

Now just then the wife of the youngest brother, Palo, had gone towards that field to throw away the sweepings of the cowshed and she thought Ret Mongla was calling her name; this surprised her and made her very angry; and she made up her mind to pay him back and then if she were scolded for not paying proper respect to her husband's eldest brother to explain that he had insulted her first. So that morning when she took out their breakfast to the men working in the field, she pretended to be in great hurry, and putting down her basket near the place where the three brothers were ploughing, called out to them: "Come, stop ploughing," and then with scarcely an interval: "Look sharp and come and eat; or if you don't I will take your breakfast away again." So the brothers stopped their work and ate their breakfasts.

But when Palo had gone back and they were sitting having a chew of tobacco, the eldest brother began: "Did you notice how that girl behaved to me just now; she spoke to me in a most rude way as if I were not a person to whom she owed respect." The other two said that they had noticed it themselves, and her husbands Chapat Champa said that he would punish her for it when he got home. Directly he got to the house he began scolding her and she made no answer, but that night when they were alone together she told him that what she had done was because Ret Mongla had insulted her by calling her by name. The next day her mother-in-law took her to task but Palo gave the same explanation.

Then Ret Mongla's mother went to him and asked him whether there was any truth in this counter-charge; he saw at once what had happened and explained that he had never called out his sister-in-law by name; he had called out for the plough: "Pal ho! Pal ho! because his brothers had not got the ploughs ready; when Palo understood what a mistake she had made, she was covered with confusion and they brought water and she washed Ret Mongla's feet as she had done on the day of her marriage, and they salaamed to each other and peace was restored But if the mistake had not been explained Palo would have been turned out of the family.

CXXXVI. THE WOMEN'S SACRIFICE

This is a story of the old days when the Santals both men and women were very stupid. Once upon a time the men of a certain village had fixed a day for sacrificing a bullock; but the very day before the sacrifice was to take place, the Raja's *sipahis* came to the village and carried off all the men to do five days forced labor at the Raja's capital. The women thus left alone suffered the greatest anxiety; they thought it quite possible that their husbands and fathers would never be allowed to return or even be put to death; so they met in conclave and decided that the best thing they could do would be to carry out the sacrifice which the men had intended to make and which had been interrupted so unexpectedly.

So they made haste to wash their clothes and bathe, and by way of purification they fasted that evening and slept on the bare ground. Then at dawn they made ready everything wanted for the sacrifice and went to the jungle with the bullock that was to be the victim. There at the foot of a sal tree they scraped a piece of ground bare and smeared it with cow dung; then they put little heaps of rice at the four corners of a square and marked the place with vermilion; then they sprinkled water over the bullock and led it up to the square.

But here their difficulties began for none of them knew what incantations the men said on such an occasion; they wasted a lot of time each urging the other to begin, at last the wife of the headman plucked up courage and started an invocation like this: "We sacrifice this bullock to you; grant that our husbands may return; let not the Raja sacrifice them but grant them a speedy return." Having got as far as this she wanted the other women to take a turn, but they said that her invocation was capital and quite sufficient; and they had better get on to the sacrifice at once. Easier said than done; they none of them knew how to do it; as they all hung back the headman's wife scolded them roundly and bade them take the axe and kill the beast; then they all asked where they were to strike the animal: "Where its life resides," said the headman's wife. "Where is that," asked the women. "Watch and see what part of it moves," answered she, "and strike there." So they looked and presently the bullock moved its tail: "That's where its life is," shouted they; so three or four of them caught hold of the rope round the animal's neck and one woman seized the axe and struck two blows at the root of the animal's tail. She did it no harm but the pain of the blow made the bullock pass water. "See the blood flowing," cried the women, and eagerly caught the stream in a vessel; then the sacrificer dealt another blow which made the bullock jump and struggle until it broke loose and galloped off. The women followed in pursuit and chased it through a field of cotton; the bullock knocked off many of the ripe cotton pods and these the women thought were lumps of fat fallen from the wounded bullock, so they took them home and ate them; such fools were the women in those days.

CXXXVII. THE THIEF'S SON

This upon a time a goat strayed into the house of a certain man who promptly killed it and hid the body. At evening the owner of the goat missed it and came in search of it. He asked the man who had killed it whether he had seen it, but the latter put on an innocent air and declared that he knew nothing about it but he invited the owner of the missing animal to look into the goat house and see if it had accidentally got mixed up with the other goats. The search was of course in vain.

Directly the owner had gone the thief brought out the body and skinned and cut it up, and every one in the house ate his fill of flesh. Before they went to sleep the thief told his sons to be careful not to go near any of the other boys when they were grazing the cattle next day, lest they should smell that they had been eating meat.

Next morning the thief's son took his goats out to graze and was careful not to go near any of the other boys who were tending cattle; whenever they approached him he moved away. At last they asked him what was the matter; and he told them that they must keep at a distance lest they should smell what he had been eating. "What have you eaten?" The simpleton replied that he had been eating goat's flesh and that there was still some in the house. The cowherds at once ran off and told the owner of the lost goat. The news soon spread and the villagers caught the man who had killed the goat and searched his house and found the flesh of the goat. Then they fined him one rupee four annas and made him give another goat in exchange for the one he had stolen.

CXXXVIII. THE DIVORCE

There was once a man who had reason to suspect his wife's faithfulness. He first tried threatening and scolding her; but this had no good effect, for far from being ashamed she only gave him back harder words than she received. So he set to work to find some way of divorcing her without making a scandal. One day when he came home with a fine basket of fish which he had caught he found that his father-in-law had come to pay them a visit. As he cleaned the fish he grumbled at the thought that his wife would of course give all the best of them to her father; at last an idea struck him. As he handed over the fish to his wife he told her to be careful not to give her father the heads of the *mangri* fish nor the dust of tobacco, as it was very wrong to give either of those things to a visitor. "Very well," she answered; but to herself she thought "What does he mean by forbidding me to do these things? I shall take care to give my father nothing but the heads of the fish" for her pleasure was to thwart her husband. So when the evening meal was ready she filled a separate plate for her father with nothing but the fish heads. As her husband heard the old man munching and crunching the bones he smiled to himself at the success of the plot. When his father was about to leave he asked for some tobacco, and the woman brought him only tobacco dust which she had carefully collected out of the bottom of the bag. The old gentleman went off without a word but very disappointed with his treatment.

A few days later the woman went to visit her father's house, and then he at once asked her what she meant by treating him as she had done. "I am sorry," said she: "I did it to spite my husband; he went out of his way to tell me not to give you the heads of the fish and the dust of tobacco, and so I picked out nothing but heads for you and gave you all the tobacco dust I could collect because I was so angry with him." From this her father easily understood that husband and wife were not getting on well together.

Time passed and one day her mother went to visit the troublesome wife. As she was leaving, her daughter asked whether there was any special reason for her coming. Her mother admitted that she had come hoping to borrow a little oil to rub on the cattle at the coming Sohrae festival, but as her son-in-law was not there she did not like to mention it and would not like to take any without his consent. "O never mind him!" said the woman and insisted on her mother taking away a pot-not of cheap mowah or mustard oil,—but of ghee.

Now a little girl saw her do this and the tale was soon all over the village but the undutiful wife never said a word about it to her husband, and it was only after some days that he heard from others of his wife's extravagance. When it did reach his ears he seized the opportunity and at once drove her out of the house, and when a panchayat was called insisted on divorcing her for wasting his substance behind his back. No one could deny that the reason was a good one and so the panchayat had to allow the divorce. Thus he got rid of his wife without letting his real reason for doing so be known.

CXXXIX. THE FATHER AND THE FATHER-IN-LAW

There was once a Raja who had five sons and his only daughter was married to a neighbouring Raja.

In the course of time this Raja fell into poverty; all his horses and cattle died and his lands were sold. At last they had even to sell their household utensils and clothes for food. They had only cups and dishes made of gourds to use and the Raja's wife and sons had to go and work as day labourers in order to get food to eat. At last one day the Raja made up his mind to go and visit his married daughter and ask her husband's family to give him a brass cup (*baati*) that he might have something suitable to drink out of, Off he went and when he reached the house he was welcomed very politely by his daughter's father-in-law and given a seat and water to wash his feet, and a hookah was produced and then the following conversation began.

"Where have you come from, father of my daughter-in-law?"

"I have walked from home, father of my son-in-law?"

"You come here so often that you make me quite frightened! How is it? Is it well with you and yours? with body and skin? Would it not be well for us to exchange news?"

"Yes indeed; for how can you know how I am getting on if I do not tell you. By your kind enquiries my life has grown as big as a mountain, my bosom is as broad as a mat, and my beard has become as long as a buffalo horn."

"And I also, father of my daughter-in-law, am delighted at your coming and enquiring about me; otherwise I should wonder where you had settled down, and be thinking that you did not know the way relations should behave to each other; at present, I am glad to say, the seed left after sowing, the living who have been left behind by death, by your favour and the goodness of God, are all doing well. Is it not a proverb. "The eye won't walk, but the ear will go and come back in no time. Now the ear is the visitor and so far as it has looked our friends up, it is well with all, so far as I know."

The other answered; "Then I understand that by the goodness of God, all is very well with you all, O father of my son-in-law. That is what we want, that it may be well with us, body and soul."

"Life is our wealth; life is great wealth. So long as life lasts wealth will come. Even if there is nothing in the house, we can work and earn wealth, but if life goes where shall we obtain it?"

The visitor answered "That is true; and we have been suffering much from the 'standing' disease; (*i.e.* hunger) I have tried to get medicine to cure it in vain; the Doctors know of none. I should be greatly obliged if you could give me some medicine for it."

"The very same disease has overflowed this part of the country" was the reply:- at this they both laughed; and the visitor resumed,—

"Don't they say we asked after them and they did not ask anything about us in return;'? it is right now for me to ask how you are getting on" and so saying he proceeded in his turn to put the same questions and to receive the same answers.

Then they went out and bathed and came back and had some curds and rice and sat for a while smoking their hookahs. Then a goat was killed and cooked and they had a grand feast. But the Raja did not forget about the *bati,* and he took his daughter aside and told her to sound her mother-in-law about it. She brought back a message that if he wanted anything he should ask for it himself. So he went very shamefacedly to his host and told him that be must he leaving: "Well, goodbye, are you sure you only came to pay us a visit and had no other object?" The Raja seized the opening that this reply gave him and said "Yes, I had something in my mind; we are so poor now that we leave not even a brass cup to drink out of, and I hoped that you would give me one of yours."

"My dear Sir, you say that you have gourds to drink but of: we have not even that; we have to go down to the stream and drink out of our hands; I certainly cannot give you a *bati.*" At this rebuff the poor Raja got up and went away feeling very angry at the manner in which he had been treated.

When he reached home the Raja vowed that he would not even live in the neighborhood of such faithless friends so he went with all his family to a far country. In their new home his luck changed and he prospered so much that in a few years he became the Raja of the country.

Meanwhile the other Raja—the father-in-law,—fell into such poverty that he and his family had to beg for their living.

The first Raja heard about this and made a plan to attract them to the place where he lived. He ordered a great tank to be dug and promised the workers one pice for each basket of earth they removed. This liberal wage attracted labourers from all sides; they came in such numbers that they looked like ants working and among them came the father-in-law and his family and asked the Raja for work. The Raja recognized them at once though they did not know him; at first the sight of their distress pleased him but then he reflected that if he cherished anger Chando would be angry with him, so he decided to treat them well and invited them to his palace. The poor creatures thought that they were probably doomed for sacrifice but could only do as they were bid. Great was their amazement when they were well fed and entertained and when they learnt who their benefactor was they burst into tears; and the Raja pointed out to them how wrong it was to laugh at the poor, because wealth might all fly away as theirs had done.

CXL. THE REPROOF

A poor man once went to visit his daughter's father-in-law who was very rich. The rich man was proud of his wealth and looked down on poverty; so he made no special entertainment for his visitor and only gave him rice and dal for his dinner. When they went out to bathe he stood on the bank of the tank and began to boast. "I made this tank; all the land over there belongs to me; all those buffaloes and cattle you see, belong to me; I have so many that I have to keep two men to milk them".

The visitor said nothing at the time but that afternoon as host and guest sat smoking together they saw a beggar standing in front of the house. The sun was very powerful and the ground was so hot that the beggar kept shifting from one foot to another as he stood out in the sun. Then the poor visitor spoke up and said "It is strange that when you made such a nice house you made the roof without eaves." "Where are your eyes? Cannot you see the eaves?" asked the host in astonishment. The other answered "I see that you have made a house as high as a hill but if it had any eaves, surely that poor beggar there would not be standing out in the sun; and this morning you must have been mistaken in saying that that tank was yours for otherwise you would have given me fish for dinner; and I think that they were only rocks and tufts of grass which you pointed out to me as your flocks and herds for otherwise you would have offered me some milk or curds." And the rich man was ashamed and had no answer to make.

CXLI. ENIGMAS

Once upon a time a man and his son went on a visit to the son's father-in-law. They were welcomed in a friendly way; but the father-in-law was much put out at the unexpected visit as he had nothing ready for the entertainment of his guest. He took an opportunity to go into the house and said to one of his daughters-in-law. "Now, my girl, fill the little river and the big river while I am away; and polish the big axe and the little axe and dig out five or six channels, and put hobbles on these relations who have come to visit us and bar them into the cow house. I am going to bathe and will come back with a pot full of the water of dry land, then we will finish off these friends."

The two visitors outside overheard this strange talk and began to wonder what it meant. They did not like the talk about axes and digging channels, it sounded as if their host meant to kill them as a sacrifice and bury their bodies in a river bed; rich men had been known to do such things. With this thought in their minds they got up and began to run away as fast as their legs could carry them. But when the young woman saw what they were doing she ran after them and called them back.

They reluctantly stopped to hear what she had to say; and when she came up they reproached her for not having warned them of the fate in store for them. But she only laughed at their folly and explained that what her father-in-law meant was that she should wash their feet and give them a seat in the cow house; and make ready two pots of rice beer and polish the big and little brass basins and make five or six leaf cups and he would bring back some liquor and they would all have a drink. At this explanation they had a hearty laugh and went back to the house.

CXLII. THE TOO PARTICULAR WIFE

There was once a man with a large tumour on his forehead and his wife was so ashamed of it that she would never go about with him anywhere for fear of being laughed at. One day she went with a party of friends to see the *Charak Puja*. Her husband wished to go with her but she flatly declined to allow him.

So when she had gone he went to a friend's house and borrowed a complete set of new clothes and a large pagri. When he had rigged himself out in these he could hardly be recognized; but his forehead with the tumour was quite visible. Then he too went off to the fair and found his wife busy dancing. After watching her for some time he borrowed one of the drums and began to play for the dancers; and in particular he played and danced just in front of his wife.

When he saw that his wife was preparing to go home he started off ahead, got rid of his fine clothes and took the cattle out to graze. Presently he went back to the house and asked his wife whether she had enjoyed the fun. "You should have come to see it for yourself," said she.

"But you would not let me! Otherwise 1 should have gone."

"Yes," answered his wife, "I was ashamed of the lump on your forehead but other people do not seem to mind, for there was a man there with a lump just like yours who was playing the drum and taking a leading part in the fun and no one seemed to laugh at him: so in future I shall not mind going about with you."

CXLIII. THE PAHARIA SOCIALISTS

Formerly before the Santals came into the country the four *taluqs* of Sankara, Chiptiam, Sulunga and Dhaka formed the Paharia Raj and the whole country was dense jungle. Then the Santals came and cleared the jungle, and brought the land under cultivation. The Paharia Raja of Gando was named Somar Singh and he paid tribute to the Burdwan Raja.

Once ten or twelve Paharias wept to Burdwan to pay the annual tribute. After they had paid in the money the Raja gave them a feast and a room to sleep in and sent them one bed. The Paharias had a discussion as to who should sleep on the bed and in order to avoid any ill-feeling about it they decided that they would all sleep on the ground and put their feet on the bed and then they could feel that they had all an equal share of it. This they did and in the morning the Burdwan Raja came in and found them all lying in this strange position and was very much amused. He explained that he had sent the bed for the use of the chief man among them and asked whether they had no distinctions of rank. "Yes" they said "we have in our own villages; but here we are in a foreign land and as we do not all belong to one village who is to decide which is the chief among us. Away from home we are all equal."

CXLIV. HOW A TIGER WAS KILLED

In the days when the Santals lived in the jungle country there was once a man who had a patch of maize by the bank of a stream; and to watch his crop he had put up a platform in his field. Now one day he stole a goat and killed it; he did not take it home nor tell his family; he took it to the maize patch with some firewood and fire and a knife and a hatchet; and he hoisted all these on to his platform and lit a fire in the bottom of an earthen pot and cut up the goat and began to cook and eat the flesh. And a tiger smelt the flesh and came and sat down under the platform.

As the man ate he threw down the bones and as he threw them the tiger caught them in its mouth; and after a time the man noticed that he did not hear the bones strike the ground; so he looked down quietly and saw the tiger; then he was very frightened for he thought that when he could no longer keep the tiger quiet by throwing down bits of meat, the tiger would spring up unto the platform and eat him.

At last a thought struck him and he drew the head of his hatchet off the handle and put it in the fire till it became red-hot; and meanwhile he kept the tiger quiet by throwing down pieces of meat. Then when the axe head was ready he picked it out of the fire and threw it down; the tiger caught it as it fell and roared aloud with pain; its tongue and palate and throat were so burnt that it died.

Thus the man saved himself from the tiger and whether the story be true or no, it is known to all Santals.

CXLV. THE GOALA'S DAUGHTER

There was once a man of the *Goala* caste who had an only daughter and she grew up and was married, but had no child; and after twenty years of married life she gave up all hope of having any. This misfortune preyed on her mind and she fell into a melancholy. Her parents asked her why she was always weeping and all the answer she would give was "My sorrow is that I have never worn clothes of "Dusty cloth" and that is a sorrow which you cannot cure." But her father and mother determined to do what they could for their daughter and sent servants with money into all the bazars to buy "Dusty cloth". The shopkeepers had never heard of such are article so they bought some cloth of any sort they could get and brought it to the Goala; when he offered it to his daughter she thanked him and begged him not to waste his money:

"You do not understand" said she — "what I mean by "Dusty cloth." God has not given it to me and no one else can; what I mean by 'Dusty cloth' is the cloth of a mother made dusty by the feet of her child." Then her father and mother understood and wept with her, saying that they would do what man could do but this was in the hands of God; and they sang:—

> "Whatever the child of another may suffer, we care not:
> But our own child, we will take into our lap, even when it is covered with dust."

CXLVI. THE BRAHMAN'S CLOTHES

There was once a Brahman who had two wives; like many Brahmans he lived by begging and was very clever at wheedling money out of people. One day the fancy took him to go to the market place dressed only in a small loin cloth such as the poorest labourers wear and see how people treated him. So he set out but on the road and in the market place and in the village no one salaamed to him or made way to him and when he begged no one gave him alms. He soon got tired of this and hastened home and putting on his best *pagri* and coat and dhoti went back to the market place. This time every one who met him on the road salaamed low to him and made way for him and every shopkeeper to whom he went gave him alms: and the people in the village who had refused before gladly made offerings to him. The Brahman went home smiling to himself and took off his clothes and put them in a heap and prostrated himself before them three or four times, saying each time. "O source of wealth: O source of wealth!" it is clothes that are honoured in this world and nothing else."

CXLVII. THE WINNING OF A BRIDE

Formerly this country was all jungle; and when the jungle was first cleared the crops were very luxuriant; and the Santals had large herds of cattle, for there was much grazing; so they had milk and curds in quantities and *ghee* was as common as water; but now milk and curds are not to be had. In those days the Santals spent their time in amusements and did not trouble about amassing wealth, but they were timid and were much oppressed by their Rajas who looted any man who showed signs of wealth. Well, in those days the winters were very cold and there used to be heavy frost at nights. And there was a man who had seven grown-up daughters and no son; and at the time of threshing the paddy he had to undergo much hardship because he had no son to work for him; he had to sleep on the threshing floor and to get up very early to let out the cattle; and as the hoar frost lay two inches deep he found it bitterly cold.

In those days the villagers had a common threshing floor; and one day this man was talking to a friend and he jestingly asked whether he would spend a night naked on the threshing floor; and the friend said that he would if there were sufficient inducement but certainly not for nothing. Then the father of the seven daughters said "If you or any one else will spend a night naked on the threshing floor I will give him my eldest daughter in marriage without charging any bride price." —for he wanted a son-in-law to help him in his work. A common servant in the employ of the village headman heard him and said "I will accept the offer;" the man had not bargained for such an undesirable match but he could not go back from his word; so he agreed and said that he would choose a night; and he waited till it was very cold and windy and then told the headman's servant to sleep out that night. The servant spent the night on the threshing floor without any clothes in spite of the frost and won his bride.

PART IV

The following stories illustrate the belief in Bongas, *i.e.* the spirits which the Santals believe to exist everywhere, and to take an active part in human affairs. Bongas frequently assume the form of young men and women and form connections with human beings of the opposite sex.

At the bidding of witches they cause disease, or they hound on the tiger to catch men. But they are by no means always malevolent and are capable of gratitude. The Kisar Bonga or Brownie who takes up his abode in a house steals food for the master of the house, and unless offended will cause him to grow rich.

CXLVIII. MARRIAGE WITH BONGAS

There have been many cases of Santals marrying *bonga* girls. Not of course with formal marriage ceremonies but the marriage which results from merely living together.

In Darbar village near Silingi there are two men who married *bongas*. One of them was very fond of playing on the flute and his playing attracted a *bonga* girl who came to him looking like a human girl, while he was tending buffaloes. After the intimacy had lasted some time she invited him to visit her parents, so he went with her and she presented him to her father and mother as her husband. But he was very frightened at what he saw; for the seats in the house were great coiled up snakes and on one side a number of tigers and leopards were crouching. Directly he could get a word alone with his wife he begged her to come away but she insisted on his staying to dinner; so they had a meal of dried rice and curds and gur and afterwards he smoked a pipe with his *bonga* father-in-law and then he set off home with his *bonga* wife. They were given a quantity of dried rice and cakes to take with them when they left.

After seeing him home his wife left him; so he thought that he would share the provisions which he had brought with a friend of his; he fetched his friend but when they came to open the bundle in which the rice and cakes had been tied, they found nothing but *meral* leaves and cow dung cakes such as are used for fuel. This friend saw that the food must have been given by bongas and it was through the friend that the story became known.

In spite of this the young man never gave up his *bonga* wife until his family married him properly. She used to visit his house secretly, but would never eat food there; and during his connection with her all his affairs prospered, his flocks and herds increased and he became rich, but after he married he saw the bonga girl no more.

The adventures of the other young man of the same village were much the same. He made the acquaintance of a *bonga* girl thinking that she was some girl of the village, but she really inhabited a spring, on the margin of which grew many *ahar* flowers. One day she asked him to pick her some of the *ahar* flowers and while he was doing so she cast some sort of spell upon him and spirited him away into the pool. Under the water he found dry land and many habitations; they went on till they came to the *bonga* girl's house and there he too saw the snake seats and tigers and leopards.

He was hospitably entertained and stayed there about six months; one of his wife's brothers was assigned to him as his particular companion and they used to go out hunting together. They used tigers for hunting-dogs and their prey was men and women, whom the tigers killed, while the *bonga* took their flesh home and cooked it. One day when they were hunting the *bonga* pointed out to the young man a wood cutter in the jungle and told him to set the tiger on to "yonder peacock"; but he could not bring himself to commit murder; so he first shouted to attract the wood cutter's attention and then let the tiger loose; the wood cutter saw the animal coming and killed it with his axe as it sprang upon him.

His *bonga* father-in-law was so angry with him for having caused the death of the tiger, that he made his daughter take her husband back to the upper world again.

In spite of all he had seen the young man did not give up his *bonga* wife and every two or three months she used to spirit him away under the water: and now that man is a *jan guru*.

CXLIX. THE BONGA HEADMAN

Sarjomghutu is a village about four miles from Barhait Bazar on the banks of the Badi river. On the river bank grows a large banyan tree. This village has no headman or *paranic*; any headman who is appointed invariably dies; so they have made a *bonga* who lives in the banyan tree their headman.

When any matter has to be decided, the villagers all meet at the banyan tree, where they have made their *manjhi than*; they take out a stool to the tree and invite the invisible headman to sit on it. Then they discuss the matter and themselves speak the answers which the headman is supposed to give. This goes on to the present day and there is no doubt that these same villagers sometimes offer human sacrifices, but they will never admit it, for it would bring them bad luck to speak about it.

The villagers get on very well with the *bonga*. If any of them has a wedding or a number of visitors at his house, and has not enough plates and dishes, he goes to the banyan tree and asks the headman to lend him some. Then he goes back to his house, and returning in a little while finds the plates and dishes waiting for him under the tree; and when he has finished with them he cleans them well and takes them back to the tree.

CL. LAKHAN AND THE BONGAS

Once a young man named Lakhan was on a hunting party and he pursued a deer by himself and it led him a long chase until he was far from his companions; and when he was close behind it they came to a pool all overgrown with weeds and the deer jumped into the pool and Lakhan after it; and under the weeds he found himself on a dry high road and he followed the deer along this until it entered a house and he also entered. The people of the house asked him to sit down but the stool which was offered him was a coiled up snake, so he would not go near it; and he saw that they were *bongas* and was too frightened to speak. And in the cattle pen attached to the house he saw a great herd of deer.

Then a boy came running in and asked the mistress of the house who Lakhan was; she said that he had brought their kid home for them. Lakhan wanted to run away but he could not remember the road by which he had come. Two daughters of the house were there and they wanted their father to keep Lakhan as a son-in-law; but their father told them to catch him a kid and let him go; so they brought him a fawn and the two girls led him back and took him through the pool to the upper world: but on the way they put some enchantment on him, for two or three weeks later he went mad and in his madness he ran about from one place to another and one day he ran into the pool and was seen no more, and no one knows where he went or whether the two *bonga* maidens took him away.

CLI. THE HOUSE BONGA

Once upon a time there was a house *bonga* who lived in the house of the headman of a certain village; and it was a shocking thief; it used to steal every kind of grain and food, cooked and uncooked; out of the houses of the villagers. The villagers knew what was going on but could never catch it.

One evening however the *bonga* was coming along with a pot of boiled rice which it had stolen, when one of the villagers suddenly came upon it face to face; the *bonga* slunk into the hedge but the villager saw it clearly and flung his stick at it, whereupon the *bonga* got frightened and dropped the pot of rice on the ground so that it was smashed to pieces and fled. The villager pursued the *bonga* till he saw it enter the headman's house. Then he went home, intending the next morning to show the neighbours the spilt rice lying on the path; but when the morning came he found that the rice had been removed, so he kept quiet.

At midday he heard the headman's servants complaining that the rice which had been given them for breakfast was so dirty and muddy that some of them had not been able to eat it at all; then he asked how they were usually fed "Capitally," they answered "we get most varied meals, often with turmeric and pulse or vegetables added to the rice; but that is only for the morning meal; for supper we get only plain rice." "Now, I can tell you the reason of that" said the villager. "there is a greedy *bonga* in your house who goes stealing food at night and puts some of what he gets into you pots for your morning meal." "That's a fine story" said the servants: "No, it's true" said the villager, an told them how the evening before he had made the bonga drop the rice and how afterwards it had been scraped up off the ground; and when they heard this they believed him because they had found the mud in their food.

Some time afterwards the same man saw the bonga again at night making off with some heads of Indian corn; so he woke up a friend and they both took sticks and headed off the *bonga*, who threw down the Indian corn and ran away to the headman's house, Then they woke up the headman and told him that a thief had run into his house. So he lit a lamp and went in to look, and they could hear the *bonga* running about all over the house making a great clatter and trying to hide itself; but they could not see it. Then they took the headman to see the Indian corn which the *bonga* had dropped in its flight. The next day the villagers met and fined the headman for having the *bonga* in his house; and from that time the *bonga* did not steal in that village, and whenever the two men who had chased it visited the headman's house the *bonga* was heard making a great clatter as it rushed about trying to hide.

CLII. THE SARSAGUN MAIDEN

There was once a Sarsagun girl who was going to be married; and a large party of her girl friends went to the jungle to pick leaves for the wedding. The Sarsagun girl persisted in going with them as usual though they begged her not to do so. As they picked the leaves they sang songs and choruses; so they worked and sang till they came to a tree covered with beautiful flowers; they all longed to adorn their hair with the flowers but the difficulty was that they had no comb or looking glass; at last one girl said that a *bonga* Kora lived close by who could supply them; thereupon there was a great dispute as to who should go to the *bonga* Kora and ask for a mirror and comb; each wanted the other to go; and in the end they made the Sarsagun girl go. She went to the *bonga* Kora and called "Bonga Kora give me a mirror and comb that we may adorn our hair with *Mirjin* flowers." The Bonga Kora pointed them out to her lying on a shelf and she took them away.

Then they had a gay time adorning their hair; but when they had finished not one of the girls would consent to take back the mirror and comb. The Sarsagun maiden urged that as she had brought them it was only fair that someone else should take them back; but they would not listen, so in the end she had to take them. The Bonga Kora pointed to a shelf for her to place them on but when she went to do so and was well inside his house he closed the door and shut her in. Her companions waited for her return till they were tired and then went home and told her mother what had happened. Then her father and brother went in search of her and coming to the Bonga Kora's home they sang :—

"Daughter, you combed yourself with a one row comb
"Daughter, you put *mirjin* flowers in your hair
"Daughter, come hither to us."

But she only answered from within —

"He has shut me in with a stone, father

"He has closed the door upon me, father
"Do you and my mother go home again."

Then her eldest brother came and sang the same song and received the same answer; her mother's brother and father's sister then came and sang, also in vain; so, they all went home.

Just then the intended bridegroom with his party arrived at the village and were welcomed with refreshments and invited to camp under a tree; but while the bridegroom's party were taking their ease, the bride's relations were in a great to-do because the bride was missing; and when the matchmaker came and asked them to get the marriage ceremony over at once that the bridegroom might return, they had to take him into the house and tell him what had happened. The match maker went and told the bridegroom, who at once called his men to him and mounted his horse and rode off in a rage. Now it happened that the drummers attached to the procession had stopped just in front of the home of the *Bonga* Kora and were drumming away there; so when the bridegroom rode up to them his horse passed over the door of the Bonga Kora's home and stamped on it so hard that it flew open; standing just inside was the Sarsagun girl; at once the bridegroom pulled her out, placed her on his horse and rode off with her to his home.

CLIII. THE SCHOOLBOY AND THE BONGA

There was once a boy who went every day to school and on his way home he used always to bathe in a certain tank. Every day he left his books and slate on the bank while he bathed and no one ever touched them. But one day while he was in the water a *bonga* maiden came out of the tank and took his books and slate with her under the water. When the boy had finished bathing he searched for them a long time in vain and then went home crying. When the midday meal was served he refused to eat anything unless his books were found: his father and mother promised to find them for him and so he ate a very little. When the meal was finished his father and mother went to the *bonga* maiden and besought her — singing

"Give daughter-in-law, give
Give our boy his pen, give up his pen.

The *bonga* maiden sang in answer

"Let the owner of the pen
Come himself and fetch it."

Then the boy's eldest brother and his wife went and sang

"Give, sister-in-law, give,
Give our brother his pen: give up his pen."

The *banga* maiden sing in answer

"Let the owner of the pen
Come himself and fetch it."

Then the boy's maternal uncle and his wife went and sang the same song and received the same answer. So they told the boy that he must go himself.

When he reached the tank the *bonga* girl came up and held out his books to him; but when he went to take them she drew back and so she enticed him into the tank; but when once he was under the water he found he was in quite a dry and sandy place. There he stayed and was married to the *bonga* girl. After he had lived with her a long time he became homesick and longed to see his father and mother. So he told his *bonga* wife that he must go and visit them. "Then do not take your school books with you," said she, "perhaps you won't come back." "No, I will surely return," he answered; so she agreed to his going and said that she would sit on the door step and watch for his return; and he must promise to be very quick. She tied up some cakes and dried rice for him and also gave him back his school books.

She watched him go to his home and sat and watched for his return but he never came back. Evening came and night came but he did not return: then the *bonga* girl, rose and went after him. She went through the garden and up to her husband's house in a flame of fire: and there she changed herself into a Karinangin snake and entering the house climbed on to the bed where the boy lay sleeping and climbed on to his breast and bit him.

"Rise mother, rise mother,
The Karinangia snake
Is biting me."

He called —

But no one heard him though he kept on calling: so he died and the *bonga* girl went away with his spirit.

CLIV. THE BONGA'S CAVE

There was once a young *bonga* who dwelt in a cave in the side of a hill in the jungle ; and every day he placed on a flat stone outside, a pot of oil and a comb and a looking glass and some lamp black or vermilion; any woman who went to the jungle could see these things lying there; but they were never visible to a man. After a time the girls who went to the jungle began to use the comb and looking glass and to dress and oil their hair there; it became a regular custom for them to go first to the flat stone before collecting their firewood or leaves.

One day five girls went together to the jungle and after they had combed and dressed their hair it happened that one got left behind; and seeing her alone the *bonga* came out of the cave and creeping up quietly from behind threw his arms round her; and although she shouted to her friends for help he dragged her inside the cave. Her companions were just in time to see her disappear; and they begged and prayed the *bonga* to let the girl go for once; but the *bonga* answered from within that he would never let her go but was going to keep her as his wife; and he drew a stone door over the mouth of the cave. News of the misfortune was sent to the girl's parents and they came hastening to the place; and her mother began to sing:

"My daughter, you rubbed your hair with oil from a pot:
My daughter, you combed your hair with a comb with one row of teeth,
Come hither to me, my daughter."

And the girl sang from within the cave:

"Mother, he has shut me in with a stone
With a stone door he has shut me in, mother
Mother, you must go back home."

Then her father sang the same song and got the same answer; so they all went home. Then the girl's father's younger brother and his wife came and sang the song and received the same answer and then her mother's brother and father's sister came and then all her relations, but all in vain. Last of all came her brother riding on a horse and when he heard his sister's answer he turned his horse round and made it prance and kick until it kicked open the stone door of the cave; but this was of no avail for inside were inner doors which he could not open, so he also had to go home and leave his sister with the *bonga*.

The girl was not unhappy as the wife of the *bonga* and after a time she proposed to him they should go and pay a visit to her parents. So the next day they took some cakes and dried rice and set off; they were welcomed right warmly and pressed to stay the night. In the course of the afternoon the girl's mother chanced to look at the provisions which they had brought with them; and was surprised to see that in peace of cakes was dried cowdung and instead of rice, leaves of the *meral* tree. The mother called her daughter in to look but the girl could give no explanation; all she knew was that she had put up cakes and dried rice at starting, Her father told them all to keep quiet about the matter lest there should be any unpleasantness and the *bonga* decline to come and visit them again.

Now the girl's brother had become great friends with his *bonga* brother-in-law and it was only natural that when the *bonga* and his wife set off home the next morning he should offer to accompany them part of the way. Off they started, the girl in front, then the *bonga* and then her brother; now the brother had hidden an axe under his cloth and as they were passing through some jungle he suddenly attacked the *bonga* from behind and cut off his head . Then he called to his sister that he had killed the *bonga* and bade her come back with him; so the two turned back and as they looked round this saw that the *bonga's* head was coming rolling after them. At this they started to run and ran as hard as they could until they got to the house and all the way the head cartels rolling after until it rolled right into the house. There was a fire burning on the hearth and they plucked up courage to take the head and throw it into the fire where it was burnt to ashes. That was the end of the *bonga* but eight or nine days later the girl's head began to ache and in spite of all medicines they applied it got worse and worse until in a short time she died. Then they knew that the *bonga* had taken her away and had not given her up.

CLV. THE BONGA'S VICTIM

Once upon a time there were seven brothers and they had one sister. Every day they used to go out hunting leaving their wives and sister at home. One very hot day they had been hunting since dawn and began to feel very thirsty; so they searched for water but could find none. Then one of them climbed a tree and from its summit saw a beautiful pool of water close by: so he came down and they all went in the direction in which he had seen the water; but they could not find it anywhere; so another of the brothers climbed a tree and he called out that he could see the pool close by, but when he came down and them in what he thought was the right direction he was equally unable to find the water; and so it went on; whenever they climbed a tree they could see the water close by, but when on the ground they could not find it; and all the time they were, suffering tortures from thirst.

Then they saw that some *bonga* was deluding them and that thet must offer some sacrifice to appease him At first they proposed to devote one of their wives to the *bonga*; but not one of the brothers was willing that his wife should be the victim; and they had no children to offer so at last they decided to dedicate their only sister as the sacrifice. Then they prayed " Ye who are keeping the water from us, listen; we dedicate to you our only sister; show us where the water is." No sooner had they said this than they saw a pool of water close beside them and hastened to it and quenched their thirst. Then they rested and began to discuss how they should sacrifice their sister; and at last they decided that as they had devoted her to the *bonga* because they wanted water, it would be best to cast her into the water; and they planned to go and work one day near a pond of theirs and make their sister bring their breakfast out to them and then drown her.

So they went home and two or three days later the eldest brother said that the time had come for the sacrifice; but the two youngest loved their sister very much and begged for a little delay. Out of pity the others agreed ; but almost at once one of the brothers fell ill and was like to die. Medicines were tried but had no effect; then they called in an *ojha* and he told them that the *bonga* to whom they had made the vow while out hunting had caused the illness and that if they did not fulfil the vow their brother would die. Then they all went to the sick man's bedside and poured out water on the ground and swore that they would fulfil their vow; no sooner had they done so than the sick man was restored to health.

So the very next day they arranged to go and level the field near their pond and they told their wives to send their sister to them with their breakfast. When the time came the girl took out their breakfast and put it down by them and they sent her to draw water for them from the pond but when she put her water pot down to the surface it would not sink so as to let the water run in. The girl called out to her brothers that the pot would not fill they told her to go a little further into the water; so she went in till the water was up to her thighs but still the pot would not fill : then they called to her to go in further and she went in waist deep but still it would not fill ; then she went in up to her neck and still it would not fill ; then she went in a little further and the water closed over her and she was drowned. At this sight the brothers threw away the food which she had brought and hastened home.

Some days later the body rose and floated to the bank and at the place where it lay a bamboo sprang up and grew and flourished. One day a Dome went to cut it down to make a flute of; as he raised his axe the voice of the girl spoke from within the bamboo " O Dome, do not cut high up; cut low down." The Dome looked about but could not see who it was who spoke; however he obeyed the voice and cut the bamboo close to the ground and made a flute of it. The sound of the flute was surpassingly sweet and the Dome used to play on it every day. One day he was playing on it at a friend's house and a Santal heard it and was so taken by its sweet tone that he came at night and stole it.

Having got possession of it he used to play on it constantly and always keep it by him. Every night the flute became a woman and the Santal found her in his house without knowing where she came from and used to spend the night talking to her but towards morning she used to go outside the house on some pretext and disappear. But one night as she was about to depart the Santal seized her and forced her to stay with him. Then she retained her human form but the flute was never seen afterwards; so they called the girl the flute girl and the Santal were betrothed and soon afterwards married.

CLVI. BAIJAL AND THE BONGA

Once upon a time there was a young man named Baijal and he was very skilful at playing on the bamboo flute. He played so sweetly that a *bonga* girl who heard him fell deeply in love with him and one day when Baijal was alone in the jungle she took the form of a pretty girl and pretended that she had come to the jungle to gather leaves. The two met and acquaintance soon became love and the two used to meet each other every day in the jungle. One day the *bonga* girl asked Baijal to come home with her; so they went to a pool of water and waded into it but when the water had risen to the calf of his leg Baijal suddenly found himself on a broad dry road which led to his mistress's house. When they reached it the *bonga* girl introduced Baijal to her father and brothers as her husband and told him not to be afraid of anything he saw; but he could not help feeling frightened, for the stools on which they sat were coiled-up snakes and the house dogs were tigers and leopards.

After he had been there three or four day his brothers-in-law one morning asked him to come out hunting pea fowl. He readily agreed and they all set out together. The *Bongas* asked Baijal to lead the dog but as the dog was a tiger he begged to be excused until they reached the jungle. So they hunted through the hills and valleys until they came to a clearing in which there was a man chopping up a tree. Then the *bongas* called to Baijal " There is a peacock feeding; take the dog; throw a stick and knock the bird over and then loose the dog at it." Baijal pretended not to understand and said that he could see no peacock; then they told him plainly that the man chopping the log was their game. Then he saw that he was meant to kill the man and not only so, but that he would have to eat the flesh afterwards. However he was afraid to refuse, so he took the tiger in the leash and went towards the clearing but instead of first throwing his stick at the man he merely let the tiger loose and cheered it on. The wood cutter heard the shout and looking round saw the tiger; grasping his axe he ran to meet it and as the animal sprang on him he smote it on the head and killed it. Then Baijal went back and told his brothers-in-law that the peacock had pecked their hound to death. They were very angry with him for not throwing his stick first but he explained that he thought that such a big dog as theirs would not need any help.

Two or three days later Baijal told his *bonga* wife to come home with him, so they set off with a bundle of provisions for the journey. When they had passed out through the pool Baijal opened the bundle to have something to eat but found that the bread had turned into cowdung fuel cakes; and the parched rice into meral leaves; so he threw them all away. However he would not give up the *bonga* girl and they used to meet daily and in the course of time two children were born to them. Whenever there was a dance in the village the *bonga* girl used to come to it. She would leave the two children on Baijal's bed and spend the whole night dancing with the other women of the village.

The time came when Baijal's parents arranged for his marriage, for they knew nothing of his *bonga* wife; and before the marriage the *bonga* made him promise that if he had a daughter he would name. the child after her. Even when he was married he did not give up his *bonga* wife and used to meet her as before. One night she came with her children to a dance and after dancing some time said that she was tired and would go away; Baijal urged her not to go but to come with her children and live in his house along with his other wife. She would not agree and he tried to force her and shut the door of the house; but she and her children rose to the roof in a flash of light and disappeared over the top of the house wall and passed away from the village in a flame of fire. At this Baijal was so frightened that from that time he gave her up and never went near her again.

By and bye his wife bore him a daughter but they did not name the child after the *bonga* and the consequence was that it soon pined away and died. Two or three more were born but they also all died young because he had not named them after the *bonga*. At last he did give a daughter the right name and from that time his children lived.

CLVII. RAMAI AND THE BONGA

Once a *bonga* haunted the house of a certain man and became such a nuisance that the man had him exorcised and safely pegged down to the ground; and they fenced in the place where the *bonga* lay with thorns and put a large stone on the top of him. Just at the place was a clump of "Kite's claws" bushes and one day when the berries on the bushes were ripe, a certain cowherd named Ramai went to pick them and when the stone which covered the *bonga* he stood on it to pick the fruit and the *bonga* called out to him to get off the stone; Ramai looked about seeing no one said "Who is that speaking?" and the voice said, I am buried under the stone; if you will take it off me I will give you whatever boon you ask"; Ramai said that he was afraid that he *bonga* would eat him but the *bonga* swore to do him no harm, so he lifted up the stone and the *bonga* came out and thanking Ramai told him to ask a boon.

Ramai asked for the power to see *bongas* and to understand the language of ants. "I will give you the power," said the *bonga* ,but you must tell no one about it, not even your wife; if you do you will lose the power and in that case you must not blame me." Then the *bonga* blew into his ear and he heard the speech of ants; and the bonga scratched the film of his eye balls with a thorn and he saw

Kisar bonga = brownie

the bongas: and there were crowds of them living in villages like men. In December when we thresh the rice the *bongas* carry off half of it; but Ramai could see them and would drive them away and so was able to save his rice.

Once a young fellow of his own age was very ill; and his friends blew into his ears and partially brought him to his senses and he asked them to send for Ramai; so they called Ramai and he had just been milking his cows and came with the tethering rope in his hand; and when he entered the room he saw a bonga sitting on the sick man's chest and twisting his neck; so he flogged it with the rope till it ran away and he pursued it until it threw itself into a pool of water; and then the sick man recovered.

But Ramai soon lost his usual power; one day as he was eating his dinner he dropped some grains of rise and two ants fell to quarrelling over one grain and Ramai heard them abusing each other and was so amused that he laughed out loud. His wife asked why he laughed and he said at nothing in particular, but she insisted on knowing and he said that it was at some scandal he had heard in the village; but she would not believe him and worried him until he told her that it was at the quarrel of the ants. Then she made him tell her how he gained the power to understand what they said: but from that moment he lost the powers which the *bonga* had conferred on him.

CLVIII. THE BOUNDARY BONGA

There was once a man who owned a rich swampy rice field. Every year he used to sacrifice a pig to the boundary *bonga* before harvest; but nevertheless the *bonga* always reaped part of the crop. One year when the rice was ripening the man used to go and look at it every day. One evening after dusk as he was sitting quietly at the edge of the field he overheard the *bonga* and his wife talking. The *bonga* said that he was going to pay a visit to some friends but his wife begged him not to go because the rice was ripe and the farmer would be cutting it almost at once. However the *bonga* would not listen to her advice and set off on his journey.

The farmer saw that there was no time to be lost and the very next day he sacrificed the usual pig and reaped the whole of the crop. That evening when work was over he stayed and listened to hear whether the *bonga* had come back, but all was quiet. The next day he threshed the paddy and instead of twenty bushels as usual he found that he had got sixty bushels of rice. That evening he again went to the field and this time he found that the *bonga* had returned and was having a fine scolding from his wife, because he had let the farmer reap the whole crop. "Take your silly pig and: your silly plate of flour from the sacrifice," screamed the *bonga's* wife, throwing them at her spouse, "that is all you have got; this is all because you would go away when I told you not to do it; how could I reap the crop with the children to look after? If you had stayed we might have got five *bandis* of rice from that field."

CLIX. THE BONGA EXORCISED

A very poor man was once ploughing his field and as he ploughed the share caught fast in something. At first he thought that it was a root and tried to divide it with his axe; but as he could not cut it he looked closer and found that it was a copper chain. He followed the chain along and at either end he found a brass pot full of rupees. Delighted with his luck he wrapped the pots in his cloth and hurried home. Then he and his wife counted the money and buried it under the floor of their house.

From that time the man began to prosper; his crops were always good; and his cattle increased and multiplied; he had many children and they grew up strong and healthy and were married and had children of their own.

But after many years luck changed. The family was constantly ill and every year a child died. The *jan guru* who was consulted declared that a *Kisar bonga* was responsible for their misfortunes. He told the sons how their father had found the money in the ground and said that the *bonga* to whom the money belonged was responsible for their misfortunes and was named Mainomati.

He told them how to get rid of the *bonga*. They were to dig up the buried money and place it in bags; and load it on the back of a young heifer; and take five brass nails and four copper nails, and two rams. If the *bonga* was willing to leave the house the heifer would walk away to another village directly the bags were placed on its back; but if the *bonga* would not go the heifer would not move.

So they did as the *jan guru* advised and when the bags were placed on the heifer it walked away to a large peepul tree growing on the banks of a stream in another village and there it stopped. Then they sacrificed the rams and uttering vows over the nails drove them into the peepul tree and went home, turning the heifer loose. From that time their troubles ceased.

But that evening a man driving his cattle home saw a young woman nailed to the peepul tree; and not knowing that she was a *bonga* he released her and took her home and married her.

PART V

The legends and customary beliefs contained in this part are definitely connected with the Santals.

CLX. THE BEGINNING OF THINGS

In the days of old, Thakur Baba had made everything very convenient for mankind and it was by our own fault that we made Thakur Baba angry so that he swore that we must spend labour in making things ready for use.

This is the story that I have heard.

When the Santals lived in Champa and the Kiskus were their kings, the Santals were very simple and religious and only worshipped Thakur. In those days the rice grew ready husked, and the cotton bushes bore cloth all ready woven and men did not have to pick the lice out of each others' hair; men's skulls grow loose and each man could lift off his own skull and clean it and then replace it. But all this was spoilt by the misdeeds of a serving girl of one of the Rajas. When she went into the field for purposes of nature she would at the same time pick and eat the rice that grew by her; and when she had made her hands dirty cleaning out a cow house she would wipe them on the cloth which she was wearing. Angered by these dirty habits Thakur Baba deprived men of the benefits which he had conferred upon them and the rice began to grow in a husk and the cotton plants only produced raw cotton and men's skulls became fixed so that they could not be removed.

In those old days too the sky was quite close to the earth and Thakur Baba used to come and visit men in their houses. So it was a saying among our forefathers, "Do not throw your dirty leaf plates near the front or back door and do not let your brass plates and dishes remain unwashed at night; for if Thakur Baba come along and' see them so, he will not come into the house but will be angry and curse us." But one day a woman after finishing her meal threw the used leaf plate out of the door, and a gust of wind carried it up to the sky; this displeased Thakur Baba and he resolved no longer to dwell in the neighbourhood of men as they were so ill-mannered as to throw their dirty leaf plates at him and so he lifted the sky to its present height above the earth.

To this day men who have heard of this scold those who throw their refuse into the street and bid them heap it up in some out-of-the-way place.

The misdeeds of men at length made Thakur Baba so angry that he resolved to destroy them all. Now Thakur Baba is Sing Chando or the Sun, and the Moon is his wife: and at first there were as many stars by day as there are by night and they were all the children of the Sun and Moon who had divided them between them. So Sing Chando having resolved to destroy mankind blazed with a fierce heat till man and beast writhed under the torture of it. But when the Moon looked down and saw their sufferings she was filled with pity and thought how desolate the earth would be without a living beings on it. So she hastened to Sing Chando and prayed him not to desolate the earth but for all her beseeching the utmost that she could obain was a promise from her Lord that he would spare one or two human beings to be the seed of a future race. So Sing Chando chose out a young man and a young woman and bade them go into a cave in a hill side and close the mouth of the cave with a raw hide and when they were safely inside he rained fire from heaven and killed every other living being on the earth.

Five days and five nights it rained fire and the man and woman in the cave sang—(to the Baha tune)

"Five days and five nights the fire will rain, ho!
Five days and five nights, all night long, ho!
Where will you two human beings stay?
Where will you two take shelter?
There is a hide, a hide:
There is also a hill:
There is also a cave in the rock!
There will we two stay:
There will we two take shelter."

When they came out of the cave the first thing they saw was a cow lying burnt to death with a *karke* tree fallen on the top of it and near it was lying a buffalo cow burnt to death; at the sight they sang:—

"The cow is glowing cinders, glowing cinders:
The *karke* tree is burnt:
The buffalo cow has fallen and has been burnt
to ashes, to ashes."

And as they went on, they sang a similar lament over the remains of each living being as they saw it.

Although these two had been spared to raise up a new race, Ninda Chando, the Moon, feared that the Sun would again get angry with the new race and destroy it; and so she made a plan to trick him. She covered up all her children with a large basket and smeared her mouth and lips with red and going to Sing Chando told him that she had eaten up every one of her children and proposed that he should now eat up his. At first Sing Chando declined to believe her but she pointed to her lips and said that they were red with the blood of the children; so Sing Chando was convinced and agreed to eat up his children except two whom he would keep to play with. So they devoured all but two and the two that were saved are the morning and evening stars.

Thus Sing Chando was deprived of the power to again burn up the earth; but when that night Ninda Chando let out her own children from under the basket she warned them to beware of the wrath of their father when he found out the trick that had been played him. When Sing Chando saw Ninda Chando's children still alive he flew to her in a passion and the children at the sight of him scattered in all directions and that is why the stars are now spread all over the sky; at first they were all in one place. Although the stars escaped , Sing Chando could not restrain his wrath and cut Ninda Chando in two and that is why the Moon waxes and wanes; at first she was always full like the sun.

Some men say that the man and woman whom Thakur hid in the cave were Pilchu Haram and Pilchu Budhi and they had twelve sons and twelve daughters and mankind is descended from them and has increased and filled the earth; and that it was in that country that we were divided into twelve different races according to the food which our progenitors chose at a feast.

CLXI. CHANDO AND HIS WIFE

Once upon a time Chando went to the hills to fashion a plough out of a log of wood; and his wife was left at home alone, Chando was so long in coming back that his wife grew impatient; so she made some mosquitos and sent them to worry him and drive him home; but Chando made some dragon-flies and they ate up the mosquitos and he went on with his work. His wife made various other animals and sent them out, but Chando destroyed them all. At last she made a tiger and sent it to frighten him home; but Chando took up a handful of chips from the log he was cutting and threw them at the tiger and they turned into wild dogs and chased the tiger away. Ever since that no tiger will face wild dogs.

Then Chando's wife shut up a locust in an iron pot and when Chando at last came home she asked him "Why have you been so long? Who is to give food and drink to all the living creatures if you don't attend to business. Chando answered that he had fed them all.

"No you have not you have not fed the locust!"

"But I have" said Chando.

Then she took the lid off the iron pot and showed him the locust eating grass inside; and Chando had nothing to say.

CLXII. THE SIKHAR RAJA

Santals say that the Sikhar Raja was a *bonga* and this is the story they tell about him. A certain woman was with child but could not say by whom she was pregnant so she fled into the jungle and at the foot of a clump of bamboos gave birth to twins, a boy and a girl; and then went home leaving the children lying in the jungle. The children lay there crying very pitifully. Now a herd of wild bison was grazing in the jungle and they heard the crying and one of the cows went to see what was the matter and took pity on the children and suckled them. Every day she came three times and fed them; and under her care the children grew up strong and healthy. If any man came to hunt in the jungle the bison cow used to attack him and drive him away; she used to bring the bows and arrows which the hunters threw away in their flight to the boy that he might learn how to shoot. And when any basket makers passed by the jungle on their way to market to sell their wares she used to charge out at them and then bring to the girl the winnowing fans and baskets they threw down in their fright, so that she might learn to sift rice.

Thus the children prospered; and the boy was named Harichand and he and his sister looked like gods.. When they grew up they married each other and then the bison cow left them . Then Thakur sent from heaven sixteen hundred *gopinis* and the *gopinis* said that Harichand and his wife should be king and queen in that land of Sikhar. Then they took counsel together as to where the royal fort should be. Three scribed sat down to study the books with Harichand and his wife in their midst; on the right sat the scribe Hikim, and on the left the scribe Bhuja and the scribe Jaganath opened the book to see where the fort should be; and all the *gopinis* sat round in a circle and sang while the book was read.

"Raja Harichand of the Sikhar stock, of Jhalamala,
Where is his abode !
Raja Harichand of the Sikhar stocks, of Jhalamala,
In the bamboo clump is his abode !"
"Raja Harichand of the Sikhar stock of Jhalamala"
In the banyan-tree field, in his abode !
Raja Harichand, of the Sikar stock, of Jhalamala,
In the brinjal corner is his abode !."

And they found in the book that the fort should be in Pachet hill; then they sang in triumph:—

"It will not do, 0 Raja, to build a fort here:
We will leave Paras and build a fort on Pachet hill:
There in the happy Brinda forest."

Then they brought the Raja and Rani from the jungle to Pachet and on the top of the Pachet hill a stone fort sprang up for them; and all the country of Sikhar acknowledged their sway, After that the Santals made their way from Champa and dwelt in Sikhar and cleared all the jungle in it and abode there many years. They called the Sikhar Raja a *bonga* because no one knew his father or mother. Under Raja Harichand the Santals were very contented and happy, and when he celebrated the Chatar festival they used to sing this song, because they were so contented:—

"Harichand Raja was born of a bison-cow,
Sirguja Rana was born of a snake."

CLXIII. THE ORIGIN OF TOBACCO

This is the way that the chewing tobacco began. There was once a Brahmin girl whose relations did not give her in marriage and she died unmarried. After the body had been burned and the people had gone home, Chandu thought "Alas, I sent this woman into the world and she found favour with no one; well, I will confer a gift on her which will make men ask for every day," so he sowed tobacco at the burning place and it grew up and flourished. And there was a boy of the cowherd caste who used to graze his cattle about that place; he saw his goats greedily eating the tobacco leaf and he wondered what the leaf was and tasted a bit but finding it bitter he spat it out. Some time after however he had tooth-ache and having tried many remedies in vain he bethought himself of the bitter tobacco and he chewed some of that and kept it in his mouth and found that it cured the tooth-ache ; from that time he formed the habit of chewing it. One day he saw some burnt bones or lime and he picked up the powder and rubbed it between his fingers to see what it was and after doing so he ate some tobacco and found that the taste was improved, so from that time he always chewed lime with the tobacco. He recommended the leaf to other men who had tooth-ache and they formed the habit of chewing it too and called it tobacco; and then men who had no tooth-ache took to it; and acquired a craving for it.This is the way tobacco chewing began, as our forefathers say.

CLXIV. THE TRANSMIGRATION OF SOULS

All the cats of Hindus have believed and believe, and the Santals also have said and say, that Thakur made the land and sky and sea and man and animals and insects and fish and the creation was complete and final: he made their kinds and castes once for all and did not alter them afterwards; and he fixed the time of growth and of dwelling in the body; and for the flowers to seed and he made at that time as many souls as was necessary and the same souls go on being incarnated sometimes in a human body and sometimes in the body of an animal; and so it is that many human beings really have the souls of animals; if a man has a man's soul he is of a gentle disposition; but if he gets the soul of a dog or cat then he is bad tempered and ready to quarrel with everyone; and the man with a frog's soul is silent and sulky and those who get tiger's souls when they start a quarrel never give up till they gain their point. There is a story which proves all this.

There was once a Brahman who had two wives and as he knew something of herbs and simples he used to leave his wives at home and go about the country as a quack doctor; but whenever he came home his two wives used to scold him and fault with him for no reason at all till they made his life a burden. So he resolved to leave two such shrews and one day when they had been scolding as usual he put on the garb of a *jogi* and in spite of their protests went out into the world.

After journeying two or three days he came to a town in which a pestilence was raging and he sat down to rest under a tree on the outskirts. There he noticed that many corpses has been thrown out and he saw two vultures fly down to feed on the bodies; and the he-vulture said to his mate "Which corpse shall we eat first?" Now the Brahman somehow understood the language of the birds—but the mate returned no answer though the he-vulture kept on repeating the, question; at last she said " Don't you see there is a man sitting at the foot of the tree? "Then the both approached the Brahman and asked why he was sitting in such a place and whether he was in distress; he told them that trouble had driven him from his home and that he was wandering about the world as chance led him, because the continual quarrelling of his two wives was more then he could bear. The vultures said " We will give you a means by which you may see your wives as they really are" and one of them pulled out a wing feather and told him when he went to any house begging to stick it behind his ear and then he would see what the people were really like; and they advised him to marry a woman who gave him alms with her hands. Then he got up and went away with the feather, leaving the birds to prey on the corpses.

When the Brahman came to a village to beg he saw by the aid of the feather, that some of the people were really cats and some were dogs and other animals and when they gave him alms they brought it in their teeth; then he made up his mind to go home and see what his wives really were; and he found that one was a bitch and one was a sow; and when they brought him water they carried the cup in their mouths; at this sight he left the house again in disgust, determined to marry any woman who offered him alms with her hands.

He wandered for days till at last the daughter of a Chamar, when he begged, brought him alms in her hands; and he at once determined to stay there and marry her at all costs; so he sat down and when the Chamar asked why he did not go away he said that he meant to marry the girl who had given him alms and live in his house as his son-in-law; the Chamar did all he could to remonstrate at such an extraordinary proposal as that a Brahman should destroy his caste by marrying a Chamar; the Brahman said that they might do what they liked to him but that he would not leave till he obtained his bride. So at last the Chamar called in his castefellows and relations to advise him whether he would be guilty of any sin in yielding to the proposal of the Brahman; and they called into council the principal villagers of all the other caste and after fully questioning the Chamar and the Brahman the judgment of the villagers was that the marriage should take place and they would take the responsibility. Then the Brahman was made to give a full account of himself and where he had come from, and when this was found to be true, the bride price was fixed and paid and the marriage took place and the Brahman became a Chamar.

CLXV. THE NEXT WORLD

This is what the Santals say about the next world. After death men have a very hard time of it in the next world. *Chando bonga* makes them work terribly hard; the woman have to pound the fruit of the castor oil plant with a pestle; and from the seeds Chando bonga makes human beings. All day long they have to work; those women who have babies get a little respite on the excuse of suckling their babies; but those who have no children get no rest at all; and the men are allowed to break off to chew tobacco but those who have not learnt to chew have to work without stopping from morning to night. And this is the reason why Santals learn to chew tobacco when they are alive; for it is of no use to merely smoke a *huka*: in the next world we shall not be allowed to knock off work in order to smoke. In the next world also it is very difficult to get water to drink. There are frogs who stand on guard and drive away any who comes to the water to drink; and so when Santals die we send drinking vessels with them so that they may be able to run quickly to the water and fill the vessels and get away before they are stopped. And it is said that if a man during his lifetime has planted a peepul tree he gets abused for it in the next world and is told to go and pick the leaves out of the water which have fallen into it and are spoiling it and such a man is able to get water to drink while he is picking the leaves out of it; but whether this is all true I cannot say.

CLXVI. AFTER DEATH

Then grown-up people die they become ancestral *bongas* and sacrifices are offered to them at the Flower and Sohrai festivals; and when children die they become *bhuts*. When a pregnant woman dies, they drive long thorns into the soles of the feet before the body is burned for such women become *churins*. The reason of this is that when the *churin* pursues any one the thorns may hurt her and prevent her from running fast: and so the man who is pursued may escape; for if the *churin* catches him she will lick all the flesh off his bones; they especially attack the belly and their tongues are very rough.

There was once a man who had been to get his ploughshare sharpened by the blacksmith and as he was on his way home it came on to rain, so he took shelter in a hollow tree. While he was waiting for the weather to clear he saw a *churin* coming along singing and she also came to take shelter in the same tree. Fortunately she pushed in backwards and the man took the ploughshare which was still nearly red hot and pressed it against her back; so she ran away screaming and he made good his escape in the other direction; otherwise he would assuredly have been licked to death.

CLXVII. HARES AND MEN

In former days hares used to eat men and a man presented himself before Thakur and said " 0 Father, these hares do us much damage; they are little animals and hide under leaves and then spring out and eat us; big animals we can see coming and can save ourselves. Have pity on us and deliver us from these little animals." So Thakur summoned the chief of the hares and fixed a day for hearing the case; and when the man and the hare appeared he asked the hare whether they ate men and the hare denied it and asserted on the contrary that men ate hares; but the man when questioned denied that men killed hares. Then Thakur said "O hare and man, I have questioned you both and you give contradictory answers; and neither admits the charge; the matter shall be decided in this way; you, hare, shall watch a *Kila* tree and if within a year you see a leaf fall from the tree you shall be allowed to eat men; and you, man, shall watch a *Korkot* tree and if you see a leaf fall, then men shall be allowed to eat hares. Begin your watch to-day and this day next year bring me your leaves." So the man and the hare departed and each sat under a tree to see a leaf fall but they watched and watched in vain until on the last day of the year a *korkot* leaf fell and the man joyfully picked it up and took it to Thakur; and the hare failing to see a leaf fall bit off a leaf with its teeth and took it to Thakur. Then Thakur examined the two leaves and said to the hare, "This leaf did not fall of itself; see, the tip of the stalk is quite different from the stalk of the leaf this man has brought; you bit it off." And the hare was silent. Then Thakur rubbed the legs of the hare with a ball of cleaned cotton and passed this sentence on him, that thenceforward he should skip about like a leaf blown by the wind and that men should hunt hares wherever they found them and kill and eat them, entrails and all.

And this is the reason why Santals do not clean the hares they kill, but eat them entrails and all.

CLXVIII. A LEGEND

Once upon a time a woman was found to be with child by her own brother, so the two had to fly the country. In their flight they came to the Mustard Tank and Flower Lake, on the banks of which they prepared to cook their food. They boiled water and cooked rice in it; and then they boiled water to cook pulse to eat with the rice. But when the water was ready they found that they had forgotten to bring any pulse. While they were wondering what they could get to eat with their rice they saw a man of the fisher caste (Keot) coming along with his net on his shoulder. Then the woman sang—

"The son of a Keot is standing on the bank of the tank:
The fish are jumping: the son of a Keot is catching the fish.',

So the Keot caught them some fish, which they ate with their rice.

Then they went on and by the side of the road they saw a date palm the juice of which had been tapped; and they wished to drink the juice but they found that they had brought no drinking vessel with them. The woman looked about and saw near by a fan palm tree and she sang:—

"The peepul's leaves go flicker, flicker:
The banyan's leaves are thick and fleshy:
Of the fan palm's leaf, brother, make a cup.
And we will drink the juice of the date palm,"

So her brother made a drinking vessel of a palm leaf and they drank the date juice and went on their way. At nightfall they rested at the foot of a Bael tree and fell into a drunken sleep from the date juice they had drunk.

As the woman lay senseless her child was born to her and no sooner was the child born than a bael fruit fell on to its head and split it into four pieces which flew apart and became four hills. From falling on the newborn child the bael fruit has ever since had a sticky juice and the tree is covered with thorns which are the hair of the child. In the morning the man and woman went on and came to a forest of *Tarop* trees and the woman wiped her bloody hands on the *Tarop* trees and so the *Tarop* tree ever since exudes a red juice like blood.

Next morning they went on and came to a spring and drank of its water and afterwards the woman bathed in it and the blood stained water flowed over all the country and so we see stagnant water covered with a red scum. Going on from there they reached a low lying flat and halted; almost at once they saw a thunder storm coming up from the South and West; and the woman sang—

"A storm as black as the so fruit, brother,
Is coming, full of danger for us:
Come let us flee to the homestead of the liquor seller."

But the brother answered—

"The liquor seller's house is an evil house:
You only wish to go there for mischief."

So they stayed where they were and the lightning came and slew them both.

CLXIX. PREGNANT WOMEN

Pregnant women are not allowed to go about alone outside the village; for there are *bongas* everywhere and some of them dislike the sight of pregnant women and kill them or cause the child to be born wry-necked.

A pregnant woman may not make a mud fire-place for if she does her child will be born with a hare-lip; nor may she chop vegetables during an eclipse or the same result will follow. She may not ride in a cart, for if she does the child will be always crying and will snore in its sleep; if she eats the flesh of field rats the child's body will be covered with hair and if she eats duck or goose flesh the child will be born with its fingers and toes webbed. Nor may a pregnant woman look on a funeral, for if she does her child will always sleep with its eyes half open.

CLXX. THE INFLUENCE OF THE MOON

If a child is born on the day before the new moon the following ceremony is observed. After bathing the child they place an old broom in the mother's arms instead of the child; then the mother takes the child and throws it out on the dung heap behind the house. The midwife then takes an old broom and an old winnowing fan and sweeps up a little rubbish on to the fan and takes it and throws it on the dung hill; there she sees the child and calls out. " Here is a child on the dung heap" then she pretends to sweep the child with the broom into the winnowing fan and lifts it up and carries it into the house; and asks the people of the house whether they will rear it. They ask what wages she will give them and she promises to give them a heifer when the child is grown up.

If this is not done the child will be unlucky when it grows up; if it is a boy, however often he may marry, his wife will die and so, if it is a girl, her husbands will die.

Another fact is that they always shave a child's head for the first two times during the same moon; if it is shaved first during one moon and then during the following moon; it will always have a headache once a month.

Similarly when they tie the knots in a string to fix the date of a wedding the wedding must take place in the lunar month in which the knots are tied or else the children born of the marriage will die.

CLXXI. ILLEGITIMATE CHILDREN

If a woman has an illegitimate child and from fear or shame will not name its father the bastard is called a child of *Chando*. At its birth there is no assembly of the neighbours; its head is not ceremonially shaved and there is no *narta* ceremony. The midwife does what is necessary; and the child is admitted into no division of the tribe. If it is a boy it is called Chandu or Chandrai or sometimes Birbanta and if a girl Chandro or Chandmuni or perhaps Bonela. Sometimes after the child is born the mother will under seal of secrecy tell its father's name to her mother or the midwife; and then between themselves they will call the child by a name taken from the father's family but they will never tell it to anyone else. When the child grows up he is given some nickname and if he turns out well and is popular his name is often changed again and he is recognised as a Santal.

Often if a father will not acknowledge a child the mother will strangle it at birth and bury the body. Men who practise sorcery dig up the bones of such murdered infants and use them as rattles when doing their sorceries and are helped by them to deceive people.

CLXXII. THE DEAD

Santals are very much afraid of burial grounds; for dead men become *Bongas* and *bongas* eat men. If a man meet such a *bonga* in a burial ground it is of little use to fight for the *bonga* keeps on changing his shape. He may first appear as a man and then change into a leopard or a bear or a pig or a cat: very few escape when attacked by such a being.

It is said that the spirits of young children become bhuts and those of grown-up people *bongas* and those of pregnant women *churins*.

CLXXIII. HUNTING CUSTOM

Formerly when the men went to a hunt the mistress of the house would not bathe all the time they were away and when the hunters returned she met them at the front door and washed their feet and welcomed them home. The wife of the *dehri* used to put a dish of water under her bed at night and if the water turned red like blood they believed that it was a sign that game had been killed.

Finding that he would not be able to get rid of the Potter by any such devices, the Raja then persuaded the faithless wife to put the Potter to death. She accordingly set up an idol in her house and prayed daily to this that her husband might become blind and die. One day the Potter overheard her prayers: the next day be hid behind the idol and when the woman came and prayed he answered from behind the idol that her prayer wars granted and that in two days her husband would become blind. Accordingly, two days later the Potter pretended to become blind. Then the woman sent word to the Raja that her husband was blind and that they had nothing to fear from him. The Raja accordingly came one night to visit the woman, and the Potter killed them both with an axe. He buried the body of his wife, but he was in great trouble as to how to dispose of' the body of., the Raja: for he knew; that there would be a hue and cry when the disappearance of the Raja was discovered. At last he decided to put the body in a field of *brinjals* belonging to a neighbour. Toward morning , the owner of the field came to see that his property was all right, and seeing some one among the *brinjals*, thought that it was a thief . He accordingly hit the supposed thief on the head and when be came to examine the body, he was shocked to find that he had, as he thought, killed the Raja. In great distress he went to consult his friend, the Potter; the Potter advised him to put the body among the buffaloes belonging to a Goala At dawn the Goala came to look at his buffaloes and seeing the body of the Raja thought that it was a thief stealing the milk of the buffaloes: catching up a club, he inflicted a blow which caused the body to fall over. When the Goala, found that the body was that of the Raja and that he had apparently killed him, he was in great fear and went to his friend, the Potter, for advice. It was finally decided to dispose of the body by putting it down a well. The next day great search was made for the missing Raja and the body was found in the well by a Brahman, Preparations were made for the obsequies and a funeral pyre erected. The Potter saw his opportunity and digging a hole in the ground under the pyre hid himself in it. When the body had been cremated and the mourners were still collected at the spot, the Potter began to speak from the hole in which he was concealed: the bystanders thought that they heard the voice of the Raja declaring that the Potter had always been his true friend and that he desired that he should be given half the kingdom and the hand of his daughter in marriage. The supposed wishes of the late Raja were obeyed and the Potter lived in luxury for the rest of his life.

PART VI

The belief in witchcraft is very real to the present day among the Santals. All untimely deaths and illness which does not yield to treatment are attributed to the machinations of witches, and women are not unfrequently murdered in revenge for deaths which they are supposed to have caused, or to prevent the continuance of illness for which they are believed to be responsible.

The Santal writer in spite of his education is a firm believer in witchcraft, and details his own experiences. He has justification for his belief, for as was the case in Mediaeval Europe, women sometimes plead guilty to having caused death by witchcraft when there appears to be no adequate motive for a confession, which must involve them in the severest penalties.

Mr. Bodding is aware that Santal women do actually hold meetings at night at which mantras and songs are repeated, and at which they may believe they acquire uncanny powers; the exercise of such powers may also on occasion be assisted by the knowledge of vegetable poisons.

The witch may either herself cause death by 'eating,' or eating the liver of, her victim, or may cause her familiar "*bonga*" to attack the unfortunate. That witches eat the liver is an old idea in India mentioned by the Mughal historians.

The Jan guru is employed to detect who is the woman responsible for any particular misfortune. His usual method is to gaze on a leaf smeared with oil, in which as in a crystal he can doubtless imagine that shapes present themselves. The witch having been detected, she is liable to be beaten and maltreated until she withdraws her spells, and if this does not lead to the desired result she may be put to death.

CLXXIV. WITCHCRAFT

The higher castes do not believe in witchcraft. If a man is ill they give him medicines and if he dies in spite of the medicine they do nothing further. But all the lower castes believe in witchcraft and know that it is a reality. The Santal women learnt the craft first from Marang Buru by playing a trick on him when he meant to teach their husbands. And now they take quite little girls out by night and teach them so that the craft may not die out.

We know of many cases to prove that witchcraft is a reality. Pirthi who lives in Pankha's house was once ill: and it was an aunt of his who was "eating" him. One night as he lay ill the witch came and bent over him to take out his liver: but he woke up just in time and saw her and catching her by the hair he shouted for the people in the house. They and the villagers came and took the woman into custody. When the Pargana questioned her she confessed everything and was punished.

Another time a boy lay ill and senseless. A cowherd who was driving cattle home at evening ran to the back of the house where the sick boy lay, after a cow which strayed there. There he found a woman in a state of possession (rum) he told the villagers what he had seen and they caught the woman and gave her a severe beating: whereupon the sick boy recovered. But about two months afterwards the cowherd suddenly fell down dead: and when they consulted *jan* as to the reason he said that it was the witch who had been beaten who had done it.

CLXXV. OF DAINS AND OJHAS

Once upon a time Marang Buru decided that he would teach men witchcraft. In those days there was a place at which men used to assemble to meet Marang Buru and hold council with him: but they only heard his voice and never saw his face. One day at the assembly when they had begun to tell Marang Buru of their troubles he fixed a day and told them to come to him on it, dressed all in their cleanest clothes and he would teach them witchcraft.

So the men all went home and told their wives to wash their clothes well against the fixed day, as they were going to Thakur to learn witchcraft. The women of course all began to discuss this new plan among themselves and the more they talked of it the less they liked it; it seemed to them that if the men were to get this new strange power it would make them more inclined to despise and bully women than ever; so they made a plot to get the better of their husbands. They arranged that each woman should brew some rice beer and offer it to her husband as he was starting to meet Marang Buru and beg him to drink some lest his return should be delayed. They foresaw that the men would not be able to resist the drink; and that having started they would go on till they were dead drunk: it would then be easy for the women to dress themselves like men and go off to Marang Buru and learn witchcraft in place of their husbands. So said, so done;—the women duly made their husbands drunk and then put on *pagris* and *dhotis* and stuck goats' beards on their faces and went off to Marang Buru to learn witchcraft. Marang Buru did not detect the imposition and according to his promise taught them all the incantations of witchcraft.

After the women had come home with their new knowledge their husbands gradually recovered their senses and bethought them of their appointment with Marang Buru. so they hurried off to the meeting place and asked him to teach them what he had promised. "Why, I taught it all to you this morning," answered Marang Buru, " what do you mean by coming to me again?" The men could not understand what he meant and protested that they had not been to him at all in the morning. "Then you must have told your wives what I was going to do!" This they could not deny: "I see," said *Marang* Buru "then they must have played a trick on you and learnt the mantras in your place." At this the men began to lament and begged that they might be taught also: but Marang Burn said that this was impossible; he could only teach them a very little; their wives had reaped the crop and they could only have the gleanings; so saying, he taught them the art of the *ojha* and in order that they might have the advantage of their wives in one respect and be able to overawe them he also taught them the craft of the *jan* and with that they had to be content. This is why only women are witches.

CLXXVI .INITIATION INTO WITCHCRAFT

When girls are initiated into witchcraft they are taken away by force and made to lead tigers about. This makes them fearless. They are then taken to all the most powerful *bongas* in succession; and are taught to invoke them, as school boys are taught lessons, and to become possessed (*rum*). They are also taught *mantras* and songs and by degrees they cease to be afraid. The novice is made to come out of the house with a lamp in her hand and a broom tied round her waist; she is then conducted to the great *bongas* one of whom approves of her and when all have agreed she is married to that *bonga*. The *bonga* pays the usual brideprice and applies sindur to her forehead. After this she can also marry a man in the usual way and he also pays the bride price. When a girl has learnt everything she is made to take her degree (*sid alang*) by taking out a man's liver and cooking it with rice in a new pot; then she and the young woman who is initiating her, eat the feast together; a woman who has once eaten such a stew is completely proficient and can never forget what she has learnt.

This is the way in which girls learn witchcraft; and if any girl refuses to take the final step and will not eat men she is caused to go mad or die. Those however who have once eaten men have a craving for it.

Generally it is only women who are witches; but there are men who have learnt witchcraft and there are others who without being initiated have kept company with witches. For instance in Simra village there is Chortha who was once a servant of the Parganna. He says that the Parganna's wife used to take him out with her at night. The women used to sacrifice fowls and goats and make him skin them and cut them up: he had then to roast cakes of the flesh and give them to the Parganna's wife who distributed them among the other women.

Sometimes also witches take a man with them to their meetings to beat the drum: and sometimes if a man is very much in love with a girl he is allowed to go with them and is taught witchchaft. For instance there was a man who had a family of daughters and no son and so he engaged a man servant by the year to work for him.

After being some years in service this man servant one night was for some reason unusually late in letting the buffaloes out to graze, and while doing so he saw all the women of the household assembled out of doors; they came up to him and told him not to be afraid and promised to do him no harm provided he told no one what he had seen. Two or three days later the young women of the house invited him to go to a witches meeting He went but felt rather frightened the whole time; however nothing happened to him, so he got over his fear and after that he used to go with them quite willingly and learnt all about witchcraft. At last they told him that he must *sid atang* by "eating " a human being. He objected that he was an orphan and so there was no relation whom he could eat. This was a difficulty that seemed insurmountable; and he suggested that he should be excused the full course and taught only a little such as how to " cat " fowls. The women agreed but it was arranged that to deceive people he should go for two or three days and study with a *jan guru* and be initiated by him. Thus it would be thought that he learnt his magic from the guru but really he learnt it from the witches who taught him everything except how to "eat" human beings. He learnt how to make trees wither away and come to life again; and to make rain fall where he wished while any place he chose remained quite dry; he learnt to walk upon the surface of water without getting wet; he could exorcise hail so that none would touch his house though it fell all around. For a joke he could make stools stick fast to his friends when they sat on them; and anyone he scolded found himself unable to speak properly. All this we have seen him do; but it was no one's business to question him to find out how much he really knew.

Once at the shield and sword dance they cast a spell on a youth till his clothes fell off him in shreds and he was ashamed to dance. Then this servant had the pieces of cloth brought to him; and he covered them with his own cloth and mumbled some *mantras* and blew on it and the pieces joined together and the cloth was as good as ever. This we have seen ourselves.

He lived a long time with his master who found him a wife; but because his first child died he left the place and went to live near Amrahat where he is now.

Another case is Tipu of Mohulpahari. They say that an old witch Dukkia taught him to be an *ojha*. No one has dared to ask him whether he also learnt witchcraft from her but he himself admits that she taught him to be an *ojha*.

Although it is true that there are witches and that they "eat" men you will never see them except when you are alone.

The son-in-law of Surai of Karmatane village, named Khade, died from meeting witches; he told us all about it as he lay dying. He was coming home with some other men: they had all had a little too much to drink and so they got separated. Khade was coming along alone and had nearly reached his house when he saw a crowd of witches under a tree. He went up and asked who they were. Thereupon they turned on him and seized him and dragged him away towards Maluncha. There they did something to him and let him go. Next morning he was seized with purging and by mistake some of the witches' vengeance fell also on the other men and they were taken ill too. They however recovered, but Khade died. If you meet witches you die, but not of course if they take you with them of their own will and teach you their craft.

CLXXVII. WITCHCRAFT

Girls are taught witchcraft when they are young and are married to a *bonga* husband. Afterwards when they marry a man they still go away and visit the *bonga* and when they do so they send in their place a *bonga* woman exactly like them in appearance and voice; so that the husband cannot tell that it is not his real wife. There is however a way of discovering the substitution; for if the man takes a brand from the fire and burns the woman with it, then if it is really a *bonga* and not his wife she will fly away in a flame of fire.

CL. XXVIII. WITCH STORIES

I will now tell you something I have seen with my own eyes. In the village of Dhubia next to mine the only son of the Paranik lay ill for a whole year. One day I went out to look at my *rahar* crop which was nearly ripe and as I stood under a mowah tree I heard a voice whispering. I stooped down to try and see through the *rahar* who was there but the crop was so thick that I could see nothing, so I climbed up the mowah tree to look. Glancing towards Dhubia village I saw the third daughter of the Paranik come out of her house and walk towards me. When about fifty yards from me she climbed a big rock and waited. Presently an old aunt of hers came out of the village and joined her. Then the old woman went back to her house and returned with a lota of water. Meanwhile the girl had crome down from the rock and sat at its foot near a thicket of *dhela* trees. The old woman caused the girl to become possessed (*rum*) and they had some conversation which I could not hear, Then they poured out the water from the lota and went home.

On my way home I met a young fellow of the village and found that he had also seen what the two women did. We went together to the place and found the mark of the water spilled on the ground and two leaves which had been used as wrappers and one of which was smeared with vermilion and *adwa* rice had been scattered about. We decided to tell no one till we saw whether what had been done was meant to benefit or injure the sick boy. Fifteen days later the boy died: and when his parents consulted a *jan* he named a young, woman of the village as the cause of the boy's death and she was taken and punished severely by the villagers.

It is plain that the boy's sister and aunt in order to save themselves caused the *jan* to see an innocent woman. I could not bring the boy back to life so it was useless for me to say anything, especially as the guilty women were of the Paranik's own family. This I saw myself in broad daylight.

Another thing that happened to me was this. I had been with the Headman to pay in the village rent. It was night when we returned and after leaving him I was going home alone. As I passed in front of a house a bright light suddenly shone from the cowshed; I looked round and saw a great crowd of women-witches standing there. I ran away by the garden at the back of the house until I reached a high road; then I stopped and looked round and saw that the witches were coming after me; and looking towards the hamlet where my house was I saw that witches were coming with a bright light from that direction also. When I found myself thus hemmed in. I felt that my last hour had come but I ran on till I came to some jungle,

Looking back from there I saw that the two bands had joined together and were coming after me. I did not feel safe there for I knew that there were *bongas* in the jungle who might tell the witches where I was. So I ran on to the *tola* where an uncle and aunt of mine lived. As I ran down the street I saw two witches at the back of one of the houses. They were sitting down; one was in a state of possession (*rum*) and the other was opposite her holding a lamp. So I left the street and made my way through the fields till I came to my uncle's house. I knocked and was admitted panting and breathless; my uncle and aunt went outside to see what it was that had scared me and they saw the witches with the two lights flashing and made haste to bolt the door. None of us slept for the rest of the night and in the morning I told them all that had happened.

Since that night I have been very frightened of witches and do not like to go out at night. It was lucky that the witches did not recognise me; otherwise I should not have lived. Ever since I have never stayed at home for long together; I go there for two or three months at a time and then go away and work elsewhere. I am too frightened to stay in my own village. Now all the old women who taught witchcraft are dead except one: when she goes I shall not be frightened any more. I shall be able to go home when I like. I have never told any one but my uncle and aunt what I saw until now that I have written it down.

So from my own experience I have no doubt about the existence of witches; I cannot say how they "eat' men, whether by magic or whether they order "bongas to cause a certain man to die on a certain day. Some people say that when a witch is first initiated she is married to a bonga and if she wants to "eat" a man she orders her *bonga* husband to kill him and if he refuses she heaps abuse on him until he does.

CLXXIX. WITCH STORIES

Young girls are taught witchcraft against their wills and if they refuse to "eat their father or brother they die or go mad. There was a girl in my own village and she went out gathering herbs with another girl who was a witch. As usual they sang at their work and the witch girl sang songs the tune of which the other thought so pretty that she learnt them by heart. When she had learnt them the witch girl told her that they were witch songs and explained to her their meaning The girl was very angry at having been taught them unawares but the witch girl assured her that she would never be able to forget the songs or their interpretation; then she assigned her to a *bonga* bridegroom and then told her to *sid atang* and all would be well with her otherwise she would have trouble.

When the girl learnt that she must *sid atang* by "eating" her father or brother or mother she began to make excuses; she could not kill her father for he was the support of the family; nor her only brother for he was wanted too at the *Baha* and *Sohrai* nor her mother who had reared her in childhood. The witch girl said that if she refused she would die; and she said that she would rather die than do what was required of her. Then the witch did something and the girl began to rave and talk gibberish and from that time was quite out of her senses. *Ojhas* tried to cure her in vain until at last one suggested that she should be taken to another village as the madness must be the work of witches living in her own village. So they took her away and the remedies then cured her. She stayed in her new home and was married there. A long time afterwards she went back to pay a visit to her father's house: but the day after she arrived her head began to ache and she fell ill and though her husband came and took her away she died the day after she reached her home.

There was another girl; her friends noticed that when she came home with them in the evening after planting rice she was very careful not to fall behind or be left atone and they used to laugh at her for being a coward. But one day she was gathering Indian corn with a friend and as they talked she said "You will all have lovely dancing at the *Sohrai.*" "You !" said her friend: "won't you be there? Are you going away?" Then the girl began to cry and sobbed out that her mother had taught her witchcraft and married her to a *bonga*; and it was for fear of the *bonga* that she did not like to be alone in the dark; and because she had refused to "eat" any one her mother intended to "eat" her and so she had no hope of living to see the Sohrai. Three days later the girl fell ill and died, and after her death her friend told how she had foreseen it.

CLXXX. WITCH STORIES

In the village of Mohulpahari there was a youth named Jerba. He was servant to Bepin Teli of Tempa and often had to come home in the dark after his day's work. One night he was coming back very late and, before he saw where he was, suddenly came upon a crowd of witches standing under a hollow mowah tree at the foot of the field that the dhobie has taken. Just as he caught sight of them they seized hold of him and flung him down and did something which he could not remember—for he lost his senses when they threw him down. When he came to himself he managed to struggle free and run off. The witches pursued but failed to overtake him and he reached his home in a state of terror. The witches however had not finished with him for two or three days after they caused him to fall from a tree and break his arm. *Ojhas* were called in but their medicines did him no good. The arm mortified and maggots formed and in a few days Jerba himself told them that he would not recover; he told them how the witches chased him and that he had recognised them as women of his own village and shortly afterwards he became speechless and died.

My own brother-in-law lived at Mubundi. One night he and several other men were sitting up on the threshing-floor watching their rice. In the middle of the night they saw lights shining and flickering in the courtyard of my brother-in-law's house and he went to see what was the matter. When he got near, the lights went into the house: he went up quietly and as he looked in found the house full of women who extinguished the light directly they saw him and rushed out of the house. Then he asked my sister what the light was; but she could only stammer out "What light? I saw no light," so he struck her a blow and went back to the threshing-floor and told the others what he had seen. That night he would not tell them the names of the women he had seen; and before morning his right arm swelled and became very painful; the swelling quickly increased and by noon he lost consciousness and a few hours later he died.

CLXXXI. THE TWO WITCHES

There were once a woman and her daughter-in-law who were both witches. One night during the annual *Sohrai* festival the men of the village were going from house to house singing and getting rice beer to drink; and one young man named Chandrai got so drunk that when they came to the house where the two witch- women lived he rolled himself under the shelf on which rice was stored and fell asleep. Next morning he came to his senses but he did not like to come out and show himself for fear of ridicule so he made up his mind to wait till a party came round singing again and then to slip out with them unperceived.

He lay waiting and presently all the men of her house went away to join in the danka dance ; leaving the mistress of the house and her daughter-in-law alone. Presently the two began to talk and the elder woman said, "Well what with the pigs and the goats that have been sacrified during this Sohrai we have had plenty of meat to eat lately and yet I don't feel as if I had any." "That is so," answered her daughter-in-law; "fowls' and pig's flesh is very unsatisfying." "Then what are we to do?" rejoined the old woman, "I don't know unless you do for the father of your grandchild." When he heard this Chandrai shivered with fright and hid himself further under the rice shelf, for he saw that the two women must be witches.

That day was the day on which a bullock is tied to a post outside each house and at noon the husband of the younger witch began to dig a hole outside the house to receive the post. While he was working Chandrai heard the two women begin to talk again. "Now is your opportunity,," said the younger woman "while he is digging the hole." "But perhaps the *ojha* will be able to discover us," objected the other. "Oh we can prevent that by making the *ojha* see in the oiled leaf the faces of Rupi and Bindi naming two girls of the village —and we can say that my husband had seduced them and then declined to marry them and that that was why they killed him." The old woman seemed to be satisfied, for she took up a hatchet and went out to where her son was digging the hole. She waited till he bent down to thorw out the earth with his hands and then cut open his back and pulled out his liver and heart and brought them into the house. Her unfortunate son felt a spasm of pain when his mother struck him but he did not know what had hurt him and there was no visible wound. The two women then chopped up the liver and heart and cooked and ate them.

That night when the village youths came round to the house, singing Chandri slipped out with them unperceived and hastened home. Two or three days later the bewitched man became seriously ill: medicines and sacrifices did him no good; the *ojhas* were called in but could make nothing of the illness. The villagers were very angry with them for the failure and the headman told them that they must ascertain by means of the oiled leaf who had caused the illness, or it would be the worse for them. So the *ojhas* went through their ceremonies and after a time declare that the oiled leaf showed the faces of the two girls Rupi and Bindi; and that it was they who were eating up the sick man. So the two girls were sent for and questioned but they solemnly swore that they knew nothing about the matter. No one believed their protestations and the head man ordered that filth should be put into their mouths and that they should be well beaten to make them confess. However before any harm was done them Chandrai spang up and called out to the headman: "You have proof that these girls are witches, but I will not let you beat them here. Let us take them to yonder open field; the token of their oath is there and we will make them first remove it. If we beat them first they will probably refuse to remove the oath." "How do you know about their oath? " asked the headman. " Never mind, I do know." The villagers were convinced by his confident manner and all went with the two girls to the open field.

Chandrai's object was to get away from the witches house for he was afraid to speak there; but when they were out in the open he stood up and told the villagers all that he had seen and heard the two witches do; they remembered that he had been missing for a whole day during the Sohrai festival and believed him. So the sick man's wife and mother were fetched and well beaten to make them the sick man to health; but his liver and heart had been eaten so that the case was hopeless and in a few day he was dead. His relations in revenge soon killed the two witches.

Rupi and Bindi whose lives had been saved by Chandrai went and established themselves in his house for they declared that as they owed their lives to him it was plain that he must marry them.

CLXXXII. THE SISTER-IN-LAW WHO WAS A WITCH

There were once two brothers who lived together; the elder was married but the younger had no wife. The elder brother used to cultivate their lands and his wife used to draw water and fetch fuel and the younger brother used to take the cattle out to graze. One year when the elder brother was busy in the fields the younger one used to take his cattle to graze near where his brother was working and the wife used to bring out the breakfast for both of them. One day the younger brother thought he would play a trick on his sister-in-law by not answering when she called him to his breakfast; so when her husband had finished his meal and she called out for the younger brother to come he gave no answer; she concluded that the cattle were straying and would not let him come so she took up her basket and went to look for him; but when he saw her coming he climbed up a tree and hid himself and for all her calling gave no answer, but only sat and laughed at her although she came quite close to where he was.

At last the woman got into a passion and putting down the breakfast by the side of a pool which was close to the tree up which her brother-in-law had climbed she stripped off her clothes and began bowing down and calling. " Ho, Dharmal Chandi I come forth !" When he saw this the man was amazed and waited to see whom she was calling, meaning to let her know he was there directly she turned to go away home with the breakfast. But the woman kept on calling to Dharmal Chandi and at last out of the pool appeared an immense bearded *bonga* with long and matted hair. When the woman saw him her tongue flickered in and out like a snake's and she made a hissing noise, such as a crab makes, Then the woman began "Dharmal Chandi I have a request which you must promise to grant." And when the *bonga* had promised she proceeded. "You must have my brother-in-law killed by a tiger the day after tomorrow; he has put me to endless trouble making me go shouting after him all through the jungle; I wanted to go back quickly because I have a lot of work at home; he was wasted my time by not answering; so the day after tomorrow you must have him killed." The *bonga* promised to do what she asked and disappeared into the pool and the woman went home.

While the younger brother was up in the tree his cattle had got into a *gundli* field and eaten up the crop: and the owner found it out and got the brothers fined. So that evening the elder brother asked him where he had been that he had not looked after the cattle properly nor eaten any breakfast. In answer the younger brother only began to cry; at that his sister-in-law said. "Let him alone; he is crying for want of a wife; he is going silly because we have not married him;" and so nothing more was said. But the elder brother was not satisfied and the next day when they went together to work he asked the younger what was the real reason for his crying.

Then the younger answered. "Brother, I am in great trouble; it makes me cry all day; if you wish ever to look on my face again, you must not work in the fields tomorrow but keep me company while I tend the cattle; if we are separated for a moment a tiger will kill me; it will be quickly over for me but you I know will miss me much and so I am grieving for you; if you have any tenderness for me do not leave me tomorrow but save me from the tiger." His brother asked the reason for this foreboding but the younger man said that he would explain nothing and accuse no one until the events of the next day had shown whether he was speaking the truth; if a tiger really came to stalk him then that would be proof that he had had good reason for his apprehension; and he begged his brother not to speak a word about it to anyone and especially not to his wife.

The elder brother promised to keep the matter a secret and cheered his brother up and told him to be of good heart; they would take their bows and axes and he would like to see the tiger that would touch them. So the next morning the two brothers went off together well armed and tended the cattle in company; nothing happened and at mid-day they brought the cattle home; when the woman saw them with bows in their hands she asked where they had been. Her husband told her that he had been to look for a hare which he had seen on the previous day but he had not a been able to find it. Then his brother said that he had seen a hare in its form that very morning but had not had time to shoot it. So they pretended to arrange to go and hunt this hare and after having eaten their rice they drove out the cattle again.

As they went along they kept close together with their arrows on the string, so that the tiger which came to stalk the younger brother got no opportunity to attack; at last it showed itself at the edge of the jungle; the cattle were thrown into a turmoil and the brothers saw that it was really following them; and the elder brother was convinced that there was some reason for his brother's fears. So they turned the cattle back and cautiously drove them home, keeping a good look out all they way; the tiger prowled round them hiding in the bushes, sometimes in front and sometimes behind, but found no opening to attack while they for their part did not dare to shoot at it. The tiger followed them right up to the house; but the elder brother did not leave the other for a moment nor let him go outside the door and at night he slept on the same bed with him.

The next morning he begged his brother to tell him all that had happened and explain how he knew that a tiger would seek his life on the previous day. "Come then" said the other, "to yonder open ground. I cannot tell you in the house;" so they went out together and than the younger told all that had happened and how his sister-in-law had ordered the *Bonga* to have him killed by a tiger; "I did not tell you before till my story had been put to the proof for fear that you would not believe me and would tell your wife; but now you know all. I cannot live with you any longer; from this very day I must go and find a home else-where. "Not so" said the other, "I will not keep such a woman with me any longer; she is dangerous; I will go home now and put her to death," and so saying he went home and killed his wife with an axe.

CLXXXIII. RAMJIT BONGA

Once upon a time a man went out to snare quail: he set his snares by the side of a mountain stream and then sat down under a bush to watch them. As he waited he saw a young woman come along with her water pot under her arm to draw water from the stream. When she got to the *ghat* she put down her pot and made her way up the stream, towards where the snares had been set; she did not notice the hunter but went to the stump of an ebony tree near him and looking round and seeing no one she suddenly became possessed and started dancing round the ebony tree and singing some song which he could not clearly catch; and as she danced she called out "The Pig's fat is overflowing: brother-in-law Ramjit come here to me." When she called out like this the quail catcher quietly crept nearer still to her. Although the woman repeatedly summoned him in this way the Bonga would not come out because he was aware of the presence of the onlooker; the woman however got into a passion at his non-appearance and stripping off her clothes she danced naked round the tree calling out " The Pig's fat is overflowing: brother-in-law Ramjit come hither at once." At last out of the *nala* appeared the bonga, dark, enormous and shaggy; and approached the woman: Then the woman said "Brother-in-law Ramjit there is something that you must do for me; my nephew is ill; he must die on such and such a day; that day I must see the smoke of his funeral pyre; but you must save me from the witch-finder; let the blame fall not on me but on so and so; this is what I came to urge on you; that you protect me from discovery and then we shall always to friends."

The Bonga at first knowing that they were being watched would not make the promise but when the woman insisted he promised in a low voice and then disappeared into the *nala*; and the witch went back to the ghat, filled her water pot and went home. The quail catcher also went trembling home and he remembered the day fixed for the death of the nephew of the witch and he decided to wait and see what happened before saying anything to the villagers. Sure enough on the day before that fixed by the witch the invalid became unconscious and was obviously at that point of death. When he heard this the quail catcher went to the sick man's bedside and seeing his condition told his relatives to collect all the villagers to beat the woman whom he had seen with the Bonga and he told them all that had passed; the villagers believed him and summoning all the women of the village they scolded them; and then being excited by this they rose up and began to beat the women; to each they gave one blow with a stick, but the woman whom the quail catcher pointed out they beat till she fainted.

Then they ordered her to cure the sick man and threatened to burn her along with him if he died, but she insisted that she was innocent. Then they told her that they knew all that had passed between her and the Bonga Ramjit, she persisted that it was all a mistake. So they started to beat her again; they beat her from her heels to her neck and then from her neck down to her heels till the blood flowed and they swore that they would not let her go unless she cured the sick man and that if he died they would cut her to pieces. At last the torture made her confess that it was she who was eating the sick man; and she promised to cure him; so they first made her tell the names of all the other witches in the village and then tied her a post and kept her there, and did not write her till in four or five days the sick man recovered. When she was let loose the quail catcher ran away from the village and would not live there any more.

But the villagers threatened the witch woman that if her nephew or any of his family got ill again they would kill her; and they told her that as her secret had been found out she was hence forth to be their *ojha* and cure their diseases; and they would supply her with whatever she wanted for the purpose; they asked what sacrifice her nephew must make on his recovery; and she told them to get a red cock, a grasshopper: a lizard; a cat and a black and white goat; so they brought her these and she sacrificed them and the villagers had a feast of rice and rice beer and went to their homes and the matter ended.

CLXXXIV. THE HERD BOY AND THE WITCHES

Once upon a time a cowherd lost a calf and while looking for it he was benighted in the jungle; for the was afraid to go home lest he should be scolded for losing the calf. He had with him his bow and arrows and flute and a stick but still he was afraid to stay the night in the jungle; so he made up his mind to go to the *jahirthan* as *More Turuiko* would protect him there; so he went to the *jahirthan* and climbed a tree in which a spirit abode; he took his bow and arrows up with him but he was too frightened to go to sleep.

About supper time he saw a number of women who were witches collect from all sides at the *jahirthan*: at this sight he was more frightened than ever; the witches then called up the bongas and they also summoned twos tigers; then they danced the lagre dance and they combed the hair of the two tiger. Then they also called *More Turniko* and when they came, one bonga said "I smell a man" and *More Turniko* scolded him saying "Faith, you smelt nothing until we came; and directly we come you say you smell a man; it must be us you smell"; and the chief of the *bongas* agreed that it must be all right. Then while the women were dancing the boy took his bow and shot the tow tigers, and the tigers enraged by their wounds fell on the witches and killed them all;

and then they died themselves; and as they were dying they roared terribly so that the people in the villages near heard them. When it grew light the boy climbed down and drawing the arrows from the bodies of the tigers went home.

Then the people asked him where he had spent the night and he said that he was benighted while looking for his calf and as he heard tigers roaring near the *jahir than* he was frightened and had stayed in the jungle. They told him that when the tigers began to roar the calf had come running home by itself and this was good news to the herd boy. Then he found that all the children in the village were crying for their mothers and the men were asking what had become of their wives; then the herdboy said that in the night had seen some women going in the direction of the *jahirthan* but he had not seen them come back and they had better go and look there. So the villagers went off and found their wives lying dead by the *jahirthan* and the two tigers also dead; and they knew that the women must have been witches to go there at night; so they wept over them and burned the bodies. And a long time afterwards the boy told them all that he had seen and done; and they admitted that he had done right in destroying the witches and that it would be well if all witches met the same fate.

This story whether true or not is told to this day.

CLXXXV. THE MAN-TIGER

There was once a young man who when a boy had learnt witchcraft from some girl friends; he was married but his wife knew nothing about this. They lived happily together and were in the habit of paying frequent visits to the wife's parents. One day they were on their way together to pay such a visit and in passing through some jungle they saw, grazing with a herd of cattle, a very fine and fat bull calf. The man stopped and stripped himself to his waist cloth and told his wife to hold his clothes for him while he went and ate the calf that had stirred his appetite. His wife in astonishment asked him how he was going to eat a living animal; he answered that he was going to turn into a tiger and kill the animal and he impressed on her that she must on no account be frightened or run away and he handed her a piece of root and told her that she must give it him to smell when he came back and he would at once regain his human shape.

So saying he retired into a thicket and took off his waist cloth and at once became a tiger; then he swallowed the waist cloth and thereby grew a fine long tail. Then he sprang upon the calf and knocked it over and began to suck its blood. At this sight his wife was overwhelmed with terror and forgetting everything in her fear ran right off to the her father's house taking with her husband's clothes and the magic root. She arrived breathless and told her parents all that had happened. Meanwhile her husband had been deprived of the means of regaining his own form and has was forced to spend the day hiding in the jungle as tiger; when night fell he made his way to the village where his father-in-law lived. But when he got there all the dogs began to bark and when the villagers saw that there was a tiger they barricaded themselves in their houses.

The man-tiger went prowling round his father-in-law house and at last his father-in-law plucked up courage and went out and threw the root which the wife had brought under the tiger's nose and he at once became a man again. Then they brought him into the house and washed his feet; and gave him hot rice-water to drink; and to drinking this he vomited up lumps of clotted blood. The next morning the father-in-law called the villagers and showed them this blood and told them all that had happened; then he turned to his son-in-law and told him to take himself off and vowed that his daughter should never go near him again. The man-tiger had no answer to make but went back silently and alone to his own home.

NOTE :— The following is a prescription for making an *Ulat bag* or were-tiger.

"The fibre of a plant (Bauhinia vahli) beaten out and cooked in mustard oil in a human skull."

GLOSSARY

Adwa........................Rice husked without having been boiled.
Arta..........................Red pigment applied to the feet for *ornament*.
Baha Porob.............The flower festival; the spring festival held about February.
Bandi.......................A receptacle for storing grain, made of straw rope.
Bharia.................... A bamboo carried on the shoulder with a load slung at each end.
Bhut........................A ghost, a harmful spirit, not originally a Santal word.
Bonga.....................The name for all gods, godlings and supernatural beings. Sing bonga is the sun god; the spirits of ancestors are bongas, there are bongas of the hills, streams and the forest; others are like fairies and take human form. Sacrifices are offered to bongas of all occasions.
Brinjal.................... The egg plant.
But..........................Grain, a kind of pulse.
Chamar.................. A low caste, workers in leather.
Chando................... The sun, the supreme god of the Santals.
Champa.................. A country in which according to their traditions, the Sandals once lived.
Charak Puja.......... The festival at which men are swung by hooks from a pole.
Chatar.................... A festival at which dancing takes place round an umbrella.
Chowkidar.............. A watchmen.
Churin.................... The spirit of a woman who has died while pregnant, her feet are turned backwards. Not originally Santal.
Chumaura...............A ceremony observed at marriage, and Sohrae festival.
Dain.......................A witch. Witches are supposed to use their powers to cause sickness and death; women accused of withcraft are often murdered.
Dehri.....................The president of the annual hunt; he presides over the Court which during the hunt hears appeals against

unjust decisions of paganas.

Dewan.................... The chief minister of a Raja.

Dhobi..................... A washerman.

Dhoti...................... The waistcloth worn by men.

Dom....................... A low caste, scavengers, basketmakers and drummers.

Gamcha................. A small piece of cloth worn round the neck, or when bathing.

Ghat........................ The approach to a pool or river at which people bathe; the crossing place of a river.

Ghormuha.............. A horse-headed monster; not a Santal name.

Goala...................... A man of the cow keeping caste.

Godet..................... The village constable, the official mesenger of the headmen

Goondli................. A small millet.

Gosain.................. A religious ascetic, usually of the Vishnuite persuasion.

Gupini.................... A celestial milkmaid, such as those who danced with Krishna; not a Santal creation.

Gur......................... Juice of sugar cane, molasses.

Hadi........................ A low caste of scavengers.

Jan or Jan guru..... A witch finder. When a man is ill the Jan is consulted as to what witch is responsible. The Jan usually divines by gazing at an oiled leaf.

Fadirthan............... The group of sacred trees left in each village for the accomodation of the spirits of the forests when the jungle is cleared.

Fai tuk..................... A bullock given to a woman at her marriage.

Fhalka.................... A boastful man.

Fogi or Fugi........... A religious ascetic, a mendicant.

Lota........................ A small brass water pot.

Lakh....................... One hundred thousand.

Mahadeo................ The great God, *i.e.* Shiva.

Mahajan................. A moneylender.

Mahuli.................... A tribe akin to the Santals, basket makers by profession.

Malhan.................. A cultivated leguminous plant.

Manjhithan............. The little pavilion in the centre of every Santal village at which the spirits of dead headmen are worshipped and where village councils are held.

Mantra.................... An incantation, sacred or majic formula.
Marang Burn.......... The great spirit, the original chief god of the Santals.
Marwari................. A trader from Rajputana and the adjoining parts.
Maund....................A weight, 40 seers or 82 pounds.
Meral.......................A small tree. Phyllanthus emblica.
More Turuiko.......... Lit.: The five or six—certain Santal godlings.
Mowah................... A tree, Bassia latifolia, the fleshy flower is eaten and spirit is distilled from it.
Musahar..................A semi-aboriginal caste which catches and eats rats.
Nala........................A water course with steep banks.
Narta......................The name giving ceremony observed three or five days after birth, by which the child is formally admitted into the tribe.
Chando...................The moon goddess, wife of Sing Chando, the Sun god.
Kat.......................... A dry measure used for grain.
Kisar Bonga........... A spirit which takes up its abode in the house, frolicsome and mischevious.
Kisku....................... One of the twelve exogamous septs of Santals, by tradition it was formerly the royal sept.
Koeri.......................A cultivating caste of Hindus.
Kora.......................A youth or young man, the hero of a story is often called so throughout, and I have for convenience adopted it as a proper name.
Kos.........................A measure of distance, two miles.
Ojha.......................An exorcist, a charm doctor, one who counteracts the effects of withcraft.
Pachet.....................A place in the Manbhum district which the Santals occupied in the course of their immigrations.
Panchayat...............A council primarily of five which meets to decide a dispute.
Pagri.......................A cloth worn round the head, a turban
Paharia...................A hill, man; the Saurias of Male of the Rajmahal hills.
Pai..........................A wooden or metal measure containing half of seer.
Pan ....Betel used for chewing.
Parganna................A santal chief having jurisdiction over a number of villages.
Paranic...................The assistant headman of a village.

Parrab.................. A festival.
Peepul or Pipal...... A tree, ficus religiosa.
Pilchu Haram.........
Pilchu Bhudi........... The first man and woman.
Rahar...................... A cultivated crop, a kind of pulse.
Raibar..................... A marriage go-between, a man employed to arrange a marriage.
Rakas...................... An ogre. Sanskrit Rakhshya.
Rum...................... To be possessed, to fall into a cataleptic state.
Sabai......................A kind of grass used for making rope.
Sal...........................A forest tree. Shorea robusta.
Seer.........................A weight, about two pounds.
Sid atang.................To take the final step, to be completely initiated.
Sing bonga............. The Sun god.
Sipahi......................An armed guard, a soldier, armed messenger.
Sohrai.....................The great winter festival of the Santals
Taluq......................A revenue division of the country.
Tarop tree............... A small tree, Buchanania latifolia.
Thakur.................... The supreme Being.
Tika.........................A mark on the forehead, the giving of which corresponds to coronation.
Toba.......................A hamlet, a detached quarter of a village.

APPENDIX

INTRODUCTION

The Kolhan forms the western half of the district of Singhbhum in Chota Nagpur. The Hos or Larka Hos who form the bulk of the inhabitants are a branch of the Mundas of the Chota Nagpur Plateau. They are one of those Kolarian tribes of which the Santals are perhaps the best known. I have collected some of the Folklore stories current among them, the recollection of which would, however, appear to be dying out.

The Rev. A. Campbell of the Free Church of Scotland, Santal Mission, has printed a volume of Santal folk tales collected by him in Manbhum, a neighbouring district to Singhbhum. As might be expected there is considerable resemblance between those Santal Tales and the ones now reproduced. I have heard some of Mr. Campbell's Santal stories told by Hos precisely as he relates them, and there are many incidents common to both collections. On the other hand there is no resemblance between these Kolarian tales, and the Bengal stories published by Rev. Lal Behari De. In the latter I only notice one incident which appears in the Kolhan stories, the bringing together of two lovers through a long hair floating down a stream, but in Bengal it is the lady's hair that floats to her lover, while in the Kolhan it is always the long hair of the hero which inspires love in the heart of the Raja's daughter.

The stories may be divided into two groups the animal stories in which the principal characters are animals, for the most part denizens of the jungles, and the stories which deal with a settled state of Society with Rajas, priests and members of the different Hindu castes following their usual occupations. It is interesting, but perhaps scarcely profitable, to try and deduce from the latter some hints of the previous history of the Hos, who, as we know them, are a strongly democratic race, with a well developed tribal system. They look on themselves as the owners of the soil and are unwilling to admit the claims of any overload.

I have made no attempt to put the following stories into a literary dress; I merely bring them as a few stones to the hands of the builders who build the structure of comparative mythology.

(1)—The River Snake

Once upon a time a certain woman had been on a visit to a distant village. As she was going home she reached the bank of a flooded river. She tried to wade across but soon found that the water was too deep and the current too strong. She looked about but could see no signs of a boat or any means of crossing. It began to grow dark and the woman was in great distress at the thought that she would not be able to reach her home.

While she thus stood in doubt, suddenly out of river came a great snake an said to her: "Woman, what will you give me if I ferry you across the river?" She answered: "Snake, I have nothing to give you." The snake said I cannot take you across the river unless you promise to give me something. Now the woman at the time was pregnant and not knowing what else to do, she promised that when her child was born, if it were a daughter she would marry her to the river snake and if it were a son that, when the boy grew up he should become the "*juri*" or "name friend" of the snake. The woman swore to do this with an oath and then the snake took her on his back and bore her safely across the flooded stream. The woman safely reached her home and in a little time a daughter was born to her. Years passed away and the woman forgot all about the snake and her oath. One day she went to the river to fetch water and the snake came out of the stream of and said to her: "Woman, where is the wife whom you promised to me?" The woman then remembered her oath and going back to her house she returned to the river with her daughter. When the girl came to the bank of the river the snake seized her and drew her underneath the water and her mother saw her no more. The girl lived with the snake at the bottom of the river and in the course of years bore him four snake sons.

Afterwards the girl remembered her home and one day she went to visit her mother. Her brothers when they came home were astonished to see her and said: "Sister, we thought that you were drowned in the river." She answered: "No, I was not drowned, but I am married and have children." The brothers said: "Where is this brother-in-law of ours?" Their sister said: "Go to the river and call him." So they went to the river and called and the snake came up out of the water and went to their house with them. Then they welcomed the snake and gave him great quantities of rice beer to drink. After drinking this the snake became sleepy and coiling himself in great coils went to sleep. Then the brothers who did not like a snake brother-in-law took their axes and cut off the head of the snake while he slept, and afterwards their sister lived in their house.

(2)—The Sons of the Tigress

Once upon a time a cow and a tigress lived in a jungle and were great friends, they were never separated. Now in those days tigers did not eat flesh, but grazed like cattle, so the tigress never thought of doing any harm to her friend the cow. The tigress had given birth to two men children who were growing up fine and sturdy lads. One afternoon the cow and the tigress went down to a stream to drink, the cow went into the stream and drank and the tigress drank lower down. The cow fouled the water of the stream and the tigress tasting the water found it sweet and thought if the cow can make the water so sweet how sweet the flesh of the cow must be. So on the way back from the stream the tigress suddenly sprang on the cow and killed her and ate her up, leaving nothing but the bones. When she got home her sons asked her where the cow was, but the tigress said that she did not know and that the cow must have deserted them, but afterwards the boys found the bones of the cow and they guessed what had happened. Then they thought, if our mother has killed her friend the cow, she will surely kill and eat us next. So when the tigress was asleep they killed her with axes. Then they ran away after going for many days thought the jungle they reached a city and they found all the people in great distress because a tiger was devastating the kingdom and killing all the inhabitants and no one could kill the tiger. The Raja of the city made a proclamation that any one who could kill the tiger should have half the kingdom and his daughter in marriage. The two boys being the sons of a tigress were able by their knowledge of tiger ways to kill the tiger. So they were given half the kingdom and the elder of them married the king's daughter and they lived happily ever after.

(3)—The Tiger's Marriage.

Once upon a time there lived a Raja who had one son and many daughters. One day the Raja went into the jungle to cut grass. He cut a great deal of grass and tied it up in a big bundle and then he found that he had cut so much that it was more than he could carry. As he was wondering what he should do a tiger came by that way and seeing the Raja in difficulties asked what he could do to help him. The Raja explained that he had cut a bundle of grass which was too heavy to carry. The tiger said that he would carry the grass if he were rewarded for it: the Raja asked him what reward he wanted. The tiger said that he wished for one of the Raja's daughters in marriage. The Raja reflected that he had many daughters and agreed to the proposition. Thereupon the grass was placed on the tiger's back and he carried it to the Raja's palace. Now the Raja was ashamed to give his daughter openly to the tiger so he told the tiger to wait by the water hole, and sending for one of his daughters bade her go and fetch water; the girl went to the water hole where the tiger was waiting and was carried off by the tiger. But the Raja's son missed his sister and went in search of her. After searching some time he came to a cave in the jungle and looking in he was the tiger finishing the remains of the girl whom he had killed. Then the Raja's son ran home as quickly as he could, and told the Raja what he had seen.

The next day the tiger came openly to the Raja's palace and asked to see the Raja. He was taken to the Raja and treated politely. Then the tiger said to the Raja: "I am sorry to say that the wife whom you gave me has died, so you must give me another. * The Raja said he would think about the matter and invited the tiger to stay at the palace. So the tiger was given a good bed, and quickly went to sleep. In the night the Raja's son boiled some large vessels of water and poured the scalding water over the sleeping tiger and killed him. And in this way the tiger died.

(4)—The Jackal and His Neighbours.

Once upon a time a jackal killed a kid in a village and taking it to a little distance began to enjoy a good meal. But the crows who always make a noise about other people's business, gathered in a tree over his head and made a great cawing, so the villagers went to see what was the matter and beat the jackal severely and deprived him of his feast. On this account the jackal was very angry with the crows and determined to be revenged.

Shortly afterwards a great storm came on with wind and heavy rain and all the birds and animals were in danger of being drowned. Then the jackal pretended to be sorry for the crows and invited them all to come and take shelter in his house. But when the jackal had got them safely into his house he killed and ate them all; all except one *nilkanth* bird which he decided to keep for his breakfast the next day, so he tied the *nilkanth* bird, on to his tail and went away from that part of the country. But the *nilkanth* bird pecked and pecked at the jackal's tail until it not only pecked itself loose but hurt the tail so much that it became festered and swollen.

As the jackal went along with his swollen tail he met a potter going to market with earthen pots for sale. Then the jackal put on a bullying air and said that he was a *sipahi* of the Raja, and one pot of those being taken to market must be given to him; at first the potter refused, but being frightened he in the end gave one to the jackal.

Into this the jackal pressed the matter which had accumulated in his swollen tail and covered it over with leaves. Going on, the jackal met a boy tending goats, he told the boy that he had arranged with the boy's father to buy one of the goats in exchange for a pot of ghee, the boy believed this and took the chatty with its contents from the jackal and gave him a fine goat.

* This is quite in accordance with Ho notions. If a man buys a wife there is an implied warranty that she is to last a reasonable time. If she dies shortly after marriage a sister or cousin has to be given to replace her.

The jackal went off to his home in triumph with the goat. His friends and neighbours were very jealous when they saw that he had so fine a goat and waiting till his back was turned, they killed and ate the goat, and then they filled the skin with stones and gravel so that it might seem that the whole goat was still there. The jackal found out what his neighbors had done and he took the goat skin to a *muchi* and got the *muchi* to make it into a drum. Then he went to the banks of a deep river and began to play the drum. All the other jackals collected round and were lost in admiration of the tone of the drum. They wanted to know where so beautiful a drum was got, the first jackal said that there were many drums as good at the bottom of the river, and if they tied stones round their necks and jumped in they would find them. So the other jackals in their anxiety to get such drums jumped into the river and were drowned, jackal was revenged on all his enemies.

(5)—The Jackal and the Tigers

Once upon a time a pair of tigers lived in a jungle with their two cubs, and every day the two tigers used to go out hunting deer and other animals that they might bring home food for the cubs. Near the jungle lived a jackal, and the found it very hard to get enough to live upon; however, one day he came upon the tiger's den when the father and mother tiger were out hunting, and there he saw the two tiger cubs with a large piece of venison which their parents had brought them. Then the jackal put on a swaggering air and began to abuse the tiger cubs for having so much venison, saying: "I am the sipahi of the Raja and the Raja has demanded venison and none can be found, while low people like you have a fine piece like this: give it at once or I will take it and report against you to the Raja." Then the tiger cubs were frightened and gave up the venison and the jackal went off gleefully and ate it. The next day the jackal came again and in the same way took off more meat. The jackal continued taking their meal from the tiger cubs every day till the cubs became very thin: the father tiger determined to find out why this was, so he hid himself in the bushes watched: he saw the jackal come and take away the meat from the cubs. Then he was very angry and ran after the jackal to kill him and the jackal ran away very fast and the tiger ran after as fast as he could: at last the jackal ran into a cleft between tow rocks and the tiger running after him stuck fast between the two rocks and could not come out and so was starved to death. But the jackal being smaller ran out on the other side.

Then the jackal went back to the tiger's den and told the tigress that her husband had been caught by the Raja and thrown into prison for interfering with his sipahi. The tigress and her cubs were very unhappy at this news for they thought that they would starve. Then the jackal comforted them and told them not to be afraid as he would stay with them and protect them, and help them with their hunting. So the next day they all four went hunting. They arranged that the jackal should wait at a certain place, while the tigers beat the jungle and drove the game towards him. The jackal had boasted about the amount of game that he could catch and when a herd of deer broke by him he tried to seize one but they easily escaped then the jackal was ashamed but in order not to be detected he lay down and pretended that he had been suddenly taken very ill. And when the tigers came up they were sorry for him and forgave him for catching no game. The next day it was arranged that the tigress should be in wait and the jackal and the two young tigers should beat: the tigress soon killed a fine deer. When the others came up the tigers wanted to eat it at once, but the jackal would not let them and said that they must go to a little distance while he did puja to make the food wholesome. The tigers obeyed and under pretence of doing puja the jackal ate up all the tit bits and then allowed the tigers to come and eat the rest. This happened daily and the jackal lived in comfort all his days.

(6)—The Wild Buffaloes

There was once a man so poor that he had no land, no plough and no plough cattle: all that he had was a pair of fine goats. This man determined to plough with the goats, so he made a little plough and yoked the goats to it, and with it he ploughed a piece of barren upland. Having ploughed he had no seed paddy to sow; he went to try and borrow some paddy form the neighbours, but they would lend him nothing. Then he went and begged some paddy chaff, and a neighbour readily gave him some. The man took the chaff and so sowed it as if it had been seed. Wonderful to relate from this chaff grew up the fines crop of paddy that ever was seen. Day by day they man went and watched with joy his paddy grow and ripen. The morning when he went to see it he was horrified to find that in the night wild buffaloes had come and eaten and destroyed the whole crop. Having now no other resource the man determined to follow the wild buffaloes into the jungle: he readily tracked them and came to a large open space where every night the wild buffaloes used to sleep. As it was very dirty he made a broom of twigs and brushed the place clean. At nightfall he heard the buffaloes coming back and he went and hid in a hollow tree. When the buffaloes saw how clean their sleeping place had been made they were very pleased and wondered who had done it. The next morning the buffaloes all went away into the jungle to graze, and the man came out of his hollow tree and again swept up the place: the buffaloes on their return saw that the place had again been swept and decided to leave one of their number to watch and see who did this. They left a buffalo who was lame to watch:

when the day got hot however the lame buffalo went to sleep, and the man then came out of his tree and swept up the place and hid himself again without being discovered. So the next day the buffaloes left a blind one behind.

The blind buffalo was of very acute hearing and he heard the man come out and sweep the place and return to the tree: so when the other buffaloes came back he told them of the man's hiding place. The buffaloes made him come out and arranged that they would provide for him if he would stay with them and sweep their sleeping place daily. The next day the buffaloes lay in wait for a band of merchants who were travelling through the forest and suddenly charging down upon them put the merchants to flight: they fled leaving behind them all their goods and provisions: these the buffaloes took on their horns and carried to the man, and in this way they from time to time supplied him with all he needed. As he was alone all day they gave him a pair of horns, and said that wherever he was if he blew on the horns all the buffaloes in the forest would come to his assistance. But one day when he was bathing he put the horns down on the Bank of the stream and crows flew away with them and he did not care to tell the buffaloes that he had lost them.

One day he went to bathe in the river and after bathing he sat and combed his hair on the bank. Now his hair was so long that it reached to his knees. One of his long hairs came out and so he took it and splitting open a *loa* fruit he coiled the hair inside and closed the fruit up and then set it to float down the river. A long way down the stream a Raja's daughter happened to be bathing and the *loa* fruit floated past her: she caught hold of it and when she opened it she found the long hair inside. At once she went to her father and vowed that she would marry no one except the man to whom the long hair belonged. As nothing would alter her determination the Raja sent men up the river to search for the owner of the long hair. One of them found the man at the home of the buffaloes and brought him to the Raja. He was at once married with great grandeur to the princess and promised the succession to the kingdom. So our hero began to live in great luxury. One day as he was standing in the courtyard of the palace some crows flew overhead and dropped the pair of horns that he had lost. He picked them up and boasted that if he blew on them the whole town would be at once destroyed. The bystanders laughed at him. Whereupon he got angry and blew on the horns. Then there was a great noise and an enormous herd of wild buffaloes was seen rushing down to destroy the town. However before they could do any damage he ran out and assured them that he was unhurt; at this the buffaloes were pacified; then all the straw and grain in the palace was brought out and given to the buffaloes to eat: after eating all they wanted they went back into the jungle, all except one pair which stayed behind in the palace; and from this pair are descended all the tame buffaloes which we see to-day.

(7)—The Grateful Cow

Once upon a time there were two brothers who were very poor and lived only by begging and gleaning. One day at harvest time they went out to glean. On their way they came to a stream with muddy banks and in the mud a cow had stuck fast and was unable to get out. The young brother proposed that they should help it out, but the elder brother objected saying that they might be accused of theft: the younger brother persisted and so they pulled the cow out of the mud. The cow followed them home and shortly afterwards produced a calf. In a few years the cow and her descendants multiplied in a marvellous manner so that the brothers became rich by selling the milk and *ghi*. They became so rich that elder brother was able to marry; he lived at home with his wife and the younger brother lived in the jungle grazing the cattle. The elder brother's son used every day to take out his uncle's dinner to the jungle. This was not really necessary for the cow used to supply her master with all sorts of dainties to eat, so the younger brother, when his nephew brought out the rice used to give the boy some of the sweetmeats with which the cow supplied him, but he charged him not to tell his parents about this nor to take any home. But one day the boy hid some of the sweetmeats in his cloth and took them home and showed them to his mother. His mother had never seen such sweetmeats before and was convinced that her brother-in-law wished to poison her son. So she took the sweetmeats away and the next day she herself took out the dinner to her brother-in-law and after he had eaten it she said that she would comb his hair and pick out the lice from it; so he put his head on her lap and as she combed his hair in a soothing way he went off to sleep. When he was asleep the woman took out a knife and cut off his head. Then she got up and leaving the head and body lying at the place went home. But the cow had seen what occurred and with her horns she pushed the head along until it joined the neck: whereupon the man immediately came to life again and learned what had happened to him. So he drove off all the cattle to a distant part of the jungle and began to live there.

Every day he milked his large herd of cows and got a great quantity of milk; he asked his friend the cow what he was to do with it and she told him to pour it into a hole in the ground at the foot of a pipal tree Every day he poured the milk into the hole and one day as he was doing so out of the hole came a large snake and thanked him for his kindness in supplying the milk and asked him what reward he would wish to receive in return. Acting on a hint from the cow the man said that he would like to have all the milk back again.

Whereupon the snake vomited up all the milk which it had drunk and died on the spot. But the milk mingled with poison fell over the man and imported to his body a glorious and shining appearance, so that he seemed to be made of fire.

After this the man used every day to go and bathe in a river, and each day when he bathed he threw one of his hairs into the water: and his hairs were very long. Lower down the river a princess used to bathe and one day the saw one of the hairs come floating down and vowed that she would marry no one but the owner of the hair. So the father of the princess sent a Brahman up the river to look for the man with the long hair. The Brahman was a very thin man with his ribs showing through his skin. After some days he found our hero and was amazed at his shining appearance. He told him that a princess wished to marry him: he was invited to stay some days; he did so, living on the milk from the herd of cows and in a short time became very fat. The cow told the man to take a basket and creep into the hole from which the snake had come he did so and at the bottom he found a heap of gold and silver: he filled his basket with this and came back and gave it all to the Brahman, and told him to go home and inform his master that he would come in a few days and marry his daughter. When the Raja saw the gold and silver and how fat the Brahman had got he was very pleased to think what a son-in-law he was getting. In a few days the cow said that it was time to start and as he had no other conveyance he set out riding on the cow. When they reached the boundary of the Raja's kingdom the man woke up one morning and found that a great retinue of elephants and horses and *palkis* and *sipahis* had appeared during the night. This was owing to the magic of the cow. So the man mounted an elephant and went in state to the Raja and married his daughter with great ceremony. After staying some days he decided to return home and started off with his wife and grand retinue. When they reached the boundary of the kingdom all the elephants and horses and *palkis* and *sipahis* vanished into air, and the princess found that she and her husband had nothing but an old cow to ride upon. At his she was very unhappy but she was ashamed to go back to her father, so she went on with her husband and helped to tend to the cows in the jungle.

One morning they woke up and found that in the night a grand palace had sprung up fitted with wealth of every kind, this was the last gift of the cow which soon afterwards died. Thus the man became a Raja and founded a kingdom and he gave a rupee to every one who would come and settle in his kingdom. Many people came and among others his brother and sister-in-law who had fallen into great proverty. When they saw their brother they were afraid and thought that they would be killed, but he forgave them and gave them clothes and land and they all lived happily ever after.

(8)—The Belbati Princess

Once upon a time there were seven brothers the youngest of whom bore the name of Lita. The six elder brothers were all married but Lita refused to marry and when questioned he said that he would not marry any one but the Belbati Princess. His sisters-in-law laughed very much at the idea that he would marry a princess and worried him so much that at length he decided to set out in search of the Belbati princess. So one day that started off and after some time came to a jungle in which was sitting a holy *muni*. Lita went to him and asked if he knew where he would find the Belbati princess. The *muni* said that he did not know but that a day's journey farther on was another *muni* who might be able to tell him. So Lita travelled on for a day and found another *muni* who was in the midst of performing a three month's spell of fasting and meditation. Lita had to wait till the muni returned to thoughts of this world and then made his enquiry. The *muni* said that he did not know but that three days journey farther on was another muni who might be able to help him. So Lita went on and found the third muni who was in the midst of a six months fast. When this *muni* came to himself and heard what Lita wanted he said that he would be very glad to help him. The Belbati princess was at the time imprisoned in the biggest *bel* fruit growing on a *bel* tree which was guarded by Rakshasas. If he went and plucked this fruit he would secure the princess, but if he took any but the biggest fruit he would be ruined.

Lita promised to bear this in mind and then the *muni* changed him into a *biti* bird and told him the direction in which to fly. Lita flew off and soon came to the tree, which was covered with fruit; he was very frightened when he saw the Rakshasas there, so in a great hurry he went and bit off the first fruit that he came to; but this was not the biggest on the tree and the Rakshasas immediately fell upon him and ate him up. The *muni,* when Lita did not come back, knew that something must have happened to him so he sent a crow to see what was the matter. The crow came back and said that one *bel* fruit had been picked but that he could not see Lita. Then the *muni* sent the crow to bring him the droppings of the Rakshasas. The crow did so and from the droppings the *muni* restored Lita to life. The muni reproved Lita for his failure and told him what if he wished to make a second attempt *he* must remember his behest to pick only the biggest bel fruit. Lita promised and the *muni* turned him into a parroquet. In this form Lita again flew to the bel tree and picked the biggest fruit on the tree. When the Rakshasas saw the parrot making off with the fruit they pursued him in fury; but the *muni* turned the parrot into a fly so small that the Rakshasas could not see it, so they had to give up the chase.

When they had departed Lita recovered his own form and went to the *muni* with the *bel* fruit and asked what more was to be done in order to find the princess. The *muni* said that the princess was inside the fruit; that Lita was to take it to a certain well and very gently break it open against the edge of the well. Lita hurried off to the well and in his anxiety to see the princess he knocked the fruit with all his force and split it suddenly in two. The result of this was that the princess burst out of the fruit in such a blaze of light that Lita fell down dead. When the princess saw that her brightness had killed her lover she was very distressed and taking his body on her lap she wept over him. While she was doing so a girl of the Kamar caste came by and asked what was the matter. The princess said: "My lover is dead, if you will draw water from the well I will revive him by giving him to drink," but the Kamar girl at once formed a wicked plan. She said that she could not reach the water in the well. Then said the princess: "Do you hold this dead body while I draw the water." "No," said the Kamar girl, "I see you mean to run away leaving me with dead body and I shall get into trouble." Then said the princess: "If you do not believe me take off my fine clothes and keep them as a pledge." Then the princess let the Kamar girl take off all her jewellery and her beautiful dress and went to draw water from the well. But the Kamar girl followed her and as the princess leant over the edge she pushed her in, so that she was drowned. Then the Kamar girl drew water from the well and went back to Lita and poured some into his mouth, and directly the water touched his lips he came back to life, and as the Kamar girl had put on the dress and jewellery of the Belbati princess he thought that she was the bride for whom he had sought. So he took her home to his brother's house and married her.

After a time Lita and his brothers went to hunt in the jungle; it was very hot and Lita grew very thirsty; he found himself near the well at which he had broken the *bel* fruit and went to it for water. Looking down he saw floating on the water a beautiful flower; he was so pleased with it that he picked it and took it home to his Kamar wife; but when she saw it she was very displeased and cut it up into pieces and threw the pieces out of the house. Lita was sorry and noticed shortly afterwards that at the place where the pieces of the flower had been thrown a small bel tree was sprouting. He had this planted in his garden and carefully watered. It grew well and after a time it produced ripe fruit. One day Lita ordered his horse, and as it was being brought it broke loose and run away into the garden: as it ran under the bel tree one on the *bel* fruits fell on to the saddle and stayed there. When the syce caught the horse he saw this and took the fruit home with him. When he went to cut open the fruit he found inside it a beautiful woman; he kept the woman in his house. At this time the Kamar woman fell ill and was like to die. Lita was very distressed at the thought of losing his Belbati princess. At last the Kamarin said that she was being bewitched by the girl who was living in the syce's house and that one or other of them must die. Lita at once ordered the girl to be taken into the jungle and killed. Four Ghasis took her away and put her to death. Her last request to them was that they should cut off her hands and feet and put them at the four sides of her grave. This they did. After the death of the girl the Kamar wife recovered her health.

After a time Lita again went hunting and at nightfall came to the place where the girl had been put to death. There he found standing a fine palace. He went in but the only living creatures he saw were two birds who seemed to live there; he lay down on a bed and went to sleep. While he slept the birds sat by him and began talking. One told the other the story of the search for the Belbati princess and how the Kamar girl had thrown her into the well and taken her place. When Lita heard this he awoke and was very unhappy. The birds told him that once a year the Belbati princess visited the palace in which he was; her next visit would be in six months. So Lita stayed there and at the end of the six months he hid behind the door to await the princess. She came and as she passed through the door he caught her by the hand, but she wrenched herself away and fled. Lita was very depressed but the birds told him to be more careful the next time. So he waited a year and when the princess was expected he hid himself: the princess came and seeing no one entered the palace and went to sleep. While she slept Lita secured her. They were married and lived happily ever after, and the wicked Kamar girl was put to death.

(9)—The Bread Tree

There once was a boy who lived with his mother and was engaged all day in tending cattle. Every morning when he started his mother gave him two pieces of bread called "hunger bread" and "stuffing bread,"—one to satisfy hunger with and the other to over-eat oneself on. One day the boy could not eat all his bread and he left the piece that remained over on a rock. When he went back the next day he was surprised to see that from the piece of bread a tree had gown which bore loaves of bread instead of fruit. After that the boy no longer took bread from his mother, but lived on the fruit of his tree.

One day he had climbed his tree to pick a loaf when an old woman came by with a bag over her shoulder and saying that she was very poor begged for a piece of bread. The old woman was really a Rakshasi. The boy was kindhearted and told her that he would throw her down a loaf, but he old woman objected that it would get dirty if it fell on the ground. Then he told her to hold out her cloth and he would throw it into that: but she said that she could not see well enough to catch the loaf: he must come down and give it to her: so the boy came down to give her the loaf and when the Rakshasi had him on the ground, she seized him and put him in her bag and went off with him.

After going some way she came to a pool of water and as she was rather thirsty from carrying such a burden, she put down her bag and went to drink. Opportunely some travellers came by and hearing the boy's shouts let him out of the bag. The boy filled the bag with stones and tied it up as before and made the best of his way home. The old Rakshasi went off with the heavy bag and when she got to her abode told her daughter with whom she lived that she had captured a fine dinner but when the daughter opened the bag she found in it nothing but stones: at this she was very angry and abused her mother: then the old woman said that the boy had escaped on the road: so the next day she went back to the place where the boy was tending cattle and by the same trick she caught him and put him in her bag and this time went straight home. She made him over to her daughter and went out to collect fire wood with which to cook him. The boy being left alone with the daughter began to ask how he was to be killed; she said that his head was to be pounded in a *Dhenki.* He pretended not to understand and asked how that was to be done. The girl not understanding such stupidity put her head under the striker of the *Dhenki* to show him what would happen. Then the boy at once pounded her head in the *Dhenki* and killed her: he then put on her clothes and cut her body up in pieces ready for cooking. When the old woman came back with the fire wood she was pleased to find that her daughter, as she thought, had got every thing ready; and the meal was soon cooked and eaten. After the old woman had thus made a hearty meal off the remains of her own daughter she felt sleepy and took a nap. While she slept the boy struck her on the head with a large store and killed her; thus he saved his life and took all the property of the old Rakshasi and live happily ever after.

(10)—THE ORIGIN OF SABAI GRASS (ISCHEMUM ANGUSTIFOLIUM)

Once upon a time there were six brothers who lived with their sister. The brothers used to spend their days in the jungle hunting while the sister minded the house and cooked the dinner against their return.

One day while the brothers were hunting the girl went to cut herbs to cook with the dinner: as she was doing so she chanced to cut her finger and some drops of blood fell on the herbs, which were put in the pot. When the brothers came home to dinner they noticed how very sweet the food was and asked the reason. The girl said that she was afraid that it must be because some drops of her blood had fallen on it. Then the brothers took counsel together and agreed that if a few drops of her blood were so sweet, she must be very nice to eat. So they agreed to murder her and eat her. But the youngest brother named Lita, though he did not dare to oppose his elders, was sorry for the decision. The next day when the brothers came from the jungle they brought with them a beautiful flower of seven colours and gave it to their sister. She was delighted with it: she had never seen so beautiful a flower before and wanted to know where it grew and whether were others like it. They said that if she liked to come with them they would take her to the tree on which the flowers grew and she could pick as many as she liked. So the next morning she gladly went with them and they took her to the tree with the seven-coloured flowers. She climbed the tree to pick the flowers and when she was up in the tree they shot arrows at her to kill her; but though they shot many arrows they could not kill her. Then they compelled Lita to shoot and he with his first arrow killed his sister.

Then they cut up the body of the girl ready for cooking and sent Lita to a well to fetch water in which to cook the flesh. Lita went to the well and overcome with sorrow sat down and wept. As he wept a large frog came to the surface of the water and asked him what was the matter; he said that he had been made to kill his sister and that now they were going to cook her flesh. The frog told him to be comforted and gave him a large *rohu* fish. Lita took this back and when his brothers told him to cook the food, he hid the pieces of his sister's body and cooked the *rohu* fish. The brothers ate his thinking that it was their sister. Then they went on into the jungle hunting. After going a short way Lita said that he had forgotten to recover his arrow and that he must go back and fetch it. He went back to the place, and taking his sister's body buried it and building a hut near, spent the days in weeping over the grave. After he had spent some time thus the girl appeared alive out of the ground. Lita was overjoyed and he and his sister remained happily in the jungle.

One day a Raja hunting in the jungle passed that way and seeing the girl at once fell in love with her and took her away and married her. Lita he also took with him and made him ruler of half the kingdom.

In honour of his marriage the Raja resolved to construct an enormous tank: and people came from far and near to work at it. Among others came Lita's five elder brothers, who had fallen into great poverty, owing to their wickedness. When their sister saw them she forgave them and sending for them bestowed on them food and clothing. But they were so ashamed and repentent that they could only kneel on the ground and beat the earth with their hands. As they continued to do so the earth with their hands. As they continued to do so the earth opened and swallowed them up: only their hair stuck out of the ground and that became *sabai* grass, and this was the origin of all the *sabai* grass which exists.

(11) The Faithless Sister

Once upon a time there was a man who had a son and daughter: he used to cultivate his land and his son and daughter used to take his dinner to him. One day the man went to plough and while ploughing he stuck the spear which he had brought with him into the ground. As the man ploughed a tiger came and waited an opportunity to spring upon the man: but from whichever side the tiger approached, the spear which was stuck in the ground bent its point towards the tiger and so protected its master. Just then the boy and girl came along with their father's dinner. The baffled tiger was hiding in some bushes by the field. As the children went along they saw a paddy bird on the ground. The boy of course had his bow and bird arrows with him and he shot an arrow at the paddy bird: he missed the bird, but it happened that the tiger was just in the line of fire; the arrow pierced the eye of the tiger and killed it instantaneously. When the girl saw the tiger lying dead she said that it was clear that their father had enticed them there in order that the tiger might kill them when they brought him his dinner: clearly the only way for them to save their lives was to leave their home at once. The boy agreed; drawing his arrow from the tiger's head and taking the tiger's eyes with him, he went away with his sister as fast as they could run. After going some little distance they met in the way two tigers. The boy threw at the tiger the eyes of the first tiger which he had brought with him. The tigers at once fell down dead, but from the body of one proceeded, a hare, and from the body of the other, two dogs which peaceably followed the boy and his sister. Having escaped to a distance they lived in the jungle happily for some time with their three animal friends. One day the hare said that he would like to have a spear, so the boy went with him to a blacksmith and got a spear made. As they were returning they met in the way a giant *Rakshasa* who wished to devour them, but the hare holding the spear kept jumping in and out of the giant's mouth with such speed that the *Rakshasa* was dumbfounded and surrendered at discretion, promising to be a faithful servant to them henceforth. With the help of the *Rakshasa* they had great success in hunting. The boy with the hare and the two dogs used to beat the jungle and drive the game towards the *Rakshasa* who caught it in his mouth. One day they thus caught a monkey, whose life they spared and who joined their band. The monkey took a large drum and caught in it a nest of wild bees, which he preserved.

One day while the others were away a Raja who was hunting in the jungle found the girl sitting alone and at once fell in love with her and wanted to marry her. The girl said that she was willing but that she was sure that her brother would never consent. The only thing was to kill her brother and the Raja could never do that as the faithful animals would protect him. At last the girl consented to try and compass her brother's death. To this end she became very melancholy and seemed to put away: her brother asked what was the matter and she said that she would never recover unless he could fetch her a certain flower which grew in the midst of a certain lake. Now this lake swarmed with gigantic fish and poisonous snakes. But the brother, never daunted, went to the lake and began to swim out to the centre where the flower grew. Before he got half way there one of the gigantic fish swallowed him up. The *Rakshasa* however saw this and set to work to drink the lake up: he soon drank the lake dry and not only caught the big fish but also was able to gather the flower that had grown in the lake. They then cut open the fish and took the boy unharmed from its belly. The *Rakshasa* then vomited up the water he had swallowed and filled up the lake again. Meanwhile the Raja thinking that the boy had died, carried off his sister. But the boy setting out with the hare and the dogs and the *Rakshasa* and the monkey proceeded to attack the Raja's capital and recover his sister. The monkey opened his drum and the bees issued forth and attacked the Raja's army so that it fled. The Raja had to capitulate and give the boy half his kingdom and his own daughter in marriage, then peace was declared and the animals all disappeared into the jungle and our hero lived happily ever after.

(12) The Cruel Sisters-in-law

Once upon a time there lived six brothers who had one sister. The brothers were all married and their wives hated their sister-in-law. It happened that the brothers all went away to trade in a far country and her sisters-in-law took the opportunity to iliterate the girl. They said "If you do not obey us and do what we tell you we will kill you." The girl said that she would obey their behest to the best of her ability. They said "Then go to the well and bring this earthen pot back full of water." The khalsi had a large hole in the bottom so that as fast as it was filled the water ran out. The girl took the pot to the well and sitting down began to weep over her fate. As she wept a large frog rose out of the water and asked her what was the matter She said "My last hour has come. If I cannot fill this pot with water I shall be killed and it has a hole in the bottom." The frog said, "Be comforted. I will cure that: I will sit on the hole and stop it up with my body and you will be able to fill it." This it did and the girl took the water back to the house. The sisters-in-law were very angry but could say nothing so they set her another task. They told her to go the jungle and bring home a full bundle of sticks: but she was not to take any rope with which to tie them. The girl collected a large quantity of sticks and then sat down and cried because she was unable to carry them home: as she cried a large snake came up and asked what was the matter. The girl told him, whereupon the snake said that he would curl himself round the sticks and serve as a rope. This he did and the girl was able to carry the sticks home on her head. Defeated in this attempt the sisters-in-law the next day told the girl to go to a field of pulse which had been sown the day before and bring back all the grain by the evening. The girl went to the field and picked up a few grains but it had been sown broadcast and the girl soon saw that the task was hopeless: she sat down and cried and as she cried a flock of pigeons flew to her and asked her what was the matter: she said that she could not pick up all the grain in the field. They said that was easily managed, and the pigeons spreading over the field soon picked up all the grain and put it into the girl's basket, so that by evening she returned with the basket full. The sisters-in-law were more than ever enragaed. They gave her a pot and told her that she must go to the jungle and bring it back full of bear's milk. The girl went to the jungle and being very frightened sat down and began to cry: a large she bear came by and asked what was the matter. The girl explained and the she bear, sorry for the distress willingly allowed herself to be milked without doing the girl any harm. The sisters-in-law then resolved to make a more direct attempt on the girl's life. They took her into the jungle and told her to climb a certain tree and pick them the fruit. The tree had a tall smooth trunk and the girl had to climb the tree by driving pegs into the trunk. When she reached the branches the sisters-in-law pulled the pegs out of the tree and went home leaving the girl to starve. Night came on an the girl stayed in the tree: it so happened that day the six brothers were returning home and being benighted stopped to sleep under that very tree. The girl thought that they were dacoits and stayed still. She could not help crying in her despair and a warm tear fell on the face of one the brothers sleeping below and woke him up. He looked up and recognized his sister. The brothers soon rescued her and when they heard of the cruelty of their wives they went home and put them all to death.

(13) The False Rani

Once upon a time a Raja who had just married was returning with his bride to his kingdom. It was hot weather and a long journey and as they passed through a jungle the Raja and all his men went down to a stream to drink leaving the bride sitting in her *palki*. As the bride thus sat all alone she was frightened at seeing a she-bear come up. The bear asked the bride who she was and where she was going. When she heard, she thought that she would like to share so agreeable a fate, so by threats she made the Rani get out of her *palki* and give her all her fine clothes and jewellery and go away into the jungle. The bear dressing herself in the Rani's clothes, got into the *palki*, and when the men came back they took up the *palki* and went on their way without noticing any change, nor did the Raja detect the fraud: he took the bear to his palace and installed her as his wife. Meanwhile the real bride had picked up the walking stick of the Raja and a cloth which he had lift on the road when he went to the stream, and ran into the jungle. She made her way to the house of a Ghasi woman who lived by the Raja's palace with her daughters. The daughters earned a living by selling flowers and one day one daughter, as she sold the Raja a garland, told him that his real bride was living in their house. The Raja was very distressed and at once went to see his bride and was satisfied of her identity when she produced his stick and cloth. The real Rani refused to go to his palace until the she bear had been put to death. Thereupon the Raja gave instructions to his followers and sent word to the palace that he was dead. The officers and servants at the palace then prepared a big pit and lit a large fire in it: they then sent for the she bear and told her that she must perform the funeral ceremonies of her husband. They made her take off her fine clothes and told her to kneel down by the burning pit and make salaam to it. As she was doing so they pushed her into the pit and she was burned to death. Then the Raja brought home his real bride in triumph. But from that time bears attack men when they get the chance.

(14) The Jackal and the Kite

Once upon a time a jackal and a kite agreed to join forces and get their food together. In pursuance of their plan they sent word to a prosperous village that a Raja with his army was marching that way and intended the next day to loot the village. The next morning the jackal took an empty *kalsi* and marched towards the village drumming on the *kalsi* with all his might, and the kite flew along overhead screaming as loud as he could. The villagers thought that the Raja's army was approaching and fled into the jungle. The jackal and the kite began to feast on all the good things that had been left in the houses. There was however one old woman who was too infirm to run away with the other inhabitants: and had hid herself inside her house. When she saw that no army came but only a jackal and a kite she crawled away into the jungle and told her friends. They came back, and surrouding the village, caught the jackal: they began to beat the jackal with sticks to kill it: the jackal uttered no sound and pretended that it did not mind being beaten: after a time it began to jeer at its captors and told them that they could never kill it by beating. The asked how it could be killed and it said by burning. So they tied a bunch of old cloths on to its tail and poured oil over them and set them on fire: the jackal run off with the burning bundle at the end of its tail and jumping on to the nearest house set fire to the thatch: the fire spread and the whole village was burnt down. The jackal then ran to a tank and jumping into the water extinguisehed its blazing tail. But if you look you will see that all jackals have a burnt tip to their tail to this day.

(15) The Sons of the Raban Raja

The was a Raja who used to bathe daily at a certain tank. In the tank was a great fish: as the Raja washed his mouth this fish used daily to swallow the rinsings of his mouth. In consequence of this the fish after a time gave birth to two human children. As the two boys grew up they used to go into the village near the tank and play with the other children. One day however, a man beat them and drove them away from the other children jeering at them because they had no father. Much disturbed at this they went to the fish and asked whether it was true that they had no father. The fish told them that their father was the Raban Raja. The two boys resolved to go in search of the Raban Raja: they set out and after a time met a man and asked him if be knew the Raban Raja The man asked why they wished to know. They said that they were his sons. Then the man at once killed them because the Raban Raja was an enemy of his country. From the place where the bodies of the dead boys lay, two large bamboos grew up. When the bamboos had grown very big Jogi came by that way and cut them down, making from them two flutes. These flutes produced such beautiful music that every one was charmed and the fame of the Jogi spread far and wide: so when in his wanderings the Jogi reached the kingdom of the Raban Raja the Raja sent for him and the Jogi came to the palace with his two bamboo flutes. When the flutes were brought into the presence of the Raja they burst open and from them appeared the two boys. When the heard their history he recognized them as his sons, and sent the Jogi away with large rewards.

(16) The Potter's Son

Once upon a time there was a Kumhar whose wife was about to have a child. As they were very poor the pair resolved that if the child should prove to be a boy they would abandon it, but if it were a girl they would bring it up.

When the child was born it was found to be a son, so the Kumhar took it into the jungle and left it there. There it was found by a tiger and tigress whose cubs had just died and who determined to bring up the man child as their own. They accordingly fed it and looked after it; the boy grew up strong and healthy. When he got big, the tiger went to a blacksmith and had made for him a bow and arrows of iron with which he used to hunt. When the boy became a young man the tiger decided that his marriage must be arranged for. So he went to the capital of a neighbouring Raja, and when the Raja' s daughter came to a tank to bathe, the tiger seized her and carried her off the jungle, where she was married to the Kumhur's son. The princess was very pleased with her new husband, but found the life with the tigers in the jungle very irksome. She constantly begged her husband to run away, until at last he agreed. One day when the tigers were at a distance they started off and soon arrived at the palace of the princess' father. Leaving her husband by the palace tank, the princess went ahead to see how matters stood and to prepare a welcome for her husband. He being left alone decided to bathe in the tank. Now a dhobi was there washing the palace clothes, and seeing a stranger he concluded that it was a thief come to steal the clothes. He accordingly killed him and then in fear threw the body into the water. When the princess returned she was disressed to find no sign of her husband but his iron bow and arrows. Search was made everywhere and the tank was netted but no trace could be discovered of her missing spouse.

Shortly afterwards a Ghasi girl came to catch *chinris* in the tank, and while doing so suddenly laid hold of a large fish. In great delight she took it home. When she came to cut it up she found inside the belly of the fish a living child. Pleased with its appearance she decided to adopt it. She put it in a basket, and tying the basket under her cloth pretended to be pregnant, and shortly afterwards announced that she had given birth to a child. The boy grew with marvellous rapidity.

Meanwhile the father of the widowed princess insisted that she should marry again. But she was faithful to the memory of her husband and declared that she would only marry the man who could draw the iron bow. Many suitors came but they all failed to draw the bow. At length the reputed son of the Ghasi woman came and pulling the bow with ease announced himself as the true husband of the princess with whom he lived happily ever after.

(17) The Wonderful Cowherd

Once upon a time there was a Raja who bad seven daughters. The seven princesses used to bathe daily in a tank and when they bathed they used to put the scrapings from their bodies in a hole in the ground. From this hole there grew a tree, and the eldest princess announced that she would marry the man who could tell her what had caused the tree to grow; many suitors came and made guesses but none divined the truth; her father was anxious that she should be married, and insisted on every one in the kingdom being questioned. At last a miserable, poverty stricken and sickly cowherd was asked; he had always grazed his cattle on the banks of the tank and had often seen the princesses bathing so he knew from what the tree had spring. The princess being bound by her oath had to marry the measurable cowherd and go and live with him in his hut.

All day long the cowherd used to be groaning in sickness and misery; but at night he used to come out of his skin and appear as a beautiful and shining man, in this form he used to go and play and dance in the moonlight in the court yard of the Raja's palace. One night the princess's maid-servant saw her master return and creep into his ugly skin; she told her mistress who resolved to keep watch the next night; when she saw her husband assume his shining form and go out of the house leaving his ugly skin lying on the ground, she took the skin and burnt it in the fire. Immediately her husband came rushing back declaring that he was suffering the agonies of burning; but the skin was burnt and the former cowherd retained his glorious and shining appearance; and on the application of oil the pain of the burning ceased. The princess then began to live with pleasure in the company of so glorious a husband, who however only went out of the house at night as his body was too bright for ordinary eyes to look upon.

It began however to be whispered about among the neighbours that a shining being was to be seen at the princess's house and that rumour eventually reached the ears of the Raja. The Raja sent a messenger to see who the being was, but when the messenger saw the shining man he was blinded and driven out of his senses and returned to the Raja in a state of madness. Two or three other messengers successively met the same fate. At length the resolved to go himself; when he saw the shining form of his son-in-law he fell down in a faint; the princess's husband ran and lifted up the Raja in his arms and revived him. After this the former cowherd became only bearably bright, and being recognized as the heir to the kingdom went to live with his wife in the Raja palace.

(18) The Strong Prince

There was once a king who, though he had two wives, had no son. He was very anxious to have a son and heir and went away into the midst of the hills and jungles and there began a course of worship and sacrifices. His prayers were heard and while he was away it was found that both his wives were pregnant. In due time the senior Rani gave birth to a son and sent a Brahman to the king with the welcome news. The Brahman was a very holy man and he had to pray and bathe so often that he made very slow progress on his journey. A day or two later the younger Rani also gave birth to a son and she sent a low caste Ghasi to give the news to the Raja. The Ghasi travelled straight ahead and reached the Raja some time before holy Brahmin. On hearing the news that the younger Rani had given birth to a son the Raja had at once declare that this boy should be his heir. He was therefore much put out when the Brahman arrived with the news that the senior Rani had given birth to a son first.

The Raja returned home and entering the palace saw the senior Rani sleeping with her babe beside her. The boy had sore eyes and the Raja, declaring that the child bore no resemblance to himself said that it was not his son and that the Rani had been unfaithful to him.

The Rani indignantly denied the accusation and said that if the two brothers fought her son would prove this parentage, Accordingly the two boys were set to wrestle with each other. The struggle was an even one. As they swayed to and from it happened that the elder boy caught hold of the Raja and pulled him to the ground. This incensed the Raja more than ever and he ordered the senior Rani to leave the kingdom with her child. On the road by which they had to pass the Raja stationed a mast elephant in order that they might be killed, but when in due course the elephant attacked them the boy caught hold of it and threw it to a distance of four *kos*. After this feat the prince and his mother journeyed to another kingdom. There they took tip their quarters near the ground where the Rajas *palwans* wrestled. The prince went to wrestle with them and easily overcame the most renowned *palwans*. In many ways he showed his strength. One day he went to a mahajan's shop and the mahajan instead of serving him promptly kept him waiting. In indignation the boy took up the entire building and threw it to a distance; hearing of these feats the Raja of the country sent for him and took him into his service; but here also he caused trouble. He insisted on being treated with deference. Going up to the highest officials he would tell them not to twist their moustaches at him , and knock them down. On the throne in the palace when the Raja was absent a pair of the Raja's shoes was placed and every one who passed by had to salaam to these. This our hero flatly refused to do. In fact he became such a nuisance that he was promised that he would be given his pay regularly if he would only stay away from the palace. After this he spent his days in idleness and by night he used to go to the shore and disport himself in the sea.

One night the goddess Kali came to the Raja's palace and knocked at the gate: but no one would come to open it. Just then the prince came back from bathing in the sea. Seeing, him, Kali Ma said that she was so hungry that she must eat him, though she had intended to eat the people in the palace. She, however, promised him that though eaten he should be born again. The boy agreed to form a meal for the godess on these terms and was accordingly eaten. Afterwards gaining admission to the palace Kali Ma ate up everyone in it except the Raja's daughter. Then our hero was born again and marrying, the Raja's daughter succeeded to the kingdom, and lived happily ever after.

(19) The Prince who became King of the Jackals

Once upon a time there lived a Raja whose son formed a great friendship with a barber. For some reason the Raja quarrelled with his son and ordered him to leave the kingdom. Accordingly the prince departed to a far country in company with his friend, the barber. In order to earn a living the barber opened a school and the prince took service with a mahajan. They were in such straits that the prince had to submit to very hard terms, it was arranged that his wages were to be one leaf plate full of rice a day: and that if he threw up the service he was to lose a piece of his skin a span long. After a short time the prince who had been brought up in luxury found the work so hard and the food so scanty that he resolved to leave the mahajan: but before he went he had to submit to a piece of skin being cut off, in terms of the agreement. The prince then went to the barber and told him how ill he had fared. The barber vowed that he should be avenged. So he went and offered himself as a servant to the mahajan: he was engaged and it was agreed that whichever party first proposed to terminate the contract should lose a piece of skin a span long. The barber worked so badly and ate so much that one day the mahajan in a fit of rage ordered him to leave the place and in consequence forfeited a piece of his skin.

Having repaid the mahajan in his own coin the prince and the barber left those parts and journeyed to the land of the king of the jackals. They found the king of the jackals asleep in front of his cave. While he still slept the barber shaved all the hair of his tail. Then the two friends hid in the cave, drawing a cart in front of the entrance. When the jackal awoke and found that he had been shaved he concluded that there were *bongas* (spirits) about, and ran away in terror. After going a short distance he met a bear who asked where he was going in such hurry. The king of the jackals said that some *bongas* had taken possession of his cave and shaved off his hair. The bear agreed to go back with the jackal and see if hair he could exorcise the spirits. Going to the cave the bear climbed on to the cart to offer a sacrifice. As he sat there the barber caught hold of his tail and held on to it while the prince began to stab the bear with a knife. The bear howled and groaned but could not get away. The king of the jackals who was looking on was delighted, for he concluded that the *bongas* had taken possession of the bear who would learn who they were and how they were to be exorcised. At last the bear broke free and ran away: the jackal ran after him and asked him what the *bongas* had told him: but the bear only said 'ugh' 'ugh' and ran into the jungle. Then the jackal met a tiger and telling his story persuaded the tiger also to try his hand at exorcising the spirits. The tiger was treated in the same way as the bear had been and ran off without giving the jackal any information.

Then the king of the jackals resolved to try himself and mounted on to the cart. But the barber stabbed him through the bamboos and killed him. Then the prince succeeded to the kingdom of the jackals, and not only so, but replaced the piece of skin which he had forfeited to the mahajan by a piece of the skin of the dead jackal.

(20) The Mongoose Boy

Once upon a time there was a Raja who had seven wives but no children. In hope of issue he retired to the jungle and began a course of prayers and sacrifices. While he was so engaged a Brahman came to him and told him to take a stick and with it knock down seven mangoes from a neighbouring tree, and catch them before they reached the ground: he promised that if the Ranis ate these mangoes they would bear children. The Raja did as he was directed and took the mangoes home and gave one to each of his wives.

The youngest Rani happened at the time to be sweeping out a room and so she put her mango in a niche in the wall. Just then a neighbour sent a mongoose, who was her servant, to ask for a light. While the Rani was fetching a firebrand from the hearth the mongoose saw the mango and climbing up nibbled part of it without being seen. After this the Rani ate the mango. In due time the seven Ranis each gave birth to a son: but the son of the youngest Ranis was the most beautiful with a face like a mongoose. The elderst Rani was jealous of the beauty of the youngest Rani's son so one day she sent the youngest Rani to fetch some water: and during her absence took up the mongoose boy and putting a stone and a broom in its place took the child away and buried it in the pit from which the potters dig their earth. When the Raja heard that his youngest wife had given birth to nothing but a stone and a broom he was very angry and turned her out of the palace.

Meanwhile a potter had found the mangoose boy still and had taken him to his home. There the child grew up and became a strong boy. One day he asked the potter to make him an earthen-ware horse. On this horse he used to ride about, for directly he mounted it, it was endowed with life. One day the mongoose boy took his earthenware horse to water it at a tank near the palace and there his six brothers saw it and insisted that they also should have earthenware horses to ride. Horses were accordingly made for them but when they mounted, the horses would not budge an inch. Enraged at this the princes complained to their mothers. The Ranis at once suspected the identity of the potter's boy and told their sons to kill him.

So one day when the young princes met him at the tank they killed the mongoose boy and buried his body. At the place where the body was buried there grew up a bamboo of extraordinary size and a bush with sweet and beautiful flowers: many people tried to cut down the big bamboo and to pluck the beautiful flowers but every arm that was raised to do so was restrained by some unseen power. Eventually the news of this portent reached the cars of the Raja who went to see what was happening. When the Raja trid to pluck a flower he succeeded at the first attempt. The Raja then cut down the bamboo and out of it stepped the mongoose boy who told of the ill treatment which he had received at the hands of the six Ranis and their sons. The Raja wished him to come to the palace but he insisted that his mother should first, be sent for. This was at once done.

Then the Raja had a wide and deep well dug and announced that a Puja was to be performed at the opening of the well. To the ceremony came the six Ranis and their sons. As they all knelt at the edge of the well doing puja the Raja had them pushed into it, so that they were all drowned. Thus the wicked were punished and mongoose boy eventually succeeded to his father's kingdom.

(21) The Prince and the Tigers

Once upon a time there was a Raja who had seven sons. One day a tigress came to the palace and asked the Raja to allow one of his sons to be her servant and look after her cattle. The Raja consented and ordered his eldest son to go with the tigress. The young man took his axe and bow and arrows and went with the tigress to her cave. When he got there he asked where were the cattle which he was to tend. The tigress pointed out to him all the bears which were roaming in the jungle and said that they were her cattle. By the cave stood a large rock and the tigress told the prince to take his axe and cut it in two. The prince tried, but the rock only turned the edge of his axe and he quite failed to cut it. The tigress being thus satisfied that the prince had no superhuman powers sprang upon him and killed him and devoured his body.

Then she went back to the Raja and said that she had too much work to be done, that she wished him to give her a second son. The Raja agreed, but this prince met the same fate as the first; and in succession, all the sons of the Raja. except the youngest, went with the tigress and were devoured by her. At last the youngest son went with the tigress: when bidden to cut the rock in two, he easily accomplished the task. Then the tigress knew that she had met her master and ran into her cave. Looking into the cave, the prince saw the bones of his dead brothers. Gathering the bones together, he prayed for fire to burn them, and fire fell from above and burned the bones.

Then he climbed a tree in order to be out of the reach of the tigress, and the tigress came and sat at the foot of the tree so that he could not descend. Then he prayed again and wind arose and wafted him away and set him down by a house where lived an old man and his wife. The tigress followed in pursuit, but the aged couple hid the prince and assured the tigress that he had not been seen; so the tigress returned disappointed. The prince stayed with the old people and worked on their land. One day as he was ploughing, the tigress came and killed, one of the bullocks that were drawing the plough. The prince at once ran to the house to fetch his bow and arrow that he might kill the tigress. When he returned, he found that several tigers were sucking the blood of the bullocks and with them a wild boar. He shot an arrow which wounded the boar. The boar maddened by the pain turned on the tigers and killed them all; including the tigress which had killed the Raja's sons.

The prince then being no longer in danger from the tigress returned to his farther's palace.

(22) The Cunning Potter

Once upon a time there lived at the gate of a Raja's palace potter who had a pretty wife. The Raja fell in love with the Potter's wife and schemed to get rid of the husband. He could not bring himself to commit a cold blooded murder, but he tried to accomplish his object indirectly by setting the Potter impossible tasks which he was to accomplish on pain of death. The Raja accordingly sent for the Potter and ordered him to bring him the heads of twenty-four jackals.

The Potter went away to the jungle and began to dig a large hole in the side of a hill. A jackal presently came by and stopped to ask why he was digging the hole. The Potter said that it was go to rain fire from heaven, and that every one who had not such a shelter would be burnt. At this the jackal became very frightened ; the Potter thereupon said that he was so sorry for them that he would allow the jackal and his friends to share the hole which he was digging. The jackal gratefully ran away and returned with a number of other jackals. They all went into the hole and the Potter closed the entrance. After a time the Potter looked out and said that the fire was over; he then stationed himself at the mouth of the hole and as the jackals came out he cut off their heads with a knife; in this away he beheaded twenty-three jackals; but the last jackal saw what was happening and dodged the knife and escaped. The Potter took the twenty-three heads to the Raja; but the Raja pretended to be angry and said that if the Potter did not at once procure a twenty-fourth head, he would be beheaded himself. The Potter took a pot of *gur* and went to a pool of water which lay in the direction in which the twenty fourth jackal had fled. Smearing his body all over with *gur*, he lay down by the water and pretended to be dead. Presently the jackal which had escaped passed that way with a friends. Seeing the body the second jackal proposed at once to go and eat it; but the first jackal warned the other that there was probably some plot and related how twenty-three of his friends had lost their lives of the hands of this very Potter. But the second jackal would not listen to advice and going to the supposed corpse smelt it and then began to lick it: finding; the taste of the *gur* very pleasant it set to work lick the body all over beginning at the feet it licked the feet and then the legs, when it reached his waist it was within reach of his hand and the Potter stabbed it with his knife and took the head to the Raja.

Foiled in this design, the Raja next ordered the Potter to bring him a jar of tiger's milk. Taking some loaves of bread, the Potter went into the jungle and soon found a cave in which was a pair of tiger cubs whose parents were away hunting. The Potter told the cubs that he was their uncle and gave them the bread to eat; they liked the taste of the bread very much. Then the Potter hid himself in a tree near the cave. Presently the tigress came back but her cubs refused to suck her milk as usual, the tigress asked the reason of this and the cubs said that their uncle had come and fed them with something nicer than milk and they were no longer hungry. They then pointed out the Potter in the tree and the tigress wanted to know what he had given her cubs to eat. He told her that it was bread: the tigress said that she would like to try some herself, whereupon the potter replied that he would give her some if she would first give him some of her milk. The tigress agreed and also consented that her legs should be tied while she was being milked in order that she might not be able to harm the potter. The tigress having been milked, the Potter gave her a loaf of bread and then ran away as fast as he could.

Finding that he would not be able to get rid of the Potter by any such devices, the Raja then persuaded the faithless wife to put the Potter to death. She accordingly set up an idol in her house and prayed daily to this that her husband might become blind and die. One day the Potter overheard her prayers: the next day be hid behind the idol and when the woman came and prayed he answered from behind the idol that her prayer was granted and that in two days her husband would become blind. Accordingly, two days later the Potter pretended to become blind. Then the woman sent word to the Raja that her husband was blind and that they had nothing to fear from him. The Raja accordingly came one night to visit the woman, and the Potter killed them both with an axe. He buried the body of his wife, but he was in great trouble as to how to dispose of the body of the Raja: for he knew; that there would be a hue and cry when the disappearance of the Raja was discovered. At last he decided to put the body in a field of *brinjals* belonging to a neighbour. Toward morning, the owner of the field came to see that his property was all right, and seeing some one among the *brinjals*, thought that it was a thief. He accordingly hit the supposed thief on the head and when be came to examine the body, he was shocked to find that he had, as he thought, killed the Raja. In great distress he went to consult his friend, the Potter; the Potter advised him to put the body among the buffaloes belonging to a Goala At dawn the Goala came to look at his buffaloes and seeing the body of the Raja thought that it was a thief stealing the milk of the buffaloes: catching up a club, he inflicted a blow which caused the body to fall over. When the Goala, found that the body was that of the Raja and that he had apparently killed him, he was in great fear and went to his friend, the Potter, for advice. It was finally decided to dispose of the body by putting it down a well. The next day great search was made for the missing Raja and the body was found in the well by a Brahman, Preparations were made for the obsequies and a funeral pyre erected. The Potter saw his opportunity and digging a hole in the ground under the pyre hid himself in it. When the body had been cremated and the mourners were still collected at the spot, the Potter began to speak from the hole in which he was concealed: the bystanders thought that they heard the voice of the Raja declaring that the Potter had always been his true friend and that he desired that he should be given half the kingdom and the hand of his daughter in marriage. The supposed wishes of the late Raja were obeyed and the Potter lived in luxury for the rest of his life.